Hearing Double

Hearing Double

Jazz, Ontology, Auditory Culture

BRIAN KANE

Oxford University Press is a department of the University of Oxford. It furthers
the University's objective of excellence in research, scholarship, and education
by publishing worldwide. Oxford is a registered trade mark of Oxford University
Press in the UK and certain other countries.

Published in the United States of America by Oxford University Press
198 Madison Avenue, New York, NY 10016, United States of America.

© Oxford University Press 2024

All rights reserved. No part of this publication may be reproduced, stored in
a retrieval system, or transmitted, in any form or by any means, without the
prior permission in writing of Oxford University Press, or as expressly permitted
by law, by license, or under terms agreed with the appropriate reproduction
rights organization. Inquiries concerning reproduction outside the scope of the
above should be sent to the Rights Department, Oxford University Press, at the
address above.

You must not circulate this work in any other form
and you must impose this same condition on any acquirer.

Library of Congress Cataloging-in-Publication Data
Names: Kane, Brian, 1973– author.
Title: Hearing double : jazz, ontology, auditory culture / Brian Kane.
Description: [1.] | New York : Oxford University Press, 2024. |
Includes bibliographical references and index.
Identifiers: LCCN 2024002008 (print) | LCCN 2024002009 (ebook) |
ISBN 9780190600501 (hardback) | ISBN 9780190600525 (epub)
Subjects: LCSH: Jazz—Philosophy and aesthetics. | Jazz—Analysis, appreciation.
Classification: LCC ML3506.K364 2024 (print) | LCC ML3506 (ebook) |
DDC 781.65—dc23/eng/20240119
LC record available at https://lccn.loc.gov/2024002008
LC ebook record available at https://lccn.loc.gov/2024002009

DOI: 10.1093/oso/9780190600501.001.0001

Printed by Sheridan Books, Inc., United States of America

For Miles

Contents

Acknowledgments	ix
Introduction: Why Standards?	1
PART I ONTOLOGY	15
1. The Metaphysics of Musical Structure	17
2. Replication	60
3. Nomination	93
4. The Ontology of Musical Networks	125
PART II AUDITORY CULTURE	153
5. The Soundscape of Standards	155
6. The Aesthetics of Standards, or Hearing Double	214
Discography	275
References	279
Index	287

Acknowledgments

Some books are written quickly, and some books take a long time to complete. And some books are written quickly *and still* take a long time to complete. That is the case with *Hearing Double*. I wrote most of Part I on a sabbatical in 2015, reworked it and developed Part II in Munich in the summer of 2019, and completed the final pieces in 2022. These fits and starts tended to echo life's highs and lows—adoption, tenure, illness, pandemic—but through it all, colleagues and friends helped to keep the project alive.

I want to recognize the professors and graduate students who invited me to talk about jazz and ontology. You shaped this book with your generous questions and thoughts. I appreciated the chance to share my ideas at the Peabody Conservatory at the University of Cincinnati College-Conservatory of Music; at the Barwick Colloquium at Harvard University; and at the University of Texas, Austin. Also, I want to thank the panelists, organizers, and respondents at a session held at the American Musicological Society Meeting in Vancouver in 2016, where I talked about *Your Hit Parade* and the "soundscape of standards."

I reached major milestones while on two fellowships in Germany. I want to thank Magdalena Zorn for an invitation to the Center for Advanced Studies at Ludwig Maximilian University, in Munich. I also want to thank Carmel Raz for an invitation to the Max Planck Institute for Empirical Aesthetics, in Frankfurt, where this book was completed.

At Yale, I want to acknowledge my dear colleagues in the Department of Music, who have been patiently awaiting this book for a long time. In particular I thank Michael Veal, Ian Quinn, and Gary Tomlinson for their support and conversation. I also give special acknowledgment to James Hepokoski, the "prose bear," for listening sessions and for innumerable conversations about American music. I benefited from the graduate students at Yale who helped me think through both halves of the book in two different graduate seminars: Jazz and Musical Ontology (in the spring of 2014) and Music, Radio, and Mediation (in the fall of 2017). Thanks also goes to my colleagues in Film and Media Studies who have supported my work on sound and let me travel up and down the dial of radio studies—in particular, Francesco

Casetti, John MacKay, and John Durham Peters. I am grateful to participants and co-organizers of the Yale Sound Studies Working Group (my personal "burrow") for the chance to share ideas about what sound studies and auditory cultural studies could be. Additional thanks to Paul North, Matt Jacobsen, and Michael Denning for formative conversations along the way. And, of course, I cannot talk about Yale without acknowledging the amazing Daphne Brooks, my co-director in the Black Sound and the Archive Working Group. Sessions with our working group have been the closest thing to pure joy I've experienced in the academy. Your support for this project has meant the world to me.

I want to acknowledge two brilliant scholars who have profoundly shaped my own thinking about the ontology of music. Thank you to Lydia Goehr for getting me interested in the issue of musical ontology as an undergraduate, and for your support and friendship during my time at Columbia University. Thanks also to Georgina Born, for soliciting an article, "Jazz, Mediation, Ontology," for a special issue of *Contemporary Music Review* (vol. 37, no. 1) on music and mediation, and for a number of conversations in person and over email about music and philosophy. Your thinking about the social dimensions of music and has been an inspiration and a model.

Thanks also to friends and family: Todd Cronan, Karen Handler, Adrienne Kane, Bruce and Ellen Kane, Debbie Kane, and Miles Kane. You've been there not just for the fits and starts but for the highs and lows; for that, I am grateful.

Introduction

Why Standards?

When jazz musicians get together to play, their repertory often consists of "standards"—well-known songs like "Stella by Starlight," "All the Things You Are," or "Body and Soul." For the young jazz musician, it can be a challenge to learn this repertory because there are no definitive sources by which to acquire it. Many of these standards might circulate as "lead sheets"—musical scores notated with only a melody and chord symbols—found online, or in various songbooks. The most ubiquitous source for lead sheets is a "fakebook."[1] For those unfamiliar with the term, a fakebook is a collection of lead sheets that musicians might use as an aide-memoire when practicing or on the bandstand. Fakebooks first emerged in the 1950s, and for most of the history of jazz they circulated illegally since they did not pay royalties on the music they reproduced. Although the raison d'être of a fakebook is to gather the songs that are most often needed by working musicians, they are always documents of their time and place, and they reflect the tastes of their (often unknown, often obscured) compilers. Many are full of idiosyncratic selections or are rife with inaccurate chord changes or melodies. Today, legal fakebooks abound and you can guarantee that almost any young jazz musician will have a few on their bookshelf, or their hard drive, or in "the cloud." But fakebooks are the hallmark of neophytes. Once graduated from their years of apprenticeship, most jazz musicians no longer lug them around from gig to gig. Experts simply know this repertory and are capable of reproducing a vast number of these songs by memory. They also expect those they work with to do the same.

To learn the jazz repertory requires much more than the acquisition of a few fakebooks. It demands a lot of listening, tracking down the famous recorded performances of these tunes, and getting a sense of the typical ways that these songs have been played. Many jazz musicians work closely with recordings, transcribing harmonies or solos note-by-note and, in doing so, acquiring an embodied knowledge of how those in the past have played these tunes. Musicians also teach songs to one another. Over time, the neophyte gets a grip on the repertory—the keys in which these tunes are typically played, the chord changes that are used (often with common variants and substitutions), and the tempo or groove or "feel" most associated with them.

My own attempt to learn the jazz repertory began in the years when I worked in San Francisco and Oakland as a jazz guitarist, from the 1990s until the mid-2000s. I was thankfully gifted with a good ear for harmony, so I could hear a chord progression once or twice and follow its basic moves. If I could not grab all the details the first time, the rest could be gleaned from listening to records, consulting lead sheets, or asking other musicians. For a while I worked in the "house band" at a regular Sunday afternoon jam session, at the Birdcage, on Telegraph Avenue in Oakland. The leader of the band was a trumpeter named Robert Porter, who was an institution in the Oakland jazz scene. Porter, small in stature but big in personality, would always show up in a three-piece suit, with his vest buttoned tight. During the jam sessions, he would watch over the happenings from a spot at the side of the bandstand. You could gauge his opinions of the music being made by watching the features on his smooth, brown, bald head. His style of playing trumpet was rooted in the Miles Davis records of the early 1950s (think "Solar" or "When Lights Are Low"). When inspiration hit, he could improvise with a kind of spare beauty and elegance of ideas that was inspiring.

The repertory played at the Birdcage was associated with bebop and hard bop. Oakland, located across the bay from San Francisco, was a magnet for African American migration in the years around World War II. Like many predominantly black cities, Oakland had many clubs and venues where you could hear neighborhood music—jazz, soul, funk, and R&B. On a Sunday at the Birdcage, you would have likely heard songs like "Out of Nowhere," "Star Eyes," "On Green Dolphin Street," a handful of Charlie Parker heads, "'Round Midnight," Horace Silver tunes like "Nica's Dream" or "Doodlin,'" "Watermelon Man," or "Invitation" (with straight-eighth notes on the A-section and swinging the bridge). Porter understood that the Sunday session was an informal classroom, where young musicians would come to learn how to play the music. He was always open to us "college kids," wryly incredulous that we wanted to learn to play jazz even as he would point us in the right direction. On a couple of occasions, I visited him in his one-bedroom apartment in downtown Oakland. The apartment had a small kitchen and a large record collection. He would heat up a saucepan of okra or beans and pull records off the shelf and onto the turntable. Sometimes he would trace the influences or genealogies of some musician's style, but more often than not he'd tell me, "you gotta hear this," or "if you don't know this recording then you don't know shit!"

At the Birdcage, it was not uncommon for some of Oakland's famous local musicians to sit in. On rare occasions, Pharoah Sanders, who had made his home in Oakland, would drop by. Most weeks, the brilliant pianist and organist Ed Kelly would sit in for a few numbers.[2] Quiet and mild-mannered, Kelly knew all the repertory cold, and he had developed his own reharmonizations of standards that had become like little idioms in the Oakland jazz scene. I learned a lot of these from working in an organ trio with Kelly for a couple of months in Jack London Square. He would nudge these changes my way on the first chorus, playing them clearly and definitely so I could catch them, before making things more abstract. Watching him play the Hammond organ was unforgettable. I would sit just a little bit behind him and to the side so I could see his hands as he performed. He'd slowly build his solos by changing registrations, pulling stops, adding percussion, or inching up the speed of the Leslie speaker. Our repertory was similar to that of the Birdcage but with additions that made sense for the organ trio. We played lots of blues and "Rhythm Changes" numbers, R&B-influenced songs like "Sunny" or "Red Clay," as well as tunes that slowly built toward climactic shout choruses ("Shiny Stockings") and plenty of modal jazz.

In the Oakland jazz scene, the repertory functioned as a common coin, one that allowed for the musicians to play together on the bandstand. Once you had a grip on it, you could go almost anywhere and make music with any of the musicians on the scene. Knowledge of the repertory was a way of entering into the social and cultural world of Oakland's black community. If you could survive on the bandstand, after the gig you would likely end up at a table at Mrs. Kelley's restaurant, eating red beans and rice and talking with the musicians. You'd learn all about their upbringing and education in the music, about the musicians they grew up with or worked with in the past, and about all the clubs that were no longer around. Although the repertory wasn't absolutely specific to Oakland, there was a sense that these musicians had been playing these well-worn tunes for a long time. The repertory was incorporated into both their shared history and their everyday interactions. These songs were just part of the local culture, like long-standing inside jokes or nicknames, all things that helped facilitate a sense of being together.

* * *

The house band at the Birdcage started doing a Monday night jam session at the Café du Nord on Market Street in San Francisco. Porter would lead the band and, in typical style, would bring people up to play. One night I recall him clearing his throat into the microphone and telling the audience, "We've got a real legend in the house tonight, Mr. Frank Jackson. Frank is going to come up and play a song, so you better SHUT UP AND LISTEN!" Frank was a pianist and singer, originally from Texas, who had come to California after enlisting in the military, as part of the African American migration to the West Coast in the years around World War II. During the heyday of San Francisco's Fillmore District, Frank had been one of the scene's bedrock musicians. He worked in house bands in various clubs, backing up traveling musicians from the likes of Ben Webster to Slim Gaillard to Sarah Vaughan. He played jam sessions at Jimbo's Bop City. He worked breakfast joints from early in the morning until noontime. He played on cramped bandstands behind go-go dancers and at hotel lounges, singing the standards. It was not uncommon for these to be lined up one after another. Musicians in the Fillmore might work twelve hours or more in a row—starting at a lounge, then backing up musicians from out of town, then off to an after-hours jam session or early morning breakfast gig.

When I met him at the Café du Nord, Frank had been at the edges of the jazz scene for a while, mostly surviving as a solo act in cabarets and piano bars. Tastes had changed and there was not the same audience for Frank's music. But San Francisco was in the midst of a swing music revival and, as I would later learn, Frank saw it as an opportunity to start performing with a small group. After Porter's introduction, Frank came up to the stage, sat down at the piano, and called out the tune "Route 66." Without even counting it off, he launched into an introduction at the piano that reminded me of the famous Nat Cole recording. As the song went on, I could hear him quoting more and more of that recording, and when it came time for the ending, I could anticipate where he was going. I played all the riffs and hits with him, as if we had practiced it, and that cemented our musical relationship. He asked me if I would be interested in working with him, and if I knew any good bass players. I was, and I did. I ended up working with him for over a decade in a small trio of piano, guitar, and bass. That trio was my master class in the jazz repertory.

I was in my late twenties and Frank was an octogenarian, but his youthful voice and wrinkle-free face seemed incongruent with his age. He didn't read music very well and didn't need to. He had a near photographic memory for popular songs and an ear that would allow him to harmonize at the keyboard whatever he heard in his head. He was a favorite performer of fans of the Great American Songbook. On a regular Monday night gig in Palo Alto, Frank would take requests from the audience, and I would wait, not without a small touch of terror, to discover *what song I would be playing momentarily that I had never heard of before!* Nearly every week the owner of the café, a restaurateur named Freddy Maddalena, would dredge up some obscure number from the past to try and stump Frank. Although it sounds like an exaggeration, I cannot recall a single instance where he ever succeeded. If Frank didn't know the words of a song, he could play its melody and harmony at the piano; and if he did know the words, he would often surprise the requester with a verse, or extra choruses of lyrics, or witty musical quotations.

Frank's repertoire was different from what was played at the Oakland jam sessions. He was like an embodied archive of popular music from the 1930s and 1940s. Aside from all the Gershwin, Berlin, Rodgers and Hart, and Cole Porter songs that one might expect, Frank would croon Ellington ballads like "I Didn't Know about You," "My Little Brown Book," and "All Too Soon." His true inspiration was Nat "King" Cole—not the later incarnation, the celebrated pop vocalist in front of orchestras and big bands, but the young, piano-playing leader of the King Cole Trio. He knew *everything* in the Nat Cole catalog: the classics ("The Frim Fram Sauce," "Straighten Up and Fly Right," and "Sweet Lorraine"), the humorous ones ("I'm a Shy Guy," "Can't See for Lookin'," and "Bring Another Drink"), the obscure ones ("A Boy from Texas—a Girl from Tennessee," "Vom Vim Veedle"), and the overlooked ballads ("Beautiful Moons Ago," "I'm Lost," "I Realize Now"). He knew songs associated from long-forgotten movies ("Six Bridges to Cross" comes to mind, which he associated with Sammy Davis Jr.), old hit parade favorites, like "Indian Summer" or "Poinciana," and even commercial jingles from his youth. (I think I recall one about Listerine.) But he also transformed them through his own musical sensibilities. As all jazz musicians do, Frank had his own habits of harmonization, his collection of vamps and endings and introductions that might be deployed as needed, and his ways of building drama through form, dynamics, and vocal-tonal coloring.

In Frank's hands the jazz repertory was more than a shared social coin within the jazz community, an object that would facilitate musicians to get a jam session going. He knew the history of these songs, their original context and the ways that they had circulated. He could recall when he had first heard them; which versions of the tunes he liked and disliked; and how the songs had, through use, acquired new chord changes, additional verses, or unique introductions and vamps. Through working with him, I came to realize that the social dimension of a jazz repertory, which was so important to functioning of the Oakland scene, was supplemented with an historical dimension. Not only did these songs facilitate performance, but each performance was inscribed within a horizon of past performances. Those two dimensions—the social and the historical, if I can call them such—were not simply orthogonal, defining a social and historical grid on which to map the jazz repertory, but they were also intertwined. Frank's re-performances of the past were not historicist in nature but were archives of the sedimentation of previous forms of sociality, of ways that the music had circulated in the past. At the same time, the sociality central to the Oakland scene's use of the repertory was historically rooted; its forms of sociality had been shaped through the experiences that the musicians in that scene had shared. The standards that formed the center of the jazz repertory could not be mapped on a simple grid because they were not fixed entities.

* * *

A standard is not just a song, or a composition, or a set of chords with a melody—something simple and easy to conceptualize—but something else entirely, a changing thing that is irreducible to any one of its performances even as it is shaped through its performances. Unlike the traditional notion of the "musical work," standards are not fixed entities; their mode of being is not reducible to something notated, scored, published, recorded, and then re-performed again and again. Standards are protean. They are musical entities that differ over time, that slide into the contours of diverse social situations, and that accrue and shed musical properties (and musical meanings) through transformative cycles of performance and re-performance. And yet, for all of their malleability, standards have a palpability that is indisputable. These songs are called on the bandstand every day, at almost every gig and jam session; they are shared across communities of musicians; they are loved (or hated) by listeners; they trigger memories for some and are forcefully memorized by others. Standards, protean as they are, have solidity and reality because they have stakes: if you are a jazz musician and do not know the standard being called, you might be ashamed, or embarrassed, or outclassed, or lose the gig. But if you know it, you might find entrance into a community that had seemed inaccessible, or performance opportunities that could be garnered in no other way. Knowing standards matters. If not your life, then your livelihood might depend on it.

To articulate what is so singular and odd about standards—and why they are an object worthy of patient inquiry—we must differentiate a standard from a song. A song might get played and replayed quite a lot, but for a song to become a standard requires not only that it be treated in multiple performances by multiple performers but also that it has become familiar in the jazz tradition to do so. A tune played only once could not be regarded as a standard; nor could a musician intend to produce a standard by playing a single tune repeatedly. Because standards are widely interpreted, different performances diverge greatly from one another in terms of their musical aspects—tempo, harmony, melody, form, and the like. Moreover, it is precisely those divergences that are valued and cultivated by both performers and listeners. By comparing different performances of the same standard, one is invited to compare and evaluate qualities of virtuosity or originality. Standards, while part of the jazz "canon," have no canonic form. They do not evoke a single, past performance or fixed aural images; rather, they are built upon a basis of multiple performances, each differing in degrees from the others. To fix this idea in our minds, a standard might be depicted as a *network*, one in which the nodes represent distinct performances and in which node-to-node relations (or edges) represent similarities and differences among performances. And yet, a standard is not any particular node in this network, but a permissive set of protocols, rules, strategies, and customs that emerges from the network in its holism.

At the very least, that is my intuition, and it has been an abiding one that has shaped my own transition from a jazz musician into a jazz scholar. This book is an attempt to transform that intuition into a theory.

***

Hearing Double is a book about the ontology of the jazz standard. Musical ontology is the study of the kinds of entities that comprise music, its composition, and its performance. The majority of writing on the ontology of music has focused on the "musical work," in contrast to musical performances, which are usually thought to be performances *of* a work. Because performances are typically assumed to be performances *of works*, philosophers of music have focused more of their attention on works, which would logically (if not temporally) precede performances. Debates in musical ontology are often about what kind of thing best defines the nature of the musical work: for example, is it a structure instanced in performances, or a universal with particulars, or a type with performance tokens, and why?

In one respect, *Hearing Double* is no different. I will be arguing that the jazz standard is best understood as an emergent entity, one that *requires but is irreducible to* a network of performances. In other respects, *Hearing Double* is different from many musical ontologies. First, my consideration is wholly focused on jazz, with very little reference to classical music and other musical traditions. By bracketing out classical music, I have tried to stay focused on what is unique and specific to the ontology of standards.[3] Second, I have tried to make the argument hinge, as much as possible, on the actual practices of musicians, critics, and engaged listeners. Lastly, my approach to musical ontology differs in that I do not strictly separate ontological questions from issues in culture, history, and aesthetics. Nor would I assert that ontology describes the way the world *is* apart from those who live in the world. Rather, I believe that ontology captures the basic entities, types, and kinds that are implicit in the engagements of agents and actors with the shared world in which they live.

My approach to ontology is shaped by two scholars I greatly admire, Lydia Goehr and Georgina Born. I was an undergraduate at Berkeley when Goehr's first book, *The Imaginary Museum of Musical Works*, appeared. It shook the musicological world (or at least the musicological world of Morrison Hall). Its premise, one that has been so influential as to now appear commonsensical, is that the idea of the "musical work" is an historical concept that primarily regulates behavior. The idea that musical works were part of an historical horizon, that its concept had perhaps surpassed its usefulness, shaped my thinking as an undergraduate at Berkeley. What I learned from Goehr was that ontology can be understood historically, that ontological concepts have a lifespan. Moreover, there is no need to inoculate ontology from history and that to do so is often suspect.[4] *The Imaginary Museum of Musical Works* generated extensive debates about the nature, history, and social function of the "musical work." It solicited more questions than could be answered in its scope. One issue that engaged me concerned a reconstruction of ontological thinking. For instance, given that the "musical work" with its paradigm of *Werktreue* is a regulative concept, one that came into being historically and may be nearing its end, what might we say about the ontology of other music, especially musics that do not fit snugly under the category of the musical work or *Werktreue*? Jazz seemed to me to be a robust and complex place to think about other musical ontologies—just as historical, and just as regulative perhaps, but regulating us in ways that might be more salubrious and permissive than the strictures of *Werktreue*.

In considering various reconstructions of musical ontology, I have also been deeply influenced by Georgina Born's writings, and through conversations and correspondence. Her work on the ontology of music is rooted in social-scientific methods (from sociology, anthropology, and science and technology studies). The strong ethnographic focus that is a hallmark of her work on the study of institutions (e.g., IRCAM and the BBC) carries over into her anthropologically influenced work on ontology. In her essay "On Musical Mediation," Born develops an ontological model of the work of art rooted in the writings of the anthropologist Alfred Gell. Gell's *Art and Agency* envisages art objects not as singular, integral entities, but as distributed objects, which are produced and reproduced across complex networks of overlapping agency. Using the language of Husserl on time, artworks retain the past and protend the future in a dynamic system of references. Although music is not considered in Gell's suggestive work, Born's application of Gell's ideas to the world of jazz and improvised music has been a source of inspiration for my own work on ontology. While we both share an intuition that musical ontology is best rendered in the shape of a network, I have tried use the large canvas of a book to explicate aspects of that idea that simply could not find their proper space within the tight constraints of an essay, nor have I used the explicit language of Gell (or of Husserl) to make my case. In addition to our shared affinity for networks, my approach to music generally has been shaped by Born's attention to jazz, improvised music, and sound art as sites for the analysis of music's sociality. Her articulation of the layers of mediation at work in every musical work and musical performance (from the microsocial level of the individual musicians engaged acts of musicking, to the macrosocial level of music's institutions and norms) has honed my eye and my ear to the traces of mediation found in all acts of musicking.

If this book cites Goehr and Born too infrequently, it is because their influence is operative at a level deeper than the endnotes. They have influenced my thinking about the ontology of music altogether. I may have been prepared for the influence of Goehr and Born because of long-standing interest in Adorno's writing—starting from the time I was an undergraduate. This may seem like an odd influence to cite in a book about jazz, given Adorno's own famously low esteem for the music. But I have always felt that, without excusing Adorno's often uninformed and mistaken judgments about jazz, there were methodological insights to be gained from his approach to both music and philosophy more generally. In Adorno's philosophical writings, concepts are always already historical and socially mediated. They do not simply appear outside of the historical flow but are themselves engaged with the vicissitudes of history, politics, and society. If concepts are understood historically, then, just as a diminished seventh chord might become shopworn and ineffective from use, concepts too might lose their critical grip on reality and become worn tokens incapable of maintaining the potential they once had. Like Adorno—and Goehr and Born—I would assert that, in part, *ontology is historical. At the very least, this book will argue that the ontology of standards can only be adequately understood in relation to history.*

In addition, Adorno's musicological writings always emphasize how the musical work—and musical performance—is mediated by social forces. It is as if every piece of music is held suspended in a field of conflicting social forces; to interpret a work is then, in part, an attempt to read the forces that are present, and to see how they have formed and deformed the work at hand. For me, the mechanisms of replication and nomination—the two main processes that I will theorize as involved in the reproduction of the jazz repertoire—are thoroughly social in nature. If the ontology of the standard emerges from ongoing acts of replication and nomination, the social forces that structure the success or failure of these are integral to ontological consideration. Like Adorno—and Goehr and Born—I would assert that, in part, *ontology is social. At the very least, this book will make the case that the ontology of standards can only be understood in relation to social forces.* An underlying motivation for writing this book is to explicate the *social and historical ontology* of jazz.[5]

***

The book is organized into two large parts. After acquainting the reader with the relevant philosophical and music-theoretic debates about the ontology of jazz, Part I presents the main philosophical argument of the book: the development of a non-essentialist, network-based ontology of standards. To make that argument, I focus on two operations—*replication* and *nomination*—that are crucial to the performance and reproduction of standards. Part II considers the historical, economic, and cultural forces that shaped the "soundscape of standards," which I locate roughly between the years 1930 and 1960. These forces help to explain why the ontology described in Part I emerged when it did, why the repertory of jazz standards contains the kind of music it does, and why additions to this corpus appear to be ever-diminishing. The final chapter considers the aesthetic evaluation of standards and argues that a network-based ontology specifies many of the implicit values of jazz criticism. It also theorizes a mode of listening that is geared to a network-based ontology of music, which I call "hearing double." When critically listening to standards, I will argue, we are always hearing double.

As an aid to the reader, here are a few words about the book's style. *Hearing Double* tends toward analytic and expository prose—for some readers, perhaps overly so. But this mode of writing permitted me to realize two desiderata. First, it allowed me to offer an account of the ontology of standards that was as clear and comprehensive as I am able to be. Some readers may grow tired of reading about "corrigible" structures, "network-based ontology," or "sufficiently work-determinative properties" and long for lither figurations. Moments where I have eschewed figurative speech for the repetition of specific terms are moments where I have tried to hold fast to delimited concepts in order to move them patiently along the path of an argument. I hope that the reader may find some compensation for occasionally dry prose in the pleasure of following a clear line of thought and an unfolding argument. Second, the analytic and expository style allowed me to draw together musical practice, music theory, and "Theory" (as it is sometimes called in "the academy") more broadly. The idea that there is philosophical insight to be gained from things as commonplace as a chord substitution or an improvisation is one that I find appealing. I am committed to the belief that musical practice is an unassuming yet rich site of insight and wisdom— not only philosophical, but social, ethical, and historical. Employing a style that could be both musically theoretic and philosophically theoretic is a part of my attempt to realize that commitment.

The analytic and expository mode is most palpable in the book's *content*, in its sentence-by-sentence connection of ideas and in the long thread of argumentation that gives them direction. But the book's *form* is less indebted to philosophy's forms (the essay, the treatise, or the tome) than to music's forms. *Hearing Double* takes inspiration from music's forms—with its repetition of sections, its linking of phrases, its obligatory contrasts and developing variations—as well as the formal affordances of music's media. At times, I have imagined the two halves of the book to be like two sides of a long-playing record. The argument of the book sweeps along continuously, like the involuted spiral on the record's surface, but it is marked halfway by a pause, a turnover, and a change of direction. After Part I's patient exposition of the standard's ontology, Part II flips the argument over in an attempt to explicate the historical and cultural conditions that led to the emergence of the standard. Throughout the whole "album"—to extend the metaphor—ontology is the keynote, but the second side tries to show the strong affiliations that bind ontology to auditory culture and history. Ontology and auditory culture are not, nor cannot be, isolated domains; they must be considered together if our ontologies are to be relevant to the actual practices and beliefs of musicians and listeners. They are as inseparable as the two sides of a phonograph disc.

There are other musical metaphors that came to mind while writing *Hearing Double*. In addition to its "two sides," I often sensed an affinity between the section-by-section organization of the book and the organizational protocols of jazz. After an extended vamp (Chapter 1), the book could be read as playing a set of choruses on the theme of the standard. Chapter 2 and Chapter 6 both address that standard of standards, "Body and Soul," which would function as the book's "head"—the melody and chord progression upon which the rest of the book cycles through, chorus after chorus, wringing new changes and bringing novel aspects to light. We might read each chapter as a collection of connected ideas that, like an improvisation, start and end unexpectedly against the bar lines and abut short motives against long, arcing lines. Rather than provide subheadings within each chapter (except in Chapter 5), the prose accumulates like the phrases of a soloist. Each phrase picks up from the last, even as it negotiates new progressions and responds to the ensemble. Although we might want to stop the record and listen to one particular phrase again, the esteem for a solo is never found in a single phrase but in the overall sweep of ideas. I might ask a similar indulgence on the part of the reader: even if there are individual phrases that may draw attention (for good or ill), or even as the solo feels like it is beginning to wander, please stick with it. I hope that the long arc of the argument, the sweep of ideas, will be worth the attention.

Speaking of indulgence, I also ask one last favor of the reader. Please listen to the recordings discussed in the book. If you do not already know some recording being addressed—or even if you do—please put the book down and turn on the music. A common joy of musicology is the pleasure of going down the proverbial "rabbit hole" of a song's history and corpus of performances. Even though I am in the enviable position of being able to claim that I do this "for research," there is always something both edifying and pleasurable in the apparently idle activity of listening to recording after recording of the "same song." I have never re-emerged from the rabbit hole without surprise, without having learned something unexpected, or without new or renewed appreciation of an aspect of a performance or of a standard. *Hearing Double* is, in some sense, the fruit of those excursions, those moments when the rabbit hole turned out to be an underground complex of rooms and chambers, or a burrow of densely interconnected passageways. Familiarity with these recordings and performances will not only make the book more enjoyable to read, you will get the much more important benefit of knowing these songs and performances in musical detail, in historical depth, and as part of an ever-transforming network of relations. Put on the music, the prose can wait.

PART I
ONTOLOGY

1
The Metaphysics of Musical Structure

In the 1990s, near the end of a long and distinguished career, the music theorist Allen Forte turned his attention to American popular music. Famous for his work on atonal music and Schenkerian theory, Forte's sudden shift of focus was bound to look like an about-face. But the Great American Songbook had been one of his long-standing interests and, in print, he offered a wry explanation: "My experience with the classic American popular song extends back to a misspent childhood during which, in addition to subjecting me to a traditional training in music, my mother made me play popular music and jazz on the piano. Subsequently I played that music professionally, before seeing the error of my ways and entering the cloistered academic life."[1] But even within the cloister, those who knew Forte can recall the many occasions when he would sit and the piano and engagingly play through some of his favorite standards.

Forte's analyses of "classic American song" employed techniques first introduced by the Viennese music theorist Heinrich Schenker, techniques that Forte himself had helped to popularize among music theorists. Although these techniques were designed to analyze the "masterworks" of Western music—Bach, Beethoven, Chopin, Schumann, and so forth—Forte, alongside other postwar American music theorists, began to champion Schenker's ideas in the service of quite differing repertories. Schenker's analytic techniques drew attention to aspects of the music's configuration often obscured by the welter of surface detail. They focused on a work's simple but powerful underlying structures—archetypes, one might say—capable of expansion and repetition at various hierarchical levels. By reducing down the music's surface or foreground, analysts could glean long-range linear structures spanning a phrase, section, movement, or even an entire work. These structures could be prolonged or elaborated through a variety of contrapuntal and harmonic means. Even the relationship among musical motives, which often appeared on the foreground of the music, could be argued by the analyst to originate in a work's middleground or background.

Hearing Double. Brian Kane, Oxford University Press. © Oxford University Press 2024.
DOI: 10.1093/oso/9780190600501.003.0002

18 HEARING DOUBLE

In *The American Popular Ballad of the Golden Era, 1924–1950*, Forte applied these techniques to ballads written by some of Tin Pan Alley's and Broadway's most celebrated composers: Jerome Kern, Irving Berlin, George Gershwin, and Richard Rodgers, among others. He did not intend his book to be read cover to cover; rather, readers were encouraged to study their favorite songs or composers from the Great American Songbook by means of detailed analytical graphs and commentary. Aside from the general boundaries of 1924 and 1950—the former year being "as close to the beginning of the modern popular ballad as I could determine ... also the year of the famous Paul Whiteman concert in Aeolian Hall, in which Gershwin's *Rhapsody in Blue* made its debut," and the latter year marking "the beginning of the rock 'n' roll idiom that was to assume the ascendant in the popular field ... also mark[ing] the closing of the careers of many of the major songwriters and lyricists of the Golden Era"—the songs representing each composer reflected both Forte's personal taste and the general fame of the tune.[2] In the chapter on Rodgers, for example, he discussed "Thou Swell," "My Heart Stood Still," "You Are Too Beautiful," "My Funny Valentine," and "Where or When"—all common standards in the worlds of jazz and popular music—as well as the lesser-known "A Ship without a Sail."

Forte focuses on two large-scale linear structures in his analysis of "My Funny Valentine." The first is the ascending melody line, which slowly rises from middle c (c^1) in measure 1 to its climax, $e♭^2$, in measure 31. However, the melody does not simply rush to the climax. Rather, it unfolds in a slow ascent across the song's AABA' form, utilizing the interval of an ascending third motivically and structurally. Starting on c^1, the melody pushes upward a third to $e♭^1$ across first A-section (mm. 1–8). The second A-section follows suit, sequencing the opening melodic idea up the interval of a third, spanning from $e♭^1$ to g^1. The trajectory of these two phrases can be seen in the upward stemmed notes in the treble clef of Forte's analytical sketch (see Figure 1.1, systems 1 and 2). The melodic leaps in the A-sections (to $b♭^1$ and d^2, respectively) open up the space that the melody will soon occupy in more systematic ways. The song's bridge or B-section (mm. 17–24) picks up A-section's $b♭^1$ and, after leaping down to $e♭^1$, initiates a series of melodic skips, each higher than the last. These leaps produce a stepwise line ($b♭^1$, c^2, d^2) that spans the interval of a third and fills in the gap between $b♭^1$ and d^2, the two highest pitches of the first two A-sections. Since "My Funny Valentine" oscillates between C minor and E♭ major, the arrival of d^2, the leading tone in E♭, initiates the expectation of the arrival of $e♭^2$. (This can be seen in measure 21 of Figure 1.1, where a broken

THE METAPHYSICS OF MUSICAL STRUCTURE   19

Figure 1.1 Analytical sketch for "My Funny Valentine." Reproduced from Forte, *The American Popular Ballad of the Golden Era, 1924–1950*, p. 198.

beam followed by the annotation "m. 31" indicates where this linear structure will eventually be continued.) The arrival of that projected eb^2 is delayed until the final A-section (mm. 25–32). Beginning with a reprise of the opening two phrases in a condensed form, the last A-section re-initiates the ascending linear motion of the song thus far and drives it to completion in measure 31. In typical Schenkerian fashion, the arrival of this eb^2 does not coincide with the arrival of tonic harmony in E♭, but rather eb^2 appears as a consonant tone over a C minor chord. The song's ending or "codetta," in Forte's terminology (mm. 33–36), puts everything aright by setting up a small descent (g^1, f^1 eb^1) that corresponds with song's final and perfect authentic cadence in E♭.

Counterpointed against the melody's large-scale linear ascent is a second linear structure, a descending chromatic figure that accompanies the A-sections of "Valentine." Forte calls this a "traditional lament feature," one that "is strongly reminiscent of the ancient ground-bass lament."[3] An inner voice, which begins in unison with the initial c^1 of the melody, descends a semitone each measure until measure 5, where it stops on a♭. (See the upward stemmed and beamed notes in Forte's analytical sketch, bass clef, first system.) The anticipated continuation of this linear descent, to g, is realized neither in measure 6 of the first A-section, nor in the restatement of this phrase in the second A-section. Rather, the a♭ is simply absorbed into the F-minor chord of measure 6 and its force is temporarily neutralized. However, in the final A-section of the song, the descent is reinitiated and reaches its goal, g, in measure 30—just one measure before the melody reaches its goal, eb^2, in measure 31. In Forte's sketch, the completion of this inner line appears on the fourth system; the descending inner voice arrives at a♭ in 29, then Forte traces it to the bass voice where its goal, G, finally arrives. (The diagonal line in measure 29 notes the shift in the lament's register from inner voice to bass.) The double completion of these two linear structures, first the "lament" in measure 30 and then the ascending melody in measure 31, with their slight temporal displacement, triggers the song's tiny ending. By extending across the refrain's thirty-six measures, these linear structures reveal the song's large-scale organization. Attention to large-scale features thus cuts against surface-oriented analyses that rely too heavily on the standard AABA organization common to many songs in the Great American Songbook. According to Forte, "It is these long-range melodic features as well as the eloquent harmonic and contrapuntal detail of *My Funny Valentine* that endow it with its special quality."[4]

***

A cultural critic reading Forte's text might readily note—and it is hardly far from the surface—that his Schenkerian approach to popular song carries along with it a set of implicit values. By analyzing popular music with tools designed for the "masterworks" of classical music, Forte appears to be engaging in an exercise of cultural esteem. The implication could hardly be clearer: popular music and jazz will only get the respect they deserve when they claim for themselves the institutional and cultural distinction that accrues to classical music—a distinction revealed, it seems, by well-entrenched academic analytic methods.[5]

And yet Forte insists that his analyses are not intended to forward this argument. "I have tried," he writes, "to avoid comparing these songwriters . . . just as I have avoided any comparison of this music with classical music of any kind."[6] Forte's esteem for American popular music is not a conclusion to be proven by the application of the analytic technique but rather a premise, the very reason for analyzing the music in the first place. In his characteristic tone of understatement, Forte writes, "To take popular music seriously in this way has required a certain reorientation from my ordinary pursuits, which concern music theory and analysis of a more recondite kind and music that other scholars might regard as better suited to more traditional research endeavors. I trust that I have done this without in any way conveying an attitude of condescension, which, in any event, would not represent my basic intuitive and intellectual approach to this music."[7] The use of Schenkerian techniques for the analysis of popular music is explicitly distinguished from Schenker's own evaluation of classical masterworks and his vehement aesthetic rejection of music that did not live up to his standards. Where Schenker intertwined the analysis of musical structure and the evaluation of musical work, Forte repeatedly insists on the separation of the two. The value of Schenkerian theory, for Forte, is in demonstrating the salient features of the structure of tonal music, of which American popular music represents a late efflorescence. "As far as we know, however, Schenker never expressed any interest in the American popular ballad; and if he had it would no doubt have been negative. . . . The primary relations between Schenker's remarkable and path-breaking work is to be found in the analytical approach, not in any shared interest in musical repertoire, except insofar as the American popular ballad exhibits the basic structural characteristics of classical tonal music."[8]

While Forte's writings on American popular song separate issues of aesthetics from the analysis of musical structure, it is the latter term, "structure," that remains central and unquestioned. Forte assumes musical structure as the primary object of study for the disciplines of musicology and music theory. Diagnosing the situation in 1995, the year *The American Popular Ballad of the Golden Era* was published, Forte observes that "there appears to be a distinct split between scholars who are interested in a music-analytic approach to the study of popular music and those who regard popular music a sociological artifact."[9] Steering clear of the cultural politics or business of popular music, Forte remains a staunch defender of the perception and analysis of musical structure, seeing it as endangered or belittled by sociological inquiry into the cultural conditions surrounding the production of popular music. Casting the argument in bellicose terms, "musicology cannot afford to neglect studies of popular music as music, for otherwise the sociological view, which often tends to disregard musical content, will prevail."[10] The implication is that those sociological approaches to American popular music that ignore musical structure are aligned with modes of musical knowledge that disregard features of the music found at "the large-scale" or at levels of "depth" beyond the music's surface. Cultural and sociological theorists, insofar as they take musical structure into consideration, remain stuck at the surface, in distinction from those possessing what Forte clearly regards as the proper musicological and music-theoretic training.

This used to be a fairly common argument. Forte's interesting twist on it is this: rather than simply opposing music-theoretical "deep structure" against sociological "surface," Forte argues that practitioners of popular music—composers, performers, and improvisers—are aligned with musicologists and music theorists in their attentiveness to structure. While the economic and cultural constraints on American popular song dictate that the "song must be easy to grasp," Forte notes that

> There are often important stylistic features of the music—substructures—that transcend the immediate perceptual experience of the casual listener. Of these perhaps the most obvious and at the same time the most familiar is the harmonic skeleton that generations of jazz performers have abstracted—"analytically," it should be emphasized—for the complete musical object. It is the melodic manipulation of this substructure that sometimes causes critics to question the relation between the improvised variation and the original. How often does one hear—especially now—the complaint that a Charlie Parker improvisation bears little relation to the harmonic prototype from which it purportedly derives?[11]

Since Forte does not often address jazz improvisation in his book, this short passage is suggestive. First, note the identification between the jazz performer and the music theorist through the use of the appositive clause: "'analytically,' it should be emphasized." Are these "abstracted" "harmonic skeletons" with which jazz performers work akin to the "structures" that Forte discovers as professional analyst? Does it matter that Forte's Schenkerian techniques are not the same techniques passed down in the various traditions—oral and written, institutional and informal, classroom and bandstand—of jazz pedagogy? Are the structures that Forte identifies (large-scale, linear structures) akin to the kind of structures that jazz musicians use as the basis for their improvisations? Given Forte's own time as a performer of popular music ("I played that music professionally, before seeing the error of my ways"), is he suggesting that his own late work on popular music makes explicit a set of implicit or practical analyses that began in his days as a performer?

Moreover, one wonders about the ontological status of these structures. If it is true that jazz performers are making their "improvised variations" on the basis of structures abstracted from an original, must we come to an agreement about the objectivity of these structures? Is Forte, in analyzing "My Funny Valentine," showing us the structures that are objectively present in the song or are they simply the structures that he *hears in* the music? Is one to assume that the presence of these abstract structures makes a jazz performance of "My Funny Valentine" an instance of that work? In other words, is an ontological claim being asserted that the shared presence of certain musical structures (or "substructures") grounds the identification of two performances of "My Funny Valentine" as performances of one and the same work? If so, then how are we to specify these structures and determine their properties?[12]

Forte claims that a shared "substructure" links the "improvised variation and the original." But what, exactly, is "the original"? The problem becomes acute when we consider the musical sources—the sheet music—employed in Forte's analysis. Composers involved with Tin Pan Alley, Broadway, and Hollywood film wrote much of this music. Each of these systems, whether intertwined or distinct, had developed an elaborate apparatus for the production, publication, and distribution of music. Newly composed songs, after leaving the hands of the composers and lyricists, would often go through a series of additional hands (additional composers, editors, orchestrators, arrangers, engravers, as well as the input of executives, directors, audiences, performers, preview audiences, etc.) before making their first appearance.

Publishers of popular music would often work with in-house arrangers to produce sheet music designed for a variety of consumer needs. Simple arrangements for piano and voice were sold to consumers to play at home; ukulele or guitar chords were added above the vocal line; standard stock orchestrations were purchased by dance bands or theater orchestras, and reviewed in trade journals; novelty arrangements were created for pianists or theater organists, employing the full panoply of registrations and, literally, bells and whistles available on some instruments; song pluggers peddled these tunes, altering them in their own performances and encouraging others to do the same in order to promote the product; recording sessions were organized, often by multiple performers as companies marketed songs to distinct audiences; Hollywood tie-ins were cultivated. This is the problem of mediation, a problem that any scholar of American popular music must face squarely. It leads to a useful methodological maxim: the more one looks into the history of a standard, the harder it is to identify the "original."[13]

Consider the case of "My Funny Valentine." The song first appeared in the Richard Rodgers and Lorenz Hart show *Babes in Arms*. Based on Forte's graphs and reductions, it appears that he worked with an arrangement of the song for piano and voice published originally by Chappell & Co. in 1937, the year of the show's premiere, and reproduced often throughout the supervening years.[14] The arrangement itself is quite thin in texture; the presentation of the first phrase of the refrain only barely goes beyond three voices: the melody, the bass, and the descending inner line. The thinness of the arrangement resembles the reductions used in Schenkerian analysis, exemplified by Forte's analytical sketch, where inessential notes on the surface of the music are excised in order to clarify the music's structural features. In making his argument about the significance of the linearly descending middle voice (the "lament")—one of the voices preserved in the piano and voice arrangement—Forte appeals to the intentionality of the composer, arguing that, "In the sheet music, the composer even supplies that note [i.e., the b in measure 2, Figure 1.2] with an accent so that the pianist will not overlook its importance."[15] Yet, what evidence is there to show that the accent was indeed drawn by the hand of the composer? Does this accent appear in the original orchestration of the song for the 1937 show? And if it does, how do we know it is the work of Rodgers and not the hand of an orchestrator or arranger? Moreover, additional harmonies, countermelodies, and changes in orchestration—all of which one would have surely heard at a performance of *Babes in Arms* on Broadway—are not to be found. Neither are features of the

Figure 1.2 "My Funny Valentine," sheet music, for voice and piano. Reproduced with permission of Alfred Music.

song that one might have grown to expect based on the commercially successful recordings of "My Funny Valentine" from the 1950s, such as the lush string harmonies heard on the famous Columbia recording of *Babes in Arms* with Mary Martin from 1951 or on Frank Sinatra's rendition from his first Capitol release, *Song for Young Lovers*.[16] I mention these not to distract from the point about sources but because it is likely that "My Funny Valentine" would never have made it into Forte's volume without the success of these later renditions.[17] The song was not one of the show's original hits. If one can judge the popularity of the tune by the number of recordings made, "My Funny Valentine" eked out a meager existence throughout the 1940s. After the appearance of the Columbia cast recording, the song underwent a resurgence, spawning versions by Frank Sinatra, Chet Baker, Gerry Mulligan, and Miles Davis, in quick succession.

In comparison with these performances, the piano arrangement seems very thin indeed. Yet from an analytic perspective, that thinness might represent something quite powerful and advantageous. By reducing the music down to its minimal elements, by stripping away the lush orchestration, ornate countermelodies, and rich harmonizations, the piano arrangement functions like a reduction, not only in the music-theoretical sense but also in the philosophical sense. In metaphysics, reduction is an important technique for separating an object's essence from its accidents or inessential properties. Essences are those features or properties of an object that are permanent, durable, and unchanging in nature. It is in virtue of its essential features that an object is what it is. Essences are gleaned by reducing away all that is changeable, contingent, or peripheral. Typically, one reduces away relations, accidents, or secondary qualities in order to determine an object's essence. In musical cases, reduction works similarly; by reducing away the orchestration and ornamentation to its bare structure, one might argue that inessential features of the song are distinguished from essential features. Thus, the stripped-down elements—the unadorned melody line, the linear contrapuntal inner voice, and the bass line—present just the "essentials," only those features that are necessary and requisite for the song to be what it "is."

***

Works of jazz and popular music, especially those considered standards, appear in an astonishing variety or forms. The same song performed by Guy Lombardo, Louis Armstrong, Paul Whiteman, or Glenn Miller might also appear in versions by Billie Holiday, Charlie Parker, Miles Davis, Thelonious Monk, or Cecil Taylor. These versions differ radically in their properties, some remaining close to the melody and harmonies found in the scores and sheet music, others incorporating wild flights of improvisation or daring reharmonizations. Often, little seems to link the more adventurous jazz versions of these tunes with those we hear on original cast recordings, in Hollywood films, or in the popular music of the 1930s to 1950s, the era in which many of the tunes now considered "standards" were composed. Forte alludes to this situation when he mentions the "complaint that a Charlie Parker improvisation bears little relation to the harmonic prototype from which it purportedly derives."[18]

Given the wide-ranging performances of these tunes and difficulty of determining why (or if) these performances are instances of one and the same song, standards provide a genuine philosophical problem for those interested in the question of the ontology of the musical work. While works of classical music typically have been the focus of the ontology of music, there is far less variability in the way that works of classical music are performed today than in jazz and popular music. And yet, works of classical music have received the lion's share of attention by philosophers. This is odd, since the challenges of the ontology of standards is greater and thus presents a more robust philosophical problem.

There are two basic positions among philosophers who have tackled the ontology of standards. The first denies that the notion of the musical work is relevant to the performance of standards. Given the wide variability of performances and the fact that the aesthetic interest in listening to standards is often directed at the quality of improvisation and the performer's originality, there is little sense in demanding that a musical work, rather than performances, be the object of ontological concern.[19] I disagree with this view. Performances of standards are not like performances of free improvisations, in that performers not only base their improvisations on pre-existing performances and works, but also intend to do so. While granting that much of our aesthetic interest as listeners is focused on the quality of the improvisation, the creativity of the reharmonizations, and the nature of the performance, we still need to account for why two different-sounding performances of "My Funny Valentine" are performances of one and the same work. Without some basis for comparison—a basis that goes beyond the evaluation of the quality of the improvisation and performance—the actions of jazz musicians who perform standards would simply be opaque or unintelligible. When listening to performances of standards, the invocation of comparisons to other versions of the tune is a central phenomenon, not an incidental one.

The second position is that standards can be reduced to a small set of essential, work-determinative properties. Philosophers have sought to account for the identity of standards across their diverse performances, well aware that such performances often employ drastically distinct instrumentation, harmonization, form, and arrangement, while still remaining performances of one and the same work. Perhaps two widely divergent performances of a standard are linked through a shared but minimal set of invariant properties present in both performances. This has been an attractive position for musical ontologists because, on a first consideration, it seems capable of accounting for the wide variability of performances of standards while also providing grounds for their identity. The properties shared might be quite minimal indeed. The philosopher Stephen Davies, in his comprehensive tome *Musical Works and Performances*, has dubbed this kind of minimal structure a "thin" musical work.[20]

Consider, for example, Frank Sinatra's recording of "My Funny Valentine" from the LP *Songs for Young Lovers*.[21] The recording is replete with musical properties, comprising every detail from the contour and rhythm of the melody line, to the specific harmonization used to accompany Sinatra, to formal aspects of the performance (such as the shift from alla breve time [2/2]—the norm for popular ballads of the era—into 3/4 time for the bridge). While some of these musical properties can be easily notated on a score, the recording will also contain properties that are much harder to notate, like the micro-timing of Sinatra's phrasing, or the specific timbre of the orchestra or of Sinatra's voice at any particular moment in the performance. Of the properties captured by the recording and made available to listeners, a philosopher might argue that only a select few of them are essential for identifying Sinatra's performances as an instance of the musical work "My Funny Valentine." Those properties that are constitutive of the musical work would be deemed essential or "work-determinative."

"Works for performance can be 'thick' or 'thin' in their constitutive properties," Davies writes. "If it is thin, the work's determinative properties are comparatively few in number and most of the qualities of a performance are aspects of the performer's interpretation, not of the work as such. The thinner they are, the freer is the performer to control aspects of the performance."[22] The thickness or thinness of a musical work depends on the amount of determinative properties that a performance requires in order to be a performance of a specific work. "If a work is thick, a great many of the properties heard in a performance are crucial to its identity and must be reproduced in a fully faithful rendition of the work. The thicker the work, the more the composer controls the sonic detail of its accurate instances."[23]

As Davies notes, no work, thick or thin, is quite as thick in properties as its accurate rendition or performance. Even the most fastidiously notated works of classical music will be thinner in properties than their accurate performances because there are always additional properties of a performance that are attributable to the performer and that go beyond the notation or work. Davies argues that musical works designed for performance, unlike those designed for recording alone, always allow the performer or conductor some control over the final result. Musical ontologists have often considered properties like tempo, phrasing, rubato, vibrato, and so forth to be inessential since they vary from performance to performance without normally affecting a listener's ability to identify the work performed.[24] Thus, every performance of a musical work will invariably contain two different kinds of properties, "those that should be ascribed to the musician's interpretation" and those that should be ascribed to "the work itself."[25]

The difference between thick and thin works is reflected in various musical traditions and their performance practices. If we consider works of classical music that have been taken as paradigmatic, such as Beethoven's Fifth Symphony, or other works from the symphonic tradition, we find a fairly uniform system of production: composers wrote scores that included specific instructions for each of the instrumentalists in the orchestra, and performers and conductors seek to realize the work in performance. While there are naturally many counterexamples to this paradigm, works in the classical tradition (as we have come to know them) tend to be thick. Traversing the interval from the nineteenth century until the heyday of postwar Serialism, works tend to become thicker. As Davies notes, Stravinsky's compositions, with his detailed attention to timbre and orchestration, are thicker than a divertimento of Mozart but not as thick as a work like Varèse's *Déserts*, an electro-acoustic work that includes the playback of a magnetic tape. Davies correctly observes, "the contribution made by the tape is both essential to the work's identity and extremely specific."[26] In contrast, popular standards tend to be thin in their constitutive properties. "Pieces specified only as a melody and chord sequence are thin. Some tin pan alley songs are of this kind. For them, the player creates the larger structure of the performance by deciding on the number of repeats, variations, elaborations, links and the like."[27] Clearly, Davies has in mind something like the lead sheets that one might find in a "fakebook," where songs are "specified only as a melody and chord sequence." Figure 1.3, a "lead sheet" for the standard tune "But Not for Me," might stand in as representative of this notational practice. This particular chart comes from one of the earliest fakebooks (*Volume 1 of over 1000 Songs*), popular in the 1950s.[28] Jazz musicians might have used such charts as an aide-mémoire on the bandstand, reminding them of the tune's melody and providing a rough harmonic framework on which to base their solos and improvisations.

While thick and thin works differ in their relevant notational and performance practices, the difference can be overstated. Considering performances of jazz and popular music as performances of thin works allows them to be placed along a continuum with thicker works. The difference between a thin work and a thick work is a difference in degree, not of kind. Both are considered by Davies to be of the same type, broadly speaking, "works for performance," although the ratio of work-determinative properties to performance properties differs between thick and thin works. Thus, his view

Figure 1.3 "But Not for Me," reproduced from *Volume 1 of over 1000 Songs*. From the collection of the author.

supports the intuition that performances of jazz and popular music are, broadly speaking, in the same category as other kinds of works for live performance, like those of the classical tradition. It would also support the intuition that two performances of "My Funny Valentine"—one by Miles Davis and one by Ahmad Jamal—are both performances of the same work, despite the very significant differences between them, differences that include not only the use of improvisation but also the pre-performance decisions about the arrangement, chord changes, time signature, and tempo. Once again, the core idea behind the notion of a thick or thin work is that across a set of various performances persists an invariant structure, a skeleton, or a schema present in every instance. This invariant structure, whether maximally or minimally specified, determines which properties are to be ascribed to the performance and which are to be ascribed to the work. The invariant structure offers a rule for parsing properties and thus grounds an account of the identity and individuation of morphologically distinct performances. For the ontologist, this can be an intuitively appealing way of accounting for identity in the performance of jazz and popular music.

***

To summarize, Davies claims that a work for performance, no matter how thick or thin it may be, specifies a set of work-determinative properties that must be present in any performance that instantiates the work. A musical work is akin to metaphysical objects like forms or substances, which through their permanence and incorrigibility ground claims about identity.[29] Performances are akin to accidents, secondary properties, relations, and the like. While performances can differ, they are ultimately predicated upon something unchangeable. The properties ascribed to musical works are essential or work-determinative, while those of performances are inessential or secondary. The properties that matter ontologically need not be those that matter aesthetically. Thin works, in possessing very few determinative properties, leave much to the performer. As listeners, our aesthetic interest may be almost entirely focused on the nature of the performance, not on the work itself. For instance, in many of Art Tatum's performances, extraordinarily banal songs are transformed, through the brilliance of Tatum's inventiveness, into objects that strike many listeners as deeply compelling. Thus, there is an important difference between an ontological account of musical works and their aesthetic evaluation or esteem. However, to argue for this difference requires that we know what properties are to be referred to works and what properties are to be referred to performances. How are the properties prescribed by a work communicated to performers and listeners?

In the classical tradition, where works are predominantly thick, we might consider the musical score as a kind of instruction manual that conveys most of the work-defining properties. But when it comes to thin works, like those in jazz or popular music, one cannot always rely on the presence of a score—or at least a score that can be considered "reliable" or virtually "definitive," as with classical works. Davies, attentive to this situation, describes three methods by which a work's prescriptions can be communicated to the performer: (1) via a score; (2) orally; or (3) via a "performance with the status of a model."[30]

In the first method, a score specifies a work by "instructing performers on how to produce a performance."[31] The score, which *precedes* the performance of the work, is the primary vehicle for communicating the work-determinative properties. However, the work and the score must be distinguished. "Typically, not everything indicated in the notation has the status of a work-determinative instruction, and not everything work determinative is notated."[32] There are two things worthy of note here. First, because not everything work-determinative will appear in a score, a performer must also understand the "appropriate notational conventions" and "performance practices" assumed by its composer. Davies is attuned to the fact that a score is not simply an algorithm for the production of works but rather, like any set of instructions, relies on the conventions and practices involved in the grammar of following instructions. To perform a work from a score requires acculturation and familiarity with the relevant practices assumed by the composer. Second, because not everything work-determinative appears in the score and not everything notated is work-determinative, scores are not identical to works; rather, they are simply vehicles by which works are transmitted. A simple graph can capture the causal and temporal relationships assumed in Davies' account (Figure 1.4). A musical work (notated by a dashed oval) is communicated in a score (notated by a solid diamond) that functions as the set of instructions for multiple performances (notated by solid rectangles). The arrows show the temporal and causal flow from work to score to performance.

Davies quickly discusses the second method, the oral transmission of musical works. It is akin to transmission via a score in that not everything transmitted orally is work-determinative and not everything work-determinative is transmitted orally. Performers are expected to learn the conventions and practices assumed by the composer of the work. Oral transmission of works is often an important part of the practice of jazz musicians on the bandstand. For instance, a saxophonist might call a tune that the pianist does not know. In response, the saxophonist might orally describe the chord changes to the pianist. Or they may use a kind of verbal shorthand and say something like, "Just play 'Rhythm Changes' with a 'honeysuckle bridge.'" (For readers requiring a quick primer on this kind of jazz lingo, musicians often use the term "Rhythm Changes" to refer to the standard chord progression of the well-known Gershwin standard "I Got Rhythm" and "Honeysuckle" as a shorthand for Fats Waller's popular tune "Honeysuckle Rose.") This statement

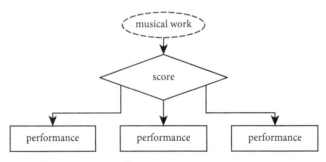

Figure 1.4 Work → score → performance.

would communicate to the pianist a simple set of instructions: they should play the standard chord progression based on "I Got Rhythm" but replace its B-section (or "bridge") with the B-section from "Honeysuckle Rose." The saxophonist's instructions do not convey everything work-determinative. For instance, nothing in the instructions refer to the melody (which we assume the saxophonist will play, so there is thus no need to convey it). To realize the instructions also requires that the pianist be properly acculturated into the performance practice of jazz. That is, he or she must know what "Rhythm Changes" and "Honeysuckle" means in this context and also know that the bridge of "Honeysuckle Rose" is not to be played in its original key but rather that it must be transposed to the key in which the song is going to be played (probably B♭, a conventional key for "Rhythm Changes"). Figure 1.5, similar to Figure 1.4, shows the parallelism between oral transmission and scores for the communication of work-determinative properties.

In the third method, the transmission of a work via model performance, a performance of a work is used as the basis for generating additional performances. According to Davies, "A model performance is not merely an accurate instance of the work, but one serving as a vehicle for the composer's work-determinative features."[33] Here a performance functions like the score in the first method, as a "vehicle."[34] Just as a score is a vehicle that communicates the work-determinative properties, a model performance communicates the work-determinative properties that allow for further accurate performances. In that sense, a model performance functions as both an instance of the work and a method for communicating the work's essential features. It is a mixture of vehicle and performance. Davies makes this parallelism clear: "A performance might achieve the status of an exemplar [i.e., an instance of the work] by following the work's score or, alternatively,

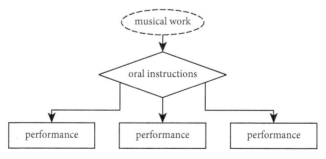

Figure 1.5 Work → oral transmission → performance.

by being based on some previous performance with the status of a model."[35] In the first case, following the score in the appropriate manner generates an instance of the work. The score *precedes* the performance of the work and the performances are instances in virtue of manifesting the work's determinative features. Davies tries to maintain this parallelism in the case of works that are based on model performances. A model performance, which functions as a vehicle for communicating the work-determinative properties, similarly precedes further performances of the work. "If the work has no score, the chain of model performances leads back to the work's first authorized performance."[36]

To show the parallelism, we could graph model performances in a manner similar to the previous two methods of communicating works (Figure 1.6). Because a model performance functions as a vehicle, we might be tempted to indicate that diagrammatically with a solid diamond. But this is not wholly accurate, since a model performance is more than a mere vehicle; it is also a performance (which, in Figures 1.4 and 1.5, was something to be sonically realized only after the presence of a notated or verbalized vehicle). Breaking the parallelism, a model performance, a hybrid of both performance and vehicle, would require a new shape in our graph to specify its unique status. On further consideration, the parallelism between scores or oral instructions and model performances is subject to even more serious challenge. As Davies notes, "When it comes to basing a subsequent performance on a prescriptive paradigm [i.e., a model performance], the musician's problem is that of extracting the qualities pertaining to the work from the welter of detail inevitably presented by the model. . . . In other words, the difficulty lies in separating the 'model' from the 'performance' in the 'model performance.'"[37] When working from a

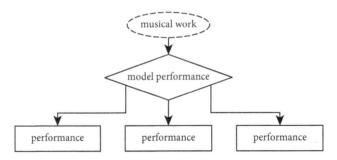

Figure 1.6 Work → model performance → performance.

model performance, how do we know which properties belong to the musical work and which to the performance? Who or what is making the determination? Without the presence of a score or explicit oral instructions, how can we know what is essential and what is inessential in a model performance? In lieu of a score or oral instructions, Davies appeals to convention. To separate the "model" from the "performance," the performer must know what is stylistically, generically, and idiomatically appropriate when following a model performance. But this appeal to convention will only get us so far.

***

We can illustrate the problem with an example. Many jazz performances function as model performances that initiate chains of further performances. Consider the case, for instance, of Miles Davis's performance of "So What," from the 1959 album *Kind of Blue*.[38] If the recording of the tune functions as model performance, what exactly are the work-determinative properties and what are the properties of the performance? One way to evade the issue would be to produce a performance of the work that follows the example slavishly, morphologically identical (or as identical as possible) to the original. By reproducing *all* of the original's properties, one would ensure as much as possible that work-determinative properties were being reproduced, without having to discriminate between properties of the work and properties of the performance. However, as Davies notes, "slavishly following the exemplar . . . may be stylistically inappropriate."[39] In cases where "conventions of the musical practice indicate that the work is of a thin kind," like in the performance practices of jazz, slavish imitation might not be the best way of performing the work.

After recording "So What," the song remained in Davis's repertoire for the next few years. Live recordings of the song reveal it to be a thin work, one that is perhaps getting thinner over time. Figure 1.7 presents a diagram of the situation.

(1) Time 1 represents "So What" at the moment of its release on *Kind of Blue* in 1959. This version of "So What" includes the introduction, the bass line, Bill Evans's famous piano voicings (doubled by the horns), and other properties. Because there is no published score that preceded it, the recording functions as a model performance. Through appeal to the conventions of the performance practice, we

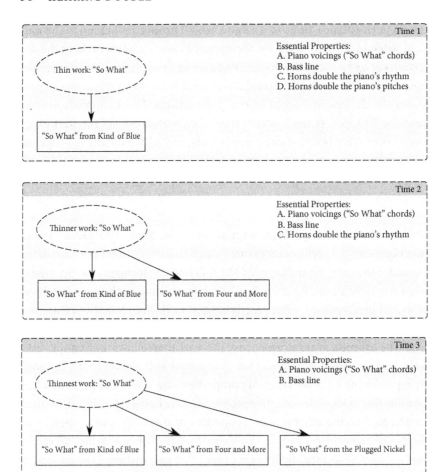

Figure 1.7 Miles Davis, "So What," progressive thinning out of the work.

might separate out the model from the performance and determine that "So What" is a thin work.

(2) Time 2 represents "So What" a few years after the release of *Kind of Blue*. To be specific, let us say that Time 2 is February 1964, the moment when Davis's group performed a version of "So What" at Lincoln Center. This performance was released on the album *"Four" and More*.[40] Comparing it with the model performance of "So What" on *Kind of Blue*, there are significant differences. In the Lincoln Center performance, the tempo of the tune has increased dramatically. This might not change any essential properties of the thin work, since it

seems to be widely accepted that tempo properties, at least within certain generous limits, are not work-determinative. (Whether that is or is not the case, the point can be conceded.) However, other properties, more likely to be work-determinative, have also changed. In this version, the bass riff and piano part are left intact, but the horns do not play in unison with the piano. Instead, Davis, on trumpet, and George Coleman, on tenor saxophone, maintain a rhythmic unison with piano's figure of a dotted-quarter and an eighth note, but both differ melodically. Pitches from the Dorian mode are selected, but they clash against the pattern played by pianist Herbie Hancock.

(3) Time 3 represents the song at an even later date, the second set of Davis's performance at the Plugged Nickel in Chicago on December 23, 1965.[41] In this performance of "So What," the tempo has again increased slightly over the Lincoln Center performance. While the piano and bass continue to play the same pattern as before, Davis changes his manner of playing the head. Instead of playing in rhythmic unison with the piano part, Davis anticipates the rhythmic figure (dotted-quarter, eighth note) creating a call-and-response pattern between the trumpet and the piano and saxophone.

As Davis's performances of "So What" change over time, the determinative properties of the work appear to be thinning out. While we might refer the increase in tempo as a property of the performance, there is a significant change in the presentation of the song's "head." If, at Time 1, we reasonably assume that the melodic unison between the horns and piano was an essential property of the song, we would have to correct that view at Time 2 and Time 3. Moreover, if we assume at Time 1 and 2 that the rhythmic unison between the horns and piano is an essential property, we would also have to correct that view at Time 3. At each successive time point, the determinative properties referred to the work seem to be getting thinner and thinner. This progressive thinning out of the work also raises additional questions. Must the bass line be present? Must the piano play the same pattern? Must the pitches played by the horns come from the Dorian mode?

Each of these changes would thin out the work more and more. But how can this be? In Davies's account there can be no evolution or change in a musical work's determinative properties and thus no change in its thinness or thickness. Davies's model requires that a musical work precede and thereby determine its performances. In order for that argument to be valid, the set of work-determinative properties initiated at the beginning of the chain must be maintained incorrigibly throughout the chain. The invariance of these properties across many performances guarantees the identity of the work. Like its cognate objects from the metaphysical tradition—forms or substances that ground the variability of accidents, relations, and secondary qualities due to their invariance and incorrigibility—the essential properties of a thin work cannot change and still do their ontological duty. Their job is to be the unchanging foundation by virtue of which divergent performances are instances of one and the same work. If works change alongside performances, on what basis can the identity and individuation of musical works be determined?

The defender of thin musical works has a response ready-to-hand. Instead of seeing each successive performance of "So What" as progressively thinning out a musical work, the ontologist might preserve the incorrigibility of the musical work by arguing the following: while it appears that "So What" was getting thinner and thinner over time, in fact the work itself had not changed; rather, we have come to realize that its properties were thinner than we first took them to be. Thus, each successive performance of "So What" does not reveal a change in the work's essential, work-determinative properties, but only a mistake in our understanding of what those properties are. Thus, any ontologist whose theory requires an incorrigible thin or thick work has, at the ready, a surefire argument. While the actual determination of properties, they may say, is simply a matter of fact, the presence of work-determinative properties, thick or thin, is necessary. Rather than concede that the work has changed and thus give up the ground for claims about identity and individuation, the ontologist can always claim that they were mistaken about the original work-determinative properties. They can keep revising these properties, thinning them out more and more to fit the current situation.

This surefire argument relies on a strange act of ontological misdirection. No matter what new performances of a thin work might arise, an updated invariant structure can be fashioned to account for it. Once that has been done, that newly formed invariant structure can be covertly placed back at the beginning of the chain of performances and said to have always already been present. The ontologist's own involvement in that process is occluded, for it is they who glean which properties are work-determinative and which are not—through a process of abstraction, reduction, or the like—and then project that structure back to the beginning of the chain. Like a magician who, at the last second, slips a ball into a cup and claims that it was always already there, the surefire argument has a strange trajectory: methodologically, the ontologist discerns a work's thin structure after a chain of performances has been instanced. But ontologically, the thin structure is posited as absolutely first, necessarily preceding the chain of performances and remaining present across all its instances. Perhaps a better word to describe this misdirection is *Nachträglichkeit*. Sigmund Freud used this term to describe the process where memories of early events are rewritten, or retroactively altered, in the light of later events. The process of revision is not explicit to the analysand, who then treats the newly formed memories as if they were original.[42] The term has been translated in various ways: retroaction, deferred action, carrying back, or, awkwardly, "afterwardness." It is a useful term for characterizing the ontologist's ready-to-hand strategy. No matter what performances appear at the end of a chain, and no matter how they may affect the set of properties that were originally thought to be work-determinative, the ontologist can retroactively revise their claim by positing an ever-thinner work in its place. This thinner work will then be said to have been always already present.

This form of musical-ontological *Nachträglichkeit* will always posit a thinner work than originally thought but will never thicken it. A set of determinative properties defines the absolutely minimal conditions for a work's successful musical instantiation. Any properties that go beyond work-determinative properties can be sloughed off as properties of the performance. And any property that is later determined inessential or non-work-determinative can be revised away. Thus, a work never changes; it is simply replaced by a better, more accurate model. But the case of "So What" challenges that view. By building a small network of performances, we can force the ontologist's hand. We see that, when faced with a thin work that seems to get thinner, the ontologist must either concede that works change, or retroactively revise the set of work-determinative properties. That is why the example of "So What," exposing the strategy of *Nachträglichkeit*, is helpful. Moreover, if the ontologist was mistaken about the work's properties to begin with, what confidence should we have that now (at Time 3, or 4, or 5 . . .) he or she has gotten it right? Why shouldn't we take the alternative view that the properties of the work are changing? Why is it so troublesome to think of a musical work as capable of change?

***

40 HEARING DOUBLE

We have considered the case where works seem to thin out over time, but what about the opposite situation where a work appears to thicken? Davies's theory should dispatch such cases easily. No matter how thick a work seems to become, new or additional properties can always be referred to the performance and not the work. Reduction is a subtractive operation; it thins but never thickens. Moreover, since the set of work-determinative properties of a thin work could be a subset of a thicker work's determinative properties, a thin work can always be found inside the thicker work like a set of Russian nesting dolls. Davies considers precisely such cases when posing the interesting philosophical question, Can a single performance simultaneously be of two works? Most theories of musical ontology assume that the work-to-performance relation is one-to-many. This captures the intuition that a performance instances only one work at a time, but there can be many performances of a single work. However, given that musical ontologists often draw an analogy between the work-performance relation and the type-token relation, we should not be surprised to see this question arise. An object can be a token of more than one type, so why might this not be the case also for certain kinds of musical works?

In considering this question, Davies offers many examples of performances that fail to instance more than one work before discussing cases that succeed. Interestingly enough, all of his successful cases concern performances of "standards."[43] And one of them, Glenn Miller's famous recording of "In the Mood," is cited as a presumably telling example. Davies observes:

> Some songs are ontologically thin, consisting of a melody and chord sequence but allowing considerable freedom to the performer as regards details and structural development. In the mid-twentieth century, many songs were performed in band arrangements. For instance, Benny Goodman's band featured George Gershwin's "Fascinating Rhythm" and Glenn Miller's band played "In the Mood" by Garland Razaf [sic]. These arrangements achieved the status of works in their own right. They were printed with due acknowledgement. Other bands played them. As a work, the band arrangement is much more detailed than the song, but it contains no material redundant to the song's identity. Everything added to the band arrangement is consistent with the song's faithful interpretation. When the band arrangement is played, the song is performed, as well as the more intensely specified piece, the arrangement, based on the song but with an independent existence.[44]

THE METAPHYSICS OF MUSICAL STRUCTURE   41

Davies is correct to note that during the Swing Era, certain arrangements became hits and were widely replicated by other bands. If a band did not have its own arranger or a relationship with various freelance arrangers, "stock" orchestrations of popular songs could be purchased from publishers or transcribed from recordings. The performance practice of using arrangements varied: sometimes arrangements would be played as is; sometimes they would be altered by cutting, re-ordering, or revising sections. In Davies's argument, there is a particular logical and temporal order that holds among thin works, thicker arrangements, and their performances; when arranging a thin work, the arrangement, with its specific instrumentation, orchestration, key changes, and insertions, is not only thicker ("more detailed") but also but also temporally later than the song it instances (see Figure 1.8). This argument is valid, however, only if there actually was a preexisting thin work. I argue that the premise that a thin work precedes a thicker arrangement cannot be assumed. And there is no better case study for this than "In the Mood."

Was "In the Mood" in fact a thin work before Miller's arrangement? That is Davies's claim, which posits Miller's performance as the performance of two works at once. But rather than providing the best solution to this problem, it might be better regarded as the solution that allows for the preservation of his ontological theory. A closer look at the historical transmission of this song complicates any account that assumes a logical or temporal sequence from thin work to thicker arrangement to performance. "In the Mood," it turns out, was the result of a complex, accumulative assemblage of a number of previous performances and recordings by other musicians. That process of accumulation, by no means unusual in this repertory, challenges any simple account of what the work at hand actually "is."

In his comprehensive book *The Swing Era*, Gunther Schuller offers a quick outline of the piece's history.[45] According to Schuller, "In the Mood" is "a riff

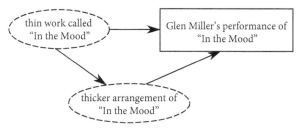

Figure 1.8 "In the Mood" as one performance of two works.

tune, built on blues changes," devised by Joe Garland, an African American arranger and multi-instrumentalist on reeds. Garland's arrangement, with some significant emendations, resurfaced in the later arrangement made famous by Glenn Miller. But Garland's arrangement was not the first time the riff we identify with "In the Mood" had been recorded. "As is so often the case in riff pieces," Schuller notes, "it was based on a motive that had kicked around a long time and was simply assembled, notated, and put by Garland in a specific copyrightable form."[46] For the sake of clarity, I will refer to this motive as the "RIFF," in capital letters (as it appears in Figure 1.10).[47] And with that we can now turn to the historical sources for "In the Mood" in order to shed light on the following questions: was "In the Mood" a thin work before Miller's performance? And, if so, how do we account for the relation between this thin work and its thicker arrangement?

The earliest recorded appearance of the telltale RIFF is on a 78 rpm disc entitled "Tar Paper Stomp," under the leadership of trumpeter Wingy Manone.[48] The session, from August 28, 1930, featured a small ensemble that included George Walters on clarinet and Joe Dunn on tenor saxophone.[49] "Tar Paper Stomp" is a mid-tempo blues with various ensemble strains. The song opens with eight measures of a riff-based introductory strain, centered harmonically on I and V, before heading into the blues (Figure 1.9). The RIFF we now associate with "In the Mood," harmonized by the horns, follows the introductory strain (Figure 1.10). There are a few differences between Manone's and Miller's presentation of the RIFF, notably the final four measures. Where Miller, at measure 9, transposes measure 5 up a step (to the dominant chord) and ends the phrase on scale degree 2, Manone ends on the leading tone (7). Also, the final two measures differ: where Miller ends the RIFF with a turnaround, a repeated-note figure accompanied by shifting harmonies, Manone plays a bluesy tag. In Manone's recording, the RIFF is played twice before the band heads off into their solos, improvised over a standard twelve-bar blues progression. After the solos are done, the RIFF never reappears; rather, the band closes with a restatement of the introductory strain.

Figure 1.9 Wingy Manone, "Tar Paper Stomp," introductory strain.

THE METAPHYSICS OF MUSICAL STRUCTURE 43

Figure 1.10 "Tar Paper Stomp," presentation of the RIFF.

Just because Manone was the first to record the RIFF, though, we should not assume that he was its composer. In Schuller's view, the RIFF must have "kicked around for a long time" and likely might have been one of those ideas that circulated within the community of jazz musicians.[50] Regardless of its origin, the recording of "Tar Paper Stomp" was the critical factor in disseminating the RIFF to the community at large. Manone recorded the tune again in 1939, a few months before Miller's famous recording, under a new title, "Jumpy Nerves."[51] While Miller's big band sounds streamlined and rehearsed, Manone's recording is with a small group playing in a hot, New Orleans style. It is definitely not "swing" music. Just as the sound of the band recalls earlier days of jazz, the pattern of "Jumpy Nerves" closely follows "Tar Paper Stomp." A new, four-bar introduction based on an arpeggiated figure (and thus foreshadowing the RIFF) is appended before the opening strain. Then comes the RIFF, followed by solos over a twelve-bar blues progression. However, instead of ending with a restatement of the opening strain, "Jumpy Nerves" introduces a new motive, based on another arpeggiated figure, which fills out two choruses of the blues and brings the tune to a close. In "Jumpy Nerves," like "Tar Paper Stomp," the RIFF appears as one among a variety of composed strains. It does not function as a typical jazz "head," presenting the melody and chord changes upon which the improvisations are based. Rather, like so many blues from the 1920s, the influence of ragtime's multi-strain form is still palpable, where distinct composed sections are distributed across the music without one having primacy over another. "Jumpy Blues" make almost no concessions to the Swing Era, except perhaps for its heavy reliance on riff-based choruses and almost complete absence of polyphonic improvisation.

Between the recording of "Tar Paper Stomp" and "Jumpy Nerves," the RIFF began appearing on other recordings. "Hot and Anxious," arranged by Horace Henderson for his brother Fletcher's band, was recorded on March 19, 1931.[52] Ambitious in conception, "Hot and Anxious" is a blues, but it plays adventurously with the formal structure of the blues. After a ten-measure introduction, Henderson presents blues choruses of fourteen, thirteen, and twelve measures, respectively. The tag from one chorus (typically, mm. 11–12 of the blues) is extended, repeated, or reharmonized, a novel technique whereby Henderson creates linking ideas that seamlessly connect subsequent choruses and thus obscure their formal boundaries. As Jeremy Magee points out, "Horace plays with the blues structure, disrupting expectations with extensions and truncations of the twelve-bar blues form," predating Duke Ellington's use of similar techniques in his 1937 recording of "Diminuendo and Crescendo in Blue."[53] The various riffs employed to create the unusual structure of "Hot and Anxious" reveal Manone's recording of "Tar Paper Stomp" as its source. The introductory strain of "Tar Paper Stomp" is recast in "Hot and Anxious" first as an introduction (ten measures long instead of eight) and then as a background riff (behind Rex Stewart's cornet solo) for a fourteen-bar chorus of the blues (see Figure 1.11). Henderson preserved only part of Manone's original melodic idea, marked by brackets in Figure 1.9 and Figure 1.11.

The next chorus of "Hot and Anxious" transforms the RIFF into a thirteen-bar-long blues chorus. The tag from measures 11 and 12 of "Tar Paper Stomp" also appears in "Hot and Anxious," but Henderson gets the number of measures to thirteen by appending an additional measure of music ending

Figure 1.11 Fletcher Henderson, "Hot and Anxious," opening strain.

Figure 1.12 "Hot and Anxious," third strain.

in a half-cadence. Eliding choruses, the tag is played again, but now fashioned into the main motive for a third chorus of the blues (Figure 1.12). After some brilliant solos and arranged interludes, "Hot and Anxious" comes to an end by riffing on the introductory strain of "Tar Paper Stomp" and adding a decrescendo.[54]

Like "Tar Paper Stomp" or "Jumpy Nerves," "Hot and Anxious" incorporates the RIFF as one idea among many arranged blues choruses. Henderson adds an additional feature to the RIFF that persists across the decade. Orchestrating the RIFF with the reed section, after each two-bar motive, the trumpets respond by punctuating a chord on beat 4 of the bar—a feature that will reappear with the trombone pedal points of Miller's arrangement (Figure 1.13). This aspect of the riff is further emphasized in a subsequent recording of "Hot and Anxious" by Don Redman, recorded in the summer of 1932.[55] Redman's recording sticks close to Henderson's arrangement, but (as usual) makes a few emendations. The tempo is notably brisker than Manone's or Henderson's, and the addition of a solo piano break between the first and second, RIFF-based chorus of blues (based on Figure 1.11) draws attention to the latter. The solo break and quicker tempo create a formal demarcation, where the RIFF now sounds like the tune's "head," arriving after an introduction. When the RIFF appears, the brass section emphasizes the punctuation at the end of each two-bar motive with more force than in Fletcher Henderson's recording.

Joe Garland enters the story in 1935. Working as a saxophonist and arranger with the Mills Blue Rhythm Band, Garland fashioned an arrangement entitled "There's Rhythm in Harlem" that prominently featured the

Figure 1.13 "Hot and Anxious," second strain, with brass punctuation.

RIFF.[56] The Mills Blue Rhythm Band was an orchestra that worked under the management of Irving Mills—who also managed Cab Calloway and Duke Ellington—and performed in many of the same venues and with a similar repertoire to Calloway and Ellington. Schuller notes that the band led a "musically distinguished career," one that has been neglected by most jazz historians, and that "the band always maintained a strong roster of fine players and arrangers."[57] Garland's "There's Rhythm in Harlem" recalls the faster tempo of Redman's "Hot and Anxious," but little else beyond that. Placing the RIFF into a new context, Garland does not play with the formal structure of the blues like Horace Henderson, but rather fashions a danceable number with the RIFF as its catchy first strain. The arrangement opens with eight measures of a simple descending bass line, played in unison by piano, slapped-tongue saxophone, and bass instruments, counterpointed with punchy riffs in the brass. Closing on a half-cadence, the band launches into a chorus of blues that presents the RIFF fully harmonized for the reed section. Garland alters the RIFF in a small but significant way. Instead of ending the arpeggio played in measures 9 and 10 on the leading tone, Garland opts for a transposition of measures 5 and 6, so that the melody ends on scale degree 2. (This alteration is later preserved in Miller's performance of "In the Mood," and with the popularity of that recording, it became the standard way to play the RIFF.) The brass punch made prominent in Redman's recording is also transformed. Instead of arriving on beat 4, Garland expands it into two syncopated brass punches on the offbeat of beats 3 and 4, the latter anticipating the harmony of the next measure (Figure 1.14). (This feature is also preserved in Miller's recording.) The final tag, used as a link by Henderson, is excised now that there is no need for links to obscure the formal boundaries. Instead, Garland introduces a repeated-note figure to close out the chorus (Figure 1.15).

After a small interlude, Garland repeats the descending bass figure to introduce a second strain, a newly composed riff-based, eight-bar phrase

Figure 1.14 Mills Blue Rhythm Band, "There's Rhythm in Harlem," the RIFF, brass punctuation.

Figure 1.15 "There's Rhythm in Harlem," the RIFF, measures 9–12.

(Figure 1.16). The phrase is repeated, given a contrasting bridge, and repeated one more time, fashioning the whole complex into a thirty-two-bar AABA chorus. The band solos over this thirty-two-bar chorus—not the blues—dividing it up between muted trombone, trumpet (with growls à la Ellington) over the bridge, and finally slap-tongued baritone saxophone (presumably played by Garland). In its next iteration (the third strain), Garland includes a shout chorus to emphasize his skill as an arranger. The first A-section is given over to the reeds, playing a fast and angular line in close harmonies in the style of Don Redman. The next eight measures introduce a dialog between the brass and the reeds (Figure 1.17).[58] Along with its accompanying chord progression, this riff appears as a contrasting strain in Miller's recording of "In the Mood." This is its first recorded appearance. After an additional thirty-two-bar AABA section, built on an additional, new riff, the tune comes to an end.

When Garland left the Mills Blue Rhythm Band with Edgar Hayes, the band's pianist, he took his arrangement with him. It is at this point that the new title, "In the Mood," appears—on a recording made under Hayes's leadership in February 1938.[59] Reflecting changes in musical taste, the new arrangement sounds less like one of Irving Mills's Cotton Club bands and more like those associated with popular swing music of the era. Yet Hayes's "In the Mood" still reflects its roots in "There's Rhythm in Harlem." The arrangements share many of the same features, although Garland's additions will eventually become iconic through Miller's recording. Now in the key of A♭, Garland omits the descending bass line that opened "Rhythm" and replaces it with the

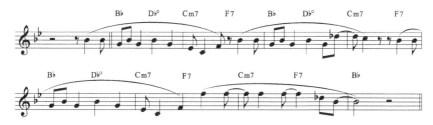

Figure 1.16 "There's Rhythm in Harlem," second strain, measures 1–8.

Figure 1.17 "There's Rhythm in Harlem," third strain, measures 9–16.

famous unison line for brass later heard in Miller's recording. The introduction leads directly into a presentation of the RIFF, played over a twelve-bar blues. Measures 11 and 12 are now replaced with the figure that would later be made famous by Miller, a repeated-note figure that sits over a series of shifting harmonies. After the blues chorus comes another riff-based phrase (8 bars long), played twice, and appended with a two-bar tag (Figure 1.18). This is followed with a strain built on Figure 1.16. The final two measures of that phrase are now replaced with the tag that one hears, again, on Miller's recording (Figure 1.19). The whole unit (riff plus tag) creates an eight-bar phrase that is incorporated as the A section of thirty-two-bar AABA chorus. The soloists (first trumpet, then clarinet) play over this thirty-two-bar form and Garland excises the riff to allow them more space to improvise. But at the end of each eight-bar phrase the tag remains, creating a call-and-response between the soloist and the band.

In 1938, Garland submitted the arrangement of "In the Mood" to Artie Shaw. Shaw never recorded it in the studio, but various radio performances from late 1938 and early 1939 have been preserved.[60] Shaw plays Garland's

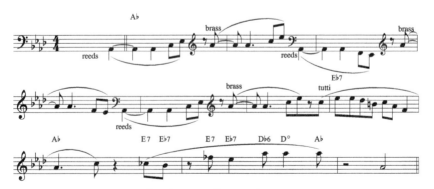

Figure 1.18 Edgar Hayes, "In the Mood," second strain.

Figure 1.19 Edgar Hayes, "In the Mood," third strain, with tag.

arrangement with only minor emendations—extending the solo section to give him more time in the spotlight. The sound of the arrangement, played in Shaw's smoother and more rounded style, shows how well the arrangement could work for a variety of swing bands. However, Shaw's slower tempo extends the arrangement to over five minutes in length. According to Schuller and Sullivan, Shaw found Garland's arrangement to be too long to fit nicely onto a 10-inch, 78 rpm disc. Shaw might have also found the music to be a too simple in its riff-based construction to fit his ambitious musical intentions.[61]

After Shaw, Garland offered his arrangement to Glenn Miller, who was in need of new material for his booking at the Glen Island Casino off Long Island.[62] The booking ran from May until August 1939 and included nightly coast-to-coast radio broadcasts, helping to raise the profile of Miller's band among swing enthusiasts. Miller and his arrangers reorganized Garland's arrangement into the iconic version recorded on August 1, 1939.[63] Keeping the opening unison phrase, Miller presented the RIFF over two choruses of twelve-bar blues (in contrast to Hayes), before heading into additional strains and solos. In a live performance from Glen Island recorded about a week before the studio recording, the second strain from Garland's original arrangement (Figure 1.18) precedes the third strain (Figure 1.17) with its new tag (Figure 1.19).[64] The second strain is wholly excised in Miller's shorter studio recording, but the motive (Figure 1.18) is still present as the background behind the trumpet solo. The solos preserve the call-and-response character of Hayes's recording by using the tag (Figure 1.19) to punctuate and complete each eight-bar unit. However, the saxophone battle between Tex Benecke and Al Klink was a new addition integrated into Garland's original arrangement. Also new to Miller's arrangement is a return to the RIFF at the end of the tune. Instead of simply playing it straight, Miller's arrangers added a few special effects: a diminuendo is prolonged across multiple choruses; the choruses are extended from twelve to fourteen bars, with the addition of a small trumpet fanfare and a pedal point in the trombones; and, after quieting

50   HEARING DOUBLE

down, the band suddenly roars back to full volume, ending the tune with a memorable coda, a triumphal fanfare for the trumpet section.

Miller's re-arrangement of Garland's arrangement puts much more emphasis on the RIFF, presenting it at both the beginning and the ending of the tune. It also repeats the RIFF far more than any of the other arrangements discussed, although Miller's arrangement varies the RIFF by using different tags in measures 11 and 12 for the beginning and ending presentations. While the opening presentation maintains the brass punctuations on the offbeats of beats 3 and 4—like in Garland's "There's Rhythm in Harlem" arrangement—the closing presentation includes a small trumpet fanfare and the famous trombone pedal point landing squarely on beat 4, recalling Redman's "Hot and Anxious." Thus, Miller's version grants the RIFF a new formal function; it is made into the "head" of the tune, conventionally played at the beginning and ending and, thus, framing the solo sections.

Miller's recording and arrangement of "In the Mood" was an enormous hit. Its popularity overshadowed the previous history of the RIFF.[65] Perhaps in that sense—in the sense of its becoming something of a permanent recorded object indelibly inscribed in American memory—Davies is correct to say that Miller's version of "In the Mood" achieved the status of a work in its own right. With its success, Andy Razaf added lyrics based on Miller's recorded version (e.g., there are no lyrics for Hayes's second strain, shown in Figure 1.18, since it was excised in Miller's studio recording), and the sheet music was quickly published.[66] Other performers began to present their own versions of the song, capitalizing on its popularity. Those subsequent versions, while re-arranging aspects of Miller's arrangement, clearly acknowledge their source by including references to its most distinctive features. In particular, the influence of Miller can be detected through the organization of the piece, which now develops a canonical form: introduction, two choruses of the RIFF, a second strain based on Figure 1.17, and solos; after the solos, there are extended repetitions of the RIFF (now 14 measures long) with a diminuendo and pedal point; and, finally, a coda that includes the famous trumpet fanfare.

Numerous versions of the tune were recorded in Miller's wake. A few examples will suffice to show how the canonical form of the tune became solidified and reproducible, a "work in its own right."

1) In late 1939, the King Sisters recorded a vocal version that closely follows Miller's arrangement.[67] Although it omits the introduction,

it reproduces Miller's arrangement, including the diminuendo, pedal point, and formal extensions; it even adds lyrics to a segment of the coda's trumpet fanfare.

2) A radio broadcast from January 31, 1940, captures drummer Gene Krupa taking a turn at the tune.[68] "In the Mood" would have been cresting in popularity at this time, first making its way onto *Your Hit Parade* on February 3 in the number 9 slot.[69] Before Krupa's performance the announcer states: " 'In the Mood' [is] the most popular piece of red hot rhythm that we've had for a long long time. You've heard it several times before . . . but haven't heard Gene Krupa do it yet." Krupa also omits the introduction, in favor of a drum-centered opening, before digging into the RIFF and second strain. Rather than solo over the chord progression of the second strain, Krupa's soloists play over the blues, building backgrounds that allude to the RIFF. On the ending, Krupa extends the chorus-extensions into repetitive drum-centered improvisations, reminiscent of Benny Goodman's performance of "Sing, Sing, Sing"—a feature piece for Krupa's drumming.

3) A live broadcast from March 1940 captures Bob Crosby and the Bobcats playing the tune.[70] Again, the introduction is replaced with a series of counterpointed ostinati, before leading to the RIFF and second strain. The solo sections are over the blues, dominated by a raggy piano improvisation and clarinet solo. The ending features all the typical bits: diminuendo, pedal point, chorus extensions—everything except the fanfare. The whole is designed to capitalize on Miller's fame while making the tune appropriate to the "modern Dixieland sound" of Crosby's orchestra, in the apt words of the broadcast's announcer.

4) The April 13, 1940, broadcast of the Camel Caravan features Benny Goodman's orchestra playing "In the Mood."[71] In a new arrangement by Fletcher Henderson, Goodman starts the tune with the Miller's introductory phrase, reharmonizing it and altering its melodic and rhythmic profile to fit the style of Goodman's band. The performance starts with a canonical presentation of the RIFF along with its repetition, then proceeds to the non-blues second strain (Figure 1.17), also heard twice (as in the Miller arrangement). Goodman then solos over the chord progression of that second strain, following the model of Miller closely. When the RIFF comes back shortly thereafter, Henderson switches its instrumentation, first giving it to the brass, before returning it to the reeds, all the while enriching the harmonies.

The phrase-extension, pedal point, and fanfare are all intact as well. But Henderson's arrangement, while sticking close to Miller's model, manages to pull the song back, in certain respects, to its pre–"In the Mood" roots. Never quite reaching the complexity and brilliance of his own performance of "Hot and Anxious," Henderson makes a small intervention to complicate Miller's schematic and standardized model.

5) Jumping a decade into the 1950s, Miller's canonical form still had a powerful grip on performances of "In the Mood." Duke Ellington recorded the tune on January 1, 1954, as part of the Capitol LP, *Ellington '55*, which featured popular songs from the big band era.[72] While being a central force in the big band era himself, Ellington here records songs associated with other bands, like Count Basie's "One o'Clock Jump," Goodman's "Flying Home," and Chick Webb's "Stompin' at the Savoy." Capturing the sound and style of Ellington's live performances, "In the Mood" opens with two chorus of Ellington, at the piano, improvising over the blues, followed by an eight-bar introduction where the band trades with the bass. Two choruses of the RIFF are followed by two statements of the second strain (with a new tag), a practice that by now seemed to have been the canonical way of beginning any "In the Mood," following the model from Miller. This material is quickly dispensed with, and Clark Terry improvises a few choruses over the blues, now elaborately reharmonized with no motivic references to the RIFF or second strain. For the next three minutes or so, solos (by altoist Rick Henderson, clarinetist Jimmy Hamilton, and trumpeter Ray Nance) alternate with choruses for the band. If a listener were to "drop the needle" at this point, the performance could be of any up-tempo Ellington blues. But in the last minute of the tune, the RIFF returns, with all the usual trimmings: diminuendo, pedal point, and phrase extensions. The final "shout chorus," when the band comes charging back to full volume, omits the RIFF entirely in favor of an Ellingtonian motive played over the blues. While incorporating the most schematic elements of Miller's canonical form, Ellington erases many details from Miller's arrangement (the unison opening, the fanfare-like coda, and the short, orchestrated breaks), filling it in with backgrounds for solos designed to show off the characteristic virtuosity of his band.

6) To end this list—which of course could include several other notable arrangements—I append one final recording of "In the Mood," the version from 1959 by Ernie Fields.[73] Translating Miller's canonical

arrangement into rhythm-and-blues instrumental, Field rephrases the RIFF and second strain to fit over a doggedly even (not swung), staccato eighth-note juggernaut, a jaggedly driving rhythm tailor-made for teens dancing "the Twist." Field's recording cracked Billboard's top 20 singles on October 26, 1959, climbing its way to number 4 by the middle of December, and vying for position against much more enduring singles like Bobby Darin's "Mack the Knife," the Fleetwoods' "Mr. Blue," and Della Reese's "Don't You Know?"[74] Beginning with an allusion to the trumpet fanfare, Fields plays the RIFF twice, then the second strain twice, now transposed to the subdominant. To get back to the tonic, the tag is replaced by a stream of steady eighth notes that moves harmonically from IV to V, reminiscent of the break from the Champs' 1958 hit, "Tequila." A few choruses of yakety sax fill out the solo section. The track is closed off by another statement of the second strain (again in the subdominant) and back to the RIFF. On the way out, many of the canonical features are in place: while the diminuendo is omitted, the pedal point, and phrase extensions, and fanfare-like tag all remain intact.

**

Can a musical work change? That question initiated this discussion of the performance history of "In the Mood." We recall that "In the Mood" was Davies's own example of a performance that instances two works at once: a thin work and a thicker arrangement of that thin work. I compared Davies's relation between the thin and thicker works to a set of Russian dolls, where the thin work sits wholly encased by the thicker arrangement. For Davies, there would be no change of essential properties since the thin work "In the Mood" is assumed to be present at the very beginning of the network of performances just described. But what is the thin work that Davies has in mind here? What is he referring to? And where in the history of the performances is it to be located?

Perhaps all Davies means by the thin work is the RIFF, the repetitive musical motive that fits over a twelve-bar blues. Historically, one might argue that it begins with Manone's "Tar Paper Stomp" or in some unrecorded model performances from which Manone got the idea. Philosophically, we might characterize this thin work as wholly defined by the set of rhythmic, melodic, harmonic, and formal properties that characterize the RIFF. The RIFF is the one piece of musical material that appears in all of the performances discussed. It is invariant, held in common across the entire network of performances, and thus seems a good candidate for grounding work-determinative prescriptions. In virtue of its presence we can consider this network of performances as instancing the same musical work.

However, we might have lingering doubts about the RIFF and how its determinative properties are fixed. While the RIFF has an identifiable rhythmic, melodic, and harmonic profile for its first eight measures, there are a variety of different ways to play measures 9–12 (or measures 9–14, if we are talking about the closing presentation in Miller's arrangement). The earliest versions—"Tar Paper Stomp" and "Hot and Anxious"—have a different melodic profile in measures 9–10 than in Garland's arrangements. Garland is the one who changes measures 9–10 to follow the same pattern as measures 5–6. We also note that there are different "tags" played in measures 11–12. "Tar Paper Stomp" and "Hot and Anxious" have one tag, "There's Rhythm in Harlem" has another, and Garland's arrangement of "In the Mood" has yet another. Given the various ways that measures 9–12 can be played, we might want to play it safe and stipulate that those measures do not establish work-determinative features. Or perhaps they are determined only by the loosest of prescriptions (viz., "when you get to measures 9–10, play a motive with the same rhythmic profile as before, make sure its melodic profile arpeggiates the harmony, and keep the voice leading parsimonious... and throw on a tag at measures 11–12").

To fix the determinative properties of the RIFF in this way raises another question. Is this thin set of work-determinative properties thick enough to do the philosophical work it was designed to do, that is, can it individuate a musical performance? I believe that the answer is no. Imagine a situation where a group of musicians playing a blues use the RIFF as a background behind a soloist. Clearly the musicians are not performing an instance of the work "In the Mood." Yet, when the work in question reaches this degree of thinness, there appears no way to differentiate a citation or "quotation" of the work from a genuine instance of the work. Moreover, the determinative properties of the RIFF do not specify anything about the musical form that a proper performance of the work should take. Should a soloist playing "In the Mood" use the blues form as the basis for solos or some other form (say AA′ or AABA)? While the canonical form of Miller's recording uses the non-blues second strain for solos, many of the versions that followed immediately upon Miller's success opted instead for a twelve-bar blues. Must the RIFF formally function as the song's "head," where it would typically frame the solo section? In Garland's original arrangement, played by both Edgar

Hayes and Artie Shaw, the RIFF only appears at the beginning. The performance comes to an end by introducing a different strain entirely—one that fits over the harmony of the second strain. The RIFF frames the solos only in Miller's re-arrangement of Garland. If we assume that an essential property of the RIFF as a thin work is that it possesses the formal function of being the "head," then we would be forced to claim that Garland's arrangement of "In the Mood" and Miller's re-arrangement were different works. But that seems counterintuitive, especially given the strong historical links that connect Miller's re-arrangement with Garland's chart.

If we decide that the RIFF, as a thin work, prescribes the formal function of the head, there seems to be no reason to say this other than the fact that the popularity of Miller's recording establishes a canonical model. But this is a conclusion that would be unacceptable to the ontologist. Since their view requires that a thin or thick work must precede its performance, it would be impervious to any future success or failure that the performance might bring. As in the classical metaphysics of forms or substances, a musical work would be immunized from such accidents and contingencies—and popular success, no matter how calculated or desired, is always contingent. The ontological features of the work must be wholly insulated from any sociological factors, like its position on *Your Hit Parade*. The establishment of a canonical model must be causally dependent on the thin work it instantiates, but not vice versa. That is precisely what Davies says when he claims that performances of "In the Mood" that follow Miller's canonical model are performances of two works at the same time (Figure 1.8). However, we may now doubt the viability of this model as we chip away at the idea that a thin work precedes and thus initiates a network of performances.

Perhaps we need to step back and thicken up the "work" a bit more in order to get a viable alternative account. Perhaps the thin work is not simply the RIFF (or the eight measures that are strictly specified plus the four, loosely prescribed measures) but must also include an additional strain (Figure 1.17) along with it. When Garland transformed "Hot and Anxious" into "There's Rhythm in Harlem," he added this strain and the AABA sections based on it. When "There's Rhythm in Harlem" was refashioned into "In the Mood," the sectional divisions were made even clearer, and this theme was given its own presentation. These features distinguish "Tar Paper Stomp" and "Hot and Anxious" from the arrangements penned by Garland. If we prescribe that the work "In the Mood" must include this second strain, that is, if we stipulate this as one of its work-determinative properties, we would get our musical work to correspond with Garland as its composer. This would also be supported by the published sheet music, which lists Garland as the composer and contains both strains.

And yet we can only place so much importance in the sheet music. It arrives too late in the story. The sheet music was published only *after* Miller made "In the Mood" into a hit, and thus its form reflects the canonical form of Miller's recording. Its purpose is both to advertise Miller's hit record and to sell sheet music in the light of its success. It thus reflects less the intentions of the composer than the market forces poised to profit on the song's success by making it available in various media. There is no good reason to accept the sheet music as the definitive statement; it is as shaped by the contingent success of Miller's recording as are any of the performances that come afterward. If anything, we might want to hold to Garland's original arrangement as the authoritative source for "In the Mood," since it is the first place where the title appears attached to the RIFF, and it is also the place where we first see the additional strain (Figure 1.17) clearly delineated into its own formal section.

But what about the other strain (Figure 1.18)? It appears in all the recorded versions of "In the Mood" before Miller's studio recording. Moreover, it is heard on Miller's live broadcast from Glen Island the week prior to making the studio recording and it is preserved as a background behind solos. If we are going to consider Garland's arrangement as the primary source for "In the Mood," what reason does he have for deciding this strain is not determinative while the other strain is? The only reason for doing so would again depend on the canonical status of Miller's recording. Since we have a live recording of Miller playing the excised strain a week prior, why should we stipulate work-determinative properties based on the vagaries of a decision made in the recording session? Perhaps the disc would have been too long with the extra strain, so it was cut. But who is to say that the other strain couldn't have been cut in its place? If so, that would have changed the canonical form. Again, from the point of view of the ontologist, all of these factors couldn't matter since the thin work is incorrigible from the very beginning. But that leads back to our original question: what is the thin work that we call "In the Mood?" Any thin work that we might decide upon will be covertly placed back at the origin in an act of *Nachträglichkeit*. Davies's example founders on the historical facts. To assume a thin work must be present from the beginning is as mistaken as identifying its composer as "Garland Razaf."

***

By being attentive to the history of recording, scores, and performances of "In the Mood," a small network can be constructed. The utility of such a network is the perspective that it grants us. What we see is not the *precedence* of a thin work deployed across the entire network; rather we see the *emergence* of a thin work. A thin work is an abstraction that emerges only when one takes the network, or a relevant part of it, as a whole and locates those properties that are invariant across it. It comes at the end of a process, not the beginning. Before Miller's recording of "In the Mood" became iconic for a generation of jitterbugs, there was no canonical form to be found in the network. Miller's recording gives the network a distinctive shape: a bottleneck. It becomes the single, central node to which all later nodes, from the King Sisters to Ernie Fields, are associated (Figure 1.20). But for how long will those "invariant" properties remain invariant? As the network grows in size, as new performances are added to the network, who can guarantee that the properties we now find invariant will remain so? Who is to predict which successes and failures will shape the future history of this network? Thin works might grow thinner or thicker; properties may become central or peripheral, depending on popularity, influence, dissemination, nostalgia, or many other "sociological" factors.

Davies and Forte, the ontologist and the music theorist, share a traditional view about musical structure. Whether determining the individuating properties of a musical work or the long-range and formal ("musicological") properties of popular songs, structure is treated like a classical metaphysical object: invariant and incorrigible, a substance or form with an essence, always already present and objective. Yet both are incorrect to think that a musical work's structure is insulated from a musical work's "sociology." The structure of a musical work is always "sociological" insofar as it is invariably formed under the influence of a network. There is no insulation of structure from the conditioning features of the social. The score that Forte uses as the basis for his analysis is just as much part of the network as the performances he neglects to consider.[75] The same would hold for the lead sheet or fakebook surely in Davies's mind when he defines a thin work as "specified only as a melody and chord sequence" and notes that "some tin pan alley songs are of this kind." Tin Pan Alley songs were not thin from the beginning. They became thin because of the way that song pluggers, jazz musicians, popular singers, and various media (Hollywood film, recording, radio, etc.) used them and performed them. They became thin because of the way that a culture of performance *replicated* them. By taking liberties, by

58 HEARING DOUBLE

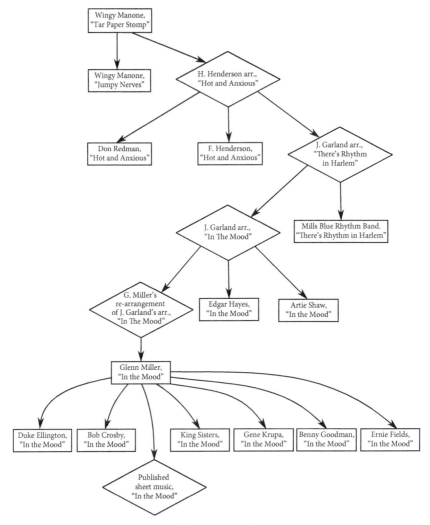

Figure 1.20 A partial network of "In the Mood."

improvising, and by making these songs their own, they added new nodes to a network of performances. Only retroactively can one imagine this network was preceded by a thin work.

Consider again the network of "In the Mood" (Figure 1.20).[76] What is gained by imagining, at the top of this graph, a thin work lording over the whole, waiting for its potential to be realized in an immense variety of performances and scores? The only thing gained is the security of a rule for deciding how to identify and individuate musical works and their performances. The thin work prescribes a set of necessary, work-determinative properties that must be present for a performance of a standard to instance a work. In that sense, it provides a standard for our judgments concerning the identity of things like jazz standards. If we chip away at the *precedence* of the work, we seem at first to lose our sure footing, our dependable foundation for judgments. It is not initially clear how to balance various considerations; for instance, how long before Miller does the work "In the Mood" persist? Does it extend back to "Tar Paper Stomp" (or earlier, if Gunther Schuller is right) or only as far as Joe Garland's arrangement for Edgar Hayes? If a work *emerges*, then what are we to say about those nodes that initiate a network? Do they instance a work or not? If indeed properties of works are affected by past, present, and future states of a network—if musical works can change—the solidity and permanence of musical works seem to evade our grasp. One musical work becomes another, or two performances of an identical work may end up as performances of different works.[77] Our categories and concepts of musical works no longer seem so certain and surefooted. We do not know which intuitions to trust.

One of the oldest and most entrenched beliefs in philosophy is that identity is guaranteed by the presence of a form. From Plato onward, the invariance and incorrigibility of form has functioned as a bulwark against ever-changeable, ever-replaceable, ever-corruptible matter. Well-entrenched, the metaphysics of structure makes its way from the heady spheres of classical philosophy to the philosophy of music. Davies provides an exemplary illustration of this view, employing it to account for the ontology of musical works. Yet the ontology of jazz standards, as I have tried to demonstrate in this chapter, presents a direct challenge to the metaphysics of substance, form, and essence. How can one go on without the metaphysical support of form? How can one ground judgments about the identity and individuation of musical works if there is no fixed structure? These are the questions I will attempt to answer in the next three chapters, by means of the interaction and relation of two distinct processes: *replication* and *nomination*.

2
Replication

If there is no preexistent thin work to which performances of standards remain faithful—if thin works *emerge* but do not necessarily *precede* their performance—how can we ever say that multiple performances of a standard are *performances of one and the same work*?

To answer that question, I need to develop some resources. In this chapter, and the following, I will present an account of two processes, *replication* and *nomination*, which together offer a solution to the ontological problem of the identity and individuation of standards. That account involves a number of steps. In this chapter, I will introduce the concept of *replication* and illustrate it by an analysis of various versions of the standard "Body and Soul." In addition, I will describe how individual replications are linked together into *chains of replications* and demonstrate their utility for offering a network-based account of identity and individuation. Although *chains of replication* will get us far into the ontology of standards, they cannot provide a full picture on their own. In addition to *chains of replication*, I will introduce a related concept, *chains of nomination*, in Chapter 3. With those two resources in hand, I will present a case study on John Coltrane's "Impressions" that will illustrate the theory's utility.

I evaluate the utility of a theory of musical ontology in a way that is perhaps distinct from other ontologists. Rather than devise a theory that produces a surefire rule for identifying and individuating works—an algorithm, as it were, that decides for us—I think a robust ontology should be sensitive in handling ambiguous cases where our intuitions about the identity and individuation of musical works are not clear-cut. I will argue that an account of musical ontology articulated in terms of *chains of replication* and *chains of nomination* can do something that the ontological theories based on musical structure cannot: it can provide reasons *why* our intuitions about musical works are sometimes unsure. In other words, it can reveal the competing intuitions provoked by ambiguous cases.

***

Whitney Davis defines *replication* as "the sequential production of similar material morphologies . . . that are substitutable for one another in specific social contexts of use."[1] The concept is best introduced through an example. Imagine a case where I am electronically transcribing a famous author's handwritten journal. As I transcribe the journal's pages, an electronic letter appearing on my computer screen represents each handwritten letter. If I transcribe accurately, and my goal is the accurate transcription of the text, the electronic file meets the criterion that Davis establishes; each electronic letter is adequately and morphologically similar to the original handwritten letter so that the two documents count as substitutable for one another. Of course, the substitutability of the two documents is context-dependent. If I simply want to read the document because I am interested in the statements written in the journal, either document would be adequate. However, if I were researching the author's "creative process," or techniques of composition, various marks in the journal that are not transcribed in the electronic document might be worthy of study. Perhaps I am interested in the words crossed out or added in the margins, in order to track the process of revision. Perhaps I am interested in the legibility of the script, knowing that this particular author tended toward sloppiness when writing faster. Thus, the legibility of the handwriting might reveal something about the pace of writing and the mental state of the author. When the context of use changes, the two documents might no longer be considered adequate substitutes for each other.

The material difference between a replication and its model, like the journal page and its electronic transcription, does not pose an insuperable problem. As Davis notes, there are no perfect substitutes, no "artifactual synonyms."[2] Every artifact has its own specific history of production—even in cases of mass-produced artifacts. There are always material differences in the properties of two artifacts; however, those differences may or may not play a significant role in the specific context of use. For instance, a musician transcribing a Louis Armstrong solo from the "Hot Five" recordings might prefer a digital copy to a shellac disc, in that the digital copy is easier to manipulate (start and stop, skip around, slow down, etc.). The record collector might want the original 78 to complete his collection. The professor of jazz history might not care if he plays a 78 or an mp3 to his class, so long as the suitable example is played. While the two recordings are "identical," broadly speaking, there are often material differences that impact the degree to which a replication is substitutable. Thus, as Davis notes, "Substitutability varies with the changing ways of using artifacts or reasons for doing so."[3]

There will always be material differences between replications; however, the more significant concern is the social context of use. We cannot know if one artifact is an adequate substitute for another without knowing how the artifact is used. Thus, we cannot know if something is a replication without understanding the practices that employ replication. The substitutability of an artifact is "an emergent, not a given, property of a tradition of production."[4] For a theory of replication, contexts of use are crucial; the substitutability of a replication is determined on the basis of the social context of use. The social context, as it were, provides the "grammar" of replication.[5] No philosophical ground more structural, substantial, or metaphysical need be invoked. Beyond social contexts of use, there is no context-free feature or property of an object that will guarantee whether or not it counts as a replication.

From my examples of replication, one might object that replication is just another name for reduction. In the first example, the interlocutor might argue that replication relies on the preservation of essential properties; the handwritten journal and typed copy are both tokens of the same type, or inscriptions of the same character-type in English. Thus, the objection goes, what a replication does is reduce an artifact to an essential property and then preserve that property in another, newly fashioned artifact. However, this objection misses a crucial point that differentiates reduction from replication. Reduction is the process of excising properties in order to arrive at necessary or essential properties, those that must be present in order for a certain thing to be the thing it is. Replication is not that process. Replication involves the selection of some, but not all, properties in order to produce a new object that is substitutable for the first. The properties selected are neither essential nor necessary. The only constraint on replication is that the properties selected be sufficient for producing a substitutable artifact. What is or is not sufficient in any process of replication depends on social factors, not on essential properties. If a community accepts an object as a substitute, then it is one. No additional appeal to necessary properties or essences is required.

Replication is not reduction because replication is relational in nature. A replication is a relation forged between two artifacts that are understood as substitutable for one another in virtue of sharing some feature relevant to the social context of use. These shared features may be properties or even aspects. Aspects are broader than properties, in that they supervene on the material properties of objects. They include affordances, or things seen-in or heard-in an object. Aspects of musical artifacts—such as their harmonic-functional meaning, or their dissonance or consonance—are not reducible to material properties of the object alone. They are an amalgam of perceptions and cognitions about objects that rely on acculturation and training. At the same time, they are not reducible to subjective projections onto an indifferent object. Artifacts, situated in cultural milieux, are aspectual. In the case of musical artifacts, we should expect this to be the case. Musical artifacts are formed (composed, improvised, etc.) *precisely* to afford such perceptions and cognitions, since they participate in larger cultures of music making and listening. Thus, aspects relate an artifact and its replication. As a third term, they mediate two primary terms, two artifacts, and forge a specific relation. An object and its replication are substitutable in virtue of some aspect they both display.[6]

***

All of this heady talk about replication is clarified by means of an example. In the case of jazz and popular music, replication is a common procedure. We need only think of the various ways that the RIFF from "In the Mood" was replicated across a network of performances to glimpse its ubiquity. By tracing the production of replications, we develop a powerful tool for understanding how basic practices of improvisation, revision, and arrangement contribute to musical ontology. To demonstrate this, for our "specific social context of use" I will address the repeated replication of a popular standard—perhaps the most recorded standard there is—Johnny Green's "Body and Soul."

Figure 2.1 reproduces the opening measures of the song's refrain, as presented in the sheet music published in 1930.[7] The passage is not complicated or difficult to describe. The song is in C major, yet the refrain begins off tonic, on a subdominant ii chord (a D-minor chord) over which the opening melodic idea sits.[8] The melody, beginning with an anacrusis to beat 2, oscillates between d^1 and e^1 before leaping, in the second measure, to a^1. Just after the melodic leap, the harmony shifts in the second half of measure 2 to G-dominant-seventh and then resolves, on the downbeat of measure 3, to a C-major triad. Just after the resolution, the oscillating melodic motive is transposed upward, now starting on g^1 . . . and the song goes on. In the following discussion, I will focus on just the first three measures of "Body and Soul" in order to describe how performers of the song create replications of these measures, each with a morphology that is distinct yet substitutable

64 HEARING DOUBLE

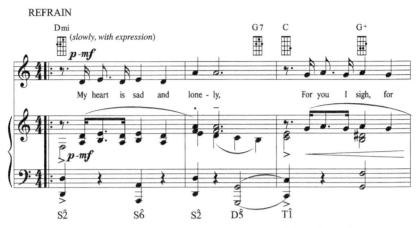

Figure 2.1 "Body and Soul," the first three measures of the refrain, from the published sheet music (1930). Reproduced with permission of Alfred Music.

for one another within the context of jazz performance. For the purposes of my discussion, I will refer to these three measures as a *model* that gets replicated.

The process of replication is central to the practice of jazz musicians, especially those who work with standards and other material generally associated with Tin Pan Alley. Jazz musicians, when creating arrangements or improvising on such material, learn various strategies for substituting one chord for another. Broadly speaking, the practices they employ discourage slavishly following a set of notated chords and encourage embellishments and reharmonizations in the moment of performance. The harmonic and melodic aspects of such practices have been often described in jazz theory and pedagogy. But the philosophical importance of such practices has not received adequate attention. Any listener familiar with the conventions of jazz improvisation and arrangement will expect to hear the "same progression" of some standard harmonized in different ways. These are instances of replications. To show how an aspect relates an improvised replication to its model, I will be focusing not at the level of individual notes and their register or voicing, but on the syntactical and functional aspects of chord progressions. Jazz musicians, in their improvisations, continually devise new ways of playing a song's chord progression. To understand that practice, and the replications involved, I will draw attention to the use that each chord has within a progression of chords.[9]

The opening three measures of "Body and Soul" follow a basic scheme in jazz, the chord progression: ii-V-I. In this case the ii-V-I resolves to the song's home key and each chord in the progression is associated with a different harmonic function: subdominant, dominant, and tonic. All three functions are represented, and the three measures establish C major as its key. In order to facilitate my discussion of the first three measures of "Body and Soul," I will introduce a few notational conventions. In addition to representing chord progressions with a Roman numeral label (which describes the root and type of chord in relation to the key, such as ii, V, or I), I will also represent chords with a "functional bass" label.[10] In the latter system, each chord is labeled with a symbol composed of two parts.

- First, a letter label representing the chord's function (S, D, or T, for subdominant, dominant, and tonic) is noted. If the chord is an embellishing chord (typically a neighbor, passing, or applied chord) it will receive a letter label noting this fact (N, P, or A). Since embellishing chords are harmonically non-functional chords, they are placed in parentheses.[11]
- Second, the scale degree of the chord's bass note is appended to each letter label. (Scale degrees are always represented by a number and a carat: i.e., $\hat{1}$, $\hat{2}$, $\hat{3}$, etc.) For example, the opening three measures of "Body and Soul" in the sheet music are represented by Roman numerals in one manner, as [ii ii64 | ii V7 | I], and in functional-bass notation differently, as [S$\hat{2}$ S$\hat{6}$ | S$\hat{2}$ D$\hat{5}$ | T$\hat{1}$].

While Roman numeral analysis is useful for showing the relationship of chords to a tonal center, functional-bass notation helps to clarify the harmonic cycle that runs through vast amounts of tonal music—a cycle of harmonic functions that typically follows a pattern of tonic, subdominant, dominant, and then back to tonic. In the discussion that follows, both systems will be employed.

(1) Art Tatum recorded "Body and Soul" many times. Figure 2.2 is a transcription of the opening measures from his 1938 recording of the tune.[12]

Given the context of jazz performance, these three measures are a replication of the song's opening three measures. For our purposes, we can posit them as replications based on the sheet music as a model, but very little will

66 HEARING DOUBLE

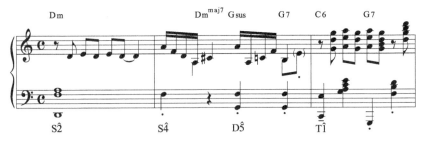

Figure 2.2 Art Tatum, "Body and Soul," 1938, Chorus 1, first A-section, measures 1–3.

ultimately hinge on what we decide is the model. We simply need there to be some artifact from which Tatum works as a precondition for the process of replication. This posit should be unproblematic since Tatum's replication follows the harmonic model of the sheet music quite closely. Melodically, Tatum plays the incipit, but upon arriving at a^1, he arpeggiates the harmony in his right hand. The harmonic progression is nearly identical to the sheet music. Tatum ornaments the D-minor chord in measure 2 by adding a descending inner voice: d^1-$c\sharp^1$-c^1-b. The notes c^1 and b are supported in the left hand by G and f, which outline the root and seventh of a G-dominant-seventh chord. The progression could be notated as [Dm | Dm Dm^{maj7} Gsus G7 | C6]. Tatum's bass line does not support the D-minor chord in measure 1 with A natural, the chord's fifth, as the sheet music does, but rather keeps the root sounding through the entire measure. In measure 2 the D-minor chord appears in inversion, with f in the bass. Represented in terms of functional-bass, the passage is notated as [Ŝ2̂ | Ŝ4̂ D5̂ | T1̂]. The old Ŝ6̂ chord is excised, but this makes very little impact. The Ŝ6̂ chord, interpolated between two instances of Ŝ2̂, was being treated like a neighbor chord and offered no novel harmonic-functional contribution to the progression. In both the sheet music and Tatum's replication, Ŝ2̂ governs the entire first measure. Tatum's alteration is to replace Ŝ2̂ with Ŝ4̂ in measure two, by inverting the D-minor chord so that f is placed in the bass. While this inversion changes the melodic contour of the passage's bass line, it does not alter the harmonic function of the passage since both chords are subdominant in function. Tatum's small alteration, while producing a phrase that is morphologically distinct, is a replication of the first in virtue of possessing the

Figure 2.3 Art Tatum, "Body and Soul," 1938, Chorus 1, second A-section.

same harmonic-functional pattern. In the context of jazz improvisation, the two phrases are substitutable.

In the next A-section, Tatum elaborates on his previous idea, by filling in the gap between S$\hat{2}$ and S$\hat{4}$ with a passing chord (Figure 2.3). On the second beat of the first measure, Tatum interpolates an inverted, rootless A7♭9 chord.[13] The gap in the bass line between D in measure 1 and F in measure 2 is filled in with the note E. This chord is a passing chord; it "passes" between S$\hat{2}$ and S$\hat{4}$ by harmonizing $\hat{3}$ in the bass. The progression in Figure 2.3 could be represented in functional-bass notation as [S$\hat{2}$(P$\hat{3}$) | S$\hat{4}$ D$\hat{5}$ | T$\hat{1}$]. However, the passing chord is not a diatonic chord; it is an applied (or secondary) dominant chord. Borrowed from the key of D minor, this chord is applied to the D-minor chord of measures 1 and 2, reinforcing that chord but making no impact on the overall harmonic progression. In both Roman numeral and functional-bass systems, we will indicate secondary dominants with an arrow that connects the applied chord to the chord it embellishes. Represented in Roman numerals, the progression of Figure 2.3 is [ii V43→| ii6 V7 | I].[14] In functional-bass notation, where we will use the letter "A" for an applied chord, the progression is represented as [S$\hat{2}$(A$\hat{3}$) → | S$\hat{4}$ D$\hat{5}$| T$\hat{1}$]. Whether interpreted as a passing chord or an applied chord, the A7 of measure two supports a walking bass line that diatonically ascends from D to G. Yet, from a functional point of view, it makes no overall impact on the harmonic function of the progression. And it is in virtue of its harmonic function that, again, this passage seems an acceptable replication, not only of the model but also of Tatum's earlier embellishment.

68 HEARING DOUBLE

Figure 2.4 Art Tatum, "Body and Soul," 1953, first chorus, first A-section, measures 1–3.

(2) In December 1953, Tatum recorded "Body and Soul" again and, as one would expect, the opening three measures of the tune appear in a new configuration (Figure 2.4).[15]

In contrast to the stepwise motion of the bass in the 1938 version, Tatum sets the incipit as a series of root-position chords. This time the A-dominant-seventh chord (V/ii) is not interpolated between two D-minor chords, but rather initiates a chain of applied chords.[16] The D-minor chord of measure 2 is replaced with D-dominant-seventh in order to prolong the chain. Thus, A-dominant-seventh is applied to D-dominant-seventh which is applied to G-dominant-seventh, the dominant chord in the home key, which resolves to the tonic, C major, on the downbeat of measure 3. The progression is represented in Roman numerals as [ii | V7/ii → V7/V → V7 | I] and in functional-bass notation as [Ŝ2̂ | (Â6̂) → (Â2̂) → D̂5̂ | T̂1̂]. The functional-bass notation clarifies the underlying harmonic-functional progression, [Ŝ2̂ D̂5̂ T̂1̂], which is replicated from the model. Again, it is a valid substitute.

In the very next A-section, Tatum further embellishes the idea. The A-dominant-seventh chord in measure 2 of Figure 2.4 is now replaced with a tritone substitution, one of the most common and effective chord substitutions in the jazz musician's vocabulary. Tritone substitution does not change a chord's harmonic function: if a chord's function is dominant it keeps that function; if it is a passing chord, it remains a passing chord; if it is an applied chord, it remains an applied chord. As a rule, tritone substitutions are function-preserving operations. (As a notational convenience, we will mark all tritone substitutions with an asterisk in functional-bass notation.)

For example, we could take a simple harmonization of the first three measures of "Body and Soul," like the following,

[dm A7 | dm G7 | C6]

[S2̂(A6̂) | S2̂ D5̂ | T1̂],

and apply two tritone substitutions, generating this progression:

[dm E♭7 | dm D♭7 | C6]

[S2̂ (*A3̂♭) | S2̂ *D2̂♭ | T1̂].

While this progression is aesthetically different from the model, it is substitutable for it and thus another replication. Perhaps the biggest conceptual challenge for readers more familiar with classical harmony is the replacement of G-dominant-seventh with D♭-dominant-seventh, or D5̂ with *D2̂♭. Within the conventions of common practice harmony, the change would be drastic indeed—so much so that the listening practices trained on common practice tonality might not accept the new passage as a genuine substitute, and thus reject it as a replication. However, I cannot emphasize enough how ubiquitous the tritone substitution is in jazz, where the progression [S2̂*D2̂♭ T1̂] is a commonplace. It is one of the oldest and dearest tricks for making stale progressions from Tin Pan Alley sound fresh and lively. The change in bass line, which is aesthetically appealing when used judiciously, does not impact the chord's harmonic function as dominant. And, given the permissive constraints on substitution in

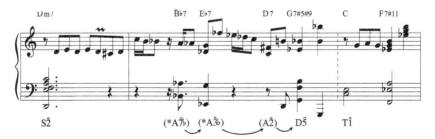

Figure 2.5 Art Tatum, "Body and Soul," 1953, first chorus, second A-section, measures 1–3.

the jazz community, [S$\hat{2}$*D$\hat{2}$♭ T$\hat{1}$] is a perfectly acceptable replication of [S$\hat{2}$ D$\hat{5}$ T$\hat{1}$].

To return to Figure 2.5, Tatum replaces A-dominant-seventh with E♭-dominant-seventh—a tritone substitution. In addition, the tritone substitution is preceded by B♭-dominant-seventh. There are two ways to analyze this additional chord:

1) The B♭-dominant-seventh is an applied chord in E♭, and thus adds one more non-functional link to the chain of applied chords: [S$\hat{2}$ | (A$\hat{7}$♭) → (*A$\hat{3}$♭) → (A$\hat{2}$) → D$\hat{5}$ | T$\hat{1}$]. Here the B♭-dominant-seventh chords sets up the arrival of the E♭-dominant-seventh chord, which prolongs the chain of applied chords until G-dominant-seventh, the dominant seventh chord in the home key is reached, and the chain resolves to the tonic, C major.

2) We might alternatively consider the B♭-dominant-seventh chord as a tritone substitution for E-dominant-seventh. In terms of functional bass, we could take the previous analysis and add an asterisk in front of the first applied chord in our previous representation: [S$\hat{2}$ | (*A$\hat{7}$♭) → (*A$\hat{3}$♭) → (A$\hat{2}$) → D$\hat{5}$ | T$\hat{1}$]. If we replace the tritone substitutions with the chords from which they theoretically derive, we generate a classical chain of applied chords, [E7 A7 D7 G7 | C], represented in Roman numerals as [ii | V7/iv → V7/ii → V7/V → V7 | I] or in functional-bass terms as [S$\hat{2}$ | (A$\hat{3}$) → (A$\hat{6}$) → (A$\hat{2}$) → D$\hat{5}$ | T$\hat{1}$].

Whether the B♭-dominant-seventh is considered an applied chord to E♭-dominant-seventh or generated through tritone substitution, the functional-bass analysis shows that the harmonic function of the original progression has again been preserved. Each example from Tatum's improvisations on "Body and Soul" maintained the model, [S$\hat{2}$ D$\hat{5}$ T$\hat{1}$], across all its elaboration, ornamentation, and chord substitution. Another replication.

***

The examples from Art Tatum demonstrate a number of ways of reharmonizing the incipit of "Body and Soul." Despite the complexity and virtuosity of Tatum's performance, the passages are all valid ways of playing

"Body and Soul" because they preserve aspects of the harmony found in the model.[17] A functional-bass analysis of each passage allows us to point out a recurring pattern, [S2̂ D5̂ T1̂]. Here, the pattern is a mediating term that forges a relation of substitution between two musical artifacts—that is, the pattern is an aspect. But what happens when the pattern is not preserved exactly? Can we still have replications?

Unlike Tatum's recordings of "Body and Soul," which are in the key given in the original published sheet music, C major, the rest of the examples that I will discuss are in D♭ major. This is a direct consequence of Coleman Hawkins's famous recording of the song from October 11, 1939. Although the song had been performed in D♭ before Hawkins, the wild success of his recording made D♭ into the standard key for the tune.[18] Like Glenn Miller's recording of "In the Mood," Hawkins's recording shaped the future performance of the tune; it became something of a bottleneck in the network, a node to which all future performances (at least, for many years) were connected.

Hank Jones, in a 1956 recording of "Body and Soul," employs a typical bebop reharmonization strategy when replicating the model (Figure 2.6).[19] In the first measure of the passage Jones supplements the ii-chord, E♭-minor-seventh, with an applied dominant neighbor chord. In the second half of measure 2, a new progression is introduced. The D-dominant-seventh chords that precedes measure 3's D♭-major-seventh chord is a tritone substitution for A♭-dominant-seventh. Omitting the A-minor-seventh chord momentarily, we would represent the functional bass of this passage as: [S2̂ (N6̂) | S2̂ *D2̂♭ | T1̂].[20] How should we analyze the Am7? I would argue that this chord is an elaboration of the D dominant-seventh chord. Since there is not a widely

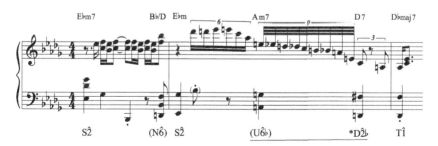

Figure 2.6 Hank Jones, "Body and Soul," 1956, first chorus, third A-section, measures 1–3

72 HEARING DOUBLE

accepted name for this kind of elaboration in the literature on jazz theory, I will call it "unpacking."[21] Here is the basic rule: any dominant-seventh chord can be "unpacked" by preceding it with a minor-seventh chord whose root is a perfect fifth above (or, via inversion, a perfect fourth below) the dominant chord; the two chords together fill the time span of the original chord (here, a half note in duration). In terms of harmonic-function, the "unpacked" chord is an embellishing chord and does not receive a functional label.[22]

A canonical example of "unpacked" chords from the bebop era is Dizzy Gillespie's reharmonization of "I Can't Get Started":

C   Am7 | Dm7 G7 | Bm7 E7 B♭m7 E♭7 | Am7 D7 A♭m7 D♭7 | C

Each of the minor chords in measures 3 and 4 are unpacked chords that embellish the dominant seventh chords they precede. We could group them as follows, where underlining groups together unpacked chords and the chords from which they were generated:

C   Am7 | Dm7 G7 | <u>Bm7 E7 B♭m7 E♭7</u> | <u>Am7 D7 A♭m7 D♭7</u> | C

If we then omitted the unpacked chords, we get a chain of descending dominant seventh chords, E7 E♭7 D7 D♭7, a progression generated by means of tritone substitution.

C   Am7 | Dm7 G7 | E7 *E♭7 | D7 *D♭7 | C

If we replaced the tritone-substituted chords with the originals, we would get an orthodox chain of applied chords, like those in the Art Tatum examples

Figure 2.7 Teddy Wilson, "Body and Soul," 1941, first chorus, first A-section, measures 1–3.

above. In Figure 2.6 the A-minor-seventh chord of measure 2 is an unpacked chord that embellishes the D dominant-seventh chord at the end of the measure. Since unpacked chords are embellishing chords, we will notate them in functional-bass notation with the letter U, for an Unpacked chord, and place them in parentheses. In terms of functional bass the progression is represented as [S$\hat{2}$ (N$\hat{6}$) | S$\hat{2}$ (U$\hat{6}$♭) *D$\hat{2}$♭ | T$\hat{1}$]. While the bass line has now been altered to generate a chromatic descent, [S$\hat{2}$ *D$\hat{2}$♭ T$\hat{1}$], this tritone-substituted version of the model, [S$\hat{2}$ D$\hat{5}$ T$\hat{1}$], is another perfectly good replication. That is, in the language of jazz harmony, these two progressions are substitutable for each other.

Another strategy for reharmonization appears in Teddy Wilson's 1941 performance of "Body and Soul" (Figure 2.7).[23] Wilson sustains the opening E♭-minor-seventh for the first measure and a half but replaces the A♭-dominant-seventh chord at the end of measure two with C7♭9, before resolving to D♭-major-sixth on the downbeat of measure three. The C-dominant-seventh harmonizes the b♭[1] in the melody beautifully and places the leading tone in the bass. Given the tendency of the leading tone ($\hat{7}$) to ascend to the tonic ($\hat{1}$), there is little difficulty in hearing this chord function harmonically as a dominant. In jazz contexts, the use of this chord as a dominant functioning harmony overrides the more classical interpretation of this chord as V/iii. (I think one would be hard pressed to find a jazz musician or acculturated listener who heard this chord as implying motion toward F minor, or iii.) If one had to derive the chord, perhaps it could be thought of as generated from an augmented V9 chord, with the root omitted (A♭, C, E, G♭, B♭). But rather than undergo a series of speculative derivations for the chord, I would rather appeal to the practice of jazz musicians to justify its use and function. Since there is no standard terminology for this class of chord in the jazz theory literature, I will refer to it as a *leading-tone dominant-seventh chord*. A leading-tone dominant-seventh chord is defined as a dominant-seventh chord whose bass note is one half-step below the chord to which it resolves. In this case, the root of the C-dominant-seventh chord is one half-step below its resolution, D♭-major-sixth. Since the chord substitutes for V7, we will include it in the family of dominant-functioning chords in functional-bass analyses. Thus, this progression is represented in functional-bass terms as [S$\hat{2}$ | S$\hat{2}$ D$\hat{7}$ | T$\hat{1}$].

The leading-tone dominant-seventh chord in Figure 2.7 is not derived from tritone-substitution, like the dominant-functioning chord in the Hank Jones example. While the *D$\hat{2}$♭ chord used by Jones approaches T$\hat{1}$

from a half-step above, the D$\hat{7}$ chord used by Wilson approaches T$\hat{1}$ from a half-step below. Both scale degrees $\hat{7}$ (the leading-tone) and $\hat{2}$ (the flatted supertonic) are tendency tones that create expected melodic motion toward the tonic, $\hat{1}$. D$\hat{7}$ and *D$\hat{2}$♭ capitalize on this tendency by generating expectations for motion to the tonic. Thus, both chords are dominant-functioning dominant-seventh chords and alternatives to the standard V7 chord.[24] They present ear-catching reharmonizations of the model's pattern [S$\hat{2}$ D$\hat{5}$ T$\hat{1}$]. But in neither case do they preserve the model's pattern wholly intact. At best, they transform it into something more general, such as [S$\hat{2}$ Dx T$\hat{1}$], where "x" is a variable denoting that one of a variety of dominant-functioning chords could be employed. Given the fame of "Body of Soul" within the jazz tradition and thus a listener's familiarity with its opening three measures, perhaps we are primed to hear almost any chord that appears at the end of measure 2 and is followed by tonic as fulfilling the role of dominant-function.[25]

However, there may be limits to how far the practice can go. An interesting example is Thelonious Monk's version of "Body and Soul." Like many of Monk's performances of standard repertoire, his harmonizations are often quite radical. In these harmonizations, it can be hard to recover the patterns they share with earlier versions. In such cases, we may not know if they constitute replications or if they go beyond replication altogether, more akin to a revision, variation, or a transformation of the original tune. "Body and Soul" is an interesting case. Monk recorded solo performances of the tune on multiple occasions, but in each case, he plays the opening three measures with the same distinctive harmonization. Figure 2.8 presents a transcription from a 1961 concert, released posthumously on *The Complete Riverside Recordings*.[26]

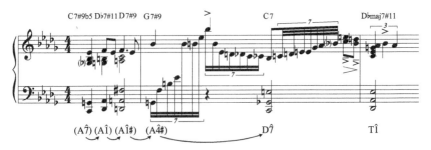

Figure 2.8 Thelonious Monk, "Body and Soul," 1961, first chorus, first A-section, measures 1–3.

Monk extends the use of the leading-tone dominant-seventh chord. The opening C-dominant-seventh is a leading-tone dominant-seventh that resolves to D♭. However, by altering the D♭ chord into a dominant-seventh chord, it too becomes a leading-tone dominant-seventh chord, one that resolves to D. Monk explores the possibility of using a leading-tone dominant-seventh chord as an applied chord. In retrospect, the opening three chords form a chain of applied leading-tone dominants that ascend to D-dominant-seventh, but the progression does not end there. The D-dominant-seventh chord at the end of measure 1 is an applied dominant-seventh chord that embellishes the G-dominant-seventh of measure 2; that, in turn, is an applied dominant to the C-dominant-seventh chord at the end of the measure. Here, C-dominant-seventh, the same chord that began the whole progression, functions not as an applied chord but as a leading-tone dominant-seventh chord that resolves, properly this time, to D♭-major-seventh on the downbeat of measure 3. In a functional-bass analysis, we represent the passage as $[(A\hat{7}) \to (A\hat{1}) \to (A\hat{1}\sharp) \to | (A\hat{4}\sharp) \to D\hat{7} | T\hat{1}]$.

What's missing from this harmonization is a clearly functioning subdominant chord—something to occupy the place of $S\hat{2}$.[27] By excising the subdominant chord that typically opens "Body and Soul," Monk's reharmonization challenges our ability to immediately accept it as a replication. The presence of the melody keeps the tune in our ears, even as the harmonization stretches chains of applied chords to a breaking point, resolving, only at the very end, by means of a leading-tone dominant-seventh chord. The passage rides a fine line between invoking the pattern from the incipit and breaking with it. Monk's version of "Body and Soul" is distinctive. It may not be substitutable in the same way that other harmonizations were. Even if we were to simplify the voicings or rewrite Monk's version in the form of a lead sheet (C7 D♭7 D7 | G7 C7 | D♭), there is a strong sense of revision at work here. Because the

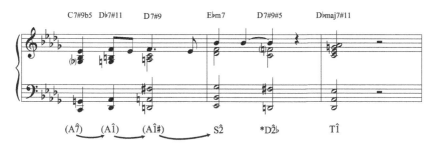

Figure 2.9 Monk's opening harmonies on "Body and Soul," reharmonized.

passage reproduces so little of the model's pattern, it seems a major alteration to the tune. It might be morphologically too remote to count as a replication. The only way to know for certain would be to consider the social context of use and see if was accepted as a replication. Given the turbulent world of jazz in early 1960s and Monk's own reputation as a high modernist and co-inventor of bebop—a composer and performer of dissonant and rhythmic yet wonderfully inventive jazz—the criteria for substitutability might be quite forgiving. That is, we might describe the culture of replication in which Monk participated as extremely permissive.

To demonstrate how far Monk pushes this harmonization, we could re-compose the passage to include $\hat{S2}$. Instead of stopping the chain of leading-tone dominant-sevenths at D-dominant-seventh, we could keep ascending to arrive at E♭-minor-seventh on the downbeat of measure 2.

This version sounds much tamer than Monk's original. The addition of $\hat{S2}$ to the progressions makes the opening measure sound like an embellishing anacrusis to the second measure. Instead of making the listener wait until the resolution in measure 3 to clarify the harmonic-functional aspects of the chord progression, $\hat{S2}$ is a clear functional marker appearing a measure earlier. I include this reharmonization of Monk's version to show, by comparison, the audacity of Monk's original harmonization. The alternate version, I think, would be accepted as a valid replication without hesitation. One reason is the inclusion of $\hat{S2}$, which restores the [$\hat{S2}$ *$\hat{D2}$♭ $\hat{T1}$] pattern found in Hank Jones's version, above.

But, if the jazz community was willing to accept Monk's harmonization as a replication—and, historically, they did—this would simply make definitive what the last two examples have shown: that not all of the features of

Table 2.1 Table of replications for the opening measures of "Body and Soul."

Johnny Green 1930:	$\hat{S2}$ | $\hat{S2}$ $\hat{D5}$ | $\hat{T1}$
Tatum 1938:	$\hat{S2}$ | $\hat{S4}$ $\hat{D5}$ | $\hat{T1}$
Tatum 1953:	$\hat{S2}$ | $\hat{D5}$ | $\hat{T1}$
Jones 1956:	$\hat{S2}$ | *$\hat{D2}$♭ | $\hat{T1}$
Wilson 1941:	$\hat{S2}$ | $\hat{D7}$ | $\hat{T1}$
Monk 1960:	| $\hat{D7}$ | $\hat{T1}$

REPLICATION 77

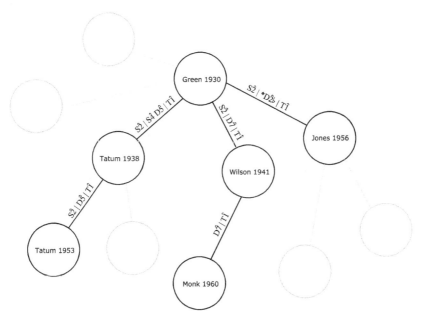

Figure 2.10 A segment of the "Body and Soul" network.

the model's pattern [$\hat{S2}$ $\hat{D5}$ $\hat{T1}$] must be preserved for successful replication. Thus, these features can in no way be considered as essential or necessary properties.

***

Across these five examples, we have seen the model's pattern [$\hat{S2}$ $\hat{D5}$ $\hat{T1}$] replicated with less and less fidelity. These cases may remind us of the discussion of "So What" from the previous chapter, where the work seemed to get thinner and thinner over time. Here we have a pattern, [$\hat{S2}$ $\hat{D5}$ $\hat{T1}$], that affords a wide variety of instantiations (see Table 2.1 and Figure 2.10). If all parts of the pattern are taken as essential or work-determinative, then the pattern cannot accommodate the examples taken from Hank Jones, Teddy Wilson, and Thelonious Monk. To include Jones and Wilson, we need to thin out the $\hat{D5}$ part of the pattern and replace it with D alone. Now the pattern is thinner: [$\hat{S2}$ D $\hat{T1}$]. To accommodate the Monk example, we need to get rid of the $\hat{S2}$ part entirely: [D $\hat{T1}$]. Thinner still. For the ontologist to keep their thin work alive, they have to keep revising the pattern. In this act of ontological *Nachträglichkeit*, there is always a thinner and wispier pattern that one could say was always already present. But where will the thinning stop? What pattern could possibly be thin enough to accommodate all the possible ways that the model could be reharmonized? And how could this wisp of pattern ever do the work of individuation and identification, which was its whole raison d'être?

The purpose of this detailed discussion of replication is that it offers us another way of accounting for the relationship between two musical artifacts, for instance, the sheet music of "Body and Soul" and Monk's daring performance of the song. Each of the examples preserved some part of an original pattern. However, there was *no need to come up with one thin pattern that accommodated all instances*. Instead, *each artifact established a distinct relation with a predecessor, a relation that might also be present elsewhere but is not requisite*. The situation can be usefully represented as a network. Each artifact functions like a node in a network, and new nodes are added when replication is successful. Each node is connected to another by a distinct edge. Each edge would define a unique relation. Some edges would associate nodes through the complete pattern, [$\hat{S2}$ $\hat{D5}$ $\hat{T1}$]; others would associate nodes through a different pattern, like [$\hat{S2}$ $\hat{D7}$ $\hat{T1}$]; others still would forge an association through a third pattern, [$\hat{D7}$ $\hat{T1}$]. Across an entire network there need be no single relation that holds between all nodes. There is no essential property to be found, no universal sign or pattern distributed equally to all its members. Rather, the network has innumerable links and connections between its nodes, each of which is sufficient and perhaps indifferent to the rest. This networked view offers a new perspective on the ontology of standards. Instead of seeking out a thin work, to understand what a particular standard is we must traverse its network of performances. To follow a standard is to trace its network of replications.[28]

We simply do not know ahead of time what features of an original will be the ones replicated. We might be surprised—a possibility that cannot arise for the ontologist and their thin, prescriptive work. The social context is the ultimate arbiter about what is or is not successful replication. As contexts change, the terms by which successful replication is assessed will also change. Monk's harmonization might have been too radical in 1939, the same year as Hawkins's recording. However, as the harmonic syntax of jazz changes—and Monk was one of the musicians whose improvisations and compositions helped to extend and complicate jazz's harmonic possibilities—so do the terms by which harmonic models can be replicated. Thus, any ontological account we are going to propose must be sensitive to these kinds of historical and cultural changes. Simply put, if the community accepts an artifact as an acceptable substitute, replication has been successful. Successful replication operates with complete indifference to the preservation of essential features. Only in contexts where replication has been successful does the ontologist, retrospectively, "discover" what a musical work's so-called essential or work-determinative features might be. Those features are only "essential" or "work-determinative" so long as the context of use continues to require them.

The hidden secret of the ontologist is that their account always assumed successful replication without acknowledging it. When the ontologist looks back over a slew of performances and claims that, at the beginning of it all, there was a thin work that prescribed work-determinative properties, they neglect to consider the practices of replication that produced the slew in the first place. To correct this view, we need to correct our language. In Chapter 1, I borrowed Davies's concept of "work-determinative" properties. These properties were defined as necessary, prescribed from the very beginning by a composer, communicated by a "vehicle" (a score, oral instructions, or model performance), and by virtue of which a performance instances a particular work. If we refrain from assuming that two performances are related by the shared presence of work-determinative properties (in the sense just defined) and start thinking about them in terms of replication, we then need to reconsider the notion of "determinative" properties. In a case like "Body and Soul," the replication of the song's harmony (among other features) helps to differentiate it from other musical works. And yet, within the culture of jazz performance, we do not know ahead of time how a standard's harmony will be transformed. In most cases, there may remain features of the harmony that we can immediately relate back to previous instances of the tune. In fact, those features would be "work-determinative," but in a new sense. They would be features by which we identify and individuate songs without being necessary or essential. (The same could be said for a standard's melody.) In other words, *for any given standard there may be features about the standard that help determine which standard it is. But that does not entail that those determinative features are essential or necessary since, in other versions of that standard, we cannot count on them being present.* All we can say is that the current determinate features of a standard depend on its history of successful replication and, thus, on their ever-changing social contexts of use. Determinative features emerge. Thus, we must revise the notion of a determinative property in the following manner: *work-determinative properties are not necessary properties; rather, they are properties that are sufficient for the purpose of replication.* Work-determinative properties are those properties to which we appeal when making a new replication. In virtue of them, we decide to include a new replication among a set of previous replications. Work-determinative properties are, in fact, network-emergent properties.

***

By distinguishing determinative properties from essential properties, and by aligning the emergence of determinative properties with processes of replication, we have made some initial strides toward establishing an ontology of standards that breaks with traditional metaphysical models. Before we complete the discussion of replication, there are two more questions about determinative properties to consider:

(1) Not all instances of replication are typical, according to the standards of a community. Some are radical, like Thelonious Monk's version of "Body and Soul." Others are conventional. How is it that a single, unique replication becomes widely replicated across a network? How does a replication establish a convention or a widely accepted, determinative property?
(2) What kinds of properties are typically selected as determinative properties of a standard? Intuitively, the most obvious candidates are properties associated with a standard's melody or its chord progression. Listeners can often identity and individuate a standard when presented with either of these features. However, if within the practices of the performance of popular song determinative properties (like a song's melody or harmony) are not essential properties but rather sufficient properties capable of being revised or even omitted, then how does replication explain these widely held intuitions?

To answer the first question—how does a replication establish a convention or a widely accepted, determinative property?—we need to return to the level of a specific song's network of performances and traverse it. Performances of standards, as we have seen, do not always remain faithful to the intent of the composer or to the prescriptions of its earliest versions, scores, or models. Sometimes standards develop performance conventions

Figure 2.11 "But Not for Me," first A section, pickup and measures 1–9. Reproduced by permission of Alfred Music.

that emerge first as unique replications and then become widely replicated. These replications of replications can ultimately change what we take to be a standard's determinative properties.

A good example of this phenomenon is found in the performance history of the Gershwin tune "But Not for Me." The song first appeared in 1930, in the musical *Girl Crazy*, although it was not originally one of the show's hit songs. Rarely recorded throughout the 1930s, the profile of "But Not for Me" rose with a resurgence of interest in George Gershwin's music after his untimely death in 1937. Deliberate and retrospective recordings of Gershwin's music helped to rehabilitate the song. An important early example of this phenomenon is the set of Gershwin recordings initiated by Lee Wiley in 1939 and in the 1943 film adaptation of *Girl Crazy* starring Judy Garland. In the published sheet music of song (see Figure 2.11), the melody of the refrain begins with a three-beat anacrusis ("They're wri-ting") that continues roving in stepwise motion over the first three scale degrees ("songs of love, but not for me").[29] The chorus, or "refrain," is organized into four phrases, eight measures each,

82 HEARING DOUBLE

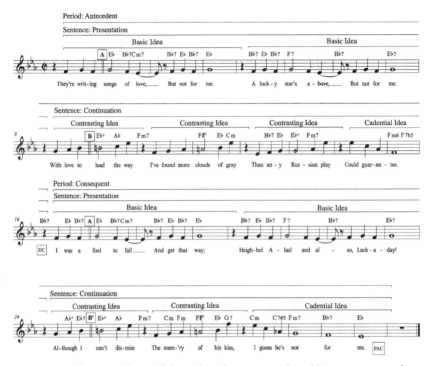

Figure 2.12 "But Not for Me," formal analysis. Reproduced by permission of Alfred Music.

built on an ABAB′ formal model (see Figure 2.12). Taken as a whole, the refrain is formally a large parallel period, divided into an antecedent phrase (AB) that ends on a half cadence, and a consequent phrase (AB′) ending on a perfect authentic cadence. Each of these phrases is sententially organized, with the repetition of a four-measure basic idea comprising the presentation (A) and a contrasting idea, a series of motivically similar two-measure ideas, in the continuation (B). The continuation begins on the subdominant (IV), returns quickly to the tonic (I), and is finished off with a cadential idea.[30]

The A-section begins on tonic harmony (E♭ in the original) and presents the basic idea. While the bass line oscillates, bouncing between scale degrees $\hat{1}$ and $\hat{5}$, the harmonies shadow the melodic contour exactly, alternating between closely spaced E♭-major chords and passing B♭-dominant-seventh chords. In measures 5–8, the basic idea is repeated but presented against a new set of harmonies, here a small cycle of applied chords (V7/V and V7). This harmonic change also affects the E♭-major chord of measure 7. Instead of a return to tonic, the E♭-major chord (I) is altered into a dominant-seventh chord (V7/IV) and sustained until the arrival of IV in measure 9, the beginning of the B-section. Due to its sentential form, the A-section, or presentation phrase, emphasizes a simple musical situation: the same melodic idea—a small stepwise idea confined to the first three scale degrees of E♭ major—is presented twice, against two different harmonizations: the first time against four measures of tonic and dominant alternation, the second time against a small cycle of applied dominant-seventh chords.

On June 29, 1954, about a quarter-century after its composition, Miles Davis—along with Sonny Rollins, Horace Silver, Percy Heath, and Kenny Clarke—recorded two takes of "But Not for Me" at Rudy Van Gelder's legendary studio in Hackensack, New Jersey.[31] Both recordings, which are considered classics of Davis's early years, include a small but significant change to the song's harmony. Instead of beginning on the tonic, as in the published sheet music (see Figure 2.11), Davis plays an F7♭5 chord just after the pickups. The opening four measures that accompany the tune's melodic basic idea are harmonized as follows: [F7♭5 | Fm7 B♭7 | E♭ | E♭]. The same progression is then repeated in measures 5–8, except for the transformation of the final E♭-major to E♭-dominant-seventh (V7/IV) in order to set up the arrival of the A♭ in measure 9. Where the sheet music presents the basic idea harmonized in two different ways (first over a tonic prolongation, then over a cycle of applied chords), Davis's version presents the basic idea twice, harmonized in the same way both times. What originally appeared in the sheet music as the harmonies of measures 5 and 6 are now, in Davis's version, substituted for measures 1 and 2.

What might be the reason for doing this? Looking at the change from a Schenkerian point of view (recalling Allen Forte's analyses of popular American ballads), there might be reasons to affirm the developmental aspects of Gershwin's original, where the same melody accrues a new harmonization. This might be a manifestation of linear structures buried below the music's surface, requiring the span of the refrain to be fully realized. But from a jazz musician's point of view, Davis's reharmonization simply offers a more challenging set of chord changes over which to improvise.[32]

As far as reharmonizations go, this is a small change to make. It is a replication as common and innocuous as those we have already seen from the incipit of "Body and Soul." Yet it made a significant impact on further renditions of the tune. Due to the popularity of Davis's bright-tempo recording of the tune, other jazz musicians appropriated his particular harmonization of "But Not for Me." We hear it replicated in the Red Garland Trio's 1957 recording.[33] Perhaps this is unsurprising since, at the time of the recording, Garland was the pianist employed in Miles Davis's quintet, and we could assume a direct line of transmission from Davis to Garland. But we find the same replication in recordings by musicians with less direct attachments to Davis. The pianist Hank Jones, in a solo performance recording session on August 8, 1956, consistently plays Davis's harmonization.[34] While Jones's tempo is slow—much closer to Gershwin's original—and the key is transposed down to C, the basic idea ("songs of love") is harmonized in parallel major thirds, emphasizing the whole-tone scale and forming a D7♭5 chord. In contrast to Jones, the popular pianist Ramsey Lewis recorded a live version of the tune with his trio at a live performance in Chicago in 1960. In this version, the tempo is faster than Davis's, and the tune is back in the original key of E♭. Unlike Davis's and Jones's versions, the opening chord is simplified from an F7♭5 chord to F-dominant-ninth chord. Other performances of the tune in the jazz tradition replicated Davis's changes. To name a few: Etta Jones (with Sonny Stitt and Gene Ammons), Sonny Rollins (with bass and drums), Stan Getz (live in Warsaw), Stanley Turrentine (at Minton's on Blue Note), Marcus Roberts, Joe Pass, "Papa" Jo Jones, Dakota Staton, Harry Connick Jr. (on the *When Harry Met Sally* soundtrack), and many others. Most jazz musicians today use Davis's reharmonization; it is even reproduced (albeit transposed) in the second volume of the Real Book (Figure 2.13).

At the same time that Davis's harmonization of "But Not for Me" was gaining traction, numerous performances of the tune remained faithful to Gershwin's original harmonization. Ahmad Jamal's commercially successful recording, from *Live at the Pershing*, remains harmonically closer to the sheet music.[35] This comes as no surprise since Jamal's repertoire reflected his deep

Figure 2.13 "But Not for Me," as presented in *The Real Book*, Vol. II. Reproduced by permission of Alfred Music.

knowledge of American popular music, often acknowledging a song's history in ways that far exceed that of the typical gigging musician. This is reflected Jamal's unusual selection of material, from Morton Gould's "Pavanne" to Richard Rodger's "Slaughter on Tenth Avenue," music that was not being widely performed by jazz musicians. In addition to Jamal, older musicians familiar with the song long before Davis's recording (such as Wild Bill Davis, Earl Hines, and Errol Garner) continued to play it beginning on the tonic. The same goes for more heavily arranged versions of the tune, like those found on Gershwin Songbook records. These recordings often preserve the verse that precedes the refrain—typically excised by jazz musicians—and the original harmonization tends to be present. This is true of Chet Baker's vocal rendition, of the Gershwin "Songbook" recordings of Ella Fitzgerald, Sarah Vaughan, Dinah Washington, and of pop singers like Eydie Gormé and Julie London. These two different ways of harmonizing the basic idea diverge over time, differentiating recordings of the tune intended for popular audiences and those for modern jazz audiences.

This bifurcation deserves further consideration. Methodologically, by assembling the performances of "But Not for Me" mentioned above into a network, we note two distinct branches in its topology: one branch where the refrain begins on tonic harmony and another that begins off tonic harmony. First, to account for the on-tonic and off-tonic branches in the network, we need to appeal to *chains of replications*. Once a new replication has been made, it is possible for others to replicate it in turn with more or less fidelity. A musician coming after Davis (for example, Hank Jones or Red Garland) can take Davis's replication and prolong it. By preserving that alteration, by strictly replicating Davis's replication, chains of replications can generate distinct traditions or styles of playing a standard. Second, whether a musician begins the chorus of "But Not for Me" on tonic (like in the Ahmad Jamal or Gershwin Songbook recordings) or off tonic (like Miles Davis), both versions count as valid replications of the song's harmony. Since replication means a valid substitution within a particular social context of use, then there is no need to say that these two different harmonizations require us to consider them as instances of distinct musical works. They are instances of the same work because they both participate in a shared network of replications. Membership in this network does not require any appeal to essential properties. It simply means that a sufficient, work-determinative property is present. Unlike essential properties, all members of the network need not share the same sufficient, work-determinative properties. For

86 HEARING DOUBLE

instance, if jazz musicians after Davis come to identify and individuate "But Not for Me" on the basis of his alterations, then those alterations are now sufficiently work-determinative.

***

The two most common sources for the work-determinative properties of a standard are its melody and its chord progression. While it is indisputable that listeners often identify and individuate standards by their melody and chord progression, we must also acknowledge the fact that in jazz performance neither the presentation of the melody nor the "original" chord changes are requisite. It is rare for both the melody and the chord changes of a tune to be drastically altered simultaneously. Often the presence of one will persist while the other is changed. For example, Monk's recording of "Body and Soul" preserves the song's original melodic contour and phrasing even as he radically reharmonizes the song. Just as common is the alteration of the melody (in more or less drastic ways) while the harmonies are preserved.

Consider Coleman Hawkins's famous 1939 recording of "Body and Soul," which replicates only the opening two measures of the melody before leaping off into one his most celebrated solos.[36] Even in Hawkins's replication of the opening melody, there are significant alterations; however, in conjunction with the chord progression, there are enough features still available that the

Figure 2.14 Opening phrase of "Body and Soul" (after Bowen 2011)

work remains recognizable. José Bowen, in an essay on the performance history of "Body and Soul," transcribes Hawkins's opening line, and shows its influence on musicians who come after him (see Figure 2.14).[37] Bowen notes the addition of the g♭^{1} in Hawkins's opening phrase (marking it *martellato*, with a large notehead). As a successful substitution of tune's melody line, Hawkins's transformation counts as a replication. Once that replication has been made it can be replicated by others, producing a chain of replications. The g♭^{1} features prominently in Jack McVea's recording from 1944, as well as in Billie Holiday's 1940 and 1957 recordings.[38] While Bowen's account focuses on the g♭^{1}, other melodic aspects of Hawkins's performance are replicated as well. McVea copies Hawkins's quarter-note triplet introduction. Blanton and McVea replicate Hawkins's sixteenth-note anacrusis to measure 4 and its implied D-dominant-seventh chord.[39]

In addition to altering a melody's pitch and rhythmic alterations, more extreme ways of handling melodies appear after Coleman Hawkins's recording of "Body and Soul." In the bebop era, there are many recordings where the melody of a tune is completely excised, like Charlie Parker's recording of "Embraceable You."[40] While Parker replicates the song's chord progression (with some alterations), the excision of the melody line and any allusions to it leads us to a unequivocal conclusion: the presence of the melody should not be taken as a determinate feature, at least by the time of bebop's emergence. Whether this practice would have been acceptable as a replication before Parker is unclear. We would have to study the practices in context to see what constituted a valid replication. In the case of Parker, either we have the institution of a new practice (based on Hawkins) or the replication of a preexistent practice in a form capable of being widely replicated because of Parker's celebrity, fame, and influence. After Parker, we find many other recordings of ballads that excise the original melody altogether. These are replications of Parker's practice; perhaps the most famous is James Moody's Parker-influenced recording of "I'm in the Mood For Love."[41]

While it is common for jazz musicians to drastically alter the melody or harmony of a tune, and thus alter what might have been considered determinative features of the tune, it is indeed rare (but not without precedent) for both the melody and the chord progression to be simultaneously revised. A good example is John Coltrane's version of "But Not for Me," from the album *My Favorite Things*.[42] Unlike Davis's small but widely replicated alteration to the basic idea of the song, Coltrane rewrites the harmony and melody in a drastic revision. *My Favorite Things* is an album of "standards," where every song on the record (other than Cole Porter's ballad "Every Time We Say Goodbye") has been significantly revised.[43] On the album's famous title track, Coltrane simplifies the harmony and adds long vamps, turning the bland Rodgers and Hammerstein song into a turbulent, modal exploration. On "But Not for Me," Coltrane applies the harmonic progressions developed in his composition "Giant Steps," to the A-section of the tune. "Giant Steps" explores the possibility of symmetrical divisions of the octave into three parts—what is sometimes referred to as "Coltrane Changes" in the jazz theory literature.[44] The entirety of "Giant Steps" is based on a series of ii-V-I progressions, or, in their reduced forms, V-I progressions, in the keys of G, B and E♭. Each key is separated by the interval of a major third (or four half-steps), which, like the augmented triad, divides the full chromatic scale into three equal and symmetrical subdivisions. This has been often noted by music theorists and theorists of jazz harmony. However, Coltrane deployed the progression in ways that go beyond "Giant Steps" by using it as a strategy for the reharmonization of popular songs.

Coltrane's application of the "Giant Steps" progressions as a strategy for reharmonization clarifies the harmonic-functional nature of the progression. Like his bebop predecessors, Coltrane often used popular standards as the basis for many of his own compositions in the late 1950s and early 1960s. On the album *Giant Steps*, Coltrane's "Countdown" is based on Miles Davis's "Tune Up," a simple piece in D major. Harmonically, the first four measures are nothing more than a simple ii-V-I progression in D major that occupies a span of four measures (see Figure 2.15). This progression is then transposed down by a whole step, tonicizing C major, and then again, tonicizing B♭ major. The final four bars set up the return of D major by emphasizing V7 in D, an A-dominant-seventh chord, which is prolonged through various means.

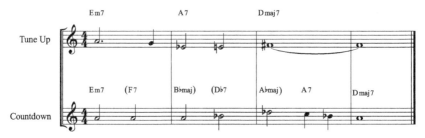

Figure 2.15 Miles Davis, "Tune Up," and John Coltrane, "Countdown."

In "Countdown," Coltrane takes the basic structure of "Tune Up" but rewrites it using the "Giant Steps" progression (see Figure 2.15). The reharmonization works as follows. The opening four measures of "Tune Up" establish D major. In Coltrane's reharmonization, he approaches the whole four-measure unit by inserting the Giant Steps progression so that it begins and ends in the key of D major. Unlike the composition "Giant Steps," which tends to give equal emphasis to its three symmetrical key areas, "Countdown" uses the "Giant Steps" progression to sustain the key of D major, even at the expense of its other, symmetrically related key areas. While B♭ major and G♭ major are rapidly suggested, they do not really challenge D major's hierarchical control over the phrase. By enclosing the "Giant Steps" progression within the key of D major, the other key areas explored become ancillary. Unlike "Giant Steps," which dutifully explores each of the three key symmetrical key areas by beginning and ending on each one in turn, "Countdown" treats the "Giant Steps" progression as a prolongation technique, one that elaborates and embellishes a key area but does not displace a tonal center.[45]

In Coltrane's version of "But Not for Me," the A-section, which (in Gershwin's original) confirms the tonic key and sets up the arrival of IV in the B-section, is now replicated by means of a "Giant Steps" progression (see Figure 2.16). A complete cycle begins on E♭ major, and it prolonged by moving quickly through G major and C♭ major. The entire cycle is completed in the space of four measures (the length of the basic idea). Rather than begin measure 5 on F-dominant-seventh, as in the sheet music, Coltrane repeats the previous four-measure cycle, altering the final chord from I to V7/IV in order to set up the arrival B-section. Like Davis before him, Coltrane develops a strategy for reharmonizing the song's basic idea and uses it for both of its appearances in the A-section. While Davis took the harmony associated with the second appearance of the basic idea and substituted it for

Figure 2.16 John Coltrane, "But Not for Me," from *My Favorite Things*, measures 1–8.

the first appearance, Coltrane does just the opposite; he takes a harmonization strategy developed for the initial basic idea and simply uses it twice. From a harmonic-functional point of view, Coltrane's version counts as a replication in that the "Giant Steps" progression, like the original Gershwin progression, begins in the tonic, embellishes it, and cadences in the tonic. In terms of its harmonic function, it establishes and prolongs the tonic over the first four measures of the tune. And yet, while we can understand how Coltrane's use of "Giant Steps" progressions acts as a tonic prolongation, it can be challenging to hear its connection to the original. It requires us to grasp the aspect preserved between the original and Coltrane's substitution as quite slim. Simply put, we have to hear the opening eight measures of "But Not for Me" as a long, tonic prolongation.

Coltrane's application of the "Giant Steps" progression to "But Not for Me" produces a replication of Gershwin's original progression, but one that is unable to support the original melody line. Thus, Coltrane writes a new melody, based on the old one, to fit over the song's new chord progression. Coltrane's melody begins with a paraphrase of the standard incipit ("They're wri-ting songs of love") but soon departs, warping it chromatically to accommodate the "Giant Steps" progression. The incipit might be sufficient to suggest to a listener that this is a version of "But Not for Me," and thus function as a work-determinate feature. Whether this is or is not the case, we should note just how radical Coltrane's version is. With a new set of chord changes in the A-section, along with a new melody line to go over it, we might say that just under half of the original tune has been substituted with some fairly radical replications.

Because Coltrane's replications are so radical, they provide a unique opportunity for considering the relationship between replication, determinative features, and ontology. By revising both the song's harmony and melody so drastically, Coltrane may also be removing features of the tune that were considered to be work-determinative. If so, why should we consider Coltrane's performance to be a performance of "But Not for Me" and not of some other work? First, the ontology of works of jazz is not determined at the level of a single replication alone. In my discussion of replication, I have been describing the phenomenon at the level of fairly small musical units, typically, those that are two, four, or eight measures long. Popular songs, at least those associated with Tin Pan Alley and the so-called Great American Songbook, are typically constructed out of these smaller units: eight-measure phrases, cadential formulae, turnarounds, bridges, codas, vamps, and so forth.[46]

Thus, we should think of the performance of a popular song as involving not one but numerous replications, linked together in time into a continuous sequences of phrases (introduction, section, bridge, turnaround, etc.) or presented simultaneously (melody and harmony). Questions of identity and individuation of works of jazz are not best handled at the level of a single replication alone.

Work-determinative properties ultimately rely on a web of associated replications. These properties might shift in relation to the whole set of replications involved in making a new version of the tune. Consider, once again, "Body and Soul." Each of the various versions of the first three measures of the tune counted as a valid substitution (and thus replication) of the model. By means of a functional-bass analysis, I demonstrated how a particular harmonic-functional pattern was preserved in each new replication. That pattern was represented as [S$\hat{2}$ D$\hat{5}$ T$\hat{1}$] and lasted for the duration of three measures. However, this is an extraordinarily common progression in the repertoire, found in the opening of many famous tunes, not just "Body and Soul." A brief list might include: "Alice in Wonderland," "Don't Worry about Me," "Fools Rush In," "I Get a Kick out of You," "I Hadn't Anyone till You," "I'll Never Smile Again," "I've Got You under My Skin," "Laura," "Once I Loved," "Poor Butterfly," "Prisoner of Love," "Tune Up," and "Under a Blanket of Blue." Considered alone, the harmonic replications of "Body and Soul" analyzed above are not specific enough to individuate "Body and Soul" from many other songs. If the opening progression is considered a work-determinative property, it simply cannot be determinative in isolation. Its power to individuate will ultimately rely on its association with other replications.

Coltrane's version of "But Not for Me," while drastically revising the A-sections, leaves the B-section intact. He presents the B-section in a manner that is completely conventional within the jazz tradition. There is no radical alteration to the melody or the harmony of the tune, other than simplifying the tune in comparison with its sheet music, a change found also in numerous other versions of the song from Miles Davis to Ahmad Jamal. Thus, the conventional presentation of the B-section helps to preserve the song's identity. Due to its conventionality, Coltrane's B-section plays the role of a work-determinate property in relation to the unconventional A-section harmonization. It signals to the listener that this performance *is* a performance of "But Not for Me." In less radical versions of "But Not for Me," other, more prominent and established properties—for example, the opening melody—might carry the brunt of individuation. But when those properties are gone, others come to the fore and the aspects they replicate suddenly become relevant. Thus, the specific properties considered work-determinative may change depending on their relation to the whole set of replications employed in a performance.

When replications are permissive they will produce artifacts that are morphologically quite distinct from their models. In contrast, impermissive (or strict) replications will produce artifacts with greater morphological similarities. When some replications in a new performance of a standard are permissive, the impermissive replications may become more important insofar as they function as markers of distinguishing features of previously accepted versions of the tune. Thus, work-determinative features of this or that version of a tune are context-dependent, holistic, and relational; the properties replicated may be deemed more or less determinative based on context and on the permissiveness or impermissiveness of the other replications to which they are associated. This is a powerful reason why work-determinative features are not essential or necessary, but simply sufficient. *If a replication or a set of replications is sufficient for identifying and individuating a work, then it possesses work-determinative properties.* If a permissive or radical replication rids a passage of its conventional work-determinative properties, the impermissive replication of other passages will take over the labor of identity and individuation.

***

Replication offers an account of the relation of performance to performance without an appeal to essential properties. Work-determinative properties are sufficient, not necessary. They are simply the properties of a work that are commonly replicated and dependent on the holism of associated replications. This new view of work-determinative properties challenges the philosophically realist view that a standard is based on a thin work—a structure or pattern with essential properties. Although a challenge to the realist view is not the same a comprehensive argument, our discussion has not been in vain. We now have some new resources: replications, chains of replications, and an account of work-determinative properties that distinguishes them from essential properties. But those resources, as I will show in the next chapter, are not yet adequate for offering a robust account of the ontology of standards. In addition to replication, we must consider nomination, or the act of giving a name to a work or a performance of a work.

3

Nomination

In addition to chains of replication, names—and acts of naming—play an important role in the identity and individuation of works of jazz. Consider for a moment the function of names in the reception, consumption, and circulation of jazz. Every piece of sheet music comes emblazoned with its name on the title sheet and above the first staff. In the earliest days of cylinder recordings, the name of the work was etched around the edge of the cylinder or shouted at the beginning of the recording. Phonograph discs come with names printed on the record sleeve and on the center label. Even contemporary digital music inscribes the name of each track in metadata included in the header of the sound file. This metadata supplies the information that scrolls across the displays of smart phones, car radios, and digital music streams. In the heyday of radio, announcers or bandleaders would tell audiences near and far the names of the compositions they played. The song's title and performer would be announced to the eager public. When titles are not present, a nagging question often follows: "What am I listening to?" Disc jockeys were often inundated with calls from listeners curious to find out what they were hearing, anxious to pin down the work before it was lost to time, fickle memory, and the airwaves. Ignorance about a title incites the desire to know what one is listening to and how to identify it so it can be heard again and again.

With shifts and developments in technology, the desire for names has not abated. Today, researchers working in the field of music information retrieval make the relationship between a recording and its name into a central problem. Their work has enabled the technology behind Shazam and SoundHound, smartphone apps that can instantly provide the names and performers of recordings based on a brief audio sample. Apple, seeking to increase its market share in distributing music, has incorporated such technology directly into its mobile operating system. Anyone with an iPhone can now ask Siri the question, "What is this?" and, holding the phone up to the ambient environment, be presented the name of the current song playing. Siri's response, while satisfying listener's curiosity to identify and individuate

Hearing Double. Brian Kane, Oxford University Press. © Oxford University Press 2024.
DOI: 10.1093/oso/9780190600501.003.0004

musical works, is intended as a vehicle for the sale of music. The song that appears on the iPhone's screen can be quickly purchased and downloaded. The curious listener is transformed into an impulse buyer. But this is a new variation on an old phenomenon. In jazz and popular song—like in other forms of American musical production—the act of naming has always been tied in with the business of music, its sale and consumption.[1] Naming and advertising join together in the titles of popular song, the token by which the musical commodity is identified and sold. Sometimes a song's title is repeated in the lyrics as a form of song "plugging." By employing music's power of repetition and memory, by embedding the titles of songs into catchy musical earworms, names remain with listeners. But there is no uniform strategy for integrating a song's title into its lyrics. Names appear in different guises and positions. The title of the song will often be stated at significant musical moments in the work, at a memorable hook or chorus. Alternatively, they might appear at the very beginning of the tune like "Long Ago and Far Away" or at the end of a set of lyrics like "All the Things You Are."

At times, the necessity to provide a name for a song is even thematized in the song itself. After becoming a hit, Sy Oliver's riff-based "Opus No. 1" was given a set of lyrics that describe the process of trying to name the song.

> I'm racking my brains to think of a name
> To give to this tune so Perry can croon
> And maybe old Bing will give it a fling
> And that'll start everyone humming the thing. . . .
>
> So we call it Opus One, It's not for Sammy Kaye, hey, hey, hey
> It's Opus One, it's got to swing not sway, baby![2]

Without a distinctive name, the song cannot make the rounds in the popular music industry. To be distinguishable in a marketplace of competing songs, the musical commodity needs a name. Once in place, it can function as a marker by which listeners can individuate it, request it, buy copies of the recordings, and—generally speaking—consume it. Undoubtedly, names play an important role in identifying and individuating musical works. But how exactly? Beyond chains of replication, what does the act of naming contribute to the ontology of standards?

***

Figure 3.1 Lead sheet with motivic analysis, George and Ira Gershwin, "Embraceable You." Reproduced with permission from Alfred Music.

The best way to understand the contribution of naming to the ontology of standards is to consider the widespread use of contrafacts by jazz musicians. The Latin term *contrafactum* refers to the practice where new texts or poems are composed to fit older, preexisting melodies or musical settings. Contemporary scholars of jazz often use the modern term *contrafact* to refer to instances where a new melody is written to fit a preexisting chord progression. The practice was ubiquitous in the bebop era, where newly written "heads" were fashioned to fit over older repertoire. Dizzy Gillespie's "Groovin' High" is a contrafact of Paul Whiteman's hit record from 1920, "Whispering." Many of Charlie Parker's most celebrated compositions are contrafacts, such as "Donna Lee" (based on "Back Home Again in Indiana"), "Ko Ko" (based on "Cherokee"), and "Bird of Paradise" (based on "All the Things You Are"). The practice existed in jazz before bebop, although it was less widespread. George Gershwin's "I Got Rhythm" spawned a glut of contrafacts, far too numerous to list here, creating a class of tunes that jazz musicians call "Rhythm Changes," denoting that the progression of the song is based on "I Got Rhythm."[3]

To begin a discussion of names and contrafacts, I will focus on a handful of Charlie Parker's performances of "Embraceable You" and contrafacts based on this source. (For reference, Figure 3.1 reproduces the opening two phrases of "Embraceable You.") Of particular interest are two takes of the tune that Parker recorded for Dial records on October 28, 1947, at the WOR studios in New York. The two takes, A and B—often identified in the musicological literature by their matrix numbers 1106A and 1106B—are remarkable for a few reasons. Rather than follow conventions by presenting the song's melody, then soloing over its harmonic progression, Parker nearly completely excises the melody on both takes, integrating it into his solo and alluding to it with

96 HEARING DOUBLE

Figure 3.2 Charlie Parker, "Embraceable You," Dial Records, take A.

various degrees of directness.[4] In addition, the two takes, which were recorded back-to-back in the studio, are often cited by jazz scholars as evidence of Parker's masterful use of motivic and thematic improvisation.[5] And masterful they are. After a four-measure introduction on the piano, take A opens with a small melodic idea, a quotation from a now-forgotten tune, "A Table in the Corner," which—as Gary Giddins notes—is repeated and developed as a motive, helping to give the solo a logical and orderly disposition (Figure 3.2). The motive is little more than a diatonic turn, sometimes initiated by the leap of a perfect fifth. It is first heard, in its entirety, in measure 1, and labeled with an "x" in the transcription. It is repeated in measure 2, with the initial leap of a fifth filled in by a diatonic run. In measure 3, the motive is transposed up a perfect fourth, but with the opening interval now expanded to a seventh, then repeated at the same pitch level, with diminution, in measure 4. According to Giddins, "Parker plays the opening motive five times in all, and variants on it appear throughout the solo." Following Giddins, we might hear this fifth presentation of the motif initiated in the anacrusis to measure 5 with the leap from the note a to d^1, followed by a few ornamental notes before completing the motive.

The melodic organization of Parker's motivic opening phrases also appears to allude, albeit indirectly, to Gershwin's original melody. "Embraceable You," as shown in Figure 3.1, is composed of two main motives, labeled α and β. Motive α is a three-note, ascending idea in quarter notes. Motive β is a rhythmically inflected descent of a perfect fifth and functions as a tail to motive α. Measures 1–4 present the basic idea, two iterations of α onto which β is appended. In measures 5–8, the same basic idea is now transposed melodically up a perfect fourth. Parker's improvisation has nothing corresponding to Gershwin's β motive, but his opening presentation of the "Table in the Corner" quote, like Gershwin, is played twice, then transposed up a fourth. It is as if Gershwin's original motive had been substituted with the quote from "A Table in the Corner," while preserving something of the logic and organization of Gershwin's melodic construction. But these kinds of structural relations are, at best, indirect allusions to Gershwin's original melody. The one direct allusion to the original melody is in measure 21, where one can hear Parker alluding to the words, "a-bove all."

The second take is played a bit faster than the first. Parker does not begin with the "Table on a Corner" motive but develops a solo that—while different from the first take—seems to me just as brilliantly logical in its design. (Figure 3.3) Parker begins with a chromatic anacrusis that leads to a central motive, c^2-c^1-$c\sharp^1$-d^1, here labeled with the letter "z." The motive is recognizable on the basis of its distinctive melodic contour, a downward leap of an octave (or, later, a seventh), followed by a rising ascent.[6] It definitively appears

Figure 3.3 Charlie Parker, "Embraceable You," Dial Records, take B.

three times in the first four measures—and even one additional time, at the triplets in measure 3, if inversions of the motive count. Unlike the "Table in the Corner" motive from take A, which tends to initiate phrases, motive z appears at the end of a phrase. A clear instance is measure 10, where Parker closes an allusion to Gershwin's original melody with motive z. In addition to this allusion, take B tends to hew closer to Gershwin's melody than take A, sounding the original melody two other times, in measures 25–28. But the allusion in measure 9, closed off with motive z, deserves a closer look. Figure 3.4 aligns measures 9 and 10 of Gershwin's original melody with Parker's two takes. Motive z appears in the same place in both takes, at the tail of the phrase that ends in measure 10. By aligning Parker's two takes, once can see how similar the final two beats of measure 9 are, and that, in fact, take A presents a highly ornamented allusion to the song's melody that was not, at first, obvious. The notes (a^1-f^1-g^1-a^1) that fill out measure 9 in the sheet music are highly elaborated in Parker's improvisations and compressed into the second half of measure 9. In take A, Parker enfolds the allusion in the midst of a rapid run of thirty-second notes, which tends to bury it into the texture of his solo. Integrated in this way, the allusion is not as audible or sharply articulated as it is in take B. In addition, the appearance of motive z in both takes A and B, and the similarity of measures 9 and 10, reveals one of Parker's musical strategies for improvising on "Embraceable You." In other performances, like a bootleg recording from a performance in Montreal from February 1953, we hear Parker play more of Gershwin's original line than in the Dial recordings. Woven between statements of the melody are improvisations through the

Figure 3.4 A comparison of measures 9–10 in Gershwin and in Parker's two Dial recordings.

changes. Melodic allusions are sometimes isolated and sometimes integrated into the larger flow of running changes, motivic ideas, quotations from other sources, and virtuosic fills.

"Embraceable You" was clearly one of the standards that Parker knew intimately.[7] Gershwin's original melody had made its way deep into Parker's approach to the tune, where it could be alluded to in various ways, more or less directly, or used as a template upon which to create startling and virtuosic improvisations. Once the general approach to the tune had been settled, many of the live recordings, like those from Montreal, simply grant Parker more time and space to demonstrate the various degrees to which he alludes to the melody or excises it altogether. Among the various versions now available to collectors of Parker's music, the Dial recordings stand out as Parker's only official studio recordings of the song. However, there is an earlier recording made by Charlie Parker's Reboppers for Savoy Records on November 26, 1945, in the very same WOR studio, that I am hesitant to identify as a recording of "Embraceable You." Released under the title "Meandering," the recording captures Parker improvising over the chord changes to "Embraceable You," this time in the key E♭, instead of the F major of the Dial Recordings, or G major of the sheet music. (Parker's solo, along with the piano introduction, is reproduced as Figure 3.5.) Like the Dial recordings that were still to come, Parker does not play the melody of "Embraceable

Figure 3.5 Charlie Parker, "Meandering."

You" at the beginning of the tune, and there is scarcely an allusion to it.[8] And again, like the Dial recordings, Parker begins his solo by developing a small motive. The motive, labeled χ, appears first in the piano introduction. It is a three-note, stepwise ascending idea. It is reminiscent of the α motive in the Gershwin's original melody (see Figure 3.1) but has been cleverly transposed so that it ends on scale degree $\hat{7}$ instead of scale degree $\hat{1}$. The motive is repeated a number of times in the piano introduction without transposition, b♭-c^1-d^1, and Parker opens his solos with it at exactly the same pitch level. But as the solo develops, he takes the idea and transposes it to fit over a variety of chords in the progression, even sequencing it by a minor third in measures 5 and 6. For some critics, like Giddins, the overall quality of Parker's solo on "Meandering" is perhaps not quite at the heights of the Dial recordings.[9] The performance is sparser, where the phrases are less liquid and forward-leaning than in the Dial recordings. But, despite some differences in overall quality, motivic organization, and allusion, "Meandering" and the Dial recordings of "Embraceable You" share many features in common, the most significant being the lack of any complete presentation of the melody line, assimilated, as it is, into Parker's basic strategies for the performance of ballads.

***

What has all of this to do with the question of contrafacts, replication, nomination, and the ontology of works of jazz? Imagine a situation where "Meandering" is played as part of a "Blindfold Test." In one of these tests, made famous by Leonard Feather in the pages of *Downbeat* and *Metronome*, a listener—usually an esteemed jazz musician—is asked to evaluate and discuss a recording without having access to any information about who is performing, the name of the track, or the circumstances of the recording. By reducing out all of the extra-musical information about a recording, the blindfolded musician is supposed to give their unadulterated musical opinion. Presented with this recording, a musician might easily identify the altoist as Charlie Parker, given his instantly recognizable tone and style. By attending to the harmony, one might recognize the chord progression as that of "Embraceable You," but it seems unlikely a listener would correctly identify the recording as "Meandering," unless they already knew about the recording. More likely, they might identify the recording simply a performance of "Embraceable You." If they knew Parker's Dial recordings of "Embraceable You," the blindfolded listener may even draw comparisons between the two recordings, remarking on the kind of differences noted in the paragraphs above—how Parker alludes to the melody line, how the solo is organized, and so on. From a purely morphological perspective, one that focuses only on the immanent musical properties of the recording, the performances "Meandering" and "Embraceable You" are indeed quite similar in approach and style. However, despite this similarity, the distinct names attached to the recordings suggest that they should be individuated. Conventionally, unique musical works are baptized with a unique name. To conflate "Embraceable You" with its contrafact "Meandering" would go against this convention. And yet, the two tunes are easily—perhaps even correctly—conflated in a blindfold test. There appears to be a divergence between the evidence provided by chains of replication and the evidence provided by acts of nomination. Where chains of replication would associate artifacts with similar musical properties, acts of nomination would associate (and disassociate) certain performances regardless of their musical properties. Contrafacts trade on the difference between acts of replication and acts of nomination, in that they replicate the chord progression of a well-known standard while, at the same time, nominating a new musical work. There might be cases where two artifacts are morphologically similar, or even morphologically identical, and turn out to be two distinct works. This feature of contrafacts has received little explicit philosophical consideration, yet it has important implications for the ontology of jazz standards. Contrafacts expose the fact that chains of replications alone are insufficient for identifying and individuating works of jazz. Names must also be considered. If we want to understand the contribution of naming to the ontology of jazz, contrafacts are crucial.

One might object that "Meandering" is a special case. First of all, we do not know who named this track, whether it was Parker or someone else. Perhaps the name was Parker's, and the performance was intended as a contrafact of "Embraceable You," and thus an instance of a new, independent work. But is just as plausible that the name was given to the recording in 1956, at the time of its commercial release on the Savoy LP *The Charlie Parker Story*. The album, described on its back cover as "The Greatest Recording Session Made in Modern Jazz History in Its Entirety," contained multiple takes, complete or incomplete, of the material recorded at Parker's Savoy session late in November 1945. "Meandering" is one of those incomplete takes, ending in the middle of Gillespie's piano solo. Given the quality of Parker's playing and the cultic status that grew up around him after his untimely death in March 1955, it was not uncommon for recording companies to release incomplete performances or alternate takes by Parker, so long as they captured his brilliant solos. There are numerous recordings of Parker playing live where only his solos have been preserved and released, many recorded on substandard recording devices, in noisy clubs, at private residences, and other less than optimal situations.[10]

Regarding "Meandering," there are various reasons why Savoy might have dubbed the incomplete take by a new name. Most obviously, by releasing "Embraceable You" under another title, the record company could avoid paying royalties to Gershwin's estate and ASCAP. In this respect, "Meandering" has much in common with "Warming Up a Riff," another incomplete take that stands in the same relationship to "Cherokee" as "Meandering" does to "Embraceable You." On Savoy's original session logs, "Warming Up" appears under the title "Savoy Tea Party," not "Cherokee," but "Meandering" makes no appearance whatsoever.[11] Given its incompleteness and the lack of documentation about its act of naming, "Meandering" might seem too impoverished an example to do the philosophical work I have ascribed to it, that is, to support the argument that morphological similarity, produced through chains of replication, is insufficient for identifying and individuating a work of jazz. If the track was intended as just another performance of "Embraceable You," one that was subsequently mislabeled or deceptively labeled as "Meandering," then it would appear to argue for the just opposite. It would legitimately be included in the network of performances of "Embraceable You," despite the name.

Without further evidence about the events that transpired between Parker's recording and the release of "Meandering," we simply do not know how much significance to place on the name of the recording. And yet, there must have been a moment of baptism where the track was dubbed "Meandering," however correctly or incorrectly, honest or duplicitous in intent that moment may have been. This is important when considering the ontology of musical works. Musical works always possess a moment of baptism, a moment when someone attaches a name to a particular work with the expectation that others will use that name to refer to it. After that moment of baptism, names of works are communicated from musician to musician or listener to listener and eventually to the audience at large by means of performance, broadcast, announcement, or publication. Communities become familiar with a name; they learn it and teach it to others by using it. The communication of a name is an historical process. Akin to the historical process of producing artifactual substitutions, that is, *chains of replication*, we can refer to the historical process of transmitting names as *chains of nomination*. Via *chains of nomination*, people learn to apply a name to different performances, but they never do so on their own or in isolation from a community. The proper use of a name to pick out a "work" depends on a speaker's (or musician's) acculturation with the ways that others use that name.

While many moments of baptism occur in private, the public nomination of a work, the moment when people begin to become familiar with it and chains of nomination begin to develop, often comes later. From a legal perspective, the moment of baptism corresponds with the moment of copyright. When an inscription of a work (either in the form of sheet music, recording, or other acceptable formats) is deposited, the work is named, identified, and protected from unlawful copy. However, few people ever see the copyright deposit. Vernacular instances of baptism are more common and often more significant for understanding how chains of nomination function in jazz and popular music. Names are learned and transmitted in a variety of different vernacular forms: as announcements during live performance or recording, or as titular inscriptions on sheet music, record sleeves, labels, or even on the sides of cylinders. Sometimes works are given names after the fact, like John Coltrane's contrafact of "Confirmation," which was eventually dubbed "26-2." Sometimes names are withheld. On Miles Davis's recording of "If I Were a Bell," he playfully teases his producer, Bob Weinstock, who is eager to keep track of the session, by saying "I'll play it and I'll tell you what it is later."[12] Frederic Ramsey Jr. describes how King Oliver would often have his band tear the names off the music on their stands in order to keep other musicians from knowing what he was playing.[13]

Because the transmission of names relies on historical chains of communication, there remains the possibility of mistakes in its transmission, ambiguity, or multiple competing baptisms of the same song. The history of jazz is rife with cases like these. Recall our previous example of the network around "In the Mood." If the name refers to the famous riff of the tune, then we might say that it was originally baptized as "Tar Paper Stomp" in Wingy Manone's recording, and later rebaptized as "In the Mood." "Mood Indigo," Duke Ellington's famous composition, was originally recorded under the name "Dreamy Blues." The tenor saxophonist Jimmy Forrest recorded the famous blues "Night Train," which is really another name for the central lick from Ellington's "That's the Blues, Old Man," which was itself later integrated into the longer composition "Happy-Go-Lucky Local." In other cases, names are incorrectly transmitted, or truncated. Even "Opus No. 1" was rebaptized as "Opus One," a fact that is thematized in its additional lyrics.

The nomination of musical works entails certain basic features: a moment of baptism initiates an historical process of transmission. But names involve more than just baptism and transmission. A name is both an *assertion* and a *solicitation*. To call a performance p by the name n is to assert that p should be associated with the network of performances associated with n. To call "Meandering" by the name "Embraceable You" is to assert that it should be included in a specific network of performances, namely, the network that goes under the name "Embraceable You." Or, to assert the difference between "Meandering" and "Embraceable You" is to assert that the former belongs to (or even initiates) a different network than the latter. Thus, to assert an association between a performance and a specific network is also to assert difference. If two performances, p and q, have different names, that is also an assertion that p and q are not substitutable for one another, even if p derives from q via a process of replication. This may seem initially counterintuitive, since replication has been defined as the production of substitutable artifacts given some specific social context of use. But not everything in p is replicated from q, just as all the musical features of "Meandering" are not simply replications of "Embraceable You." When comparing two artifacts that are morphologically similar yet with different names, the differences that are not derived from replication will often be considered as work-determinative properties, sufficient for identifying and individuating performances and works.

In addition, names are also solicitations. To call a performance p by the name n is to solicit listeners to hear the musical properties of p in relation to n, that is, to hear in p work-determinative properties associated with performances of n. To call "Meandering" by the name "Embraceable You" is to ask a listener to hear its properties in relation to the work-determinative properties of other performances of "Embraceable You." This is a fairly easy task to do, especially if one focuses on the chord progression. Or, to assert the difference between "Meandering" and "Embraceable You" is to solicit listeners to hear the performance as having distinct work-determinative properties from those of "Embraceable You." By attending to the thematic construction of "Meandering," the ascending three note motive presented in the piano introduction and echoed in Parker's opening phrase—a thematic construction that is derived yet distinct from the melody of "Embraceable You"—one might find musical properties sufficient for individuating "Meandering" from its contrafactual source.

We can develop our claims about nomination by considering another of Parker's contrafacts. On December 19, 1947, Parker and a group of all-stars went back into the WOR studio and recorded for Dial records two takes of "Quasimado," a contrafact based on "Embraceable You" (see Figure 3.6). A newly composed melody is played in unison by Parker, Miles Davis on trumpet, and J. J. Johnson on trombone, in the conventional manner typical of many bebop performances. The solo section is divided between the various musicians, and the melody is restated at the end of the performance. The unison presentation of the melody, unlike the solo statement on "Meandering," implies that the music must have been written down or orally transmitted and rehearsed ahead of the performance. It could not simply have been improvised in unison at the moment of recording. In addition, we have an explicit account of how "Quasimado" received its unusual name. According to Ross Russell, the producer of Parker's recordings for Dial, "As a rule Charlie [Parker] did not bother to title his compositions. Often, they were known to members of the Quintet by numbers. The Dial studio log listed them by means of a different series of master numbers, with a new set assigned to each session. Until it was titled, Klactoveesedstene [*sic*] was simply Dial D-1112. Usually I dreamed up some kind of a title when it was time to release the record."[14] However, Russell had a list of potential titles from which to draw. The list was relayed through Parker's agent, Billy Shaw, to Dial and contained the title "Quasimado," with its unusual spelling, along with a handful of other titles.[15] In terms of work-determinative properties, the catchy unison melody of "Quasimado" is recognizable, easily identified and individuated from its harmonic basis in "Embraceable You." Unlike "Meandering," which was not widely replicated by other jazz musicians, "Quasimado" (often with the spelling corrected) has been recorded many times by jazz musicians, another of the many bebop melodies associated with Parker. The Dial recording of "Quasimado" initiates a new network of

Figure 3.6 Charlie Parker, "Quasimado," lead sheet.

performances, and those subsequent performances, by extending chains of nomination, associate themselves to this network and solicit a listener to hear them in relation to it.

***

Two distinct kinds of chains are involved in the ontology of works of jazz: chains of replication and chains of nomination. The identity and individuation of works of jazz requires both, for two reasons. First, chains of replication might be so generic that they do not specify or identify a work as a particular work. A musician might play any number of possible "Rhythm Changes"—that is, songs that employ "I Got Rhythm" as a harmonic framework—without playing the "head" or melody at the beginning, and thus a listener would lack information that could function as a work-determinative property. There would be a bevy of songs to which that particular chord progression might be related. Thus, there would be no determinative feature specific enough to pick out the correct network to which the performance should be associated. The best one might do would be to simply say that the performance is of "some kind of Rhythm Changes," treating the work like a genre, musical type, or a super-network. Second, chains of replication are not bound by individual works. Aspects from a performance of work x might be replicated in a performance of work y. A good example of this is James Moody's version of "I'm in the Mood for Love," which replicates the general style and approach of Charlie Parker's performance of "Embraceable You." Tracing individual replications will often lead beyond one work into neighboring works. A musician, arranger, or performer may have certain generic ways of playing through common progressions, and thus chains of replication will link performances across an artist's body of work. Tracing these kinds of chains would be an important part of identifying or describing a performer's style. But the fact that a performance of a work may replicate aspects of a performance of a different work means that chains of replications, on their own, are often too prolific and gregarious to individuate works by themselves.

In contrast, names pick out particular musical works, but they do so without specifying any musical properties. Thus, chains of nomination without chains of replication can only do so much work. Without some information about the features or properties of a work that are currently taken as determinative, there is no way to check if a name is being used correctly. This is not an abstract worry. Ashley Kahn, in his book on Miles Davis's *Kind of Blue*, describes how the first 50,000 copies of the record were incorrectly labeled due to a mistake in the chain of nomination. The second side of the LP featured two tracks: "All Blues" and "Flamenco Sketches." The mistake appears to have originated with producer Irving Townsend, who worked out the order of the record's tracks on two sheets of memorandum paper. On one sheet, the titles of the five tracks recorded for the album are numbered from one to five on the left-hand side. Townsend then reordered the tracks into their arrangement on the LP with an additional a set of numbers circled on the right-hand side. Townsend used this to generate a second sheet, where the tracks are laid out by side and each includes a "CO number," a marker that identifies which takes from the recording sessions were to be used for mastering and pressing. It appears that Townsend got the CO numbers in the correct order but mistakenly swapped the titles; the take of "All Blues" was labeled as "Flamenco Sketches" and vice versa. According to co-producer Teo Macero, when the record was released Miles told him, "No, that's not the way it goes." Davis, who had ostensibly been involved in the naming the songs, was in a position to point out the mistake to others. A memo written by Macero in late 1959 corrects the mistake in further pressings of the album. Aside from requesting that the record label copy and flyleaf copy be changed, Macero also requested that the references to the tunes in the liner notes be corrected. In Bill Evans's liner notes, which appeared on the back of the album, he describes some of the musical properties associated with the various tunes. Apparently, with the confusion about track titles, Evans's note read that "*Flamenco Sketches* is a 6/8 12-measure blues" and "*All Blues* is a series of five scales, each to be played as long as the soloist wishes until he has completed the series." Macero's memo makes it explicit that these names are to be swapped. Of course, there was nothing about the name itself (other than the notion that "All Blues" might be an appropriate name for a song in blues form) that would guarantee that they were being correctly applied. Some confusion about the titles has remained and, according to Kahn, "to this day, many of the album's original fans still mention 'All Blues' while meaning to describe 'Flamenco Sketches' and vice-versa."[16]

    In most cases, chains of replication and chains of nomination will run "in parallel." By the colloquial phrase "in parallel" I mean that the evidence derived from chains of replication and from chains of nomination, evidence used to make judgments of identity and individuation, will often converge. For example, I may encounter a new version of "Body and Soul" by reading the name off the back of the record sleeve or hearing a radio announcer state it. The music I hear presents a bundle of replications, which together preserve those features of the tune that are work-determinative, that is, features sufficient for individuating the tune. Even without the name being announced, I might have recognized the song from its properties alone, even expressing my recognition by saying, "Ah, that's 'Body and Soul.'" Here, the name reinforces a judgment based primarily on chains of replication. Or, I may not have known that the song was called "Body and Soul" until I heard the announcer state it, even though I might have heard the tune before and even been familiar with its work-determinative features. In that case I might say to myself, "oh, *that* must be the name of that ballad all the tenor saxophonists play." When chains of nomination and chains of replication run in parallel, judgments about identity and individuation are unproblematic, even intuitive. However, these two chains can cross, or run obliquely. When the evidence derived from chains of nomination and chains of replication diverges, a short circuit occurs. Such cases offer tremendous challenges when making judgments about identity and individuation. If the announcer had played the same music as above but called it "The Song Is You," I might think that either they announced the incorrect tune, or that I have been confusing what I thought was "Body and Soul" for another song. I either have to relearn what name attaches to what musical properties or discount the evidence of one of the chains.

The interaction of chains of replication and chains of nomination can be diagrammed on a small grid (see Table 3.1). Columns represent the similarity and dissimilarity of two artifacts in terms of chains of replication. Rows represent the similarity and dissimilarity of the same two artifacts in terms of chains of nomination. In case 1, two artifacts are morphologically similar and have the same name. Here, based on the converging evidence of replication and nomination, it is unproblematic to identify them. In case 4, just the opposite holds. Two artifacts are morphologically dissimilar and have different names. Here, it is unproblematic to individuate them. Cases 2 and 3 are the

Table 3.1 A grid comparing chains of replication and chains of nomination.

	Chains of Replication	
Chains of Nomination	(1) Similar replications, similar names (identity)	(2) Dissimilar replications, similar names (revision)
	(3) Similar replications, dissimilar names (contrafacts)	(4) Dissimilar replications, dissimilar names (individuation)

challenging ones. In case 3, two similar sounding artifacts are presented with different names. This describes the case of contrafacts discussed above. Both "Meandering" and "Quasimado" possess morphological similarities not only to each other, but also to their source work, "Embraceable You." At the same time, the fact that they have different names evidences the claim that they are different works. Yet, as we saw in the case of "Meandering," we might not wholly trust the evidence derived from chains of nomination; the tune might have been intended as a performance of "Embraceable You" but was released under a different name. In such a situation, we are pulled in conflicting directions. The keen morphological similarities between "Meandering" and the Dial takes of "Embraceable You" seem to evidence that they should be associated as performances of one and the same work. Yet, the titles tell us something else. Chains of replication and chains of nomination run in different directions, and thus we do not have a secure footing on which to ground an ontological judgment about the work.

In case 2, morphologically dissimilar artifacts are given the same name. Here is a case of radical revision, where an unconventional performance of a standard, one that perhaps pushes the envelope on the kinds of replications that a community might accept, is asserted as an instance of the work and solicits others to hear it as such. Adventurous versions of standards would fall into case 2, such as Cecil Taylor or Sunny Murray's recordings of the Rodgers and Hammerstein song "This Nearly Was Mine," from *South Pacific*, or John Coltrane's famous modal version of "My Favorite Things," from *The Sound of Music*. A pertinent example, especially in relation to the discussion of contrafacts like "Meandering" and "Quasimado," is Ornette Coleman's version of "Embraceable You" from his LP *This Is Our Music*. The performance is the only standard that Coleman recorded on his influential albums for Atlantic Records.[17] Coleman's version of the tune is like an inversion of Parker's Dial recording. Whereas Parker barely alludes to Gershwin's melody while preserving the harmony, basing his solo on a motivic improvisation over the chord changes, Coleman's recording dispenses with the chord changes in favor of exploring, developing, and extending Gershwin's melody. In Coleman's pianoless quartet, Charlie Haden's bass lines and Coleman's improvisations both generate and manifest the harmonic dimensions of the tune. Between the two, the performance seems to oscillate between following the harmonic progression and form set out by Gershwin and following a harmonic-melodic logic that emerges from their close interplay and responsiveness. Where Parker alludes to the melody of "Embraceable

You," Coleman alludes to its harmony. For someone trained on previous versions of "Embraceable You," Coleman's version challenges listeners to hear it against a background of other performances, to glean the work-determinative properties that they have come to expect. Those expectations are sometimes satisfied and sometimes frustrated, as Haden and Coleman weave in and out of the tune—raising the possibilities of allusion and association in jazz to a new register. It is not always clear how, or if, Coleman and company are replicating previous models. There is a divergence between the morphology produced via chains of replication and the assertion and solicitation that stem from chains of nomination.

Coleman's recording was variously received. Is the performance an instance of the work and thus a legitimate addition to the network of "Embraceable You" performances? Coleman, on the liner notes to *This Is Our Music*, emphasizes the links between his performance of the tune and traditional ways of performing it, writing that "*Embraceable You* is the first standard that we have recorded, and we played it the way standards are played and with as much spontaneity as we could."[18] For some listeners, the new version was easily accepted, affirming Coleman's assertion that "we played it the way standards are played," while demonstrating his new ideas about "the shape of jazz to come." In Michael James's review of *This Is Our Music*, he writes, "the material [on the album] is varied as its quality is high, and the leader brings to each item a freshness of inspiration and a wealth of ideas.... His melodic thinking is outstanding in the Gershwin tune, which he transmutes into a statement as personal as any of his own compositions."[19] Martin Williams, one of Coleman's early supporters, drew a connection between Parker's celebrated versions of "Embraceable You" and Coleman. In a dialogue with an imaginary interlocutor, Williams argues that "the best soloists improvise with melodic order, not just the more or less automatic harmonic order that comes from running the chords.... Parker's 'Embraceable,' for example, is built around an elaboration of his opening phrase. He plays it five times at the beginning and in various ingenious permutations throughout." When his incredulous interlocutor says, "You don't mean to tell me you hear this sort of thing in Ornette Coleman?," Williams responds affirmatively, "I sure do! Just this sort of thing."[20] By drawing a connection between Coleman and Parker, by putting them into a shared "jazz tradition" (to cite the title of a famous book by Williams), he shows what exactly is being replicated in Coleman's performance, how Coleman's practice relates to Parker's practice, and why both performances of "Embraceable You" should be associated in the same network.

Others challenged Williams's and James's esteem. For some, Coleman's performance was accepted as an instance of the work but held in low esteem. The critic and poet Philip Larkin writes that those who praise Coleman "do so not so much for his musical subtlety and technical innovations as for the sheer exuberance and freedom of his playing. This is undeniable but there is a good deal of silliness mixed with it that shows in standards such as 'Embraceable You' . . . and which prevents one from taking him quite seriously."[21] Benny Carter, the saxophonist, arranger, and bandleader, panned the recording in a blindfold test. "I have heard Ornette's first album . . . and I didn't particularly care for that—that is, the playing on it, but I did think his writing was very promising, and his playing was much better than this. . . . From the very first note [of 'Embraceable You'], it's miserably out of tune." The only feature that Carter can affirm is Charlie Haden's choice of notes on which to end the performance. "Of course, one thing I did like: they wound up on a new chord, a new triad . . . on a nice augmented fifth—with the augmented fifth in the bass! I thought this was unique! This was different! I'll give it two stars for courage."[22]

The harshest critics saw Coleman's performance of "Embraceable You" as proof that he couldn't play, or worse, was a fraud. In *Downbeat*, the critic Don DeMichael gave *This Is Our Music* one star, picking out "Embraceable You" as a particular low point. "Coleman has been criticized for not playing standard tunes, especially ballads," he writes. "In this collection, however, *Embraceable You* is included. It was a mistake. If he had left it out, we still should not have recorded evidence of whether he could play a ballad. Now we know. Or perhaps he is merely putting us on: he couldn't be serious."[23] One critic even went so far as to call Coleman's performance of "Embraceable You" a "mercy killing."[24]

For others, Coleman's version simply fails to instance the work. In an interview, the saxophonist Herb Geller puts the whole situation bluntly: "I heard Ornette's recording of 'Embraceable You,' and it's a laugh. I'm sorry, but that's not 'Embraceable You.'"[25] Milt Jackson, who occasionally played Coleman's compositions as part of the Modern Jazz Quartet, was equally dismissive. When asked his opinion of Coleman's playing, the vibraphonist said, "He plays only his own music—except he plays *Embraceable You*, but it's not the *Embraceable You* that I know."[26] Alun Morgan, writing for *The Gramophone*, cites the passage from the album's liner notes about "the way standards are played," only to demur, "This is patently ridiculous. . . . Any musician worthy of the name would first make a point of getting the chords right, or at least come to an agreement with the rest of the group about any which were in dispute."[27] For Morgan, Coleman's version breaks altogether with the conventions required for replication in jazz. The problem is that appeals to the "jazz tradition" will cut both ways: Martin Williams can argue for the continuity in practices between Parker and Coleman, just as Alun Morgan can argue that Coleman fails to satisfy the basic conditions that a performance of "Embraceable You" must meet.

The grid provided in Table 3.1 offers a rough way of characterizing the relation between chains of nomination and chains of replication. But, as with any simple model, its diagnostic power is limited. There are cases that might fall between categories, where the complex, historical interaction of chains of replication and chains of nomination cannot be neatly reduced to a single category. Oftentimes, there will be gaps in the historical record that will make it difficult to reconstruct complete and intact chains. In such cases, we may not have enough evidence to confidently guarantee claims about identity and individuation. But that should not stop us from investigating such cases and pinpointing exactly where the record runs out. In that spirit, it is worth considering one more case study before making some summary observations about the joint contribution of replication and nomination to the ontology of works of jazz.

***

A curious incident occurred at the Newport Jazz Festival on July 1, 1961. As the John Coltrane Quintet took the stage, the festival's announcer, WEVD's Mort Vega, introduced the band to the audience. Listening to the recording of that introduction today, Vega's hip patter is typical of jazz announcers from the period, informing the audience about who plays what instrument, interesting bits of the performers' résumés, and what they might expect to hear.

> One by the gentlemen of our next group . . . and a rather unique instrumentation in as much as that this group houses *two* string basses [bassists?] . . . first a nice, warm welcome for Reggie Workman on bass. Reggie Workman. [Applause] There you go, Reggie Workman. And his fellow bassist, Arthur Davis. Arthur Davis. [Applause] The drummer, from a, uh, very illustrious musical family out of Detroit, Michigan . . . Thad Jones is one of the members, Hank Jones is another . . . this is *Elvin* Jones, ladies and gentlemen. [Applause] At the piano, a nice hello to McCoy Tyner. McCoy Tyner. [Applause] And the gentleman who is probably the most

influential tenor saxophonist in the world today, I know you know who I'm talkin' about . . . he's going to open with "So What" [the] Miles Davis tune, John Coltrane, ladies and gentlemen.

After a quick bit of tuning, Coltrane taps off the tempo and the band begins to play. However, instead of playing "So What" the band plays a different tune, a tune that most listeners today would identify as "Impressions." What happened?

"Impressions" is a contrafact of "So What," borrowing its form and harmonic structure. Coltrane was intimately familiar with "So What," having played on its original recording (March 2, 1959, released on *Kind of Blue*) as a member of Miles Davis's sextet. According to drummer Pete La Roca, who worked intermittently with Coltrane's quartet in 1960, Coltrane was performing "Impressions" as early as the summer of 1960.[28] The earliest recording widely available is a bootleg of the Coltrane Quintet at the Sutherland Lounge, Chicago, from March 1961.[29] Throughout 1961, "Impressions" was a staple on the bandstand—a feature for Coltrane's explorative solos of tremendous intensity over long timespans. In addition to performing "Impressions" in July at the Newport Jazz Festival, Coltrane performed it on three of the four nights recorded at the Village Vanguard from the beginning of November. The performance of "Impressions" from November 3 would eventually be released on the album *Impressions* in 1963, constituting something of a public baptism of the song.[30]

However, "Impressions" seems to have been given various names before its public baptism. Based on the circumstantial evidence, it seems that Coltrane used the working title "So What" to refer to the composition throughout much of 1961. In addition to Vega's announcement on July 1 at Newport, an article in *Downbeat*, reporting on Coltrane's September 22 performance at the Monterey Jazz Festival (with the guitarist Wes Montgomery joining the band), identifies the set as containing "My Favorite Things," "Naima," and "So What."[31] Stronger evidence can be gleaned from the complete tapes of Coltrane's performance at the Village Vanguard in November. On the November 3 performance, the one eventually released on *Impressions*, after

Figure 3.7 John Coltrane, "Impressions," measures 1–8, from *Impressions*.

the song is done Coltrane can be heard calling off the next tune on the set list. He initially calls "So What," but realizing that the band just played that, he corrects himself and calls "My Favorite Things."[32]

For the rest of November, Coltrane's group toured Europe, and "Impressions" was standard fare. Coltrane performed the tune in Paris, Copenhagen, Helsinki, Stockholm, Stuttgart, Frankfurt, and Berlin, among other cities—and many of these concerts have appeared on bootleg recordings. On December 4, the band performed in Baden-Baden at the Südwestfunk TV studios, taping a program entitled *Jazz—Gehört und Gesehen*, hosted by the jazz writer and critic Joachim-Ernst Berendt. On the program, the band performed "Impressions," which is introduced by Berendt as "Excerpts."[33] Apparently, "Excerpts" was an interim title for "Impressions," one that was used through much of 1962, replacing "So What." Between April and June 1962, Coltrane recorded a handful of sessions at Rudy Van Gelder's studio in Englewood Cliffs, New Jersey, where the band recorded many takes of "Excerpts."[34] The session logs on this recording offer evidence that "Excerpts" was the name in circulation at that time. Most important, for tracking the song's chain of nominations, is the session from June 20, where Coltrane gives the working title "Excerpts" after Van Gelder's slate announcement.[35]

Coltrane continued to play the song live throughout the rest of 1962 and far into 1963—occasionally reworking it musically. Performances grew in length and intensity, and—for a period in the summer of 1963—Coltrane tended to play the opening melody on soprano sax, but switched to tenor for his solo and closing statement. Even with Coltrane's new working title, "Excerpts," confusion remained about the song's proper name, which the public still knew as "So What," or as an unnamed contrafact of that tune. Reporting on a Coltrane concert in Chicago, from December 1962, a *Downbeat* reporter writes, "John Coltrane, with Eric Dolphy on board, did SRO business at McKie's Disc Jockey Lounge during his recent three-weeker. One night the group played 'So What?' for what must have been record endurance time—an hour and 20 minutes."[36] As mentioned above, the release of the album *Impressions* in the summer of 1963 functions as something of a public baptism of the tune. Afterward, journalists, critics, and fans start to use the name "Impressions" to refer to the tune.[37] For example, LeRoi Jones (Amiri Baraka), writing about a New Year's Eve concert at Lincoln Center's Philharmonic Hall, featuring Coltrane, Cecil Taylor, and Art Blakey, notes that "Coltrane and company, even though they went through what by now must be their standard concert repertoire (which includes the soprano

Figure 3.8 Morton Gould, "Pavanne," first strain.

treatment of *My Favorite Things*), still managed to get up on a couple of tunes—especially on their last tune of the evening, *Impressions*."[38] Perhaps Coltrane felt similarly to Baraka and grew tired of playing his standard concert repertoire, which included "Impressions," around this time. According to the various recordings (private, bootleg, and released) and information about Coltrane's concerts, starting in 1964 "Impressions" is played with far less frequency than over the preceding two years.[39]

***

If these chains of nomination are complex and confusing, the chains of replication for "Impressions" are no less complicated. It would be reductive to say that "Impressions" is simply a contrafact of "So What" since it borrows from multiple other sources. The melody on the A-sections of "Impressions" is lifted from an unlikely source, a piece by the middlebrow composer Morton Gould.[40] Gould's *American Symphonette No. 2* spawned a hit in 1938, a movement entitled "Pavanne" [*sic*]. Within a year, two swing arrangements (by the Glenn Miller band and Jimmy Lunceford's band) gained notoriety, and Gould's "Pavanne" was circulated widely through recordings, performances, and sheet music. For the next decade and a half, jazz musicians rarely performed the entire piece, but the first strain, a catchy melody in F major, was a favorite quotation for soloists. Set over a single chord, it fit nicely into situations where jazz musicians improvised over tonic prolongations extending over a few bars, such as "I Got Rhythm." Saxophonist Wardell Gray quotes "Pavanne" in his solo on "Little Pony," a Rhythm Changes tune recorded with the Count Basie band in 1949.[41] Gould's melody, when replicated and rephrased, sounds like the kind of linear melodic idea that might have emerged from Lester Young's tenor saxophone (see Figures 3.8 and 3.9). "Pavanne" eventually fell out of fashion, but it was not completely

Figure 3.9 Wardell Gray, "Pavanne," quote from his solo on "Little Pony."

forgotten by jazz musicians. The Chicago-based pianist Ahmad Jamal recorded an arrangement of Gould's "Pavanne" with his trio in 1955. Jamal's arrangement recalls the tempo of Lunceford's version but alters many aspects of Gould's original. Apparently, the arrangement stayed in Jamal's repertoire, recorded (but unreleased) at the Washington, DC's Spotlite Club in 1958 and again (this time released) in a Chicago recording studio in 1960.[42]

The resemblances between Gould's "Pavanne" and "Impressions" are too close for coincidence—and I will explore the possible historical chain of replication between the two pieces, below. However, there is disagreement about the source of the melody for the B-section of "Impressions." According to Lewis Porter, it is a quotation from Ravel's *Pavane pour une infante défunte*, which was jazzed up into a minor hit in the summer of 1939 as "The Lamp Is Low."[43] This conjunction of pavanes by Gould and Ravel has led some commentators to confusion. Martin Williams, writing about Coltrane's contributions to jazz a few months after his death in the summer of 1967, notes that "'Impressions' borrows an opening melody from Claude Debussy [sic], to revisit, two years later the same modes and song-form structure that Davis used on 'So What?'"[44] Stanley Crouch, years later, says that Jamal's arrangement of "Ravel's [sic] Pavane" provided the structure for Davis's 1959 "So What" and the melody for Coltrane's 1961 "Impressions."[45]

In addition to Gould and Ravel, there is another work relevant for Coltrane's "Impressions." In 1961, the same year as Coltrane's performance at the Newport Jazz Festival and his Village Vanguard recording of "Impressions," another song based on "So What" was circulating among jazz musicians. The tune, entitled "Why Not," was clearly a response to Davis's record. "Why Not" retains the thirty-two-bar form and harmonic structure of "So What." Like "Impressions," it too borrows the third strain from Gould's "Pavanne." In fact, the only difference between "Impressions" and "Why Not" is the B-section: "Why Not" transposes Gould's melody up a half-step, while "Impressions" includes the (disputable) Ravel quotation. In 1961–1962, "Why Not" appeared on two records. The first, *Ease It!*, recorded on March 13, 1961 (about two weeks after Coltrane's Sutherland Lounge performance), was the only studio album released by the tenor saxophonist Rocky Boyd.[46] Boyd is an obscure figure in jazz. There are accounts of him sitting in with Davis's band in Boston in late 1958 and 1959, before moving to New York City. He appears to have studied and hung out with John Coltrane in the years 1959–1961. According to Jack Chambers, a biographer of Miles Davis, Boyd even replaced Hank Mobley in Davis's band for a few months in the winter of 1961–1962, before joining "Philly" Jo Jones in early 1962. The recording of *Ease It!* corresponds with Boyd's period of closest association with Coltrane. "Why Not" is credited to the drummer Pete La Roca, who played on the session. The second recording, by the vibraphonist Dave Pike, appears on the album *Pike's Peak*, recorded February 8, 1962. Bill Evans, the pianist on the original recording of "So What," plays piano on the session. In this arrangement of "Why Not," Pike plays the melody on the vibes while Evans improvises over it. On the album's liner notes, jazz critic Ira Gitler credits "Why Not" to Pike, not La Roca, describing the tune as a "swinging, modal adventure, the title an obvious answer to Miles Davis 'So What.'"[47] To add to the confusion, La Roca, while not on this recording, also worked with Pike during 1961, thus drawing a possible link between the two recordings.

Clearly, a complicated chain of replications links "Impressions," "So What," and "Pavanne." Coltrane's "Impressions" borrows properties of these other works. Yet these chains of replication may or may not run parallel with its chains of nomination. Then, to add to the story, there is "Why Not," which functions like a strange double to "Impressions." Are we dealing with two separate works or one work with two names? How can attention to chains of replication and chains of nomination help in determining whether these works should be identified or individuated? As a method for tracing the various chains that bind and associate "Impressions" to its multiple sources, I will consider them two at a time.

1. "Impressions" and "So What." There is no question that "Impressions" is modeled on "So What." As mentioned above, Coltrane played in the band that made the first recording of "So What," and the tune was a hit. Like so many jazz standards, "So What" is structured as a thirty-two bar AABA tune and yet it reduces the harmonic complexity typical of the repertoire. Instead of complex harmonic progressions, loaded with substitutions and linked by turnarounds, each section is built around a single harmony: a D minor-seventh chord in the A section is shifted up chromatically one half-step in the B-sections. The formal structure of the tune is made apparent through the sudden chromatic shift at the bridge. No functional relation holds between the D minor-seventh and E♭ minor-seventh chords. Rather, the E♭ minor-seventh chord functions as neighbor chord, embellishing the D minor that precedes and follows it.

"So What" became *the* iconic work of "modal jazz."[48] From a harmonic perspective, modal jazz is a style that slows down the harmonic rhythm

118 HEARING DOUBLE

Figure 3.10 Bill Evans's chords on "So What," from *Kind of Blue*.

Figure 3.11 McCoy Tyner's chords on "Impressions," from *Impressions*.

typical of jazz (moving at the rate of a half- or whole-note) in favor of emphasizing a kaleidoscopic juxtaposition of non-functionally related harmonic planes.[49] Parallel chords from distantly related keys are placed in close proximity, minimizing the number of common tones between them. By slowing down the harmonic rhythm, modal jazz also emphasizes the scales associated with such chords and encourages soloists to explore the sound of various scale degrees against a static harmonic background or pedal point. It also encourages accompanists to develop new strategies for voicing chords, like Bill Evans's famous "So What" chords—voicings that emphasize the interval of a perfect fourth. On the original Miles Davis recording—discussed in Chapter 1—this chord is played in unison by the piano and the horns, but a chain of replications links them to McCoy Tyner's accompaniment on Coltrane's official recording of "Impressions" (see Figures 3.10 and 3.11).

2. **"Impressions" and "Pavanne."** Gould's composition is organized into three broad strains. The first strain, in F major, is the most recognizable and memorable theme in the piece (see Figure 3.8). Only the third strain of Gould's "Pavanne" is copied in "Impressions" and "Why Not." In Gould's original treatment, the melody of the third strain is preceded by a two-bar accompaniment figure, in G minor, played twice. The figure comprises of a set of seventh chords diatonically transposed along a G Dorian collection. The pattern begins on G minor-seventh, leaps in parallel motion to B♭ major-seventh, and then steps down to an A minor-seventh chord. In Gould's version, the rhythm is placed squarely on the beat (see Figure 3.12). In contrast, jazz arrangements of "Pavanne," like those by Glenn Miller and Ahmad

Figure 3.12 Morton Gould, accompaniment pattern from "Pavanne," third strain.

Figure 3.13 Ahmad Jamal's accompaniment pattern from "Pavanne," from *Ahmad Jamal Trio*.

Jamal, replicate the figure while syncopating it. Miller's version anticipates the G minor-seventh and B♭ major-seventh chords in the second bar of the figure. Ahmad Jamal's leaves those chords as written and anticipates the A minor-seventh chord. Jimmy Lunceford's arrangement, in contrast, plays the figure as written in Gould's original (see Figures 3.13 and 3.14).

After four bars of the accompaniment figure, the sinuous melody of the third strain unfolds over eight measures (see Figure 3.15). When its pitches are taken as a whole, it comprises a G Dorian collection. Throughout "Pavanne," Gould emphasizes minor-sixth chords—that is, a minor chord with an added tone a major sixth above the root. The addition of the sixth shifts the chord's corresponding mode from the natural minor to Dorian. This is important because, in the late 1950s, the Dorian mode became closely associated with modal jazz. "So What," "Impressions," and many other works in the style exploit the sound of the Dorian scale. Whether Gould was interested in the use of minor-sixth chords or Dorian scales is uncertain, but since the two imply one another, it is easy to hear these passages as affording either aspect.

After the G minor presentation of the strain, Gould transposes the entire passage upward by the interval of a minor third, to B♭ minor. The two presentations, first in G minor, then in B♭ minor, frustrate functional interpretations. Rather, the sequence of the two modules sounds more like a juxtaposition of non-harmonic planes. The transpositional vector of the

Figure 3.14 Glenn Miller's accompaniment pattern from "Pavanne," from a radio broadcast, 1939.

Figure 3.15 Morton Gould, third strain from "Pavanne."

sequence (up a minor third) is copied neither by "Impressions" nor by "Why Not." In "Why Not" the third strain of "Pavanne" is transposed up a half-step and presented with a replication of Gould's original accompaniment figure (see Figure 3.16). In "Impressions," the introduction of a contrasting melody over the B-section (and no accompaniment figure) diminishes the strength of the chain. In both cases, the harmonic scheme of third strain of "Pavanne" is altered to fit the model of "So What."

3. **"Impressions" and "Why Not."** There must be a chain of replications linking "Impressions" and "Why Not," but it is difficult to definitively reconstruct it. La Roca might be the source that connects the two, since he performed with Coltrane, Boyd, and Pike. Boyd is another possible source; he could just as easily have gotten the tune from Coltrane himself (or from hearing Coltrane play) as from La Roca. As mentioned above, on Boyd's recording the melodic strain from "Pavanne" is presented along with its accompaniment figure. The accompaniment figure is not present in Coltrane's various performances of "Impressions." However, the additional feature cannot be taken as evidence that "Why Not" preceded "Impressions" chronologically. We cannot assume that there was a process of progressively thinning down "Why Not," where, at first, both the accompaniment and melodic aspects were present and then, second, the accompaniment figure was excised. It is just as possible that Boyd or La Roca, knowing the original source of Coltrane's melody, decided to include the

NOMINATION 121

Figure 3.16 Rocky Boyd, "Why Not," melody and accompaniment of A-section, from *Ease It!*

accompaniment figure. Doing so might function as a way of making its source in "Pavanne" explicit.

One might be tempted to take the accompaniment figure as an essential property of "Why Not," as opposed to "Impressions." However in Pike's recording of "Why Not" the accompaniment figure has been left out entirely. In addition to whatever chains of replication link these two recordings of "Why Not," there is also a chain of nomination. The name, given on the record label, associates the two performances with one another, despite the presence or absence of the accompaniment figure (and the different composer credits). Chains of replication participate in the establishment of work identity, but in a situation like this, they are inadequate. If they were, "Impressions" and "Why Not" might be considered identical. To make a claim about work identity, we also need a baptism and historical transmission of a name. While the name "Why Not" clearly functions as a response to "So What," we might speculate that La Roca, being a possible source for the chain of replication between Boyd and Pike, was also the source for the transmission of the name.

If we take the nominations "So What," "Impressions," and "Why Not" as assertions and solicitations then the replicational differences between them become crucial, even work-determinative. While all three have the same harmonic structure and form, the differences between "Impressions" and

"Why Not" depend on the melody of the bridge and—on Boyd's recording, but not Pike's—the accompaniment pattern. And yet, if we ground the difference between "Impressions" and "Why Not" only on morphological differences, we run into problems. "Impressions" generated its own performance conventions as it was replicated again and again. For instance, Coltrane never quite settled on a definitive way of phrasing the B-section. Some later performances of the tune explicitly follow the Coltrane's presentation of the bridge from the officially released recording on the LP *Impressions* (Figure 3.17). One example is found on the album *Newport in New York '72*, a jam session record documenting the "Newport" jazz festival as it moved to New York City.[50] An "all-star" band performs "Impressions," with Rahsaan Roland Kirk playing the melody. Aside from a few alterations to the melody, Kirk replicates many of the features of Coltrane's recording from *Impressions*, including the bridge. But after a few choruses, the horns begin to play the distinctive chords and dotted-quarter plus eighth-note rhythm of "So What" behind the soloist, the trumpeter Harry "Sweets" Edison. After a final drum solo, Tony Williams leads the band back in by playing the distinctive rhythm of "So What." The pianist, Herbie Hancock, plays the chords from "So What" for a few measures before Kirk enters playing the melody from "Impressions." Although the whole performance is something of a palimpsest, the song is confusingly identified as "So What" on the record sleeve and credited to Miles Davis.[51]

In contrast to Kirk's faithful paraphrase of Coltrane's bridge, a second alternative is to simply improvise over the B-section. The guitarist Wes Montgomery, in both bootleg and commercially released performances of "Impressions" recorded at the Half Note, does just this.[52] A third alternative, one that became more common in the 1970s and after, was to drop the B-section melody entirely and replace it with a repetition of the A-section's melody, transposed one half-step higher. McCoy Tyner (Coltrane's pianist on *Impressions*) recorded a version of "Impressions" in 1975 that follows this format.[53] The lead sheet for "Impressions" appearing in the *Real Book* follows this model as well (see Figure 3.18).

Figure 3.17 John Coltrane, "Impressions," B-section (measures 17–24), from *Impressions*.

Here, we are presented with performances and scores of "Impressions" that, in terms of their morphology, are indiscernible from performances and scores of "Why Not." However, the brute fact that two artifacts are morphologically identical or indiscernible is not sufficient for making a claim about their identity. This is one of the important lessons to be learned from Arthur Danto's work. "Why Not" and "Impressions" here function like the identical red, rectangular paintings that Danto considers at the beginning of *Transfiguration of the Commonplace*.[54] Rather than identify them on the basis of morphology alone, extra-morphological features and properties of the work must be taken into consideration. "Why Not" and "Impressions" are individuated because of their distinct chains of nomination—that is, by the titles written on record sleeves and across the top of lead sheets—and their chains of replication, which track how the bridge from earlier versions was substituted and transformed in later performances. By following both chains of replication and chains of nomination, ontological judgments are rendered more nuanced than in a brute appeal to essential properties or structure alone.

***

If forced to position "Impressions" on our schematic grid, the best fit would be to call it a contrafact of "So What." And a contrafact it is. Yet that feature alone does not account for other important aspects of the song's history and relation to other works. It does not account for the repeated conflation of names, at both Newport and New York's Half Note and at "Newport in New York" (and perhaps elsewhere), where the contrafact "Impressions" is called by its harmonic source, "So What." Nor does it acknowledge that "Impressions" has sources beyond "So What," in Morton Gould's "Pavanne," and (disputably) in Ravel's "Pavane." Nor does it account for the strange relation between "Impressions" and its double, "Why Not," in which two works, minimally distinguishable, become morphologically indiscernible.

Figure 3.18 "Impressions," B-section of the lead sheet from *The Real Book*, Vol. 1.

The grid was constructed by juxtaposing in rows and columns the similarity and difference of chains of replication and chains of nomination. Yet, chains of replication and chains of nomination interact in complex ways, converging and diverging, running parallel or transversally, as demonstrated in the study of "Impressions." Both chains, taken together, provide evidence supporting ontological judgments of identity or individuation. Rather than provide a rule or fixed standard for making such judgments, the evidence provided by such chains may be ambiguous at times. As noted above, some will consider this a failing, but I would argue that it is, in fact, a virtue. Attention to the interaction of these chains provides an account of why the hard cases are hard. If ontology is to be more than an abstract game of postulating what is and what is not but rather a serious attempt to grasp what kinds of entities are entailed by our practices, then the joint consideration of chains of replication and chains of nomination has much in its favor.

4
The Ontology of Musical Networks

Philosophy has a long and venerable history of reflection on music; yet within that tradition, reflection on musical works is rare. Unlike cognate art forms such as painting, sculpture, poetry, and such, where ontological reflection on the "work of art" is of central concern, reflections on the *musical* work are often sequestered to the later chapters of dusty volumes on aesthetics. For much of the twentieth century, Anglo-American philosophers writing about the ontology of artworks felt little obligation to consider musical works. When they did, they often fit them into ontological schemes more properly suitable to explicate literature or the visual arts. However, within the Anglophone tradition, the publication of Nelson Goodman's *Languages of Art* in 1968 brought the question of the musical work front and center. Goodman's idiosyncratic and trenchant observations about musical works considered them from a nominalist point of view, placing them in relation to his broader theories of symbolism and reference.

Goodman differentiated artworks into two broad categories, *allographic* and *autographic*, characterizing the distinction this way: "Let us speak of a work of art as *autographic* if and only if the distinction between an original and forgery of it is significant; or better, if and only if even the most exact duplication of it does not thereby count as genuine. . . . Thus painting is autographic; music nonautographic, or *allographic*."[1] Autographic works are unique objects, while allographic works can be instantiated again and again. To test the difference, Goodman considered whether an artwork was capable of forgery. In the case of painting, there is one and only one original, considered to be the genuine work. While some painters may repaint the same themes again and again, like Titian's *Venus and Cupid with an Organist*, each version of the painting is singular and genuine; the significant details of the work—everything from formal arrangement of the figures, to the background, to the smallest aspects of the handling of paint—are unique. If another painter were to come along and copy the work, the forgery would not count as a genuine instance of the painting. It would be counterfeit. Even if the painter were to reproduce the smallest details of the original work, it

Hearing Double. Brian Kane, Oxford University Press. © Oxford University Press 2024.
DOI: 10.1093/oso/9780190600501.003.0005

would still be considered a fake or an inauthentic work. In contrast, there can be no forgery when it comes to *allographic* works, like those of music or literature. While a gifted forger could indeed try to pawn off a fake copy of a composer's manuscript score as original, it would still count as an instance of the work so long as all the notes are correct. The same goes for a literary work. No matter which edition of a novel I purchase, nor how the font or margins or layout may differ from edition to edition, the copy counts as an authentic instance of the work so long as all the words appear in the correct order. To copy a poem out by hand is not to forge it. It is no less genuine by being in your hand than in the hand of the author.

While the possibility of forgery offers an initial test to distinguish the autographic from the allographic, Goodman develops a more rigorous philosophical account of the distinction by focusing on the role of notation. Allographic works, like musical works, are allographic because they employ notational systems that meet specific syntactical and semantic requirements. These requirements permit a musical score to specify a work uniquely and unambiguously, and for the work to be multiply instantiated in additional scores or performances. Goodman's two syntactical conditions are disjointedness and finite differentiation. These conditions are satisfied when a notational mark, the actual inscription or mark on the page, corresponds unequivocally with a discernible "character," that is, a class of inscriptions or marks. Every mark must unambiguously be a member of one and only one class. In musical terms, this means that any mark or symbol on a score denotes a class of musical events unambiguously. A notated c^1 denotes the pitch middle C, and no other pitch. The three semantic requirements are unambiguousness, disjointedness, and finite differentiation. These conditions are met when (1) an inscription in a score denotes a musical event without ambiguity (unambiguousness); (2) every musical event that constitutes part of work is a member of one character class (finite differentiation); and (3) given two distinct musical scores, there are no accurate performances or copies that they have in common (disjointedness).[2]

By defining allographic artworks in terms of these syntactic and syntactic features of notational systems, Goodman produces rigorous criteria that musical performances and scores must meet if they are to be instances of a musical work. When performing a musical work, a performance must comply exactly with its score. Since the criteria guarantee that every musical performance will correlate one-to-one with a musical notation, which will in turn be a member of one and only one character-class, Goodman defines the relationship between scores and performances as one of exact correspondence. Musical works, as allographic, share these features with literary works. For allographic works, "all that matters is what may be called *sameness of spelling*: exact correspondence as sequences of letters, spaces, and punctuation marks."[3] Two copies of Gray's *Elegy* will instance the same literary work so long as they correspond exactly; the same holds for two performances or two scores of Beethoven's Fifth Symphony.

Goodman often speaks of musical works in terms of scores and the performances that comply with them. Scores and works, exactly correspondent, are on the same ontological level. One is not superior, or more "real" than another. Goodman treats them like perfect translations, where a performance is, as it were, carried over from the domain of musical notation to the domain of sound and back again without any loss of fidelity. Any score that can be performed should, in Goodman's theory, be translatable back into the same notation based on the performance.[4] A performance or a score *specifies* a musical work. A score specifies a work through its particular marks, and a performance through its particular sounding events. If the score and the performance meet the strict standard of translatability, that is, if a performance complies exactly with a score or a score is an exact transcription of a performance, then the two specify the same musical work. The compliance of a performance with a score (or a score with a performance) is Goodman's *only* requirement for the instancing of a musical work. There is no additional feature that makes a performance or a score an instance of a musical work, and there is nothing more to a musical work than its class of compliant performances or scores. Unlike other musical ontologists, who are realists about musical works—where a musical work is treated as a form, structure, or abstract object, present in various instantiations (i.e., scores or performances) but distinguishable from them—Goodman makes an argument designed to support his nominalist view. For Goodman, there is no such thing as an abstract object or Platonic form. There is no essence or substance that precedes a performance or a score or prescribes its properties. A musical work is not some special kind of object with metaphysical properties all its own. Nor is it some vaguely defined type that participates in a mysterious relation with its tokens or shares its properties with them. Rather, a musical work is nothing more than the exact sequence of sonic characters specified by a score or a performance.

The common objection to Goodman's theory is that it raises the standard of musical performance exorbitantly high. "Since complete compliance with the score is the only requirement for a genuine instance of a work," Goodman writes, "the most miserable performance without actual mistakes does count as such an instance, while the most brilliant performance with a single wrong note does not." The slightest deviation of a performance from its score makes it into a performance of a different work than intended. Goodman is well aware that his stringent requirement does not jibe with ordinary speech about music. "Could we not bring our theoretical vocabulary into better agreement with common practice and common sense by allowing some limited degree of deviation in performances admitted as instances of a work? The practicing musician or composer usually bristles at the idea that a performance with one wrong note is not a performance of the given work at all; and ordinary usage surely sanctions overlooking a few wrong notes. But this is one of those cases where ordinary usage gets us quickly into trouble." If we loosen our exacting standards and allow for performances of works with a few wrong notes, Goodman argues, then through a series of translations back and forth from performance to score we would end up with a different musical work. "By a series of one-note errors of omission, addition, and modification," Goodman tersely and wittily writes, "we can go all the way from Beethoven's *Fifth Symphony* to *Three Blind Mice*."[5] Even worse, "the innocent-seeming principle that performances differing by just one note are instances of the same work risks the consequence—in view of the transitivity of identity—that all performances whatsoever are of the same work."[6]

Goodman worries that the alteration of one note initiates a descent down a slippery slope, where the accumulation of alterations in a musical work will eventually undermine all criteria for its identity. Although cast in terms of musical works, Goodman's worry is quite an old one, often known as the sorites paradox, concerning the problem of predication and continual change. The paradox gets its name from the Greek work *soros*, meaning "heap." Imagine a heap of sand from which one grain at a time is extracted. The removal of a single grain does not change a heap into its opposite, a non-heap. But were the process to go on long enough we would eventually arrive at a single grain of sand. Is that single grain still a "heap?" And if not, when did the heap become something other than a heap? In Goodman's formulation of the paradox, notes are like grains of sand and musical works are like heaps. The omission of a single note may not appear to alter the musical work at first, at least according to common sense and common usage, but were the process to go on long enough, the paradox sets in: at what point in the process does Beethoven's Fifth Symphony become "Three Blind Mice"? The work, like grains of sand, slips through our fingers.

***

Languages of Art sparked a vigorous debate within Anglo-American philosophy about the ontology of musical works. Nearly everyone found Goodman's solution unsatisfactory. The stringency with which Goodman required compliance between performances and scores led to counterintuitive claims that did not correspond with musical practices. Many felt that Goodman's account was tainted by his commitment to nominalism. Because Goodman was philosophically opposed to abstract objects, he did not consider them possible candidates for musical works. While the language of types, universals, or kinds was anathema to Goodman, other philosophers considered the advantages that realist theories might have over nominalist ones in describing musical works. They used the conceptual resources of realism to develop theories of musical works that were more permissive about mistakes and wrong notes, and thus in line with common speech and musical practices.

Without going into a detailed account of the realist responses to Goodman, it is useful to characterize a few of the best-known realist theories of musical works. The utility of such a discussion is that it will help bring into relief sharp differences between nominalist ontology, realist ontology, and the network-based ontology I have been developing in the previous chapters. Realist writing on musical works is often technical and detailed, informed by shared knowledge of (and thus often tacit reference to) prior philosophical debates about the nature of objects and events, types and tokens, particulars and universals, metaphysics, theories of reference, and the like. There are many useful summaries of the debates available.[7] To facilitate my discussion of these writings, I want to introduce a framework common to all the varieties of realist musical ontology under consideration.[8]

(1) For the realist musical ontologist, a musical work is an object that is foundational and ultimate. This object can come in a variety of different guises: eternal and exemplary forms, like those in found in Plato; non-spatial, non-temporal types that can be tokened in particular spatiotemporal objects; abstract objects; sound-structures or patterns; concrete, physical sounding events; or some variant of the above. In all cases, this metaphysical object is the terminal point of the investigation; it is the

basis or foundation upon which properties and predicates are added. These ultimate objects cannot be further investigated or analyzed into smaller components. They are ontologically elementary.

(2) The realist musical ontologist is also committed to the idea that musical works have essential properties, which are to be distinguished from accidental properties. Musical works are identified and individuated by virtue of these essential properties. Different realist ontologists will select different properties as essential or accidental. Much of the debate between realists involves arguments for determining and distinguishing essential properties from accidental properties. Some candidates are: properties of ordering and arrangement in a structure, properties that are shared between a type and its tokens, properties that define a particular natural kind, prescriptions of instrumentation, and so forth. Such properties are present (or correlated) in both the work and its instances; performances and scores align with musical works because they share (or have correlate) properties with musical works.

(3) If, for the realist, musical works are real things, then it follows that there is a difference between how musical works are and how they are perceived. If there were no split between the two, then there would be no possibility of being mistaken about a musical work, since a mistake trades on the difference between how something is and how it is taken to be.[9] This difference between ontology and epistemology is a heady philosophical theme, opening the door to the split between things-in-themselves and our representation of them as phenomena. In realist musical ontology, the difference is often articulated as a question about the nature of the compositional act: does a composer create or discover a musical work? While the intuitive answer is that a composer creates a musical work, the fact that we might be wrong about this opens the door to a realist position. Works, for the realist, exist apart from the representations of listeners, performers, and so forth. How they are is different from how they are perceived.

Realist musical ontology, as I mentioned above, presented a robust alternative to Goodman's nominalist account where musical works are defined as a class of compliant scores and performances, and as not objects. In addition, the realist account offered an alternative to Goodman's rigid rules about malformed performances since, if works are real things, performances could be related to them with more or less fidelity. The difference between a work and a performance, a difference that is flattened by Goodman's nominalism, allowed for realist ontologists to explore the various relations that might hold between a work and its performance.

Nicholas Wolterstorff, in an influential essay on the ontology of artworks, argued that musical works are akin to natural kinds, and that scores and performances are examples of these kinds.[10] The relationship between kinds and examples is defined as "analogical." Properties that are ascribed to the examples are not necessarily ascribable to their kinds. In Wolterstorff's example, individual grizzly bears have the property of growling, but the kind Grizzly does not growl. This is because kinds, which are different from their spatiotemporal examples, are not capable of producing sound, or of growling. Rather when we say "the Grizzly growls," the claim is analogical. We are really saying that something cannot be a properly formed grizzly bear unless it growls. This analogical relation between kinds and their examples also holds for musical works. Ascriptions of properties to musical works are really ascriptions of properties that any properly formed instance of a work must have. These properties define the kind and all of its well-formed examples. "In botanical and zoological taxonomy books, one is not told about the features shared by all examples of a certain kind, nor about essential features shared by all examples of a certain kind, but about the features which a thing cannot lack if it is to be a properly formed example of the kind."[11] By laying out the basic features that an example of a kind must have, these properties establish "norm-kinds." Musical works are norm-kinds for Wolterstorff. They are defined as sound-sequences, a norm-kind whose examples are well-formed occurrences of that sequence. Just as there might be the occasional grizzly who does not or cannot growl, there might be the occasional performance of a musical work that does not exemplify the work's sound-sequence with absolute fidelity. Thus, Wolterstorff offers a rejoinder to Goodman's note-perfect criterion of the performance of musical works.

While appealing to works as norm-kinds provides an intuitive way of accommodating mistakes in the performance of musical works, it too has its own counterintuitive consequences. Kinds—whether norm-kinds, natural kinds, or any other kind—are non-spatial and non-temporal. When I fashion a score for a musical work, have I also fashioned the musical work itself? If the score is a spatiotemporal particular, one that I created, did I also create, along with it, the norm-kind that the score exemplifies? Wolterstorff defends a platonic realism about kinds, ultimately arguing that kinds are incapable of being created or destroyed. Thus, if a musical work is a norm-kind, it too cannot be created. Rather, it is selected from out of a stockpile of possible norm-kinds. When a composer creates a score or a performer creates a performance, he or she makes an example of the kind, and in doing so determines the norm-kind that the score or performance exemplifies. "A score would just be the composer's record of his determination [of a sound-sequence norm-kind]."[12] Thus, two composers might "compose" the same work in Wolterstorff's world, insofar as their distinct scores determine exactly the same sound-sequence norm-kind.

Jerrold Levinson's often-cited essay "What a Musical Work Is" responds, in part, to Wolterstorff's platonist account by arguing that musical works are indeed created, while also trying to defend a notion of musical works as types whose performances are tokens.[13] The challenge of this position is that types, like kinds, are non-spatial and non-temporal objects, and thus incapable of being created. Levinson's solution is to argue that a musical work is not just a run-of-the mill type, but rather something unique and special: an "initiated type." According to Levinson, "initiated types . . . begin to exist only when they are initiated by an intentional human act of some kind. All those of interest can, I think, be construed as arising from an operation, like indication, performed upon a pure structure."[14] When a composer writes a score she indicates, by the very act of writing, a specific structure. The musical work, which includes this specific structure, is not sufficiently determined by the structure alone. Rather, we must also include the act of indication as part of the musical work. A musical work is, to begin with, a "structure-as-indicated-by-x-at-t," where x is the composer and t is the moment of indication. Levinson also considers the different kinds of structures that are included in a musical work. If a musical work is an indicated type, its essential properties are not exhausted by its indicated sound-structure; one must also include a "performing-means" structure, which indicates instrumentation required for a proper performance of the work. These two structures taken together, both of which are indicated by the composer, constitute a musical work.[15] Where some realist musical ontologists may take an austere view of a work's essential properties, limiting them to the work's sound-structure alone and classing performance means as accidental properties, Levinson is more generous.

By appealing to "initiated" types, Levinson argues against Wolterstorff's view that composers simply select sound-structures. The very act of selection is also an act of indication. Since a musical work is defined as including, essentially, its act of indication, we can say that a composer is a genuine creator.

By binding sound-structures and performing-means-structures to their moment of indication, Levinson also produces an argument against the possibility that two composers could compose the same work. The "*x-at-t*" part of the indicated structure would be different in each case.

Finally, Levinson argues against Goodman's note-perfect view of performance, but without appealing to norm-kinds. His argument is to draw a distinction between a *performance* of a work and an *instance* of it. An *instance* of a musical work is defined as "a sound event that conforms *completely* to the sound/performance means structure" of a specific work. Instances are a subset of *performances*, defined as "a sound event that is *intended* to instantiate" a specific musical work.[16] Because the criterion of a performance is more permissive than an instance, there can be cases where a performance of a work, say one with mistakes in it, intends to instance a work yet fails do so. By drawing such a distinction, Levinson preserves ordinary linguistic usage concerning musical performances, and argues that Goodman confuses the more specific concept of an instance with the more general notion of a performance. One can still perform a work, even if it has mistakes in it. One has just failed to instance it.

The most parsimonious of the musical realists is Peter Kivy. In his strict platonist account of musical works, a musical work is nothing more than a sound structure, an abstract object like those found in mathematics, geometry, or exhibited in scientific laws.[17] The sound structure alone provides the essential properties of the musical work. Kivy places fewer requirements on how those properties must be exhibited in performance. For instance, he has no qualms about arrangements of works for new instrumentation, so long as the sound-structure (the proper sequence of the notes and their duration, etc.) is preserved. Thus he rejects Levinson's inclusion of a performing means structure as an essential component of musical works. This makes Kivy's view particularly amenable to arrangements, which have often been a bugbear for philosophers of music. He also rejects Levinson's claim that works are initiated types, opting for a more traditional view about types, namely, that they are timeless and uncreated. Initiated types are not required for the identity and individuation of musical works, and in fact generate counterintuitive claims. Kivy cites the example of a chromatic prelude and fugue, once thought to be the work of J. S. Bach, but later found out to be the work of his relative, Johann Christoph Bach.[18] While acknowledging that we may listen to the work differently based on our knowledge of its historical pedigree, Kivy claims that we cannot go so far as to say that it is a different work. To do so would be to conflate the distinction between how things are and how they are perceived. The different features we hear based on our knowledge of the composer are not essential features for identifying a work, important though they may be for evaluating, esteeming, or interpreting a work. If a work were to essentially include its act of indication, then novel musicological discoveries would constantly be producing new works.

Like Wolterstorff, Kivy argues that composers do not create musical works but rather discover them. As part of this argument, Kivy tries to defend the value of "discovery," claiming that our esteem for acts of creation is a romantic vestige and that composers, like scientists, mathematicians, and inventors, all participate in processes of discovery.[19] In many respects, Kivy's position is sympathetic to Wolterstorff's platonism, but he offers a more austere form of it. Rather than account for malformed performances of works in terms of norm-kinds, Kivy's approach is simpler. In cases where a musician, playing work W, makes a mistake or does not play some feature of W correctly, "then it is not a performance of W *in respect of those measures and that feature*. But it is still a performance of W *sans phrase*."[20] Kivy does not take the all-or-nothing approach stipulated by Goodman's nominalism. Rather, the performance instances the work with respect to the features that it gets right. However, by stringently keeping works and performances ontologically distinct, there is no problem with simple matter of fact that performers make mistakes. It does not affect the work.

***

Despite the internal debates between Wolterstorff, Levinson, and Kivy, all three share the realist framework outlined above. They all believe that musical works are real things, whether norm-kinds, initiated-types, or sound-structures. Musical works are specified and individuated according to their "essential" properties, whether these are features that establish a norm-kind, the properties determined by a specific sound/performing-means structure indicated by composer x at time t, or properties possessed by a specific, discovered sound-structure. Finally, musical works as such are distinct from the way they are perceived. Because all three rely on the notion of independent sound structures, they are simply discovered or selected—or much work must be done to manufacture a new kind of "indicated type" that will align the metaphysical object with intuitions about the creation of musical works.

All three also find a way of responding to the sorites paradox. The paradox is generated when a vague predicate like "heap"—that is, a predicate that does not have a clearly defined or rule-governed application—is applied to a situation that undergoes change. As the heap changes, as grains of sand are removed, there is a moment where we are no longer sure how to apply the predicate. When does a heap become a non-heap? The same holds for the problem of musical works, at least in Goodman's presentation. When does Beethoven's Fifth Symphony become "Three Blind Mice"? Goodman's solution to the problem is to remove the vagueness from the concept of a musical work, by defining it rigidly as a class of compliant scores and performances. Any change that a score or performance undergoes entails that it now complies with a new work. By fixing the predicate so sharply, all change is overcome. There *is no relation* between the note-perfect performance and the nearly note-perfect performance. They are simply two distinct works. In contrast, the realist solution to the sorites problem depends on the first two commitments in their framework. In their view, a musical work is a real thing (an abstract object, norm-kind, structure, etc.) that is individuated and specified according to its essential properties. By appealing to essential properties, the realist overcomes the issue of vagueness. Their predicates are not vague at all but are determined by the musical work's essential properties. If there is doubt about the individuation of a musical work, one must simply differentiate its accidental properties from its essential properties and consult the latter. If performances fail to display all these properties, then they are perhaps not instances of the work, but they can still be understood as performances of it, since the work is what was intended to be played. The ontological split between performances and works—a split to which Goodman as a nominalist is unwilling to appeal—allows the musical realist to be less concerned about performances with mistakes. No matter how mistaken a performance might be, it never crosses the ontological divide between works and performances, and thus never threatens to sully the work itself. This leads to a second point. While essential properties may specify the musical work and thus remove the problem of vague predication, the realist metaphysical commitment to types, universals, structures, and the like also removes the issue of change. These kinds of metaphysical objects are impervious to change or—in the philosophical sense of the term—incorrigible. This is quite clear in Kivy's and Wolterstorff's analyses, but it also holds for Levinson's initiated types. While the latter are created by composer x at time t, after that moment they are unchanging and unchangeable.

What Goodman shares with the realist musical ontologists is a belief *that a musical work cannot change*. Neither Goodman nor the realists entertain this possibility. However, in the previous chapters, we have encountered situations where it appears that musical works are indeed changing. Stephen Davies's theory of musical works falls right in line with his realist predecessors. In Davies's account, a work of music, no matter how thickly or thinly specified, is a real structure that precedes its performances and is instantiated in all of its performances. No matter how well-formed or ill-formed a performance might be, it is a performance of a work in virtue of instancing the essential properties prescribed by the work. When it came to his account of jazz, there was always a thinly specified work preceding a network of performances. The identity of each performance was guaranteed by the fact that it instanced the thin structure of the work by preserving just those features that are specific and essential to the work, while filling in the rest as needed. But we also saw the compensatory nature of this argument; that is, we saw how it responded in counterintuitive ways to works that seem to change, by projecting back, through an act of ontological *Nachträglichkeit*, an always already present thin work.

Jazz standards pose a serious challenge to nominalist and realist theories of musical works. They present a situation where we have a set of performances that are morphologically distinct from one another, sometimes in radical ways, and yet all of the agents involved (musicians, listeners, record companies, publishers, broadcasters, etc.) understand them as performances of one and the same musical work. These are the facts on the ground, and they are the facts that any adequate philosophical ontology of jazz standards must explain. Neither the nominalists nor realists have convincing arguments to account for these facts on the ground. They either say, as the nominalist does, that every jazz performance is ultimately a performance of a different work or what amounts to the same thing, no work at all; or they say, as the realist does, that every performance *must be* an instance of some vaporous, thin work that precedes it all. In contrast, the network-based account I have begun to establish can accommodate these facts on the ground and encourages the development of a theory of musical works that can not only account for their change, but also their emergence, identity, and individuation, by appealing to chains of replication and nomination.

***

I have defined replication as "the sequential production of similar material morphologies . . . that are substitutable for one another in specific social contexts of use" and demonstrated, through a series of examples concerning

"Body and Soul," how replications function in the specific social context of jazz improvisation and arrangement. Imagine for a moment an original artifact, A, that is replicated in artifact B. To A and B we will add a chain of replications. B is replicated in artifact C, and C is further replicated in artifact D. At the ends of the chain, D might be morphologically quite distinct from artifact A. Furthermore, since replication depends on contexts of use, we cannot determine whether D counts as a replication of A in the absence of social context. It may count as a valid replication, or it may not. However, along each link in the chain, from A to B, B to C, and C to D, we have legitimate replications, in that each item can be substituted for its predecessor. At the local level, identity is preserved across each link in the chain; at the ends of the chain, identity seems to be missing. This is the sorites paradox.

Neither the nominalist nor the realist has given much consideration to what happens in the middle of the chain. For the nominalist, each replication in the chain is simply new, unrelated to the others. Any mistaken performance is, according to the nominalist, a performance of a new work. There is nothing that *relates* the intended work with the performance. The nominalist finds an appeal to their similar morphologies inadequate, since any two artifacts can just as well be morphologically compared. By ignoring the fact that the artifacts are related through a process of replication the nominalist sees no good reason why the relations between A and B should be more worthy of attention than two other artifacts. Differences between artifacts are leveled. Thus, in order to account for the seeming lack of identity of A and D, all identity beyond the self-identity of any individual link in the chain is sacrificed entirely.

For the realist, the solution to the problem of the identity of A and D is to discover a structure that inheres in both artifacts. The realist jumps to the assumption that identity must be preserved *in exactly the same way across the chain*, and thus there is no good reason to consider the middle of the chain as opposed to it ends. Whatever we find, whatever thin structure or set of essential properties inheres in the artifacts, must be equally distributed across the entire chain. The realist is indeed able to give an account of the relation between artifacts, but the answer comes at a cost. By formulating the solution in terms of metaphysical types and material tokens, the realist opens up a gap between matter and form, between particulars and universals, and so forth. Thus, the realist is forced to explain how spatiotemporal particulars and invariant, eternal, universals cross this metaphysical gap. How is it that a property can be shared between a token and its type? What kinds of properties are these, and how do they bridge the abyss so as to impress tokens, instances, or particulars with the essential properties of types, kinds, or universals? We might, for the sake of brevity, refer to this as *the realist gap* between matter and form. If identity is defined as the adherence of a material token to an abstract type, then our claims of identity will always require that a gap between form and matter be crossed.

There are resources available for a more satisfactory theory. Bruno Latour, the philosopher and historian of science, presents trenchant critiques of both realism and nominalism. His network-based ontology challenges the realist and nominalist positions by (1) focusing on a critique of the epistemological gap that realists posit between form and matter; and (2) offering an account of relationality that does not demote relations to the status of mere accidental properties. To introduce Latour's thought, I will focus on his account of "circulating reference." As we will see, Latour is extraordinarily attentive to the mediating or middle links, like those we might find in a chain of replications. While the focus of Latour's discussion is the problem of reference, his argument is equally applicable and pertinent to questions of identity.

***

In Chapter 2 of *Pandora's Hope*, Latour introduces the concept of "circulating reference" by means of a case study. In the Amazon, at the point where the savanna meets the rainforest, there are a few isolated patches of forest vegetation surrounded by savanna. How did they get there? Are they the result of the savanna encroaching on the forest, or the forest expanding out into the savanna? Latour follows a group of soil scientists to Boa Vista in an attempt to answer the question. His chapter is organized around the presentation of a series of photographs of the scientists in action. Each photograph is described, contextualized, and commented on by Latour. The photographs show the various steps involved in the production of a scientific paper: procedures, techniques, methods of mapping, data gathering, archiving, discussion, and, finally, writing. There is no moment where the answer to the question is simply grasped in a glance, no disclosure or revelation of the truth in the blink of an eye. Rather, the answer to the question travels along a series of steps, across a long chain of mediations. Satellite maps of the region are consulted. Trees on the ground are numbered with small tin tags to facilitate their identification. Plant specimens from various parts of the jungle and savannah are cut, dried, and stored in shelves for further analysis and recording. The jungle floor is mapped with the use of a tool called a "pedofil," a device that spools out threads and allows for the plotting of locations. Soil samples are removed, logged in a book. They are placed into a gridded box, organized into symmetrical rows and columns, called a pedocomparator, whose regularity facilitates the comparison of samples from miles apart. The scientists consult a color chart, called the Munsell code, to compare and differentiate similar shades of soil. The samples in the pedocomparator can be reorganized, allowing patterns to emerge and data to be transcribed. The scientists begin to wonder if worms might not be playing a role in the preparation of the soil that supports these patches of the forest in the savannah.

Only at the end of this long chain of mediations do the scientists write up their report. Here, Latour warns us, we are in danger of falling prey to a classical view concerning reference. "The philosophy of language," Latour writes, "makes it seem as if there exist two disjointed spheres separate by a unique and radical gap that must be reduced through the search for correspondence, for reference, between words and the world."[21] The traditional view about language is that the words used to describe the situation on the ground in the Amazon are not of the same order as the facts about which they speak. They seem to be distinct, ideal, and different in kind from the things they denote. In writing up the report, the long chain of mediations, which lead from the initial survey of satellite maps to the final conclusions about the role of worms in transferring soil, have been seemingly erased. A diagram stands in for the facts on the ground, yet the steps involved in generating the diagram are occluded. Rather, it seems that the scientific diagrams and language employed, when functioning smoothly, simply capture the facts on the ground by corresponding with them. The diagram or language appears to work by sharing some kind of logical form or structure with the facts, isomorphic with them in some crucial respect. In contrast, Latour's description of the process puts the facts and the report on the same footing. They are all involved in a long chain of mediations. Latour's ethnography allows the reader to see how the concrete situation in the Amazon is translated into a scientific paper by means of a whole series of steps, chained together, one after another. If one only looks at the extremes—the Amazonian rainforest at one end and the scientific paper on the other—there appears a radical gap between the paper and the rainforest. The two ends of the chain look different in kind; thus, the only way to connect them is through a precarious leap across the gap between words and world.

The point of Latour's ethnography is to demonstrate that there is no gap from word to world that one must leap across. Rather, there is just a long chain that connects the extremes. In each case, Latour reinserts the chain of mediations—or what he calls the "translations"—that link the rainforest to the report. "An essential property of this chain is that it must remain *reversible*," writes Latour. "The succession of stages must be traceable, allowing for travel in both directions."[22] In the scientific account, the mediations that link the forest floor to the collection, organization, and recording of data, and finally to the complete paper, are fully traceable. Each time samples are moved, organized, or classified there is a traceable process. The same process that goes from the forest floor to the paper can be traced back the other direction, in that someone reading the paper could (if need be) work their way back through the chain that links the paper to the concrete situation of the forest floor. Once one becomes attentive to the chain that links the rainforest to the report, it no longer makes sense to think of reference as a leap. Latour encourages us to consider reference in different terms: "*The word 'reference' designates the quality of the chain in its entirety*, and no longer *adequatio rei et intellectus*. Truth-value *circulates* here like electricity through a wire, so long as this circuit is not interrupted."[23]

The contrast between classical reference and circulating reference leads to two models. In the first, two distinct and autonomous spheres are linked across an abyss by some sort of correspondence. This is the model of *adequatio rei et intellectus*. Things and ideas, different in kind, are linked together across a gap by means of *adequatio*, some isomorphic structure that guarantees the connection between the two. In the second model, we have a continuous chain. Each link in the chain functions as a small mediation or translation. For example, to categorize the color of the soil samples, color charts functioned as a tiny mediator. They allowed for the sample's property of color to be translated, preserved in a log, diagrammed, and compared, while getting rid of other properties. The soil samples and color chart have distinct morphologies, yet between the two a property was transferred. Latour is quite aware of the small gap that must be transcended in the move from soil sample to color chart; he refers to these small gaps as *hiatuses*. In each case there is a little shift from matter to form, from actual color to a color grid or system. In comparison, classical reference, holding itself to the extremes ends of the chain, encounters a massive gap that must be crossed in a single leap order to account for reference. Circulating reference breaks this gap down into tiny parts, none of which has the abyssal character of the large leap from extreme to extreme.

The philosophical power of Latour's model of circulating reference is that it can explain classical reference, while classical reference is incapable of explaining circulating reference. To generate the classical reference from circulating reference, one need only erase the middle links in the chain while preserving the extremities:

> Let us block in the extremities of the chain as if one were the referent, the forest of Boa Vista, and the other were a phrase, "the forest of Boa Vista." Let us erase all the mediations that I have delighted in describing. In place of the forgotten mediations, let us create a radical gap, one capable of covering the huge abyss that separates the statement I utter in Paris and its referent six thousand kilometers away. *Et voilà*, we have returned to the former model, searching for something to fill the void we have created, looking for some *adequatio*, some resemblance between two ontological varieties that we have made as dissimilar as possible. It is hardly surprising that philosophers have been unable to reach an understanding on the question of realism and relativism: they have taken two provisional extremities for the entire chain.[24]

The classical and circulating theories of reference embody two different ways of thinking about ontology, reference, identity, and other philosophical problems. Following Latour, we can describe the difference between these two views, using the striking language of William James, and call them the *saltatory* and *ambulatory* models. For James, classical theory of knowledge turns the relationship between objects and our knowledge of them into an "empty interval" that must be crossed. Between the object and the idea of the object, we are forced to execute a *salto mortale*, a fatal leap. James writes, "The relation between idea and object, thus made abstract and saltatory, is thenceforward opposed, as being more essential and previous, to its own ambulatory self, and the more concrete description is branded as either false of insufficient."[25]

James's critique is useful for considering the ontology of musical works as well. Rather than consider the work/performance relationship in terms of the ambulatory model, where the work and performance are involved in chains of replication—chains that transmit and preserve certain aspects of the work at the same time that they change the work and the sufficiency of its work-determinative properties—the saltatory model severs the performance from the work. In the latter, the relation between the work and its performance, "made abstract and saltatory," is also made to seem "more essential and previous." Through a kind of ontological sleight-of-hand or *Nachträglichkeit*, the salutatory view assumes that the musical work (thin or thick as it may be) is more essential than its performance, as well as prior to it. The saltatory view *is* the realist view of the relation of musical works to performances. Each performance is removed from a network of performances and compared with an incorrigible and invariant musical work. The saltatory view generates the *realist gap* between the work and its performance. Once this gap is generated, the philosophical realists finds himself, "searching for something to fill the void we have created, looking for some *adequatio*, some resemblance between two ontological varieties . . . made as dissimilar as possible." By putting the work before its performances, adherence to the work becomes the only guarantee of a performance's identity. The performance is a performance of the work in virtue of referring to it, of instantiating it, of following its prescriptions.

While this saltatory model of the musical work offers a rigid criterion for determining the identity of performances ("does a performance adhere to the prescriptions of the work?"), it does not describe the practices of jazz musicians nearly as well as the ambulatory model. In this latter view, the identity of the musical work is carried across the links of the chain. Returning to our chain of replications ($A \to B \to C \to D$), the saltatory view has limited options. By erasing all the mediating links it is left with only two nodes to consider, A and D, separated by a gap. It can either say that A and D are non-identical, which would contradict the opinions and practices of the community of musicians and listeners, or it can say that A are D are identical in virtue of possessing a structure that was always already there. The ambulatory view, on the other hand, is more robust. It does not have to be committed to the view that a structure instantiated in A and D are identical, or that this structure was always already in place.

Take, for example, our discussion of "But Not for Me." If we compare Coltrane's performance with Gershwin's score, it looks like a mistaken or faulty instance since it does not render the original accurately. Like a bad reproduction, it does not preserve the correct properties to successfully cross the gap between work and performance. The two are non-identical in that the work's essential properties do not seem to be present in Coltrane's version. But when Coltrane's performance is reinserted into a chain of mediations, a different story about identity is available. The changes Coltrane made to the song are understandable when traced across chains of replication. In every replication, there is a small *hiatus*, a shift from matter to form to matter. Two artifacts are substitutable in terms of some aspect or property they share. Thus, in replicative terms, we can describe a *hiatus* as involving a shift from artifact to aspect (and back again) to artifact. In Coltrane's substitution, the opening progression of "But Not for Me" was heard as a tonic prolongation—a shift from "matter" to "form," or from artifact to aspect— and then substituted with "Coltrane Changes," another progression with the same tonic-prolongational aspect—a shift back from "form" to "matter," or aspect to artifact. Identity is preserved across each replication, in that salient properties or aspects are preserved. Like the relation of the soil and the color chart, each replication is a valid, unproblematic substitute for its predecessor. Even if the aspects found at one end of a long chain of replications are no longer present at the other end, and thus no longer substitutable for one another, the replicative relation between individual links still holds. According to the saltatory model, there is nothing but non-identity at the extremes. However, the ambulatory model supports a different claim. By tracing the hiatuses involved in each replicative link of the chain, and by showing that the chain *is* a chain of mediations, the ambulatory model asserts that the identity of the work is not dependent on the extremes but, to borrow Latour's phrase, "*designated by the quality of the chain in its entirety.*"

The ambulatory model supports the view that standards are more accurately described in terms of networks of performances than in realist terms, where works and performances are akin to tokens and types, kinds and examples, or universals and particulars. Each performance or publication of a song constitutes a node in a network, and each node is related to some other node by virtue of replicating aspects of a previous node. The process achieves two things: from node to node, it preserves some property (or aspect) from node A to node B, although the two nodes are morphologically distinct. At the same time, node B might also introduce new, additional properties *because* of its morphological distinctness. Those new properties can then be taken as exhibitions of structure or form and further replicated in node C. While properties are preserved from any node n to another node n' directly connected with it, there is at no point a guarantee that there is some essential property or structure present across the entire network of performances or publications. This is an important observation. When we conceive of a song in terms of a network, we can see that what makes the network into a network

144   HEARING DOUBLE

is not a form, property, or structure that exists outside of the network. There is neither a transcendental structure, nor substance, nor form that grounds the network's holism. Rather, the network is generated by forging new replications.[26] Other than being related to its neighbors, a node need not possess any relations to the network as a whole. However, the addition of new nodes, especially if they develop numerous attachments, impacts our view of the network as a whole. New additions to the network can change what properties are considered sufficiently work-determinative. The properties of standards that musicians, critics, or listeners find determinative, salient, and meaningful are impacted by new additions.

***

Recall the historical and critical debates over Ornette Coleman's performance of "Embraceable You." The question at the heart of its critical reception is this: does it count as performance of the work? The answer is not easy to settle. Weighing ontological judgments on the basis of chains of nomination and chains of replication may not always lead to clear-cut answers about musical ontology. This aspect of my account differs from the realist and nominalist theories described above. In those theories, once the criteria for compliance or the determination of essential properties have been settled, there is an unambiguous rule for determining whether a performance is or is not an instance (or particular, or token) of a work. Following those rules, clear-cut results follow; either performance p is an instance of work w or it isn't. However, that is not the case in the network-based ontology that I have been describing. There are performances, like those of contrafacts and revisions, where there may very well be a vibrant critical dispute about whether performance p is indeed an instance of the work w—or, in my terms, whether it should be associated with w's network of performances. If a philosopher thinks the goal of the ontology of music is to offer immaculate, clear-cut rules for determining what is or is not an instance of a musical work, then the network-based theory proposed will be unsatisfactory.

In response, I would argue that identity and individuation are not nearly as clear-cut as realist ontologies would have it. Some may think this is a disadvantage of the network-based theory, but I disagree. I do not see how an ontological theory that automatically provides rules for the discrimination and differentiation of musical works can also be a theory that is sensitive to the actual, historical practices of improvising musicians, arrangers, and performers. If musical works change (and do so in relation to their network of performances), then we should expect cases where we cannot simply rule where one work begins and another ends. Such cases do not undermine the theory but in fact, reveal its power. By weighing the different kinds of evidence provided by chains of nomination and chains of replication, the *network-based theory can provide an account of the difficult cases by showing why they are difficult.* When chains of nomination and chains of replication do not run in parallel, judgments about the identity and individuation of musical works are challenged. Where the network-based theory can account for this challenge and describe what is challenging about it, the realist and nominalist theories fall silent. This is an asset of the network-based approach.

This feature of the theory aligns the ontology of music with recent work on "ontological politics." Annemarie Mol describes the idea of "ontological politics" as a composite, or mixed term. The combination of ontology with politics is intended to jar the reader, to propose that the fixed, immutable forms of ontology are in fact not fixed and immutable but come into being in relation with the sociality of the politics. According to Mol, "If the term 'ontology' is combined with that of 'politics' then this suggests that the conditions of possibility are not given. That reality does not precede the mundane practices in which we interact with it, but is rather shaped within these practices. So the term *politics* works to underline this active mode, this process of shaping, and the fact that its character is both open and contested."[27] Ontological politics is coined to emphasize the open and contested character of ontology, and the inseparable alloy of ontology with cultural practices. The network-based ontology that I have been describing accepts the inseparability of ontology and practice. In fact, by developing ontology in relation to cultural practices like replication and nomination, we have not assumed—as the realists do—that ontology precedes the "mundane practices" of performance, composition, and improvisation out of which it emerges. Since there is no homogeneous set of practices employed in the performance and replication of jazz standards—no assumption of a uniform bloc of musician-listeners—there will naturally be disputes about what counts as a replication, what is the proper baptism of a work, or how a name or performance should be associated with a network. These disputes will not simply be "cultural" disputes, as if culture is something isolated and independent of ontology, or something contingent and fickle; rather, they will be genuine *ontological* disputes about musical works. As we see in the disagreements about Coleman's performance of "Embraceable You," these disputes are arguments about whether that performance *is or is not* a legitimate performance of the work "Embraceable You."

* * *

Philosophers of music, with their steady commitment to the realist project, have typically considered the ontology of musical works from a theoretical perspective. Rather than investigate how it is that particular works come to be, change, or how they are performed, received, and understood in relation to particular historical and social settings, the ontology of music often stands at a degree of remove from practice. As I noted above, for Davies, Kivy, Levinson, Wolterstorff, and company, there is an unshakable commitment to the notion that musical works possess essential properties. Performances either instance these essential properties or they do not. The challenge, from their point of view, is in determining what kinds of properties are to be considered essential for musical works *in general*. That is why the philosophical debates, for example, have perpetually been focused on whether works require a performing-means structure initiated by composer x at time t (as Levinson argues) or something much more austere and parsimonious (as Kivy argues). *At no point* does their interest lie in actually enumerating, for any *specific work*, what the essential properties would be. That's all just "a matter of fact," something assumed to be easily worked out once the proper theoretical framework has been determined.

If we set out from musical practices, not from a detached viewpoint of theoretical generalization, the ontological project will look quite different. When a musician performs a musical work—whether an improvising jazz musician or a member of a string quartet—there is no moment in their practice where they worry whether or not they are properly instancing a work by transmitting its essential properties. Rather, they perform the work in the way that they know how, and in the manner that depends on a long history of performance practices into which they are acculturated. If you asked a musician to enumerate a work's essential properties, you will likely get confused looks. Or, if you receive a reply, you would likely have little consensus, with as many answers as you have performers. And yet, when jazz musicians perform some standard or a string quartet gives a concert of some piece of chamber music, works are instanced. Which makes one wonder, if essential properties were so inessential to the practice of performers, why have they been the main focus of the realist philosophy of music?

The networked-based ontology developed thus far has a different relationship to musical practice than the realist philosophy of music. Chains of replication and chains of nomination, which are the two mainsprings by which a network of associated performances is created, are generated through practice. Jazz musicians substitute one chord for another, one melodic phrase for another, or alter a work's form or time signature. This is simply part of their practice. The result is the formation of new artifacts based on previous models that, while morphologically quite distinct from the latter, are nevertheless substitutable for them. (In other words, there's a lot of different ways to play "Body and Soul.") Jazz musicians, because they participate a culture that is permissive about what counts as a replication, reveal how extensive and how transformative acts of replication can be. In this sense, the culture of jazz differs from the impermissive culture of replication that has developed around classical music. While some revisionist performers might push fairly hard against the norms—Glenn Gould, for one, comes to mind—it is uncontroversial to assert that since the age of *Werktreue* classical music has been a culture of impermissive replication. But impermissive replication is replication nevertheless. While impermissive practices keep performances of works morphologically similar over time—and thus create the stability of that fabled institution, "the imaginary museum of musical works"—they do so without appealing to any essential properties. In this respect, both the practices of jazz musicians and classical musicians dovetail.[28]

In addition to practices of replication, we also have practices of nomination. Again, this is not a theoretical issue; composers name their works. Names are emblazoned on performances, recordings, and inscriptions. They are also crucial to the kinds of negotiations made by jazz musicians on the bandstand.[29] When a bandleader calls out "Body and Soul" to the other musicians, they are not secretly identifying a set of essential properties to be instanced in their performance. Rather, they are identifying the song that they are preparing to play by associating it with a network of previous performances of that song. Unless the musicians already know *how* they are going to play the tune—are they going to play John Coltrane's arrangement, or are they going to double-time the chorus as in Roy Eldridge and Chu Berry's version, or follow some other model or arrangement?—all those decisions will be negotiated in real time on the bandstand. The experience that musicians bring with them and their familiarity with the past performances form the basis of their knowledge about the song's work-determinative properties. But we must recall that these properties are sufficient, not necessary or essential.

Any particular chord or melodic profile that, from a theoretically detached viewpoint, we might think essential *may or may not be present*. A name promises that the music we are about to play will be a successful replication, based on those previous performances yet without specifying any properties in particular.[30]

By investigating the ontology of music starting from a consideration of practices, like those of replication and nomination, we are now prepared to offer a very different answer to the realist's central question: what kind of thing is a musical work? *A musical work is an entity that emerges from a network*. A musical work is what emerges from an association of performances, recordings, scores, arrangements, and publications. A musical work is dependent not on essential properties exhibited in all members of a network but on the various connections formed through repeated practices of replication and nomination. This entails that works are produced, and that they change over time. Works are historical, not platonically real, immutable, incorrigible, or ideal. They are real in a different sense: works are real when they are effective, when they produce results. They are real when they both constrain and afford properties for future performances. A network is not the creation of one single individual but is the collective, emergent product of many hands. Works are negotiated by means of everyday musical practices—in acts of reproducing and receiving them. They can be changed through performance, arrangement, and revision. Works are passed from musician to musician and depend on such transactions for their continuing persistence. Unlike the immutable integrity of platonic forms, structures, patterns, or natural kinds, the reality of works requires care, upkeep, and maintenance. Works can lie fallow for years, until a performer, arranger, or producer decides to revisit it, change it, and make it appropriate for the current moment (just think of those late bloomers such as "But Not for Me" or "My Funny Valentine"). Single inscriptions, single performances, are networks (albeit networks of a single node) just as much as standards like "Body and Soul," which have been played and recorded innumerable times. But the relevant properties of networks—the fact that they have no essential features linking all nodes, that they possess no minimum or maximum number of nodes, that their associations and relevant properties change over time, that they are developed collectively and require constant care and renewal—all of these properties are clarified by studying standards. While all musical works emerge from networks, standards *exemplify* this ontological condition.[31] In their multiplicity of guises—constantly being revised, substituted, replaced, versioned, appropriated, and reappropriated—standards show the variety of possibilities that a work can undergo.

***

Earlier, I identified three rubrics that defined a "realist framework." How do these rubrics compare with the ambulatory model?

(1) The realist view typically sees sound-structures (or other structures, such as Levinson's initiated types) as providing the "substance" of musical ontology. That is, at bottom, a musical work *is a structure*. None of the realist philosophers investigate the question of structure more deeply; rather, structure is the ultimate stratum of a musical work, beyond which there is no need to investigate. However, in Latour's metaphysics, there are no ultimate strata. In their place, there are "black boxes."[32] A black box is a replacement for the traditional metaphysical notion of a substance. For Latour, the objects of the world are not integral and fixed; rather, objects are assembled into temporarily (and pragmatically) integral units through the association of distinct parts. Each part is, in turn, assembled from other parts. Thus, for Latour, there is no ultimate foundation or ground. Rather, everything is a black box, capable of being opened up, analyzed, and reassembled. Black boxes are assemblages that, when functioning smoothly, are treated as if they are solid and permanent and, thus, have no need to be opened up or reassembled in new ways. "While traditional substances are one, black boxes are many—we simply *treat* them as one, as long as they remain solid in our midst."[33]

American popular songs are assembled from smaller parts. Standard chord progressions are linked with melodic phrases, set to certain accompaniment patterns; various standard turnarounds are tacked on to the end of choruses; introductions and codas frame the choruses, and so forth. These songs are usefully described in terms of black boxes. Even before their premieres on radio, film, Broadway, or recordings, songs from the era of Tin Pan Alley were never integral. They would go through many alterations: a verse might be added or cut; new lyrics might be written, or rewritten; the melody line might be altered to accentuate the strengths of one singer and hide the weaknesses of another. Once in the public, the song might circulate in performances by a wide variety of musicians, each making alterations or additions to the tune. When musicians, singers, lyricists, arrangers, and improvisers rework songs, they unhesitatingly open up a black box and begin to fiddle with its parts. We have seen this again and again in our case studies. Consider the RIFF associated with "In the Mood." For Horace Henderson,

"Tar Paper Stomp" was a black box. He tore it open, taking every strain, riff, and tag, and reassembled it into a new black box, called "Hot and Anxious." Joe Garland took that black box, popped open the lid, and reassembled it again, as "There's Rhythm in Harlem" and "In the Mood." Even Garland's arrangement of "In the Mood" was unboxed by Glenn Miller and his arrangers, and through excision and addition, boxed back up in a new arrangement. For almost a decade, the RIFF was being boxed and unboxed, until the success of Miller's recording made it into something nearly impermeable. As Miller's version of the tune was played again and again, transcribed into sheet music, sold as stock arrangements, performed by others, and impressed into the memory of the public, that particular assemblage gained associations. It became a central node in the network, one to which all other further nodes attached themselves through acts of replication. The song's assemblage held together (it "remained solid in our midst") in ways that earlier versions did not. While Krupa, Goodman, Ellington, and others, in performing the tune, cracked open the black box again, refashioning the song to fit their individual bands, it was never to the same degree as in its early days. The black box began to function smoothly. It solidified. It became integral.

This leads to a proposition: *the durability of a standard is the durability of a black box, not anything platonically real.*

(2) The realist, when making claims about identity and individuation of musical works, appeals to a set of essential properties that are "work-determinative," in that they specify sound-structures or whatever other metaphysical candidate plays the role of "substance." In this view, essential properties are those attributable to the musical work and are to be differentiated from accidental properties attributable to the performance. However, as I argued above, work-determinate properties should not be identified with essential properties. Rather, work-determinative properties are emergent. They are the properties that are sufficient for the recognition and specification of the work. In the case of "In the Mood," the RIFF is a work-determinative property, but it is not an essential property. It is quite easy to imagine a version of "In the Mood" that lacked the RIFF but had all the other parts of Miller's recording intact. In that case, those other parts would emerge as work-determinative, because it would be in virtue of them a listener would recognize the work. Work-determinative properties shift in relation to the whole set of replications that constitute a song and in relation to the history of such replications. When someone opens up the black box of a standard and fiddles with it, its work-determinative properties are

likely to change. Work-determinative properties are fickle; they are sufficient to specify a work but make no transcendental guarantees.

This leads to a second proposition: *for any standard that possesses property p, there are performances (real or possible) that are performances of the work and lack* p.

The proposition is an interesting consequence of the culture of jazz performance. Given the role of permissive replication in jazz practice, and given the fact that replications are determined on the basis of social contexts of use, this proposition must be taken as theoretically true. Of course, in practice, the replications a song undergoes may or may not be all that radical. There may be famous versions of a song that, due to its influence or great number of associations, preserve certain features across a network. There may also be established performance traditions of songs that maintain certain properties across the network. Impermissive replication of aspects will preserve particular features of songs. But the preservation of properties in these situations is not *necessary* or *essential*, just matters of fact. Theoretically, we must acknowledge that there is no guarantee that an essential property is to be found across a network.

(3) The realist locates a work and its performance on opposite sides of a gap. On one side, there is the work as such, a sound-structure with essential properties; on the other, there is a performance full of potential mistakes and accidental properties of its own. The musical work is given logical and ontological precedence over the performance and the performance intends to reproduce the work by reproducing all of its essential properties. In contrast, the ambulatory view supports the notion that standards are composed of a network of performances, scores, inscriptions, and such, without positing a work that precedes it all. The large gap between work and performance is replaced by a chain or sequence of smaller gaps—those between the material properties of performances and the aspects that acculturated listeners hear in them. Each node in the network is a translation or mediation; it relays some properties forward, adds new properties of its own, and excises others. The work, and its work-determinative properties, emerges from the steady growth of the network and from the associations that nodes form with their neighbors. Arrangers, improvisers, and performers intervene in the work by adding new performances to the network and by forging associations with other nodes. In no case is a performance a distortion of the work, or unfaithful to it. Nobody is distorting anything; there are just translations and replications. These can be successful or unsuccessful, esteemed or rejected.

If a permissive replication is esteemed and becomes widely replicated through long, impermissive chains, then new determinative properties of the standard might be introduced. Otherwise, the performance is not replicated; it does not generate any additional associations. A song may have one performance, one recording, and disappear. When it does, it seems silly to analyze it in terms of a network. But a network it is, albeit a network with a single node. Standards, on the other hand, make the networked nature of jazz and American popular music apparent. Standards require multiple performances by multiple performers. They never exist as a single node. Nobody can will a standard into being. Its fate is always in the hands of others, never its composer.[34] "In the Mood" was in the hands of Glenn Miller, not Joe Garland. "But Not for Me" was in the hands of Miles Davis and John Coltrane, not George Gershwin. "My Funny Valentine" was in the hands of Chet Baker, Mary Martin, and Frank Sinatra, not Richard Rodgers. Often, the performers of standards may have no idea who the composer was. (Pop quiz: who composed "Stella by Starlight" or "Invitation"?) The songs have been so often replicated, have circulated so widely, that they become like memory traces or reflexes to jazz musicians, who have honed their skills on these tunes while carrying them far from their origins. Yet, even in performances of standards by those who have forgotten the composer, the performer is always playing a dual role: on one hand, they function as the representative of the standard, on the other, they appropriate the standard to their own ends. Every translation is a traducement, as the saying goes, but it is also a transmission.

Thus, a third proposition: *A standard requires that others participate in its perpetuation and stabilization. By reproducing the standard, it is transformed at the same time that it is transmitted.* As a corollary: *the performance of a standard does not require a thin work, but rather participates in the standard's emergence from a thick musical network.*[35]

PART II
AUDITORY CULTURE

5
The Soundscape of Standards

In the preceding chapters I have developed an account of the musical ontology of the standard that considers the practices of replication and nomination in jazz performance. Those considerations allowed me to formulate a non-essentialist ontology of musical works, where work-determinative properties of a standard emerge from a network of performances.

I now turn to consider the historical and cultural conditions that supported this particular musical ontology. In this chapter, I argue that, in the period roughly spanning the years 1930 to 1960, there existed a co-constitutive relation between musical practices and musical ontology, where practices shaped ontology, and ontology in turn guided practices. I will develop the account by considering the various protocols, or rules of the game, that both tacitly and explicitly organized the circulation, distribution, and consumption of popular music, including swing and jazz. As a recurring "case study" for the chapter, I will often consider the program *Your Hit Parade*. This may seem like something of an odd choice, given that the show was more of a popular and cultural phenomenon than one of lasting musical value—whatever that might mean. However, there are various reasons why the program proves useful. The show straddles the period of the standard's efflorescence and waning. In its rise and fall in popularity, *Your Hit Parade* is a seismograph of mainstream musical taste—it registers and responds to changing patterns in the production and consumption of music, and in so doing reflects many broad musical ontological commitments of the era. Consideration of *Your Hit Parade*, alongside other examples, helps to trace the co-constitution of cultural practices and ontological ascription in the era of the standard.

The Emergence of the Soundscape of Standards

The possibility for a show like *Your Hit Parade* to reach such a vast audience was predicated on the rise of network radio. If in the late 1920s radio in America could be described as "largely a story of separate transmitter towers, each independent, each vying for attention with countless others," radio networks harnessed these isolated transmitters into a powerful, homogeneous force. Linked together by means of leased telephone cables, stations in various parts of the country began "broadcasting the same singer, the same speaker, the same comedian, the same drama." Networks became "national distributors of voices and sounds."[1] The rise of the radio network allowed for these voices and sounds to be heard not just locally but nationally, and afforded listeners of diverse ethnicity, race, and class the experience of certain commonalities in their soundscape. Before the institution of network radio there had been hit records that had circulated widely across the nation, and specific song crazes that had national appeal. Yet network radio made available, for the first time, a *national* soundscape. It afforded listeners who were geographically widely distributed access to an ensemble of specific "voices and sounds" distributed at a national level. Superimposed over their local soundscape, this national soundscape of radio helped to constitute a palpable sonic experience of the nation, built on the shared experience of "listening in," to use the lingo of the era. In this regard, it should come as no surprise that radio played a crucial role in garnering political and affective support for American involvement in World War II. However, the commonalities in the soundscape must be understood as a construction of a homogeneous "America" by the networks and their advertisers, one that also excluded certain "voices and sounds." For instance, African Americans had limited opportunities on network radio, often constrained to playing supporting roles that perpetuated broad stereotypes. The prominent role of the sponsor to shape radio's content led many advertising agencies to veer away from producing shows that might be considered too "controversial," or that might "alienate" stations in the South. Although there were important exceptions, national radio networks emphasized middlebrow musical production, racially homogeneous comedies and dramas, quiz shows, news, and mild educational programming.

Your Hit Parade is not one of those exceptions. Its content reflected network radio's homogeneous and national focus through its survey of the most popular songs in the nation. The basic premise of the show was simple: tabulate a list of the country's most popular songs and present them on the radio in a way that was lively and engaging, mostly through use of brisk tempos and bright orchestrations.[2] The show originated the format of "counting down" America's most popular tunes. In so doing, it built on the various sales and popularity charts that appeared in entertainment industry publications such as *Billboard* or *Variety* but transformed them into their own form of entertainment by making them into a competition. What had been largely an "intramural music business activity" became a form of audience participation, where listeners would spend the week guessing about which songs would move up or down the charts, and which would be number one.[3] Originally, *Your Hit Parade* presented the top fifteen songs of the week out of sequence, but soon shifted to include only the seven (or so) most popular songs in the nation. Each broadcast would dramatically build toward the top three songs, delaying their arrival with special "Lucky Strike" extras: numbers that featured favorite melodies of yesteryear, recent hit songs no longer on the parade, or other recognizable tunes. After a drum roll, the number one song would be revealed and performed to close out the show.

Your Hit Parade held enormous significance for a generation of radio's listeners. Ray Barfield, in *Listening to Radio: 1920–1950*, documents its importance through interviews and surveys. "I waited breathlessly every week for 'Your Hit Parade' to announce which song was (drum roll) *number one*," writes one respondent. Another used to "keep a list of the 'Hit Parade' selections each Saturday night," writing each number "in its place on the list as it was announced after yet another 'Lucky Strike Extra' had added to the suspense." Another, a prisoner of war held in a liberated German camp, recalls how troops used to listen to *Your Hit Parade*, broadcast by Armed Forces Radio. All eyes would be on the "little cloth covered speaker, so as better to hear the name of the top song of the week back home in America."[4] These recollections demonstrate the kind of cultural and affective work that *Your Hit Parade* performed in its time. It held the listener's attention like a radio drama or serial, keeping listeners in suspense until the secret of America's number one song was revealed; but it also functioned like a hobby, insofar as the hit songs could be tracked and tallied and collected, as one might do with baseball statistics or as many teenagers did with the personnel of big bands during the height of the Swing Era. It also provided a common sonic thread that could link the home front with the war front, providing an imaginary space where wartime soldiers could share experiences with those back home.

Unlike the model that emerged after *Your Hit Parade*, where the top twenty or top forty *recordings* in the nation were "counted down" by disc jockeys, *Your Hit Parade* had its own staff orchestrators, singers, bandleaders, and cast members who performed these songs week after week in unique arrangements. Musically, *Your Hit Parade* stuck to the middle of the road; it dressed up popular songs with bright orchestral colors—dousing them with plenty of harp glissandi and brass fanfares—but never veered off in directions too classical and highbrow, or too jazzy and lowbrow. The arrangements were pure middlebrow fare, meant to appeal to everyone and offend none. Since many songs remained on the parade for weeks on end, they would often receive multiple arrangements. For example, in the summer of 1944 listeners might hear the number one hit, "Long Ago and Far Away," arranged to feature Frank Sinatra; on another week, performed in an arrangement for the Hit Paraders, the show's resident choir; and the following week, in a different arrangement, to highlight Joan Edwards (see Table 5.1). The arrangements themselves are typical for the time, but there are some noteworthy things to consider. First, the fact that songs were rearranged from week to week is significant. In one sense, it reflects the fact that even in the middlebrow

Table 5.1 Arrangements of "Long Ago and Far Away" on *Your Hit Parade*

Your Hit Parade, date of broadcast	Position on the countdown	Notes on the arrangements
May 6, 1944	Number Three	Instrumental chorus (B♭) followed by choral arrangement for the Hit Paraders (F). A truncated half-chorus (C) ends the arrangement.
May 13, 1944	Number One	First vocal chorus (E♭) for unnamed male singer, with choral background from Hit Paraders. An instrumental interlude sets up truncated second chorus (E♭) for the same unnamed vocalist.
May 20, 1944	Number One	Similar to previous week's arrangement, but with a new instrumental introduction, and no choral background. First vocal chorus and truncated second chorus (E♭) are sung by Frank Sinatra.
June 10, 1944	Number One	New arrangement. First and only chorus (C) for Joan Edwards with background choral singing from the Hit Paraders. Second half reharmonizes the chord progression.
June 17, 1944	Number One	Arrangement from May 20, 1944, featuring Frank Sinatra, is reused.
July 8, 1944	Number Three	Based on the arrangement of May 6, 1944, but with the first instrumental chorus (B♭) excised.

and homogeneous context of *Your Hit Parade*, it still participated in a culture of fairly permissive musical replication. While replication of lyrics and melodies tend to remain quite narrowly fixed, arrangers would often devise novel harmonizations. The three arrangements of "Long Ago and Far Away" all harmonize the tune in quite different ways. Rearrangement reflects a larger set of norms about music on the radio in this period, namely, that popular songs were often altered and tailored to suit the performers. Second, the very fact that the music on the show was performed, not reproduced from a recording, speaks to the limited role of phonography on network radio during the era of the standard.

To follow on the latter point, *Your Hit Parade* began in the era when programs on network radio generally avoided broadcasting commercial phonograph records. Unlike the pattern that would emerge by the 1950s, where record labels would send promotional copies of records to radio stations and cultivate close relationships with disc jockeys to promote new products, in the initial decades of network radio there was a clear separation between broadcasting live performances and broadcasting commercially available recordings or "electrical transcriptions," that is, discs made specifically for radio play. This may come as a surprise to anyone raised on radio after the 1950s, where commercial stations typically follow designated formats (e.g., classic rock, country, adult contemporary, urban, etc.) and confine themselves to highly specific, narrow playlists. However, the reasons for separating radio and phonography were many. I will address those reasons first, before considering how this practice contributed to the "soundscape of standards."

***

Attitudes about the use of phonographs on the radio were shaped by four factors: government regulation, internal network radio policy, record companies, and the musicians union.

Government regulation. The US government began its formal involvement with radio with through the passage of the Radio Act of 1912 and with the significant role that radio played in naval and maritime matters before and during World War I. Throughout most of the 1910s the government shared the airwaves with private companies, like American Marconi, and with civilian operators (or "amateurs"). As radio made the transition from wireless telegraphy, the sending of messages in Morse code, to wireless telephony, or the sending of voice and music over the airwaves, small commercial stations began to appear, such as: KDKA in Pittsburgh, associated with Westinghouse; WEAF in New York, associated with AT&T; and various stations sponsored by department stores.[5] Beginning in the early 1920s the government began to seize more control over the airwaves by drawing sharper distinctions between amateur and commercial stations. One reason was due to interference, caused by the rise in the number of stations competing for space on the radio spectrum and the limited bandwidth of available frequencies on which to transmit. The government also had concerns about the use of phonograph records over the air. In January 1922, a rule was issued that disallowed amateur stations to "broadcast weather, reports, music, concerts, speeches, news or other similar information or entertainment."[6] In memoranda on this rule, David B. Carson, commissioner at the Bureau of Navigation—the bureau overseeing the Radio Act of 1912—commented that "a number of amateur stations and other stations were beginning to broadcast phonograph records which had no real value as entertainment or instruction and which threatened to seriously interfere with the higher classes of service."[7] He argued that the rule did not diminish recognition of the important service provided by amateur radio operators, but rather was intended "to stop broadcasting by amateurs of phonograph records, which are not enjoyed by the public but at times becomes annoying."[8] By the end of 1922, the federal government began to enforce such distinctions through the creation of two classes of radio license. Class A stations could continue to transmit at a shorter wavelength (360 meters), while Class B stations—those who could meet more demanding technical and programming requirements only available to the non-amateur radio station—would get a better slice of the airwaves on a longer wavelength (400 meters). The rules for a Class B license specified that "the use of mechanically operated instruments is prohibited." Not only did the act of licensing draw a sharp distinction over what each class of station could broadcast, it also divided up the radio frequency spectrum like a parcel of property, confining amateurs to a small portion.[9] While live performance of music on the radio might fall under the government's rubric of information or entertainment, phonograph records were below the line. They were a sonic nuisance, something that cluttered up the airwaves—in other words, noise. The best way to abate the noise was to confine it to a small part of the spectrum. Class B stations would soon make up the various nodes of the larger radio networks. Moreover, many stations seeking the Class B license already relied on live talent. The new ruling made sure that they kept doing so and "stopped playing records altogether."[10]

Over the course of the 1920s, as the population of amateur radio operators dwindled and more high-powered experimental and commercial stations took over the airwaves, the government's regulation enforcement of the Class A and Class B distinctions became more relaxed. However, its basic attitude toward broadcasting recordings remained negative. The passage of the Radio Act of 1927 created the Federal Radio Commission (or FRC, which later became the present-day Federal Communications Commission, or FCC) as a body to oversee the rules and regulations by which all broadcasters had to comply. The Radio Act of 1927, unlike the 1922 rule, was silent on the use of phonographs on the radio, but the issue was studied by the commission not long after its creation. In the view of the FRC, the purpose of radio was to supply original programs that would entertain or inform the public, not duplicate services already available in another form. In a report from August 23, 1928, the commission noted that "the public in large cities can easily purchase and use phonograph records of the ordinary commercial type," and thus a radio station that devotes the majority of its programming to broadcasting such records "is not giving the public anything which it cannot readily have without such a station." To grant such a station a license would not ultimately be in the public's interest. Moreover, if the station were to be in a city where there "are large resources in program material"—that is, if other kinds of programming were available that did not rely on the phonograph such as live music, news, drama, or educational shows—then to grant this station a license means "that some other station is being kept out of existence which might put to use such original program material." At the same time, the commission realized that in smaller, rural communities, with less "program material" at hand, phonographs and transcribed programs might be necessary to keep such stations on the air. Taking a pragmatic approach, the commission wrote, "Without placing the stamp of approval on the use of phonograph records under such circumstances, the commission will not go so far at present as to state that the practice is at all times and under all conditions a violation." Reasserting its watchful eye over the airwaves, the commission also noted that it would "not close its eyes" to the real purpose of the use of phonograph records in most communities, which was "to provide a cheaper method of advertising for advertisers who are thereby saved the expense of providing an original program."[11]

The FRC also worried that mechanical reproduction might dupe the public into thinking it was hearing a live speaker or performer: "While the broadcasting of music performed through the agency of mechanical reproductions, such as records or perforated rolls, is not in itself objectionable, the failure clearly to announce the nature of such broadcasting is in some instance working what is in effect a fraud upon the listening public."[12] Where phonography had once been chastised as a nuisance, a source of unwanted noise on the airwaves, now it was being characterized as deceitful. A phonograph might be played in lieu of the genuine artifact and the public might be none the wiser. To safeguard against potential deception, in the late 1920s the FRC regulated that broadcasters must announce when they are using any and all "mechanical reproductions," whether music or speech. Many stations had been using phonographic music and "electrical transcription" discs of popular shows intended for radio broadcast and syndication, such as *Amos 'n' Andy*, as part of their regular programming. In the face of the new regulations, broadcasters lobbied the FRC into changing and clarifying its orders. While the broadcast of records would have to be preceded with a description such as "This is a talking machine record," or "This is a phonograph record," transcriptions discs were to be preceded by a different statement: "This program is an electrical transcription made exclusively for broadcast purposes."[13] Over the next two decades the rules for broadcasting mechanically reproduced music remained in place with minor alterations and concessions. In the 1940s through the mid-1950s, announcements were only required at the beginnings and ends of programs and need not precede each use of a recording. The exact form of the identifying announcement was no longer specified, so long as it was clear to the public and employed terms commonly used and understood. In no case could a broadcaster "create the impression that any program being broadcast by mechanical reproduction consists of live talent."[14]

Internal policies at the networks. Within the large radio networks such as NBC and CBS, attitudes about broadcasting commercial phonograph records were often in line with the government. Network executives held the belief that live programming was superior to pre-recorded transcriptions and recordings. The value created by live programming was used to justify the hefty price tag sponsors paid for network airtime. It also justified the expense required to lease the telephone lines that linked various affiliates into a network. Why bother with the cost of "chain broadcasting" if it was going to be used simply to play phonograph records? While the local independent stations could make easy money selling time to advertisers by using phonograph records as a cheap alternative to costly programming, local network affiliate stations could claim to participate in the quality and prestige of the network and its original programming. By keeping phonograph records off the air, networks possessed an audible sign of cultural distinction, where the difference between live and "canned" music was a sonic index of the difference between affiliates and local stations. However, electrical transcriptions—recordings of music and programming made specifically for broadcast—were often of high quality, so much so that listeners could not always tell the difference. This worry motivated the government's rules about "announcing" mechanical reproductions on the air. Producers of electrical transcriptions also used a similar rhetoric of distinction when selling programs to local stations. Transcription disc producers sold libraries of well-recorded, royalty-free music designed especially for broadcast, which could be used to keep competing, lower-quality phonograph recordings off the air. While NBC and CBS generally viewed records and transcriptions similarly, keeping them both off the air, other networks, such as Mutual, were not as strict.[15] On local stations, transcription discs and phonographs were used regularly, helping to fill out the broadcast day and cultivate listeners.

Record companies. Throughout the 1930s and 1940s, record companies also supported the policies of the networks. Strange as it may seem in retrospect, record companies considered radio as competition in the marketplace. (This was the case *even* when the same company owned both radio stations and recording companies, like RCA's ownership of both NBC and Victor records.) The record companies received royalties only on the sale of their records, not from their broadcast. From their perspective, they were giving away free programming to radio stations. Additionally, the Great Depression initiated a worldwide slump in record sales, at the same time that radio's popularity grew sharply. In that respect, the attitude of the record companies is understandable. They worried that audiences would not purchase records that could be heard on the radio for free. Moreover, popular recordings could be overexposed on the radio. The music publishing industry expressed concerns that such overexposure was helping to drastically shorten the sales life of hit songs. Recordings broadcast on the air were thought to compete with, and cheapen, the value of a performer's live appearances on radio and in real life. Popular artists would get paid for live appearances, and major personalities could command quite large sums. When performers were scheduled to appear live on a radio program or at a local venue, smaller stations were known to counter these appearances with programs of the artist's records. Not only did the small stations avoid having to pay, listeners could tune in for free and avoid the hassle of going out.[16] Beginning in late 1932, many record companies began to print the phrase "Not Licensed for Radio Broadcast" on the center label of their discs.[17] The strategy was designed to counter radio's "unfair practice," although it was not established that the record companies had the legal basis to assert this right. This initiated almost a decade of lawsuits to determine if the record companies or recording artists did indeed possess the right to restrict the broadcast of their records over the air, of if broadcasters, as lawful purchasers of the records, could enjoy the right to broadcast them at their choosing. An appellate court decision from July 1940 put the issue to rest: the record companies could not restrict the use of their products beyond its point of sale.[18]

The Musicians' Union. The musicians' union, and various organizations representing performers, also put pressure on the networks to keep phonographs off the airwaves and support the work of live musicians. The American Federation of Musicians (AFM) vigorously fought against the use of recordings on the radio throughout the 1930s. They lobbied the FRC to make sure that when records were played, they were announced as such and would not be used to dupe the public. They were also strong advocates for labeling phonograph records for "home use only" and supported many of the legal challenges that tried to enforce the rights of musicians to restrict the broadcast of their records. In 1937 the AFM proposed radio strikes and recording bans in order to force radio stations to either hire union musicians or keep specific numbers of musicians on the payroll.[19] The union's threats were multipronged. The networks already employed union musicians, and the threat of a strike could halt their programming (and thus their advertising revenue) as well as damage their reputation with the government and its regulators, who were seen by the networks as being supportive of labor.[20] The independent stations, which relied heavily on records and transcribed programs, did not want to be forced to hire musicians beyond what they could afford. After months of negotiations an agreement was reached between the parties. Small stations, whose average income was less than $20,000 per year, were exempt from the obligation to hire live musicians, but the networks and larger independents agreed to hire union musicians based on a percentage of their sales.[21] The agreement held until 1940 but began to unravel during its renegotiation. In addition, the Department of Justice began to look askance at the AFM's dealings and threatened to sue the union for restraint of trade.[22] Under the new leadership of James Caesar Petrillo, the strategy of the AFM shifted. Given the appellate court decision that guaranteed broadcasters free rein to play recordings on the air, the union set its sights on shutting down the supply of new records by threatening to strike, effectively creating a national recording ban. Beginning in August 1942, the AFM struck, and maintained the ban for just over two years. With a few exceptions, all recording with union musicians stopped other than for the production of V-discs, special phonograph records made for the Armed Forces Radio Service. By supporting the production of V-discs, the union could portray themselves as patriotic in their support of the war effort while resisting exploitation by radio corporations and record companies. The only sources of new discs were choral or "a cappella" recordings, since vocalists were not part of the union. In the weeks leading up to the ban, some record companies booked their studios to capacity in an effort to stockpile a cache of new recordings and weather the ban. However, as the strike lingered on individual record companies began to negotiate one by one. Decca, whose primary market was jukeboxes, was the first to settle in September 1943, followed soon after by Capitol Records. Decca and Capitol, unlike Columbia and Victor, had no specific connection to a radio network and could not sustain themselves without being able to bring new products to the market. In addition to agreeing to improvements in working conditions and pay, the record companies agreed to pay a royalty to the union on each record sold which would, in turn, be distributed back to their members through a Performance Trust Fund.

In sum, "The broadcasting of phonograph records seemed to please no one but the broadcasters who did it and the listeners who tuned in," writes media historian Michael Biel. "The networks, the quality broadcasters, the musicians' union, and the transcription producers were all against it; the federal government's edicts against *all* recordings were originally stimulated because of it, and even the record companies and the recording artists opposed it."[23] The combination of these factors contributed to the overall soundscape of network radio in its initial decades. In particular, network radio, with the various factors that helped keep phonograph discs off the airwaves, helped to forge a public association of the sound of popular music with the sound of live performance. We might say that network radio, before the rise of the disc jockey, helped to forge a soundscape of standards where songs were expected to circulate predominantly in live performance. Where there was live performance, there was also a need for arrangers. Singers of popular song required arrangements suited to their vocal range, and different network programs used different-sized bands, orchestras, or ensembles—each with their own specific sound and style. Popular songs were constantly being adapted to specific performers and performance situations. The instrumental forces might be anything from a studio orchestra, to a big band, to smaller mixed ensembles, or even to electric organ and violin, to name just one of radio's unusual instrumental combinations. A listener of popular song over the radio would have expected performances of songs to carry along with them distinct arrangements. Although there were also hit records that facilitated listeners' associations of a song with a particular recording, radio's manner of circulating songs would promote expectations for any hit song to be re-performed by others in ways that may not reference any previous recording.

The Popular Music Industry

The combination of these various negative attitudes toward phonography on the radio—those displayed by the government, networks, record companies, and the musicians' union—contributed to what I am calling the "soundscape of standards." The denigration of phonography was one important condition in the construction of a sonic field in which popular songs were typically heard as live performances or as performances that could only be heard on the radio, like those recorded specifically for broadcast via electrical transcriptions. Of course, radio did not constitute the only medium that contributed to this soundscape. Phonograph discs (heard at home or on the jukebox), sheet music, and other forms of mechanically reproduced music (such as player pianos) also contributed to the "soundscape of standards." Yet it is hard to overestimate the significance of radio in this era for constituting a popular or national musical soundscape. After the formation of the networks in the late 1920s and the subsequent boom in home receiver sales, radio was transformed from a medium of amateur, military, and maritime communications into a mass medium on a scale heretofore unseen. Pollster Elmo Roper estimated that in 1940 *Your Hit Parade* reached nearly 46 million listeners per month—about half of the potential radio audience. The population of the United States was only 132 million in 1940, which meant that *Your Hit Parade* was heard by about one third of the entire population monthly. While only a handful of programs possessed the enormous audience share of *Your Hit Parade*, radio chained together geographically dispersed stations into a web where performers of popular music could reach, potentially, tens of millions of listeners with a single performance. The music publishing industry quickly came to understand the powerful role of radio, and of radio personalities and popular bandleaders, in making a song into a "hit." In response to radio, they developed a particular model for the exposure, promotion, and exploitation of new songs. This model helped create the phenomenon where different arrangements and performances of one and the same song follow in close succession.

In his study of the "Popular Music Industry" from 1941, Duncan MacDougald Jr., working at the Princeton Radio Research Project, detailed the various stages involved in the exploitation of a popular song.[24] In the first stage, songs submitted to one of the prominent publishing houses are evaluated by various executives, managers, and other hit makers. Only a very small number of songs submitted to publishers eventually make it to market. If a song received a favorable response, promotion would begin through an initial campaign for ten to fifteen weeks. Piano-vocal scores of the song were arranged, printed, and sent to important figures on the publisher's mailing list, including: program and musical directors at radio stations around the nation, directors at advertising agencies that sponsored radio programs, singers and performers, and record companies and manufacturers of transcribed musical programs and libraries. In some cases, arrangements and stock orchestrations (or "orks" for short) would be produced and sent to the leading dance orchestras and big bands in the country, especially those with "name recognition" and a penchant for performing new material.

In stage two, which lasted about a month or two, song pluggers would "work on" the song by securing bandleaders, singers, and radio program managers to perform (or "plug") their song on radio shows both local and national. MacDougald describes song pluggers as "hardy, indefatigable, insistent and relentless individuals whose sole mission in life is to persuade, wheedle, cajole and implore band leaders and singers to 'do' their song."[25] Getting a name band or famous singer to plug a song could help to make it a "hit," and the potential economic windfall that followed motivated the whole process. In the Swing Era, where big bands dominated the soundscape, song pluggers used whatever means possible to get plugs. Song pluggers "wooed bandleaders with varied gifts as liquor, theater and baseball tickets, clothes, women, jewelry, resort vacations, musical arrangements for their band and just plain money."[26] While some leaders accepted these gifts, others resisted. The pressures placed on song pluggers to get plugs and make hits shaped their relationships with bandleaders, which could vary from the respectful to the badgering, and from honest to sycophantic. Bandleaders were not blameless either. Some enjoyed the outsized attention they received and could often demand excessive favors in exchange for performance, or even the mere consideration, of a tune.[27] Due to the song plugger's "relentless persecution of performers," MacDougald notes that "there has naturally come to be a feeling of hostility and resentment," toward the entire system.[28]

As the song is being "introduced to the nation," it might receive "fifteen to forty radio performances a week" over the major networks, being heard "three to eight times nightly ... coast-to-coast."[29] Publishers understood that the audience reaction to a new song was typically negative until the song had been sufficiently repeated. Bandleaders were often hesitant to accept a song unless it had a "head start," taking on new material only if the publisher could guarantee that it would be extensively promoted or had tie-ups with other parts of the culture industry (such as Hollywood or the record business).[30] Yet the possibility of getting in on the ground floor and being known as the "introducer" of a successful song had its benefits. Sometimes bandleaders would cut deals with the publishing houses to have their picture featured on the cover of its published sheet music along with a phrase such as "Introduced and Featured by ...". Publishers, looking to hedge their bets, might cut similar deals with multiple bandleaders, so that the covers of identical pieces of sheet music may feature different performers. These might be specifically designed to target distinct geographical regions or demographic populations. Sometimes the reason was more haphazard, where the picture would simply be changed after a certain number of copies were printed. "This accounts for the unusual fact that pictures of obscure orchestra leaders are featured as 'introducers' of big hits," even when their "part in popularizing them is a very negligible one."[31] In other cases, the publisher might agree to give a performer an "exclusive performance" right whereby they can introduce a song for a limited period of time. By recording the song and plugging it as frequently as possible on the radio, the performer tries to become closely identified with the song's success, thereby gaining higher visibility in the marketplace and creating demand for their recordings and performances.

If the song seemed to be getting favorable reception at the end of stage two, the publishers would then begin a third stage aimed at getting the song to the top of the charts. An important part of this process involved securing radio "plugs," or targeted performances of the song on the radio. Since many of the popular music charts published in industry magazines like *Billboard* or *Variety* tabulated radio "plugs," publishers and song pluggers concentrated on getting as many plugs as possible in the span of a week. This became known as "drive week." In addition to plugs on sponsored network programs, publishers would also secure performances by bands performing "remotes."

These were fifteen-minute or thirty-minute live performances from clubs, hotels, ballrooms, restaurants, or military bases, broadcast over the networks and their affiliate stations. Remotes typically appeared after evening programming was done, around eleven o'clock in the evening. Sustained by the networks or their affiliates and free of sponsors, remotes were an important part of the soundscape of popular music, where musicians could often perform without the time constraints of three-minute recordings or tightly organized variety programs. Plugs on remotes, especially those broadcast on powerful stations in cities like New York, Chicago, and Los Angeles, were tallied up alongside prime time plugs and presented on weekly charts or "sheets." If the drive week was successful, the song would break into the top ten or fifteen. Once it started appearing the charts, it might also appear on a show like *Your Hit Parade*, whose massive audience share would further expose the song and generate sales and demand. While ostensibly presenting the popular songs in the nation, *Your Hit Parade* also played an important role in influencing the very ecosystem of popular song that it was supposed to be registering. Advertisers who sponsored radio programming would rely on the charts and sheets to determine which musical selections were the most popular with their audience and would often reject anything that was not on "the hit parade." The whole system fed on itself. "Once a song is high up in the plug lists," MacDougald writes, "its 'popularity' is increased as it is played more and more on commercial programs—solely because it is a leader on the sheet." Plugging would then begin to taper off over the next few weeks as the music houses began to turn their attention to other songs ready for promotion.

If "drive week" was a success, record companies would get in on the action. Numerous labels might record competing versions of hit songs, designed to appeal to different demographics, regions, and musical tastes. The arrangements on each recording would differ—sometimes a little, sometimes quite a lot—depending on the signature sound of the performer and the intended audience. The strategy of the record companies depended on a provision that first appeared in the Copyright Act of 1909. The law granted to the copyright holder of a musical work the right to allow a company or firm to make an initial mechanical reproduction of their work for sale—which, at the time of the Copyright Act, meant a recording or piano roll. It also guaranteed the copyright holder a small royalty payment for every copy of the work made. This is known as the "mechanical right." The provision stated that once the copyright holder had granted permission for an initial mechanical reproduction of their work to be sold, any other firm or company could manufacture and sell its own versions of the work for mechanical reproduction so long as they too paid the royalty. This is known as "compulsory license," which requires the copyright holder of a musical work to license their material to others, after the first recording is sold. The law had broad implications for the replication of popular music. Historian David Suisman notes that compulsory license "is the legal basis for 'cover' songs: once a composition is recorded, it is fair game for anyone else at the same rate. The composer still received the royalty, but after the first sale, he or she had no control over who made subsequent reproductions."[32]

Once a song made its way to drive week and began to garner attention on the charts, numerous record companies might opt to produce versions of the song. These various recordings would then be tracked on charts that measured record sales, nationally and regionally, or which tabulated which records were generating the most "coin" in jukeboxes. What this meant, in terms of the soundscape, was that it was a common phenomenon for multiple recordings of a song to be on the charts simultaneously. For example, the April 29, 1944 issue of *Billboard* lists Guy Lombardo's recording of "It's Love-Love-Love" (recorded for Decca) as the top-selling record in the nation for the second week in a row. A competing recording of the song, by the King Sisters for Bluebird, was a new arrival at number nine. Cole Porter's "I Love You" was in the second spot (in a recording by Bing Crosby for Decca) as well as in the eighth spot (in a recording by Jo Stafford for Capitol). The regional differences are also telling. Where Crosby's recording was on top in the East and Midwest, it did not even break the top ten on the West Coast charts; rather, Jo Stafford's recording was number one. In the South, Lombardo was on top, but only number eight in the Midwest, behind the King Sisters' recording at number two. The jukeboxes told a different story: Bing Crosby's recording of *San Fernando Valley* and Jimmy Dorsey's "Besame Mucho" both on Decca were on top, and nudged out Lombardo at number 3; the King Sisters' recording was number eight, Crosby's "I Love You" was number nine, and Jo Stafford's disc did not crack the top twenty.

The differences on the various charts are often hard to interpret. In one respect, they represent the regional differences in musical taste at the time. At the same time, they also represent the relationship between record companies and the various markets where they sold their wares. (Decca, e.g., had a very strong hold on the jukebox market.) They also reflect how the record companies, and the music industry magazines that tracked sales, marketed their music along racially segregated lines. Beginning in the 1920s, record companies started marketing "race records" to Black audiences. These records featured jazz, blues, and boogie-woogie, mostly performed by Black musicians. Today, these race records are considered some of the most important documents we have of the development of Black music in the United States, with a roster of performers such as Louis Armstrong, Bessie Smith, and Fletcher Henderson, among others. But at the time they were designed for quick consumption and advertised with racially stereotyped imagery. The marketing of these recordings along racially segregated lines was sustained by record companies for decades after the designation "race record" had fallen out of favor, and it was reflected in the segregated charts of a magazine like *Billboard*. In the April 29, 1944, issue discussed above, the so-called Harlem Hit Parade—*Billboard*'s euphemism for tracking the sales of recordings marketed to Black audiences—lists an entirely different set of recordings: the King Cole Trio's Capitol recording of "Straighten Up and Fly Right" is in the top slot, followed by Duke Ellington's Victor recording of "Main Stem."

Given all these various ways that the popularity of a song was being measured, the task of *Your Hit Parade* to present the most popular songs in the nation was not trivial. How exactly should one determine which songs are hits given their multiple forms of mediation? How should one rate the importance of various media against one another? Should a radio plug count for more than a jukebox play, or the sale of a phonograph disc more than a piece of sheet music? If so, should a plug on a network in prime time, or on a station in a populous market, count for more than a plug on a smaller-wattage local station? Unlike the trade publications, which divided up the various media and markets to track them separately, *Your Hit Parade* emphasized that its tabulations balanced many distinct categories, "accurately and authentically."[33] Between the trade journals and *Your Hit Parade*, there were often notable differences. Such discrepancies were matters of concern to music publishers and organizations such as ASCAP, and gripes and suspicions of unfair play were aired in the music industry publications, like *Billboard* and *Metronome*. Moreover, *Your Hit Parade* did not just tally and track the popular hits—as the trade publications did—but given its massive audience share, an appearance of a song on the *Parade* also constituted a significant plug in itself and thus impacted the whole economy of popular song.

From the program's inception until the end of 1944, the method for tabulating the hits remained a well-kept secret. Legal action by song publishers against *Your Hit Parade* led to the release of an affidavit by the

American Tobacco Company, the *Parade*'s longtime sponsor, that detailed the survey's method of tabulation. Five factors were considered: (1) the retail and wholesale sale of sheet music; (2) number of radio plugs, subdivided into plugs (a) on the networks and (b) on local stations; (3) retail and wholesale record sales; (4) number of plays on jukeboxes and other coin-operated phonographs; and (5) requests made to various leading bands and orchestras throughout the country. The affidavit described in some detail which organizations were used to gather the data for each category. For instance, sheet music sales were tracked via a list of wholesale sales published by Music Corporation of America, a similar list published by the Supreme Music & Orchestra Service, reports from various retail sheet music stores across the country, and *Billboard* magazine's tabulations of sheet music sales. Requests were tallied based on "weekly information from sixty different orchestra leaders in all sections of the country" who rated their requests in numerical order. Yet, given the frequent tie-ups between bandleaders and the publishing industry, one has to wonder about the reliability of these compiled lists. Radio plugs presented the most complex medium to track. *Your Hit Parade* used a radio ratings service started by John Peatman, the director of the Office of Radio Research at City College of New York. Peatman's service had its own complex formulas for weighing the value of radio plugs in relation to their appearance on a network versus a local station, the wattage of the station, and the size of the potential audience it might reach. Given that the Peatman service drew its numbers from tracking the networks and stations primarily on the East Coast, *Your Hit Parade* also received reports from twelve stations in the Midwest and on the West Coast. While the affidavit opened up *Your Hit Parade*'s methods of tabulation to public scrutiny, it did not contain an exact formula for the ways that the five factors were weighed and combined.[34]

However, the complex methods for tabulating rankings on *Your Hit Parade* reveal the amount of labor required to pack into a neat and tidy list of the week's "hits" what was, in fact, an unruly collection of performances, recordings, scores, and requests. To unpack the various factors that were involved in the production of the list is to be attentive to the complex, variously mediated ways that popular music circulated. Those factors included: (1) the proscription against phonography on the radio, which encouraged a culture of live performance and the manufacture of electrical transcriptions designed for radio, with all of their various arrangements; (2) the phenomenon of "song plugging" and the way that it would encourage the repetition of a song in different performances in close temporal succession; and (3) the record industry and their competitive promotion of multiple recorded versions of one and the same song. Taken together, these factors contributed to a soundscape of popular music quite distinct from the one that we currently inhabit. What I have been calling the "soundscape of standards" is a soundscape where any individual song would have been heard by listeners across various media (radio, phonography, sheet music) in quite distinct and differing performances. The specific properties of the song might be quite different from version to version. Listeners would not necessarily have associated a hit song of the day with one specific top-selling phonograph record, with one specific performer, or with one specific arrangement. Rather, there were many different possible performances by which a listener might encounter and re-encounter a song, and they might hear many different versions of that song in very close succession.

This raises some challenging questions about what we mean by a "song" in this period, and the ways that listeners might have considered that question. Beyond the factors that constituted the soundscape, how did the experience of the soundscape impact and affect listeners? What did listeners hear in it? How did this shape their understanding of the ontology of popular song?

Listeners

One answer to these questions focuses on the industrial aims of the popular music business and its alleged promotion of forms of passive consumption. MacDougald's conclusion in the "Popular Music Industry" is that the procedures for making a hit song were "largely borrowed from those being used by any industry producing consumer goods which do not strictly belong to the necessities of life. The promotion and distribution of popular songs is not left to chance nor to the spontaneous success or failure of the material offered in the market. What makes this process so similar to the industrial one is its highly developed 'system,' all of whose parts are directed toward one end: the enforcement of the material on the consumer."[35] While MacDougald offers a detailed look into the specifics of "song plugging" on the radio, the industrial aspects of the production of popular music had been common knowledge to insiders of the popular music business for quite a long time.[36] What made radio different was its scale and the psychological effect it had on the public. The "whole plugging mechanism" led to a single result: "The public at large—more specifically the radio audience—has been led more and more to the point of merely accepting these songs as standardized (musical) products, with less and less active resentment and critical interest." The passive consumption of music, where the consumer has little to no choice in the music they consume, is actively pursued by the music industry. Consequently, passive consumption also has an impact on the listener's taste and ability to make aesthetic evaluations. "While the accepted songs are being incessantly hammered into listeners' heads, the prestige build-up strives to make the audiences believe that this constant repetition is due to the inherent qualities of the song, rather than to the will to sell it." In the end, "controlled repetition and manipulated recommendation" tend to the "standardization of tastes" and their "subsequent gradual eradication."[37]

If MacDougald's conclusions about the popular music industry seem eerily similar to those written about the "culture industry" by Theodor Adorno just a few years later, there is a good reason why. Adorno was MacDougald's supervisor at the Princeton Radio Research Project and played an important role in shaping the essay's form and content.[38] Published in Paul Lazarsfeld's edited collection *Radio Research 1941*, "The Popular Music Industry" immediately precedes Adorno's analysis of "The Radio Symphony." The latter traces how the conditions under which the symphony is experienced over the radio encourage listeners to fetishize its various parts, encouraging listeners to focus on its hummable themes or unusual timbres rather than understanding how the themes are developed and dialectically related to the whole, or how the specifics of orchestration might contribute to the overall content of the symphony. Taken together, the two essays divide up the field of radio music into "serious music" and "light music"—the categories used in the 1940s to describe the difference between so-called classical music and popular music—in order to show how radio music leads toward a "regression in listening," to borrow Adorno's famous titular phrase. On the serious side, new forms of musical mediation, like network radio, liquidate the holism of the symphony into fetishized and atomized pieces; on the light side, popular music, designed for the radio from its inception, offers the near-endless repetition of standardized musical structures, whose very repetition and "popularity" dupes listeners into believing in the song's quality and uniqueness.

Adorno and MacDougald's views concerning music on the radio imply a very particular understanding of the relationship between a musical work and aesthetic judgment. Both assume that listeners should be listening for, and evaluating, the properties of musical works, not properties of its performance per se. The quality of a work depends, on this view, on the properties that inhere in the musical work itself—in its properties of internal organization, thematic development, the relationship of the parts to the whole, and so forth. However, in a soundscape where a song circulates across a variety of media, in many distinct performances and arrangements, there may not be objectively fixed musical properties to evaluate in the first place. How could a thin work, like the standards described the first part of the book, possess the kinds of properties that Adorno and MacDougald want them to bear? Their criticism of popular music and its effects on the capacities of the listener are predicated on a musical culture that esteems thick musical works, one that values the work over its performance insofar as the work is the primary object of aesthetic attention.

And yet, Adorno and MacDougald are not incorrect when they describe the kinds of musical properties that are the main object of attention for listeners to popular music on the radio at the dawn of the 1940s. However, there is a crucial difference. Rather than assume that consumers of popular music are ideologically duped, many listeners were not laboring under false consciousness about what they were listening to, what they were listening for, and where their musical values lay. The composer and arranger Johnny Mandel describes his experience of listening to the radio at night—likely listening to "remotes"—and hearing different performances of one and the same song in close succession:

> Lying in bed after lights-out, I was glued to the radio, as most kids were then. . . . Every band—from Goodman to Dorsey on down—was broadcasting, and the publishers were constantly forcing songs on them. The whole idea was to get your song played on the radio. And the band's idea—especially if it was a struggling band—was to be heard more and more, so that when they went out on the road, they'd be able to get higher prices at better ballrooms. I'd hear these different bands playing the same songs. . . . I would think to myself, "What's so great about this song that's supposed to be so popular? I think it's mediocre." Then another band would play the same damned thing, because everybody is restricted to those songs on the *Hit Parade*, and it would sound wonderful. And then another band would come on a half hour later, and that song would sound dreadful. At one point, a lightbulb went on over my head. I said, "Wait a minute. It's not about the song at all, but about the way the band plays it."[39]

Mandel is aware that he is listening to different performances of one and the same song, and that the song as such is not the main focus of attention or value. He is listening is a comparative way to the arrangement, the performance, or the "way the band plays it." His comments about how song plugging constrains the repertoire evince an awareness of the functioning of the popular music industry, and not a false belief that the song's repetition is an inherent marker of its quality. Quality, for Mandel, lies in the performance and not the work. To put it in the terms previously employed, Mandel is listening for properties that are not specifically work-determinative—since, in the end, those might be quite thin and banal—but to those that differentiate performances from one another, while encouraging comparison. From Adorno or MacDougald's perspective, bound to a traditional ontology of musical works, Mandel appears as a "regressive listener." From another perspective, bound to a network-based ontology of musical works, Mandel's listening is appropriate, even exemplary. He represents a different way of considering what listeners might be hearing in the soundscape of standards. If the "passive listener" is inattentive to work-determinative properties, Mandel offers reasons why they might not care about these properties, or why an attachment to the musical work may be misplaced. In the context of the soundscape of standards, focusing too closely on properties of the musical work occludes a more tacit understanding of the ontology of song. Any specific song was heard within a network of ever-differing and ever-competing performances, recordings, arrangements, and scores. Consequently, aesthetic judgment was not primarily concerned with the song itself, but with its various arrangements, performances, and recordings. Even if listeners to popular music in the 1930s and 1940s did not engage in explicit debates about the "ontology of song," their acts of listening, their attitudes and disposition, and the knowledge disclosed in those acts and dispositions evince tacit assertions about musical ontology. Such assertions are entailed in a statement like: "It's not about the song at all, but about the way the band plays it."

The mode of listening exhibited by Mandel—the other side of "regressive listening"—is also exhibited, surprisingly, by MacDougald himself. In his discussion of the role of the arranger in popular music, MacDougald observes that "An interesting aspect of the role of the arranger in the success of popular songs is found in the importance that little known orchestras throughout the country attach to the orchestrations of the leading arrangers." Some songs are selected simply because they have been skillfully arranged. "In such cases the song itself loses all identity as a song, being de-individualized to the final degree. The actual *song* means nothing; the arrangement everything, and *any* of the endless Tin Pan Alley products would serve the same purpose." This claim relies on positing the *song itself* against its arrangement, alongside the belief that arrangements are objects of lesser aesthetic value. As the arrangement rises in significance, the *song itself* disappears from view. If the song itself is the proper object of aesthetic judgment, then its de-individualization or liquidation would mean the eradication of such judgment altogether. While Adorno might make such an argument—that arrangement, as a culinary and fetishistic way of dressing up standardized music, destroys whatever truth-content the genuine musical work might possess—MacDougald hesitates, and for good reason. Against the thrust of his own argument, he notes that "distinctive arrangements play a far greater part in the success of hits than is generally realized. Special mention must be made of the brilliant orchestrations of Duke Ellington, Fletcher Henderson and Benny Carter, who are among the most talented musicians in the entire field of 'light music,' and who are musically far superior to most Tin Pan Alley 'composers.' Accordingly their arrangements should be considered among the most important accomplishments of popular music."[40] At a moment like this, MacDougald begins to sound a lot less like Theodor Adorno and a lot more like Johnny Mandel.

***

Mandel and MacDougald, in affirming the value found on the other side of "regressive listening," are also asserting an alternative ontology where the "work," as traditionally conceived, means little. It is simply not what the music is "about." Performance, rather than the composition or the score, plays a determining role in this alternative ontology. Moreover, the alternative ontology goes against the legal ontology written into copyright law, which at the time of the Copyright Act of 1909 defined musical works in terms that did not consider the creative and intellectual contributions of the performance. Although the Copyright Act helped to institute "mechanical rights" and "compulsory license," and thus unwittingly contributed to the promotion of the soundscape of standards, the concept of the musical work inscribed in copyright law made the composer's creative and intellectual product, presented and published in the form of a score, the central object to be protected. The notion that a musical work might emerge in relation to a network of its performances implies an ontology of musical works that runs counter to the law.

In the 1930s, performers of popular music began to push back against the Copyright Act. A group of popular bandleaders and singers formed the National Association of Performing Artists (NAPA) to challenge the musical copyright laws and the way that it privileged—that is, compensated—the composer over the performer. Albin Zak, in *I Don't Sound Like Nobody*, described how Fred Waring, the bandleader and president of NAPA, aimed to "add to the copyright law *the Right of Interpretation*."[41] In 1935 Waring, via NAPA, initiated a suit against radio station WDAS. The station had played his records on the air, even though their center labels stated clearly: "not for radio broadcast." By playing Waring's records on the air small royalties were paid only to the composer of the songs, even though it was Waring's name and recording that was the object of public attention. Radio stations could play recordings like Waring's and make a profit by selling the time to advertisers, "trading on stars' names and their work without further compensation."[42] Two years later, the suit had made its way to the Pennsylvania Supreme Court, where the majority opinion ruled in favor of Waring. Justice Horace Stern, who wrote the opinion, tried to reconcile copyright law with the challenges of mechanical reproduction and radio broadcasting, challenges that the law was not designed to handle. His decision acknowledges the difficulties the case provoked, writing that, "The problems involved in this case have never before been presented to an American or an English court. They challenge the vaunted genius of the law to adapt itself to new social and industrial conditions and to the progress of science and invention."[43] Noting specifically the challenges to copyright law presented by the phonograph and radio broadcasting, Justice Stern related them to the context in which copyright law originated, the birth of printing. "Just as the birth of the printing press made it necessary for equity to inaugurate a protection for literary and intellectual property, so these latter-day inventions make demands upon the creative and ever-evolving energy of equity to extend that protection so as adequately to do justice under current conditions of life." Rather than hold recordings and broadcasting to the current legal standards first codified around print, Stern's ruling revisited the motivation for copyright protections in the first place—to equitably protect literary and intellectual property—and considered ways to extend it to new sound media. In his ruling, two factors predominate. First, he notes previous cases where an intellectual or artistic production that "perfects the original work or substantially adds to it in some manner" has been granted property rights. Second, he notes that great actors or musical interpreters have "definitely added something to the work of authors and composers," and this surplus is the basis for their fame and for their ability to command large fees for their work. With those two factors in mind, he reasons: "A musical composition in itself is an incomplete work; the written page evidences only one of the creative acts which are necessary for its enjoyment; it is the performer who must consummate the work by transforming it into sound. If, in so doing, he contributes by his interpretation something of novel intellectual or artistic value, he has undoubtedly participated in the creation of a product in which he is entitled to a right of property, which in no way overlaps or duplicates that of the author in the musical composition."[44]

While Waring's victory only held in the state of Pennsylvania, other cases were initiated by NAPA with the aim of challenging the Copyright Act. In a similar suit raised by Paul Whiteman against WNEW in New York, the trial judge noted that "The fact that Whiteman contributed something in addition to that which was already the subject of a copyright, the musical composition itself, cannot in any way detract from his right to protect what is his property, over and above existing property rights of the composer."[45] The implications of these rulings—in particular, the compensation it promised to performers of popular music—would have had a massive impact on the economics of music industry, had they held. But the rulings of the lower courts were reversed on appeal in 1940. In an opinion written by Justice Learned Hand, Chief Judge of the Second Circuit Court of Appeals, he ruled that the performers' claim to additional property rights ended with the sale of the record. Thus, the older standards of the Copyright Act were upheld.

Concerning Justice Stern's ruling and rationale, Zak writes: "The idea that a musical composition is an incomplete work was aesthetically startling and legally, it turned out, ahead of its time."[46] Yet the argument that I am making suggests that it the ruling was, in fact, *perfectly of its time*. Justice Stern's ideas about the creative contributions of the performer align with MacDougald's views about the significance of the arranger and Mandel's views about the virtues of musical performance. All three are "earwitnesses" to the soundscape of standards, voicing common intuitions about the relation of a performance to a musical work in the popular music of the 1930s and 1940s.[47] They are similar responses to an immersion in a particular soundscape of music, one that—as I have been trying to argue—is constituted in such a way that it produces a maximum exposure of ever-differing performances of one and the same song in close temporal succession. It is this sonic atmosphere where the creative contributions of the performer are brought to the foreground, against the background of a thin, emergent musical work.

Soundscape, Ontology, and Auditory Culture

If musical ontology is to actually reflect the function, use, and meaning of musical works in ordinary life, then we must be attentive to the way that views about the ontology of music are presumed in the cultural practices of listeners, as well as the way that the cultural practices of music making and music listening presume an ontology of music. What is challenging, even paradoxical, about this view is the idea that musical ontology is *both a cause and an effect* of an auditory culture. Establishing how this works will help clarify the relationship of auditory culture, musical ontology, and the soundscape.

First, consider the term "soundscape." R. Murray Schafer, in his foundational work on the concept, defines a soundscape as "any sonic field of study." "We may speak of a musical composition as a soundscape, or a radio program as a soundscape or an acoustic environment as a soundscape," writes Schafer.[48] Its scope and boundaries are established according to the aims of the listener or researcher and the kinds of things that they intend to study. Over the course of his own career, and in his work with the World Soundscape Project, Schafer studied urban soundscapes—like those documented in *The Vancouver Soundscape* and in the European villages examined in *Five Village Soundscapes*—as well as media soundscapes, musical soundscapes, and (most centrally) the history of the global soundscape in its relation with noise pollution. He also offered a set of guidelines and recommendations for the design of soundscapes, which he called "acoustic design," inspired by the functional design work of the Bauhaus, and others. Schafer's own work tends to overlay his environmentalist commitments and critiques of noise with analyses of soundscapes; however, many artists and scholars have productively borrowed from his ideas without prolonging Schafer's aesthetic values and social judgments. While the term "soundscape" has been challenged, I still find it to be useful in that it encourages historical analyses of a particular sonic field.[49] The sonic field of concern for my argument is that of popular music in all of its various, mediated forms—that is, the whole sonic ecosystem comprising the production and reproduction of popular music—from about 1930 until 1960. As we will see, changes in the soundscape are important markers for considering corresponding changes in musical production and in musical reception.

Next, when we speak of an auditory culture, we are speaking of a community of listeners who roughly: (1) share repertoires of listening techniques and (2) *hear in* sounds sets of shared likenesses. Regarding the former, listeners in a particular auditory culture often engage in similar ways of listening to the soundscape, employing one of many techniques, taken from a shared repertoire, for parsing and interpreting the soundscape. These repertoires are established through more or less established methods of pedagogy and instruction, or through more or less informal cultural processes that make up the bulk of the process of enculturation, such as imitating others. Regarding the latter, listeners enculturated in an auditory culture tend to hear certain sounds as being like (or unlike) other sounds in various common respects. Whitney Davis, in *A General Theory of Visual Culture*, has described how this process works within visual cultures, and the process for listening cultures is parallel.[50] Within a visual culture, common (but not necessarily identical) morphological likenesses can be seen in visual field. For example, two objects might look alike, or be shaped similarly, and so forth. However, Davis argues that not everything relevant to a visual culture will be constituted in terms of vision alone. Practices of seeing and practices of making artifacts are often recognized as analogous to non-visual practices. A building may not only morphologically resemble other visual artifacts or features within the visual field (this building *looks* grey and tall), it may also have analogical relations to non-visual aspects (this building *looks* regal, expensive, etc.). Beyond morphological likeness there is analogical likeness. The same holds for auditory cultures. Not only do listeners *hear in* the sonic field morphological resemblances to other sounds (that sounds like a flute, that is a ii-V-I, that piece is in sonata form, etc.), they *hear in* sound analogies to other practices and predicates in their culture (that saxophone sounds like its screaming, that chord progression feels as though it is floating, that theremin sounds eerie, etc.). These likenesses are formed in the context of (and recursively constitute) auditory cultures. They are woven together into a mesh or texture of practices that communities of listeners employ when they hear relevant features of the auditory field, communicate them to others, and pass them on through training. The employment of listening techniques is central to an auditory culture, since it encourages and maintains ways of hearing, both cognitively and bodily. To *hear in* sounds likenesses (both morphological and analogical) is to participate in an auditory culture through acquiring listening techniques. Of course, one should not assume that every listener in an auditory culture hears the same likenesses, for to do so would be to assume a degree of homogeneity that no culture possesses. However, enculturated listeners could negotiate such differences. The potential sharing of practices, the agreement and disagreement over what morphological and analogical likeness are apt, and the prolongation of techniques are the conditions of the possibility of such negotiations.

Finally, a musical ontology is an enumeration and description of the kinds of things that make up the production and reception of music (e.g., notes, chords, melodies, works, performances, recordings, broadcasts, and so forth). Rather than tackling all of musical ontology, my argument has been focused on the region that includes musical works, performance, recordings, and the like. My ontological inquiries are directed at the category of "songs," and in particular the smaller subcategory of "standards." Part I of the book attempts to establish some of ways of answering the question, What is a standard? The answer to that question depends on identifying the relevant properties, qualities, or features that standards possess, and delineating the ways that those properties, qualities, or features are determined. For the realist, a standard is a kind of structure, one that may be thick or thin in properties, one that may be initiated or discovered, but one that always preexists its performances and incorrigible. For the nominalist, a standard is a class of compliant scores, recordings, and performances, each of which can be "translated" into one another without losing any of its relevant properties. My answer to this question is that a standard is a corrigible set of sufficient musical properties that emerge from a network of multiple performances, recordings, and inscriptions. Yet, no matter what kind of answer we give— realist, nominalist, or emergent—ontology is a matter of ascription. It is an act of regarding a quality as belonging to some entity, as much as it is an act of regarding an entity as exhibiting some particular quality. Musical works do not appear as such; they are only phenomenalized in the acts of performance or inscription. From their phenomenal properties we make ascriptions that relate these properties to their kinds, types, objects, and so forth. Phenomena are related to their ontology through acts of ascription.

This is all quite abstract, but it can be illustrated by considering Johnny Mandel's quote for a moment. The soundscape here under consideration, our acoustic field of study, comprises, let's say, the sounds coming out of a radio late at night—a series of ballroom remotes of bands playing music. An enculturated listener to the popular music in the 1930s—one who possesses the relevant techniques—will select from the soundscape passages that share morphological likenesses. They might note two passages that sound similar to one another with respect to their chord progression and/or melody, and so forth. At the same time, passages that are morphologically similar may have very distinct analogical characters. The listener might note that, despite two passages' sounding similar in terms of their chord progression or melody, they have very different affects. One passage might sound "corny" or too "sweet," while the other will be "hot," "swinging," and so forth. Or, the same two passages might be heard differently, the first as "sentimental" or "nuanced" and the other as "exaggerated" or "exhibitionistic." When Mandel notes that he is hearing the same song played again and again, he is doing two acts at once: he is "carving up" the soundscape into a set of objects (musical passages or songs or performances, and so forth), and he is hearing in the "carved up" soundscape morphological and analogical likenesses and unlikenesses between its different parts. That means that he is hearing particular passages, melodies, lyrics, or chord progressions as being like or unlike one another with respect to many different qualities.

Listeners pick out various resemblances and likenesses from the totality of the soundscape. In picking out these likenesses, listeners also commit themselves to particular ways of dividing up the soundscape, parsing it, and lumping together its various qualities. Every listener, as a participant in an auditory culture, carries with them acquired sonic ontologies, that is, ways of dividing up the soundscape to facilitate the hearing of likenesses. While a sonic ontology frames the experience of sounds heard in the soundscape by offering ready-to-hand ways of parsing it, changes to the soundscape or novel listening experiences can elicit new ontological ascriptions that are not easily assimilated to previously acquired ontologies or listening practices. These changes might require the listener to make new accommodations. All three parts of this complex system are co-constitutive: the ever changing soundscape, the mutable experience of what is heard in the soundscape, and the soundscape's constantly re-evaluated ontology. Changes to one may effect changes to the other two. Everything in this dynamic system can function as both cause and effect.

The Culture of Permissive Musical Replication

General claims about the relationship of soundscape, auditory culture, and ontology come into sharp focus when we consider them in terms of the concrete musical practices addressed in previous chapters: practices such as chord substitution, melodic alteration, formal manipulation, and so forth. These are all practices of replication, where one musical bit is substituted for another, and where the success of its identity or individuation depends on its social context of use. Practices of replication are *culturally specific ways of demonstrating likenesses*. In fact, replication trades on the shared perception of likeness within in auditory culture by manifesting, or making audible, those perceptions. In cases of radical replication, new likenesses are forged, and listeners are solicited to grasp them. While a replication can produce two passages of music that are heard as morphologically similar, morphological likeness does not necessarily imply analogical likeness. Recall the striking reharmonizations of "Body and Soul" described earlier. While various listeners may have no trouble hearing all of them as valid performances of "Body and Soul"—that is, they are heard as morphologically similar in the relevant ways—there might be very different kinds of affects, attitudes, and sentiments expressed in those performances. Hearing morphological likeness does not preclude a listener from judging the musical quality and affect of those performances in starkly different terms.

Since the success of any act of replication depends on its social context of use, we must pay close attention to the concrete circumstances that shape an auditory culture when considering acts of replication. Jazz is historically unique in the ways that it has fostered a wide range of practices of musical replication, treating songs to both simple reharmonizations as well as radical transformations. In contrast with European art music, or so-called classical music, jazz embraces a wide swath of permissive replicational practices. But that raises an important question: why is jazz permissive?

To answer it, we must consider the history and the social contexts in which the practices of permissive musical replication came into being. Under the conditions of forced enslavement, and its prolongation by other means in the era of Jim Crow, Black music in America developed under a set of historically, socially, and economically unique circumstances unlike those anywhere else on the globe. Those circumstances are well known to any readers in the history of African American music but a few, select points might be worth recalling.

Musical replication is tied to issues of musical literacy, issues concerning the accessibility and reproduction of notated music. For much of the nineteenth and early twentieth-centuries, access to musical literacy for African Americans was uneven at best. While some Black musicians were well trained in score-reading and had acquired the typical forms of knowledge and competence taught in the music conservatory, others were not. And between the extremes, there are endless degrees: musicians who may have had no formal training, or only a modicum; those who taught themselves to read music, or worked through books and manuals to teach themselves harmony, orchestration, or arranging; or unique individuals who devised their own idiosyncratic techniques for notation and score-reading. In many cases, musicians who had studied in conservatories in the North faced limited professional options upon graduation, and often found employment as teachers or as performers outside the concert hall. As music teachers and as bandleaders, they disseminated what they learned, but the dissemination was never homogeneous. Given the complex role of economics, geography, and cultural norms, it is hard to generalize about the role of musical literacy in African American musicking, or to make claims about what was or was not typical. The bugbear of generalization has to give way to the acknowledgment of heterogeneity.

We are aided, though, by the work of historians like Lynn Abbott and Doug Seroff, and their detailed documentation of the routes, sites, and practices of Black musicking in the decades surrounding the turn of the century—at the moment just before jazz and blues emerged on a large scale. In *Ragged but Right*, they trace the routes that Black traveling shows took through the South and describe their venues, repertoire, and styles of performance.[51] These troupes followed the paths of migrant agricultural workers from town to town since these were the temporary locations where large audiences seeking entertainment could be found. Whether putting on tent shows, minstrel performances, or revues, musicians working on these routes played in a variety of settings and for various audiences. The size and instrumentation in these ensembles were not standardized. The makeup of the orchestra might change as new members joined or left the tours, and the repertoire was as varied as the instruments. It included overtures, arias, rags, blues, marches, and popular songs, and incorporated arrangement and improvisation. A band might parade through town in the day to advertise an evening show, playing military music and marches; they might set up on bandstands and give concerts of ensemble ragtime music, operatic overtures, and arias; in the evening, they would become a minstrel band during the shows, playing for the singers and performers in whatever style was required, or vamping and performing music between the various acts; and, sometimes, after the show was done, they would hold impromptu performances of rags, blues, and popular tunes. As the musicians traveled from town to town, bandleaders would rehearse or teach the members of the group new repertoire. Repertoire and personnel were closely linked: the virtuosity of a musician could be exploited in solos and features; but if they left, the repertoire would change to make use of the other members of the band. Musicians with less training could learn, in formal and informal ways, from their peers or elders. Bands learned to quickly sketch arrangements and adapt their repertoire for the circumstances they might encounter, using every means at their disposal. These traveling shows helped to solidify many of the basic musical skills and techniques that became requisite in the early days of jazz and blues music. In fact, many performers who performed on the early "race records" and initiated the craze for jazz and blues in the 1920s had worked on these circuits. Just to name one example, Gertrude "Ma" Rainey toured extensively in these kinds of groups before emerging as one of the seminal "blues queens" of the 1920s. It is safe to say that as jazz and blues began to emerge as a popular phenomenon, its performers exhibited a mixture of degrees of musical literacy. On any bandstand one might find non-literate, semi-literate, and literate readers of music working together. Given the need to fit the music to different settings and circumstances, the ability to adapt music in short order was often more important than the ability to read a score perfectly.[52]

I raise the question of musical literacy not to dwell, once again, on African American history and the politics of literacy.[53] My point is that if we are talking about the factors that shaped a distinctive African American culture of permissive musical replication, then we cannot ignore the issue of literacy. Musical literacy, and the perpetuation of forms of musical reproduction and performance that arose around skilled score-reading, helped to usher in the era of the "musical work." Thus, to understand why a counter-ontology of the musical work arose, we need to take account of factors like the unequal distribution of musical literacy in America. One consequence of the heterogeneous status of musical literacy was that it encouraged the use of both arrangement and improvisation. In the history of African American music, one can mine deep veins of both improvisation and arrangement: from the collective singing of sorrow songs described by Frederick Douglass, to the various arrangements of spirituals and folk melodies by Harry Burleigh or James Rosamond Johnson; or from the on-the-spot invention of blues lyrics and stanzas, like the improvised choruses of "Buddy Bolden's Blues" sung to the delight of the audience at Funky Butt Hall, to the brilliantly orchestrated rags and early jazz of James Reese Europe; or to the spontaneous head

THE SOUNDSCAPE OF STANDARDS 187

arrangements of Count Basie, and the precise, haunting timbres of Duke Ellington's "Mood Indigo" or "Creole Love Call." Improvisation and arrangement are not opposites, despite the heated debates and reams of jazz criticism that have kept the flame burning beneath this unhelpful distinction. Rather, they are two techniques in a collection of permissive replicational techniques, that is, two ways of making *one piece of music out of another*.

Beyond the issues of musical literacy—and its relation to the economic necessity and incentive for Black musicians to develop skills for adapting music to a variety of situations—we must also acknowledge additional factors that shaped Black musicking leading up to the era of the standard. We might consider the prejudicial social forces that excluded Black musicians from the concert hall or, when they overcame these forces, tolerated them as second-class participants in European "classical music" culture. We should also consider the specific way that race, geography, caste, and class shaped the distinctive musical production of cities like New Orleans, Chicago, and Harlem. These are places where Black musicians lived and worked together (not always harmoniously) and actively developed novel musical practices. Together, these factors, alongside others, created the hothouse in which the permissive replicational practices of Black musicking flowered in the first decades of the twentieth century. And, soon, those practices established the musical protocols heard all across the "soundscape of standards."

***

By the mid-1920s, when jazz and blues became the popular music of the day, many of the practices of permissive replication rooted in Black musicking were absorbed by the mainstream even as their permissiveness was narrowed.

To support this claim, you have to look not to the great Black musicians of the period, like Louis Armstrong, Fletcher Henderson, or Bessie Smith, but to the white musicians who were listening to Black music. Consider the Original Dixieland Jazz Band, the Austin High School Gang, or Paul Whiteman.[54] Whiteman, as one of the most successful bandleaders of the 1920s, is surprisingly useful on this question, because he wrote about his understanding of jazz in concert programs and in his book *Jazz*, coauthored with Mary Margaret McBride. "Jazz," he writes, "is not as yet the thing said; it is the manner of saying it.... Jazz is a method of saying old things with a twist, with a bang, with a rhythm that makes them seem new."[55] What is interesting about Whiteman's claim is that he considers jazz not as a noun—a class of music or type of musical genre—but as a verb: "to jazz." To jazz something, claims Whiteman, involves taking familiar musical material and changing its rhythm and counterpoint, or its orchestration and color. One could "jazz" some music by shifting the rhythmic profile of a melody by adding syncopations and anticipations, or by placing a melody into a new, polyphonic texture (one that might conjure up the sound of improvised polyphony that became associated with the New Orleans style). In addition, the use of percussion, saxophones, brass mutes, and unusual sonic effects are all effective ways of "jazzing" music. Emphasizing its transitivity, jazzing, for Whiteman, is something *done to* musical material and musical ideas.[56]

In this respect, Whiteman's famous "Experiment in Modern Music," presented at Aeolian Hall in 1924, is illuminating. Although the premiere of *Rhapsody in Blue* has tended to eclipse musicological consideration of the rest of the program, throughout its duration Whiteman presented selections where well-known melodies were "jazzed," so that audiences could hear the transformation. John Schoenberger's tune "Whispering," which had been an enormous hit for Whiteman, was played in two ways: so-called legitimate scoring versus jazzing. In comparison to the sheet music of "Whispering," or one of its many performances on piano rolls, Whiteman's version was notable for its slide whistle solo, and the syncopated, "jazzed" presentation of the melody, played high and powerfully on the trumpet, over the final chorus. Later in the concert, immediately preceding the premiere of Gershwin's *Rhapsody in Blue*, Whiteman presented a series of "Standard Selections" adapted to "Dance Rhythm." Familiar tunes like "To a Wild Rose," "Pale Moon," and "Chansonette" were "jazzed" for the audience. In all of these selections, Whiteman showed off his orchestra's gifts at playing syncopated figures with precision and snap, and with a thick, round sound notable for its sonic markers: the banjo's insistent strumming, muted brass, bouncy bass lines played on the tuba, and novel instruments like the saw and the slide whistle. The reason Whiteman programmed these selections was to educate his audience about the new musical, technical, and aesthetic possibilities that jazz offered. This required listeners to attend to the differences between the "original," so-called legitimate versions of these tunes (to which they were likely already familiar) and the novel, "jazzed" performances they were currently hearing. By presenting two versions of one and the same piece, Whiteman was asking listeners to pay attention to acts of replication.

This brief discussion of Whiteman raises some noteworthy points for tracing how the permissive replicational practices of Black musicking were assimilated by the mainstream in the 1920s. First, from the perspective of the present, some scholars may no longer consider Whiteman's music as "jazz," but I disagree. The term "jazz" in the 1920s was nearly synonymous with the concept of "popular music," as we might use the term today. Thinking historically, Whiteman understood what he was producing to be jazz music and so did others—from musicians, artists, and writers, to Hollywood filmmakers, and to everyday listeners. Attending to the ways that Whiteman's music employs practices of replication can help link it to other, more permissive forms of replication that are now thought of as *paradigmatic* of the jazz tradition—such as those found in Armstrong's Hot Five recordings, to name only one example.

Second, even though Whiteman's music contains very little improvisation and focuses primarily on arrangement, his views about "jazzing" speak to the prominent role of replication in the popular music of this era. Whiteman's style helped to set the tone for much of the mainstream popular music of the 1930s and 1940s. Listeners at the time might have characterized it as "sweet jazz." In contrast to the "hot jazz" of a figure like Armstrong—with its smaller ensembles, faster tempos, and prominent use of improvised solos and ensemble polyphony—"sweet jazz" was slower, timbrally nuanced, and heavily arranged. One might associate this "sweet" style with crooners like Rudy Vallee, or popular bandleaders such as Whiteman, Guy Lombardo, or Isham Jones. It became the sound of the mainstream, network radio orchestra in the 1930s.

You can hear it in a program like *Your Hit Parade*. Recall, as songs remained on the charts, they were often rearranged week after week, and doled out to different singers, or to the Hit Paraders. In the specific reharmonizations and alterations found in those weekly arrangements and rearrangements, and in the expectation that music would (and should) change from performance to performance, we can find the traces—canalized and reduced, but traces nevertheless—of the practice of permissive musical replication.

In other words, consideration of figures like Whiteman, or of shows like *Your Hit Parade*, is useful precisely because they demonstrate how the more permissive acts of musical replication that one might find in Louis Armstrong, Bessie Smith, and elsewhere were winnowed into less permissive modes. For a while, the practices of permissive replication, even in their canalized forms, became the assumed practices of American popular music. Once you add the pervasiveness of permissive replication to the other factors that helped to shaped the production, circulation, and reception of popular music the 1930s and 1940s—such as the rise of network radio, its proscription of phonography, the power of the musician's union, and the thrust of government regulatory policy—you can see why a specific configuration of the soundscape, auditory culture, and ontology that I am calling the "soundscape of standards" locked into place. But only for so long.

From the "New Sound" to the New Soundscape

In the decade and a half following the end of World War II, the culture of permissive musical replication began to change. At first, with the rise of the "new sound" of the 1950s, and its emphasis on the sound of recorded music, a "new soundscape" came into being. At the same time, replicational possibilities began to narrow. But by the turn of the 1960s, many factors converged to produce a crisis of replication altogether, one that questioned, and ultimately displaced, the entrained practices that had grounded prewar musical culture. To make this argument, I will focus on three factors: (1) changes to the nature of radio, including attitudinal changes about the broadcast of phonograph recordings, the rise of the "disc jockey," and the shift of network broadcasting from radio to television; (2) changes in the production of recordings and the development of a new aesthetics of sound recording; and (3) the bifurcation of jazz and popular music, and the self-reflexive ways that avant-garde musicians and critics began to question the assumed protocols of jazz performance.

Radio, Records, and the Disc Jockey. Learned Hand's appellate court ruling settled that neither the artist nor the record company had legal right to restrict the use of a phonograph record after it had been sold.[57] In the wake of his ruling, record companies ended the practice of labeling their discs with the warning, "not for broadcast." Radio stations could broadcast recordings without fear of legal reprisals by labels or performers. At the same time, the FCC had begun relaxing the rules on the announcement of phonograph recordings on the air, making it less cumbersome for stations and on-air personalities to comply with the law. By 1940, the commission only required the announcement of recordings twice per hour. This helped to increase the amount of recorded music broadcast on the air. But the wheels had already been set in motion; in the years just preceding Hand's judgment, some labels had begun to change their attitudes toward the use of recordings on the air and cut deals with radio stations to license the broadcast of recordings. In the late 1930s, RCA Victor began sponsoring *Music You Want*, a show that featured selections from their Red Seal line of recordings of classical music, and the *Victor Record Review*, which featured popular music releases. The shows were played over a network of about fifty stations.[58]

Record showcase programs, like those sponsored by Victor, had only a small effect in comparison with programs centered on a new type of radio figure: the "disc jockey." While familiar on-air personalities such as Arthur Godfrey had been using phonograph recordings on his popular Washington, DC, morning show in the early 1930s, the phenomenon of the "disc jockey" really began to crystallize around figures like Al Jarvis and Martin Block. Block's *Make Believe Ballroom*, which copied the concept from Al Jarvis's programs on the West Coast, began in 1935 in Newark, NJ. The premise of the show was to replicate the feeling of a ballroom remote by spinning recordings of popular bands, yet "pretending" that they were live in the studio. Everyone was in on the fiction; the title of the show made it clear that this was not an actual ballroom, but an imaginary one. Block and Jarvis had relaxed on-air personas, framing the recordings with information about the bands and the music. Most radio historians consider Jarvis and Block the first radio disc jockeys, but even if there were precedents before them, the popularity of the *Make Believe Ballroom* would make a tremendous impact on the future of broadcasting and on the record business.

Jarvis and Block set up the initial patterns that one finds prolonged by the disc jockeys of the 1950s. With their rise, and newfound power in the marketplace of popular music, song pluggers moved their attention away from program directors and advertising agencies responsible for sponsored programs and onto the disk jockey. Jarvis and Block, and others following on their heels, were becoming the new hitmakers, figures who could make or break a new song by including it in the "ballroom."[59] The rise of the DJ and the changes in attitude toward the broadcast of records on the radio initiated a change in the soundscape of radio. Less attention was centered on live performance or on transcriptions exclusive to radio, and listeners began to hear more repetition of individual recordings. The change in the soundscape reoriented the center and periphery of popular music's ecology, pushing live performance on the radio toward the margins while centering phonography, and helped to bring a windfall to the record companies. Although music publishers continued to promote piano and voice reductions and arrangements, the industry began to focus more on the use of compulsory license to produce competing recordings of hit songs.[60] If a particular recording of a song could saturate the airwaves, it would become the dominant node in a network of competing recordings and constitute the particular "aural image" recalled by listeners when the song was mentioned.[61]

Record-based programs, like *Make Believe Ballroom*, were cheap to produce and drew large audiences. Moreover, their rise was facilitated by the postwar shift of the national networks from investing in radio to the new medium of television. As television began to occupy the national role that radio once had—borrowing not only radio's organization of the broadcast day into daytime programs, news, and prime time programs, but also many of radio's biggest stars—radio shifted back toward local stations and less-expensive programming. Record shows were a low-cost, high-revenue option. Even local stations and affiliates could produce their own record shows, which led to the important rise of local disc jockey personalities in cities across the country. The economics of DJ-centered radio worked well in the new, postwar mediascape, where radio was eclipsed by television.

"The New Sound." As these events were occurring in radio and television, changes to the processes of sound recording would also make a significant impact on the soundscape of popular music. Beginning around 1950, the stream of hit songs associated with Tin Pan Alley began to be displaced from the charts, at first by a series of "novelty" records, and then by various crossover and small-label hits. These small-label recordings focused on styles and musical genres such as doo wop, rockabilly, country and western, and rhythm and blues, all of which eventually cohered under the label of rock and roll. Ben Yagoda, in *The B-Side*, a popular book about the demise of Tin Pan Alley and its subsequent resurrection (and repackaging) as the "Great American Songbook," laments the transformation. "All of a sudden, what came out of the radio wasn't Gershwin, Porter, and Berlin, but 'Come On-a My House' and 'The Doggie in the Window.' Elvis Presley and rock and roll arrived a few years later, and at that point the game was up." It was a veritable "triumph of record over song."[62]

The transformation and triumph of record over song was due, in no small part, to both technical and conceptual changes in sound recording. The evolution of studio technique in the late 1940s and early 1950s—with its use of artificial reverberation, echo, overdubbing, and mixing—afforded new sonic possibilities. Les Paul's 10-inch album *The New Sound*, released in 1950, featured heavy use of overdubbing, half-speed recording, and complicated arrangements to produce novel sonic effects. Its chart-topping popularity introduced listeners to a novel kind of soundscape and initiated a new sonic ideal in the popular music industry. "The New Sound" became a record industry moniker under which one might group the exploitation of the affordances of the recording studio. It became a staple of producers such as Mitch Miller, Sam Phillips, Phil Spector, and Norman Petty.

Rather than simply book fixed periods of studio time in order to record music that had already been well-rehearsed and honed through live performance, Elvis's Sun sessions, under the guidance of producer Sam Phillips, were created under a different approach. The master recordings were the result of a process of trial and error facilitated by the new recording technology of magnetic tape. In the studio, Presley, with guitarist Scotty Moore and bassist Bill Black, could work up versions of songs, record them, instantly audition them, evaluate, make changes to their approach, and re-record. Microphones were placed to capture the sounds of instruments in ways that would simply not be audible in venues for live performance. Then those sounds could be electronically manipulated—equalized, reverberated, or augmented with echo or slapback—before being fixed on a master and pressed into records.[63]

In the studio, sounds could be sculpted and finessed to produce a fixed aural image that simply could not be produced in live performance. The transformation of the process of making records also transformed basic precepts about sound recording. When Edison introduced sound recording, he characterized it as a documentary medium, where recordings functioned as indices of events in the real world—a way of preserving the voices of the dead, as courtroom evidence, or as family albums. Now, recordings were no longer bound to the strictures of representational fidelity.[64] As part of the "new sound," singers could sing duets with themselves (like Patti Page or Mary Ford) or create virtual and uncanny acoustic environments, free from specific spatial constraints, through the addition of echo and reverberation. According to musicologist Albin Zak, the creation of the "new sound" initiated a slow and continuous, but ultimately tectonic, shift in the popular understanding of recorded music. As he puts it:

> By the late forties, the record groove was no longer simply a container for musical performances but a musical line in itself produced through a new mode of musical composition. It became a site of musical and sonic interaction with a distinct identity and, through mass exposure, the power to shape the public soundscape as never before. The record groove did not discriminate; it welcomed all music and all sound. The gatekeepers were the recording team members who worked with the groove like a blank canvas.

As record production evolved through the fifties, the result was not only new music but a new way of making music. It was perhaps the most enduring musical concept to emerge from the postwar period: records were no longer simply aural snapshots but deliberatively crafted musical texts.[65]

This sea change in the technical and conceptual aspects of sound recording also brought with it a shift in the very ontology of music. Theodore Gracyk, in his groundbreaking *Rhythm and Noise: An Aesthetics of Rock*, draws out the ontological consequences of these new recording techniques, beginning with early rock and roll.[66] With the rise of rock and roll, "records, not simply songs or performances, are the relevant object of critical attention."[67] In particular, the sounds captured on the recording became "as relevant as any other aspect of the interpretation."[68] Gracyk argues that recordings, like the ones that Presley made for Sun Records,

> embodied a new *sound* as an **essential quality of the musical work**.... Each listener who learns these songs through these recordings grasps every aspect as properties of a *total musical work*. The timbre of Presley's voice, the phrasing, even the sound of this voice *on that particular day*, is as much a part of the musical work as the melody or the syncopation.[69]

The value suddenly given to "sound" as such—its promotion from a matter of fact of musical performances to an essential property of musical works—altered common ascriptions of musical ontology. If sound itself is an essential property of the musical work, then the distinction between performance and work loses its pertinence. For there to be a difference between a musical performance and a musical work, there must be some properties that are not shared by both, otherwise the two would be indistinguishable. Sound is "thicker" than the objects or structures that are typically heard in it: notes, tones, chords, melodies, progressions, prolongations, and the like. Structures, because they are thinner than sounds, are capable of being multiply instantiated in sounds. The same notes, chords, or melodies can be instanced in quite sonically different tokens. But if sound constitutes as an essential property of the musical work, then any modification to the sound would be considered an adulteration of the musical work. The same song released on different formats, or even heard on different sound systems, could potentially be considered different musical works, depending on how stringently or loosely one construed the identity of two sounds.

Gracyk explores these problems head-on, by considering Bruce Springsteen's album *Born to Run* (1975). Today a listener might encounter the work in one of many possible formats: LP, compact disc, or mp3.[70] "If one listens to *Born to Run* in all three formats, one will notice slight differences in the sound quality." Thus, if one accepts the strictest form of the claim that sound is an essential property of the work, each new format would ostensibly produce a different work. Gracyk offers an additional criterion to help mitigate this counterintuitive problem. "What makes each [of the three formats] count as an 'authentic' presentation of *Born to Run* is that each is causally derived from a single master tape.... One can know *Born to Run* only by playing something derived from that master tape."[71] In introducing that criterion, what he calls the "appropriate derivation" from a master recording, Gracyk commits to the idea that works of rock, *pace* Nelson Goodman, are autographic. According to Goodman, a musical forgery is impossible because any note-perfect score or performance of a musical work would count as an authentic instance of it. In contrast, Gracyk argues that forgery in rock is quite possible. The reason is that an authentic instance of a work of rock depends on being appropriately derived from the master tapes. The only form of appropriate derivation is, for all intents and purposes, duplication. To perform a song based on a transcription of its chord progression and melody would neither preserve the essential sonic features of the original nor be appropriately derived (i.e., duplicated) from the master tapes. Gracyk explains, "The *Born to Run* album is a musical work, but it is autographic because notational determination is entirely irrelevant to the genuineness of its instantiations.... If Springsteen or anyone else rerecords the songs on *Born to Run*, notational fidelity may occur (we may genuinely have the same eight songs in the same order), and it may resemble *Born to Run* as closely as two performances might. But it won't be *Born to Run*.... Notational accuracy is insufficient for access to the relevant piece of rock history."[72] The consequences of Gracyk's argument are clear: if rock recordings are autographic, if notational accuracy is insufficient for instancing the work, then we've entered a phase where every rock recording must be taken as an individual and distinct musical work. This would imply a whole new alignment of performances, works, and recordings. Recordings would be both performance and work at the same time, and would eclipse the ontological configuration of thin, emergent musical works associated with the "soundscape of standards."

While I find Gracyk's argument generally persuasive, I differ from his essentialist position—that is, his view that sonic properties of a recording, alongside "appropriate derivation," are necessary and essential in individuating the musical work of rock and roll. Rather, I would argue that an emphasis on the sonic properties of recordings—what I've been calling the "new sound"—helped sound to *become* a sufficiently work-determinative property, one that took on more and more importance in the 1950s and afterward, even to the point of excluding other, traditional candidates for work-determinative properties. The accumulation of recordings that emphasized their sound helped to bring sound's relevance in determining the specific properties of a musical work to the fore. But the argument doesn't rely on technology alone, since ontological ascriptions also rely on the beliefs and practices of auditory cultures and transformations in the soundscape. In agreement with Zak, I too would affirm that the "new sound" and its "radical transformation in American popular music" was also a transformation of "the pop soundscape" and its auditory culture of reception. While technology might have afforded this kind of attention to sound as such, sound would not have become work-determinative unless communities of listeners were convinced (recruited, assembled, joined in the stance) that it provided the most important criterion for the identity of the work.

When sound emerged as *a* (if not *the*) central work-determinative property of popular music, it precipitated something of a crisis for traditional practices of replication. How exactly is one to replicate a song if the most important criterion is sound itself? Unlike properties of melody and harmony, sound itself is not easily replicated. It either requires very talented imitators (we might even say "forgers") or requires the use of mechanical reproduction. The practices of replication—practices that were permissive in the world of jazz and popular music that preceded the turn of the 1950s—became more highly constrained. Replication, for all intents and purposes, tipped over into duplication. If replication is defined as the substitutability of one artifact for another given some specific social context of use, duplication might be understood as a narrower subset of replication: the situation where an artifact is mechanically reproduced or copied by means of a technological device. Duplication is still guided by the social context of use, just as replication is. To duplicate a "master tape" does not require mechanically reproducing its shape or its color, reel size or tape speed. Rather, only the relevant properties need be duplicated: the sounds inscribed on the tape. (That is why duplication does not require that the format remain the same. An LP record can be duplicated to a CD or an mp3, and so forth.) The sonic inscription must simply remain as close as possible to the original. While Gracyk focuses on the role of mechanical duplication, it is important to note that duplication need not be mechanical. The production of new performances that sound identical to previous ones is also an act of duplication. LaVern Baker's original 1955 recording of "Tweedle Dee" on Atlantic records was copied, note for note, by Georgia Gibbs for a Mercury release. Not only was the arrangement identical, but the same backup singers were used on both recordings, and Mercury's A&R team coached Gibbs to imitate Baker's vocal performance. And this was no isolated case. "Copy" records cropped up as fast as mushrooms throughout the mid-1950s.[73]

Yet, if the "new sound" precipitated changes in popular music's culture of replication, nudging replication toward duplication, how does one account for the fact that so many early rock and roll hits—from Elvis's "Good Rockin' Tonight," "Mystery Train," "Hound Dog," "Blue Moon," and "Blue Suede Shoes," to the Beatles' "Twist and Shout" and "Roll Over Beethoven"—were also performances of songs that had been previously recorded? How should one make sense of the relationship between these "standards" (or "covers") and the sonic emphasis of the new sound? These recordings added new nodes to an already existing network of songs. They did so by prolonging chains of nomination and chains of replication. But what was unique about *these* additions is that their emphasis on specific sonic properties only available in the studio challenged, even stymied, further replication. In their enormous popular success—and in their unique sound—these recordings helped to erase from memory the network that had preceded them or, at the very least, function as new, central nodes to which further performances refer. To put a finer point on it, one might detect in these recordings the presence of a strange paradox: on the one hand, these recordings still participate in the permissive culture of replication that preceded them; on the other hand, by placing such an emphasis on their sound, these recordings narrow the possibilities of replication altogether, winnowing it down to duplication. Yet the paradox is perfectly understandable given that these recordings sit at the beginning of a profound change to the soundscape of popular music. They contribute to an auditory culture in the process of transformation, one that is shifting away from attending to the complex networks of competing performances that constituted the ontology of song ("it's not the song, but how it is played"), toward the sonic-focused modes of listening that make the recording the primary object of musical ontology.

The effects of the paradox were felt in the television version of *Your Hit Parade*, which began in 1950. In addition to new musical arrangements week after week, the TV program also illustrated the week's top songs with stage sets and choreographed dances. The transition from radio to television coincidentally corresponded with the beginnings of the "new sound." For the first few years, the show was a television success, but its sudden demise is often attributed to the rise of rock and roll—in particular, the struggles that plagued longtime cast member Snooky Lanson when forced to sing "Hound Dog" on the show week after week. First appearing on *Your Hit Parade* on September 1, 1956, "Hound Dog"—which was so associated with Elvis's visual persona and the unique sound of the recording—did not translate well to Lanson's moderate, crooning, middle-of-the-road style. Here there were no swaying hips, no greasy pompadour, no sex appeal—just a toothy mouthful of all-American white bread. The old practices of mainstream permissive replication no longer seemed adequate to the new criterion of sonic duplication. Lanson didn't look like or sound like Elvis, and that fact began to matter as it had never before.

In interviews later in life, Lanson mentioned how grateful he was when "Hound Dog" finally fell off the charts. He was never a fan of Elvis Presley or Bill Haley or any of the early rock and rollers.[74] He had begun his career singing with Ray Noble's Orchestra in 1940 and modeled his style on Bing Crosby and Frank Sinatra. Born a bit too late, he was stuck between two different cultures of replication, rooted in the old one and unable to uproot into the new one. In 1957, Lanson and the rest of the cast of *Your Hit Parade* were replaced with a new cast of younger singers, with more ability to cover "rhythm and blues" and rock and roll. And by the summer of 1958, the show would be canceled. Who needed Snooky Lanson and the Hit Paraders, when you could simply watch *American Bandstand* and see the genuine article lip-synching to their newest single?

Jazz and criteria. The demise of *Your Hit Parade* represents the closing of a particular tradition of popular song, a mainstream tradition that both incorporated yet constrained practices of permissive replication rooted in African American music. The arc of the show's rise to popularity and eventual decline registers, like a seismograph, changes to the soundscape of popular music and the auditory cultural modes that attended to it. Changes in the culture of replication—that is, changes in the criteria by which musical properties were deemed sufficiently work-determinative—brought about something of a crisis for the older practices of making popular music. The qualities of a song that once could be permissively replicated by means of arrangement, reharmonization, or improvisation no longer functioned as such. These qualities were eclipsed by other qualities, like that of the sound of the recording. With the emergence of sound as a sufficient work-determinative property, the possibilities for replication were further narrowed.

But that is only one part of the postwar story. In addition, during the span from 1930 until around 1960, there were also significant changes in the relationship between jazz and popular music. While the two were closely associated from the mid-1920s until the beginnings of World War II—the period often referred as the "Jazz Age" and the "Swing Era"—changes within the world of jazz helped to shift the music from being a popular music with a broad, national appeal to a more specialized, niche genre. Jazz was, naturally, affected by the rise of disc jockeys and the invention of new studio recording techniques, but not to the same degree as the postwar popular song tradition. Rather, when it faced its own crisis of replication, the reasons for it were more internal than external.

Jazz began to diverge from popular music around the time that World War II came to an end. The demise of the Swing Era and the rise of the popular singer occurred simultaneously with the beginnings of bebop. Of course, the moment when bebop was born is hard to specify precisely. While many key musicians in the history of bebop were working together and jamming in the early 1940s, "bebop" recordings and press coverage begin only around 1945 and afterward. This is partially due the AFM recording ban, which coincided with the early years of bebop, leaving a gap in the documentation of bebop's development. When bebop emerged as a postwar musical phenomenon, its leading figures understood themselves to be artists and distinguished themselves from entertainers.[75] Dizzy Gillespie, who initially drew the most attention of the jazz critics and press, dressed the part: he wore a beret, goatee, and horn-rimmed glasses along with a zoot suit. He fused sartorial tastes of Black urbanites with those of European intellectuals. In front of the band, Gillespie was something of a classic trickster figure, one whose complicated music and use of jive ("ooh bop sha bam, a-klook a mop") required cultural initiation to decode it.[76] Bebop was not music for the mainstream; rather it was a kind of insider's musical language. It was powerful for those who knew how to listen to it, full of brilliance and feeling and depth, but it required work to understand it, and did not instantly accommodate listeners. Gillespie's own early critiques of Louis Armstrong's audience-pleasing behavior on the bandstand—which he later revised with more understanding—were directed at the kind of jazz that makes itself too easily available to the mass audience.

Even as bebop helped open the breach between jazz and popular music in the 1940s, it was still rooted in the culture of permissive replication that it inherited and immersed in the soundscape of standards. While Parker, Gillespie, and Monk all wrote and recorded compositions, much of their repertoire comprised popular songs of the day or contrafacts based on them. Charlie Parker is exemplary in this respect. Well-known ballads from the 1930s like "Embraceable You" or "Don't Blame Me" formed a core part of Parker's repertoire—just as they did for more transitional figures between swing and bebop, like Nat "King" Cole or Art Tatum. Contemporary songs, like "Star Eyes," "Stella by Starlight," and "All the Things You Are," were all written between late 1939 and early 1944, and all appeared in films in the early 1940s.[77] "How High the Moon," which is the basis for Parker's contrafact "Ornithology," was written for a Broadway revue in 1940 and circulated in various recordings in the years immediately following. Even the then-popular, but now forgotten, "A Table in the Corner," written in 1939 and recorded by Artie Shaw, is quoted by Parker and used as a thematic motif in one of his Savoy recordings of "Embraceable You." All these songs would have been "plugged" and promoted in the ways described by MacDougald. Even as Parker is making self-conscious artistic decisions to perform these songs, he is participating in a larger, common practice of performing new versions of popular songs of the day.

Parker's selection of repertoire, and his ability to quote contemporary melodies in his performances, demonstrates just how intimately familiar he was with the popular music of his day.[78] At the same time, Parker's radicality is grounded in the ways that he self-consciously pushes at the limits of replicational practices. In my previous discussion of "Embraceable You," "Meandering," and "Quasimado," I noted many of the ways that Parker challenges and extends conventional protocols of musical replication. By reharmonizing, by excising the melody or submerging it into florid improvisations, and by composing contrafacts, Parker expands what kinds of practices might count as replication altogether. (The same could be said for Thelonious Monk's radical reharmonization of "Body and Soul," discussed in Chapter 2.) Some listeners, when first faced with Parker's recordings or performances, were puzzled. It took time for them to learn how Parker had expanded and altered the basic protocols of jazz performance to which they had become accustomed. This aspect of bebop helped to make it something of an insider's music at first hearing. It is registered in reactions, common at the time, that bebop was "weird" or "strange." In aiming to extend and elaborate the established protocols of jazz performance, bebop functioned as an internal critique of the institutions of jazz. With cultivation of insider knowledge, alongside its complexity, strangeness, and anti-commercial stance, bebop constituted jazz's first significant avant-garde.

***

The next wave of jazz's avant-garde emerged in the years leading up to 1960, around figures like Cecil Taylor, John Coltrane, and Ornette Coleman, among others. These musicians are often associated with the "new thing" or "free jazz," and their music posed significant challenges to the conventional protocols of jazz performance while, at the same time, reflecting an historical awareness of jazz's past. Throughout the 1960s, Amiri Baraka (then writing under his baptismal name, LeRoi Jones) stood out as a staunch, articulate defender of the second avant-garde. In his book *Blues People*, and in the essays collected as *Black Music*, Baraka writes forcefully and polemically about the "new thing." His writing is full of insights about the relationship of the second avant-garde to its musical past, to its situation within the ongoing African American freedom struggle, and to the cultural and economic politics of the music industry at large.

In Baraka's advocation for the second avant-garde, jazz standards come up often as objects of critical reflection. They are described in ways that are surprising and that have not received adequate attention in the scholarly literature on jazz. Baraka associates standards with Tin Pan Alley and the commercialism of the music industry. The song "Melancholy Baby" is mentioned often, functioning as a metonymy for the music industry writ large and its antipathy to the "new thing." For Baraka, the commercialism of the popular music industry stands in contrast to the autonomous musical production of the avant-garde, even as autonomous music registers its historical rootedness in producing its social critique. Attitudes toward standards like "Melancholy Baby" are read by Baraka as condensed, focal points where one can glean the state of consciousness of the musician or listener. For instance, Sonny Rollins, when playing with musicians closely associated with the "free jazz" of Ornette Coleman such as Don Cherry and Billy Higgins, is picked out as "the one that might be capable of finally forcing understanding of *contemporary jazz* on the melancholy baby crowd."[79] Similarly, writing of John Coltrane's *Live at the Village Vanguard*, Baraka argues that the album (and perhaps more specifically the track "Chasing the Trane") "proves that the blues can still function on any level as an *autonomous* music (and is not limited to playing funky versions of 'Melancholy Baby')."[80]

Baraka's use of the terms "funky" and "contemporary jazz" are tacit references to "hard bop" and "cool jazz" respectively, which had come to be the dominant jazz styles of the 1950s. Both styles were subjected to stringent analysis in Baraka's *Blues People*. "Cool Jazz," although it had its roots in transformations brought to bebop by Miles Davis and others, became primarily associated with white musicians like Shorty Rogers, Chet Baker, and Dave Brubeck. In the middle of the 1950s, "the soft, intimate sounds and regular rhythms of such groups, along with their tendency to redo popular ballads like *Spring is Here* or *My Funny Valentine* with just a vague bop accent, made them listened to everywhere by white and black college students and [sophisticated] young-men-on-the-way up."[81] What gave cool jazz the air of being "contemporary" or "progressive" was its self-conscious adoption of "fugues, rondoes [sic], and other such consciously affected pickups from European music. This was a natural for college-bred audiences who liked a little culture with their popular music."[82]

If cool jazz brought highbrow affections to popular music, Baraka saw "hard bop" as its dialectical counterpart. The word *funky* became "the treasured adjective, where once *cool* had been, with *soul* . . . following closely behind."[83] Hard bop drew inspiration from the historical roots of Black music—spirituals, work songs, the blues, and other autochthonous African American musical forms—and incorporated the "harsher, rawer, more classic timbres of older jazz," in contrast to the smoothness of cool jazz. Where cool jazz indexes an act of bad faith on the part of the listener, mixing high culture with popular music in order to make a music perfect for conspicuous consumption, hard bop was more ambivalent. On the one hand, Baraka commends the fact that hard bop registered a change in the historical consciousness of African American music, a "return to roots" that is "not so much a return as a conscious re-evaluation of those roots." On the other hand, this re-evaluation proved to be "affected" and "emotionally arid."[84] In many cases, hard bop became "little more than a style," "a self-conscious celebration of cliché," one that "lost sight of the important ideas to be learned from bebop," and "substituted largeness of timbre and quasi-gospel influences for actual rhythmic or melodic diversity or freshness." Most damningly, "calling tunes *Dis Heah* or dropping *g*'s from titles is not going to make the music more compelling."[85]

To understand Baraka's critique of standards, as exemplified by "Melancholy Baby," one has to keep this twinned critique of cool jazz and hard bop in mind. Playing funky, hard bop versions of "Melancholy Baby," or lacing it with cool counterpoint, will never bring genuine *understanding* or *consciousness* about what is actually contemporary and autonomous in jazz and Black music—and more broadly, about the relationship of music to the ongoing African American freedom struggle. Baraka, in blunt terms, writes, "[there is] a whole world of most intimacy and most expression, which is yours, colored man, but which you will lose playing melancholy baby in B-flat, or the *Emperor Concerto*, for that matter."[86]

How, then, should one understand the continued presence of standards in the repertoire of figures such as Sonny Rollins or John Coltrane? Baraka reads the role of the standard as an index of the generational difference between musicians like Coltrane and Rollins, on the one hand, and Coleman and Taylor, on the other. Coltrane and Rollins, who came of age in the post-bop context of the 1950s, worked their way toward the second avant-garde through a complicated negotiation with standards. Both are considered performers of standards par excellence, and yet, in Baraka's interpretation, both work through the constraints of standards toward the "new thing." In so doing, they play an important role in demonstrating to critics and listeners the guiding ideas and social and aesthetic aims of the "new thing." Listeners who follow along the trajectory of Coltrane and Rollins toward the "new thing" might come to an understanding about the transitional role of the standard in eventually getting to a place where it can be discarded, where its chord progressions and cyclic forms were no longer necessary. This is one implication of the phrase that Rollins is "the one that might be capable of finally forcing understanding of *contemporary jazz* on the melancholy baby crowd."

The ability to play standards—much like the ability to "swing"—was often used as a benchmark by which to evaluate a jazz musician's competency.[87] In the "new thing," where the aim is "reestablishing the absolute hegemony of improvisation in jazz," the ability to play standards will be used as a critical weapon to dismiss its worth.[88] As we saw in the discussion of Ornette Coleman's version of "Embraceable You," critical reaction was polarized, with some citing his performance as evidence that Coleman could not play ballads and, more generally, must be "putting us on." But rather than judge Coleman and Taylor by their ability to perform standards according to its traditional protocols, Baraka considers the transitional role that standards play in "preparing" the way for the second avant-garde. Baraka writes, "People will use Coltrane to beat Ornette [Coleman] and Cecil [Taylor] over the head, not understanding that Trane functions as their hired assassin. He is using the various post-bop reactions to prepare, as it were, an area for Taylor and Coleman."[89] Musicians like Rollins and Coltrane, who have legitimacy in the eyes of critics for, among other things, their brilliant performances of standards, yet decide to abandon traditional ways of replicating standards for "free jazz," are important figures. They show that the goal is not to keep playing standards in ever more perfect ways, but to abandon them when the protocols of improvisation have outstripped the usefulness of the standard. That is why Coltrane *prepares* an area for Taylor and Coleman, even as he inhabits it.

Yet Coltrane, unlike Coleman and Taylor, keeps returning to the standard in a kind of struggle that seems rooted in his own past relationship with the jazz repertoire. Reviewing his striking performances of songs like "My Favorite Things," "Greensleeves," or "Inchworm," Baraka writes that Coltrane's "salvation will only come as a murderer or anarchist, whose anarchy seems so radical because references to the 'old music' still remain." Bordering on obsessive repetition, Coltrane continues to play out a life-and-death struggle with standards, where he "seeks with each new onslaught to completely destroy the popular song." At the same time, "Taylor and Coleman are proceeding as if Coltrane's work had been completed long ago."[90] For Coltrane, the standard keeps returning from the grave, like the undead, needing to be killed off once again; but from the perspective of the young avant-gardists, Coltrane simply "showed us how to murder the popular song," and opened up a new territory, free from its haunting.[91]

But death is never that simple. Like an *idée fixe*, the term "assassin" appears throughout Baraka's rumination on standards. At the end of his review of Sonny Rollins's 1964 recordings with Don Cherry and Billy Higgins, where standards like "Doxy" and "Oleo" (both written by Rollins) are transformed into long-form improvisational platforms, he confesses that "*Assassins* is what I've been calling this group privately. *The Assassins.*"[92] The term functions in multiple ways. It has its violent connotations, where Coltrane or Rollins appear as revolutionary figures who take up arms against the commercial music industry in order to finally do away with it. Like a regicide or the execution of a tyrant, the end of the standard's reign would then open the possibility for a new order of things—in this case, a return to the "hegemony of improvisation" and a newfound freedom from the mainstreaming and winnowing of permissive musical replication. Violence functions as a force of musical transformation as well as a counterforce to a previous violence done to Black music (through appropriation, imitation, minstrelsy, and so forth). And yet, within the traditions of African American music, there is also another connotation to the word "assassin." When a musician, like Coltrane or Rollins, is performing at such a high level of skill and brilliance, they are sometime said to be "killing it." This kind of usage goes back, at the very least, to the mid-1910s, where the future "blues queen" Gertrude "Ma" Rainey and her husband Will were billed as the "assassinators of the blues."[93] Thus the meaning of the term "assassin" is, at the very least, double. To be an assassin is to kill something off but also to be "killing it." Musical "assassination" is an act of simultaneous cancellation and preservation—a kind of musical *Aufhebung*. Its connotations must be heard against the background of Black music's history of brilliant "assassins"—like "Ma" Rainey—as well as in the militant struggle of the second avant-garde to free improvisation from the shackles of the popular song.

In that respect, there is an important lesson to be learned in listening to figures "assassinate" standards. For Baraka, the way to play standards, like "Melancholy Baby," is to make them into something entirely other, something that overwrites its relation to the original, commercial context for which the song was written. In a 1963 review of Thelonious Monk's performance at the Five Spot, Baraka notes that "almost everything heard throughout any given evening was a Monk piece, except for a few standards like 'Tea For Two,' 'Sweet Georgia Brown,' 'Don't Blame Me,' which upon hearing seem immediately and permanently transformed into Monk originals."[94] The distinctiveness and brilliance of Monk's playing performs a kind of alchemical transmutation on the song, changing shopworn standards into something completely different. But Baraka's most surprising variation on this idea appears in his review of *The World of Cecil Taylor*. From an album of mostly Taylor originals (one that is now considered one of the high points of Taylor's early period) Baraka selects out Richard Rodgers's "This Nearly Was Mine" from *South Pacific* as the "best tune" on the album—"a tune that under ordinary circumstances is one of the most terrifyingly maudlin pop tunes of our time."[95] Taylor's version "completely rearranges the melodic, harmonic and rhythmic devices of the tune and succeeds in making a music that is so personal and intimate as to give one the feeling that the original 'This' never really existed, except as a kind of dyspeptic nightmare." In his performance of the song, Taylor, from out of "old forms and old nightmares," makes "his own music," just as Monk made old standards "into Monk originals."[96] From these examples we can enrich our sense of what a musical "assassination" means for Baraka. To "assassinate" a song is to perform an act of willful erasure or appropriation, but in a subjunctive mode. The memory of the original tune is dissolved, taking on the character of a wispy memory, a dream, or a nightmare—just some old form. Instead of considering these performances as nodes in a network of previous performances, where the current performance accrues meaning through their relation to other performances of the song in the network, these new performances seem to balk at membership in a network altogether. Each new performance of these standards, in the hands of Monk or Taylor, becomes "contemporary and autonomous music," to use Baraka's own terms. Each is more akin to a monad than a network. Or nearly so. As singularities, these performances efface their relation to the past; as "assassinations" they retain their relation to the past, and present themselves *as if* the original never really existed.

One of the techniques that Taylor employs in his performance of "This Nearly Was Mine" is radical revision. I described this earlier as the production of two morphologically dissimilar artifacts that share the same nomination. This leads to a situation where there is a divergence between chains of replication and chains of nomination. In cases of radical revision, the listener is being solicited, by the name of the song, to associate it with a particular network of performances, and yet it is not clear exactly how to relate the properties of the current performance with those properties considered sufficiently work-determinative.

To illustrate, we must consider some of the basic features of "This Nearly Was Mine" and see how Taylor both works with and against them:

- Formally, the chorus of "This Nearly Was Mine" is in sixty-four-bar AABA form, with each section occupying sixteen measures.
- Melodically, the song is built from a small handful of motives (see Figure 5.1). In the A-section, the melody comprises four phrases of four measures apiece. Phrase 1 presents a neighbor note idea (motive x), starting on E♭, over the first four bars. In phrase 2, starting on B♭, motive x appears truncated (x′) but with a new tail added; the tail leaps up the interval of a perfect fourth and down a perfect fifth (motive y). Phrase 3 repeats phrase 2 but transposes it so that it starts on G natural. The fourth phrase repeats motive x at its original pitch level of E♭ and closes off the section. The bridge, or B-section, is melodically built on a new idea (motive z), which recalls motive x's neighbor motion, then leaps up a fifth and descends stepwise down a third (see Figure 5.2). In the first

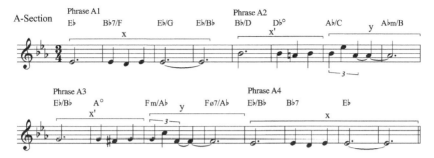

Figure 5.1 Rodgers and Hammerstein, "This Nearly Was Mine," A-section with analysis.

- phrase of the bridge, motive z starts on an A♭; in the next on E♭; and in the final phrase it returns to A♭ and ends with a melodic idea supported by a half-cadence.
- Harmonically, the song emphasizes stepwise and chromatic motion in the bass. Motive x is harmonized with an ascending, stepwise bassline, moving from root position to first inversion through a passing dominant harmony. Phrase 2 and 3 of the A-section is built over a long chromatic descent from D to A♭. The final phrase of the A-section is a perfect authentic cadence. The first half of the B-section begins on the subdominant chord, first inversion, and walks the bass line down from scale degree $\hat{6}$ to the tonic. The second half of the B-section starts the same way, but gets diverted towards a dominant half-cadence, which sets up the arrival of the final A-section.

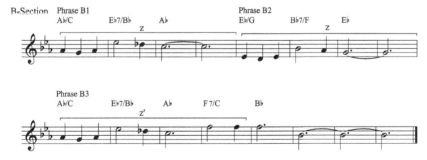

Figure 5.2 Rodgers and Hammerstein, "This Nearly Was Mine," B-section with analysis.

Table 5.2 presents a listening guide to Taylor's performance, noting the timings for each of the choruses and its sections, as well as some comments to help the reader follow along. The performance begins with a long duet between Taylor, on piano, and Buell Neidlinger on bass. There is no obvious, direct statement of the melody line, the harmony, or even the meter of the song. As a listener, one struggles to find the properties that are work-determinative. From out of the opening duet, one gets glimpses of these properties. Taylor plays the chromatic neighbor-note figure that opens the melody but weaves it into a larger chromatic field, harmonizing it with various roving chords that do not help to orient the listener harmonically to any particular location in the song's form. Neidlinger, on bass, follows Taylor's melodic profiles.

Only in retrospect does one hear the opening, neighbor-note figure of the of the melody, at around 0:30 into the recording, and realizes that they are now in the first A-section. Throughout, there is constant play with form; the trio alternately articulates and effaces the characteristic melodic and harmonic aspects of the song, or its work-determinative properties. Articulation, when it is foregrounded, comes from two sources: (1) Neidlinger often plays the chromatically descending bass line from the middle of the A-section. Following that chromatic descent can help to orient the listener to their position within the chorus and its various cycles. (2) At moments Taylor plays the corresponding bits of the $x'+y$ motive against this descending line; at other times he improvises over various chordal reharmonizations of this line. But when he does play bits of the melody, he often effaces the opening neighbor-note figure (motive x), instead choosing to emphasize motive y, with its perfect leaps. But this is a strange kind of articulation, since it tends to home in on the middle of the phrase. Clarity comes partway through the A-sections, when Neidlinger and Taylor lock into motive y and its chromatic bass line, then head off in different directions. The typical melodic and harmonic markers that emphasize the beginning and ending of a phrase are lacking. When the middle comes into focus, the listener is solicited, retrospectively, to reframe what they are hearing. The signposts don't appear at the outset (no "you are here") but always point back and forward ("you were there, and you will be somewhere else soon").

Throughout the entire performance, nearly eleven minutes long, the trio preserves the song's cyclical AABA form, but it is not always easy to follow. Listening to Denis Charles, on drums, can help, since his entrances, exits, and changes in texture (brushes, high hat, sticks on the ride cymbal) correspond with the song's formal boundaries, such as the arrival of the bridge or

Table 5.2 Listening guide to Cecil Taylor's performance of "This Nearly Was Mine," from *The World of Cecil Taylor*

Formal Unit	Start Time	Comments
Introduction	0:00	Duet between bass and piano, ascending melodic idea passed between bass and piano, roving chords.
1st Chorus: A-section	0:30	Phrase A1 (motive x), played rubato, marks beginning of the chorus, Phrase A2 and A3 (x'+y) played with growing dynamic intensity.
A-section	1:15	
B-section	1:52	The drummer enters, keeping time with brushes and hi-hat; Phrase B1 (motive z) orients the listener to the arrival of this section.
A-section	2:26	Phrase A2 (marked with an accented tremolo) helps to orient the listener, even as Taylor obscures the beginning of this section.
2nd Chorus: A-section	3:00	Phrase A3 helps orient the listener, like in the immediately preceding A-section.
A-section	3:32	
B-section	4:03	Phrase B1 is stated, but with some obscuring figuration.
A-section	4:33	
3rd Chorus: A-section	5:03	Drummer moves to sticks, and keeps time on the ride cymbal.
A-section	5:33	
B-section	6:02	Phrase B1 and Phrase B3 of the bridge are slightly obscured; this recalls the B-section of the 2nd chorus.
A-section	6:30	
4th Chorus: A-section	6:58	Phrase A3 is directly stated, recalling the 1st A-section of the 2nd Chorus.
A-section	7:27	
B-section	7:54	The end of Phrase B1 is marked with a piano flourish à la Don Shirley or Ahmad Jamal; Phrase B3 is directly stated.
A-section	8:21	
5th Chorus: A-section	8:48	The beginning of this section is extended by four bars. Taylor plays Phrases A2 and A3 (the x'+y motive) in a manner reminiscent of the 1st chorus, to reorient the band; he cues the B-section with descending figuration.
B-section	9:23	Phrase B1 (motive z) is marked with an even bigger flourish, recalling the B-section of the 4th Chorus.
A-section	9:50	Drummer returns to brushes; starting with Phrase A2 the melody is stated, rubato.
Cadenza / Outro	10:10	Recollects the introduction.

the beginning of a new chorus. In contrast to the roving, descending chromaticism of the A-section, Taylor, in the latter choruses, puts marked emphasis on the arrival of the bridge. The arrival of the subdominant chord is one clue, but Taylor does more than that: he often plays a paraphrase of the bridge's melody with a conventional harmonization. This is most obvious in the final chorus of the performance—at about 9'20" into the track—when, at the arrival of the bridge, Taylor suddenly plays the melody and harmonizes it with a big flourish, one that is humorously reminiscent of Don Shirley or Ahmad Jamal, yet still fused with Taylor's staccato attack and dissonant figuration. These moments of aural orientation and disorientation, of selecting unexpected properties of a song and making them do the work of signaling identity and individuation, of work-determination, create a radical chain of replications.

And yet, focusing on the radicality of the replication—as I did in the preceding paragraphs—will only get you so far. We can also think about what properties Taylor is pushing forth as work-determinative, how they differ from what we would have expected, and how it might shift our understanding of the ontology of the song; but that does not get to the even more profound shift of focus within the second avant-garde. With its insistence on the "hegemony of improvisation" and the freedom from preestablished forms, the second avant-garde began to pose a set of *criterial questions* about the assumed protocols and established practices of jazz performance. A criterial question emerges when one faces a situation where the conventions upon which one previously relied no longer seem to be adequate or appropriate to the task at hand. In such a situation, one is solicited to find a new solution to the situation, or to discover a way to "go on" without appealing to prior practices. In this way, criterial questions elicit improvisation. They do so not just in the sense of what notes to play over some complicated set of chord changes, but rather they demand new ways of relating to the situation altogether. For instance, what happens if you try to play jazz but get rid of the pulse, or allow all the instruments to free themselves from a time-keeping role, or have multiple pulses simultaneously? What happens if you try to improvise in a group without a preset chord progression? Or if you decide to improvise between the phrases of the melody, or use the melody as the basis for inventing new harmonic progressions? What happens to the conventional division of labor and definition of roles within the jazz ensemble if you have two drummers, or two bassists, or no chordal instruments? These are some of the ways that the second avant-garde posed, *within the music,* criterial questions—questions that challenged the very protocols and practices upon which replication was grounded.[97]

Consider Ornette Coleman's "Free Jazz" or John Coltrane's "Ascension." How might one replicate it? What would be the properties that are sufficiently work-determinative? If the point of compositions such as these is to set up a zone for collective improvisation, perhaps the best way to replicate it would be simply to collectively improvise. While that might get to the most important property of the work, it would not specify any particular sonic properties as work-determinative since the collective improvisation might go in any direction. From that perspective, Coltrane's "Ascension" might very well be a very replication of Coleman's "Free Jazz." (That is perhaps an extreme proposal, but both are structured around alternating episodes for soloists, with rhythm section, and roughly scored passages for the ensemble.) Yet if that is the case, replication has become so permissive as to do almost no individuating work. However, as a thought experiment about musical ontology it might be interesting to consider this proposition because it underscores what is shared between "Ascension" and "Free Jazz"—among other things, a certain consensus about collective improvisation as central to jazz's second avant-garde, and how such an improvisation might be roughly organized.[98]

The End of the Soundscape of Standards

The "new thing" or "free jazz" helped to encourage a significant change in the culture of replication, one that, oddly enough, seems like the dialectical opposite of that brought on by rock and roll. Through the directive of the "new sound," with the recording as its primary aesthetic object, rock and roll transformed the soundscape of popular music and narrowed down the possibilities of musical replication toward duplication; "free jazz," with its focus on the ephemerality and presence of improvisation, and through its formulation of criterial questions, entails that replication be so permissive that it is no longer clear what does or does not count as a replication or what features are sufficient for replication.

It is for these reasons that I see the end of the 1950s, and the beginning of the 1960s, as an inflection point in the soundscape of standards. In the interval that precedes and succeeds the year 1960, changes in the soundscape of popular music, the criteria of music ontology, and the culture of musical replication all underwent substantial changes. The configuration of soundscape, ontology, and auditory culture that promoted the "soundscape of standards"—where performances of a song were heard in relation to a network of other performances of the same song, and the sufficient work-determinative properties of the song emerged from out of this network—became less and less the norm. As the established protocols of musical replication were challenged, new ways of ascribing the ontology of musical works, whether rock and roll or jazz, kept pace. Rock and roll—along with the rise of the DJ, format radio, and new studio techniques, among other factors—helped encourage the ascription that musical works should be normatively understood as established by recordings. Jazz—under the leadership of its second avant-garde, with its emphasis on restoring the "hegemony of improvisation"; with its political, social, and racial aspirations to raise consciousness; and with its critique of commercialism and rejection of middlebrow jazz as a token of conspicuous consumption—helped encourage a counterview where performances are normatively understood as fundamentally improvisations based on malleable frameworks, or even based on nothing more, and nothing less, than the inspiration of the moment.

Of course, any attempt to definitively pin down the moment when the "soundscape of standards" begins or ends is a fool's errand. History has no sharp boundaries and neat periods, even if the historian posits them. The indistinct boundaries of historical periodization become even more porous when one is thinking about the history of cultural practices, protocols, and tacit beliefs. Cultural practices, like those involved in making music and in listening to it, are awfully resilient. It is not as if all the enculturated protocols of musical replication suddenly disappeared overnight, as if in some kind of meteoric extinction event. Musicians and listeners who identified neither with rock and roll nor with the second jazz avant-garde continued to produce and consume music in ways that they had been accustomed to do. At the same time that we have profound shifts in musical ontology, practices of replication associated with the world of standards persisted, albeit in a diminished form. Duke Ellington, Count Basie, and Ella Fitzgerald made records of the Beatles' music, and Pat Boone did his best to sing Elvis Presley's repertoire.[99]

While this chapter traces the inclination and declination of the "soundscape of standards" (and its related musical ontology and auditory cultural practices) from around 1930 to 1960, it is important to emphasize that auditory cultures, ontologies, and soundscapes are never homogeneous, neatly bounded things. Older practices of musicking linger beside newer practices. And yet, even as musicians grounded in the older, enculturated practices continued on, those practices still register their difficulty in completely accommodating the new situation without some degree of strain. Consider, for a moment, Ellington's performance of "All My Loving" or "I Want to Hold Your Hand" (from *Ellington '66*), Fitzgerald's swinging "Can't Buy Me Love" or soul-inflected "Savoy Truffle," or Basie's entire Beatles album (*Basie's Beatle Bag*); no matter how much they may revise, reharmonize, and translate the Beatles' hits into their own characteristic sounds and styles, there is something that makes those recordings different from the ones made 1930s, 1940s, and 1950s. In Ellington's, Fitzgerald's, and Basie's versions of the Beatles, one always has the original Beatles recording in mind as a baseline for comparison. There is one, unique, fixed, preceding sonic image indexed by these versions. As I argued above, this is one of the consequences of the rise of the DJ, the saturation of the soundscape with phonography, and the ideal of the "new sound." But this is also unlike the situation of the 1930s or 1940s, where a performance of a popular song was not necessarily bound to a preceding aural image.

6
The Aesthetics of Standards, or Hearing Double

The previous chapter had two intentions: first, to offer a set of confluent historical, institutional, and social reasons why the "soundscape of standards" came into being, effloresced, and then waned; and second, to demonstrate the ways that soundscape, auditory culture, and musical ontology are coconstitutive and corrigible. By tracing the inclination and declination of the "soundscape of standards," my goal was to follow the conditions that shaped the relationship between musical ontology and auditory culture. I did not set out to tell a story about the rise and fall of the so-called Great American Songbook. This term, an ahistorical and oftentimes defensive construction, is too often summoned up for purposes of nostalgia. I have no desire to mourn the loss of standards or lionize a "Golden Age" of American popular song. Nor do I have an investment in the championing "the song" over "the recording," or vice versa. I simply note that the estimation of the quality of the songs that comprise it (its "greatness") is not germane to my argument. While I would assert that there are remarkable performances of standards, and that the excellence of those performances should be noted and celebrated, I do not believe that the quality of such performances is predicated *in any way* on the quality on the composer's product. The story of inclination and declination of the "soundscape of standards" is, at bottom, a reminder that musical cultures change alongside their ascriptions of musical ontology and soundscapes—a matter of fact, and nothing to bemoan. The presence or absence of standards is not a marker of goodness, esteem, or musical value. It is a matter not of aesthetics, but rather of culture and ontology: a standard is simply a musical object that requires a large network of performances from which its sufficiently work-determinative properties emerge.

And yet, I cannot simply ignore all considerations of aesthetic value, nor would I want to. What, then, is the aesthetic value of standards? It is a difficult question to answer because any question concerning the aesthetic value of standards must first consider questions about why, or if, standards are still relevant. Given that the auditory cultural foundations that supported the "soundscape of standards" have changed and, concomitantly, the ontology of song has shifted with it, does the standard still matter for jazz? It is reasonable to wonder if, within the culture of jazz performance, standards function as anything other than a canon, an historical vestige, or a hollow marker of a "jazz tradition" that was always contestable. Are they still *musically* significant? Do they contribute to the future of jazz or do they simply ossify what jazz is and constrain what it might be? What are the reasons to keep listening to standards? To leave questions like these unanswered at this point would not only be disappointing, it would be negligent. It would fail to draw out the entailments concerning aesthetic value from the ontological and historical account of the standard presented thus far. To ignore aesthetics at this point would be like fashioning a stool with only two legs: we need one more point for the argument stand on its own.

To pierce our ballooning questions, we might start with one: what is the relationship of ontology to aesthetics? For many philosophers of music, the answer is simple: there is none. Moreover, the question is considered unproductive because it promotes confusion about the value of an artwork with the kind of work that it is—as if being an artwork also means that that artwork is intrinsically valuable. The question is especially pressing when considering jazz, where calling a song "a standard" is easily confused with a judgment about the song's aesthetic value.

Andrew Kania has addressed this issue in his writings on jazz and ontology, but perhaps most directly in the essay "All Play and No Work: An Ontology of Jazz."[1] Kania contends that any attempt to establish ontological terms for jazz must be congruent with the precepts of informed listeners and practitioners. "The measure of any such theory," he writes, "is coherence with jazz discourse and practice, that is, what people knowledgeable about jazz say and, even more importantly, do." Rather than stipulate an ontology for jazz by forcing it into congruence with other, related musical traditions (say, rock, or classical music, or even Indian raga), one must try to formulate the ontological categories of jazz immanently, from within the matrix of its practice and appreciation. "The underlying assumption of this methodology," writes Kania, "is that art forms, such as jazz, are social practices that depend on understandings . . . shared by most participants in the practice." Such understandings, however, "may not be directly or immediately consciously accessible."[2] For the philosopher who takes practice seriously, talk about the ontology of jazz is enmeshed with articulating how jazz musicians and educated listeners understand the music, even if that understanding has not been explicitly verbalized and theorized. This is, generally speaking, an *emic* approach to ontology, which develops ontological categories by attending to the perspective of its participants. Careful attention must be paid to the way that tacit understanding and knowledge are made explicit and how they fit into a web of coherent beliefs and practices. As both Kania and I agree, there is ontology at work wherever there is practice.

Jazz is an artform without works, argues Kania; jazz is, literally, "all play and no work." The ontological term "work" or "work of art" is not evaluative in that being an artwork carries with it no aesthetic or axiological value. To demonstrate, Kania draws on a comparison: in the art of painting the work is simply the finished painting itself, not the sketches or studies involved in its production; in music, the work is the enduring entity to which performances refer. Works only play an aesthetic role in situations where practitioners or listeners make explicit work-to-performance or work-to-work comparisons, judgments, or evaluations. In jazz, Kania notes, works do not fulfill that role. Practitioners and listeners are interested in performance-to-performance comparisons alone. "Just as rock covers are compared directly with one another, not (primarily) as performances of the same song, so jazz performances based on the same head get compared directly with one another, not (primarily) as performances of the same work." Jazz is then "a tradition without works," ontologically speaking. At first glance, Kania's language can appear counterintuitive, as if he were devaluing the aesthetic importance of jazz by tossing out the musical work. But that is not his intention: "Why should an art with *only* performances and no works be considered inferior to one with *only* works (such as sculpture) or one with both works *and* performances (such as classical music)?"[3]

I agree with certain aspects of Kania's account, but not all. I too believe that identifying something as a "work" does not entail that such "works" are of aesthetic value generally. Likewise, I too believe that when we are evaluating jazz performances we are not evaluating the intrinsic quality of the musical work as such. In contrast, I believe that the ontology of jazz *includes* works, that musicians and educated listeners *talk about* works, and that they *have an important but delimited role* to play in the formulation of aesthetic judgments. That is, I do not believe that the *emic* position will permit the wholesale rejection of works. Works do not entail but rather contribute to the formation of aesthetic judgments in that they establish the terms by which performance-to-performance comparisons are based. That is, works matter for aesthetic evaluation, even if (in themselves or as such) their aesthetic value is irrelevant.

Throughout this book, I have been arguing that the "work" in jazz is an ontological entity that emerges from a network of performances; its primary function is as a repository of determinative properties and protocols to which musicians, critics, and listeners appeal when they are identifying and individuating jazz performances. Emergence is a process by which a novel entity comes into being whose properties and functions are irreducible to the properties and functions of its constituent or subordinate parts. The opening chapters sought to explain how the emergence of the standard is *constituted by but irreducible to* a network of performances: how a work's determinative properties are sufficient but not necessary; how replication, which is an act of socially specific and contextually conditioned substitution, accounts for the corrigibility of determinative properties over time; and how chains of replication and nomination bind together performances into structures that are larger than the sum of their parts. This is what it means to say that a standard *emerges* from a network. In jazz, the musical work, in contrast to the individual performance, is an emergent entity. It is a set of durable yet corrigible protocols, of stable yet malleable routines. The work, to borrow a phrase from the anthropologist Paul Kockelman, is both root and fruit: the fruit of prior performances as well as the root of further performances.[4]

The theory I am advocating is intended to be congruent with the intuitions of practitioners and knowledgeable listeners, even if they might not have formulated it in similar language. (One motivation for lavishing so much time on the intricacies of replication and nomination was to describe its operation and effects as rigorously as possible, and—to repeat Kania's phrase—to show "its coherence with jazz discourse and practice, that is, what people knowledgeable about jazz say and, even more importantly, do.") Kania's argument that jazz is "all play and no work" rests on the assumption that musical works must be incorrigible; that they are enduring entities, objects, or structures impervious to change. The assumed fixity of the work makes it difficult to glean what role it might play in jazz performance, where songs and compositions are undergoing constant revision. From this perspective the work's incorrigibility appears to contribute little, so it is tossed out in favor of the performance. But when the assumption of fixity is removed, so is the difficulty. Emergent entities can be both enduring and corrigible. That is the case with standards. The work and the performance are responsive to one another: performances contribute to works because works emerge from networks of performances; and works contribute to performances because they codify the durable yet malleable protocols and routines for future performance. Because the work and the performance are co-constitutive, *both* works *and* performances impact the aesthetic evaluation of standards.

Surely, performance-to-performance comparisons are important for the evaluation of jazz. But they are also incomplete, in that a performance-to-performance comparison cannot wholly address what is of aesthetic interest when listening to a standard. In evaluating the performance of standards, a critical listener not only makes performance-to-performance comparisons, but also evaluates the current performance against a network of previous performances; they listen and attend to the ways that previous performances have shaped the possibilities and protocols of any current performance of the standard, and the ways that the current performance might rearrange what properties of the standard are sufficiently work-determinative. Insofar as a background of possibilities and protocols are involved in aesthetic judgment of a jazz performance, the work makes its contribution. The work plays a co-constitutive role in establishing the terms for the aesthetic estimation of any individual performance of a standard, even as the *intrinsic* aesthetic value of the work as such is irrelevant.

***

Standards emerge from networks, but not every network has the same shape. If we picture a network as a collection of nodes and edges—where nodes represent individual performances, and edges represent the chains of replication that connect nodes to other nodes—each standard will arrange those nodes and edges differently. Attention to such arrangements can be useful for identifying a standard's various protocols and in tracing the way that such protocols have come to be. The shape of the network, which forms over the long span of innumerable performances, is an ongoing articulation of the ways that musicians, through performance, negotiate with musical works. Topology is the discipline that studies the shapes of networks; and here, the topological approach will help to articulate how the musical work in jazz impacts its performances and their aesthetic evaluation.

For a standard with extensive performances, such as "Body and Soul," the sublimity of its network is daunting. But its overall shape can be gleaned.[5] Topology allows us to describe the network's shape and to distinguish its central from its peripheral nodes. In this immense system, with its countless small branches and webwork of edges, we can shift our attention to trace the network's large branches, organized around a handful of central nodes. These central nodes, replete with edges, are the inscriptions (the performances, scores, recordings, and so forth) that have come to influence and shape the song-specific protocols of a standard. These nodes need not index the earliest performances of a song, but simply the ones that have been most widely replicated, permissively or impermissively.

The topological approach to standards was broached earlier in the book, but not as explicitly or extensively as I will do so here. In Chapter 2, when introducing the idea of "chains of replication," I analyzed the first few measures of the refrain of "Body and Soul." To refresh the reader's memory, I followed three small paths through the network. Each path was an association of nodes, linked by edges representing replicated harmony. The first was a chain that linked various performances by Art Tatum over the span of about fifteen years through and emphasized his use of bass motion as a basis for reharmonization. The second path linked Teddy Wilson's 1941 recording with Thelonious Monk's solo performances of the song in the 1960s, emphasizing the use of the leading-tone dominant-seventh chord. The third path led through Hank Jones's solo performance, emphasizing the use of tritone substitutions. After considering chains of replication based on harmony, we considered permissive replications of the melody and traced the edges that lead from Coleman Hawkins's recording through performances by Jack McVea, Jimmy Blanton, and Billy Holiday. In order to explicate how replication works, I could consider only a small subset of performances and their webwork of replications. It is as if we were viewing the work through a magnifying glass, studying the fine filaments of the network as they gathered around a handful of nodes. It is useful to supplement this with a wider, synoptic view, one that considers a standard like "Body and Soul" in broad topological contours, to see what shapes are discernible.

Taking the wider view, we might note a few distinct branches within the network of "Body and Soul":

(1) There is a branch that stems from Roy Eldridge's and Chu Berry's 1938 recording for Commodore Records.[6] Chu Berry's opening statement

of the melody departs quite quickly from the written line and heads off into an improvisation that predates Coleman Hawkins's iconic performance from 1939. But the distinguishing feature of this branch appears with Roy Eldridge's solo, which is taken in "double-time" or, to use Gary Giddins's phrase, "long meter."[7] The two terms are equivalent here, in that as the tempo doubles the rate of the harmonic rhythm stays the same, thus expanding what was previously one bar into two and doubling the length of the song's refrain. Eldridge's tone, power, and range on the trumpet all exhibit the strong influence of Louis Armstrong, and yet Eldridge's "Body and Soul" makes little reference to Armstrong's 1930 recording of the tune. (If anything, Armstrong's solo on "Shine" is a more relevant model.) Because of the doubled tempo, Eldridge's solo is more "hot" than "sweet"—to use some very old parlance—and points toward the dexterous and virtuosic aspects of Armstrong's up-tempo playing. By bookending the double-time solo with ballad-tempo statements of the head, Eldridge turns "Body and Soul" into a vehicle for up-tempo improvisation and display. The chord changes, now in "long meter," allow the soloist to stretch out, to arpeggiate chords or play with their substitutions, or to invent melodic pathways through them without having to simply "run the changes."

From Eldridge and Berry's recording, a branch of recorded performances of "Body and Soul" extend outward, replicating its formal pattern: ballad-tempo head, double-time solo choruses, and a return to the ballad tempo for the final A-section of the tune. A few standouts are:

(A) Cozy Cole and His Orchestra, from 1944, with Ben Webster on tenor saxophone.[8] Cole's up-tempo drum break comes after Webster's sensitive ballad-tempo chorus of the head, and leads into another chorus for Webster, now in double-time. Webster's two choruses, one fast and one slow, highlight his gifts as an improviser at all tempos and his emotional range, from the whispering, caresses on ballads, to his powerful, driving, rounded tenor-saxophone tone on faster numbers. Webster had already displayed this kind of range on his recordings with Ellington, on moody ballads like "Chelsea Bridge" and up-tempo burners like "Cottontail," and both sides of Webster are on display in this recording.

(B) Art Tatum's trio recording from 1944 with Tiny Grimes on guitar and Slam Stewart on bass.[9] With its instrumentation, approach to the melody, and extensive use of quotations, Tatum's recording offers a knowing wink to the "King" Cole Trio recording of "Body and Soul" from earlier in the year; but it also develops aspects of Eldridge and Berry's recording.[10] Tatum tears into his double-time choruses with brilliant runs, serpentine double-octave lines, and furious riffs. By saving the double-time section for himself, Tatum uses the tune to highlight his stunning speed and facility, and rapid-fire musical ideas. Bringing the tempo back down after his solo, Tatum plays melody on the final A-section, and ends with a long quote from Dvořák's "Humoresque," a favorite piece in his repertoire.

(C) James Moody's 1956 recording on Argo records.[11] The recording begins with Moody on tenor, playing a quick up-tempo introduction. It leads directly into a few solo choruses played in double-time by Moody, and the trumpeter Johnny Coles. After Coles's solo, the band downshifts into ballad-tempo, and the trombonist (William Shepherd) solos over the bridge and the final A-section. Nowhere on the recording is the head of "Body and Soul" ever played. But the track's nomination, its distinctive and recognizable chord progression, and the protocols associated with Eldridge and Berry's recording, make this track easily identified as "Body and Soul." In listening back, there is an odd effect: like one of those wire recordings of Charlie Parker, where only parts of performances are recorded rather than entire takes, there is a sense that the slow, ballad-tempo head is omitted, left off the recording. It is as if the engineer pressed the record button only when the solo choruses began. But the fact that something as simple as a shift from ballad-tempo to a long-meter double-time could be immediately understood as a protocol of "Body and Soul," as one of the characteristic ways that it is performed, shows how pervasive and influential Eldridge and Berry's recording had become. Like a famous quotation or a common saying, it can be referenced even when parts of it are omitted, alluded to, or condensed.

(2) Another branch forms around Coleman Hawkins's iconic 1939 recording, where the melody is cast aside moments after it has been initiated.[12] Hawkins's recording become a surprise "hit," and his solo a definitive "masterpiece," one that was transcribed, memorized, and quoted by musicians for decades afterward.[13] Hawkins's performance

concretely associated "Body and Soul" with the tenor saxophone, and made it into a vehicle to demonstrate (or to test) the mettle of a tenor soloist. Because of its slower tempo, Hawkins's approach to the song demands less pyrotechnics—the kind that Eldridge sparked in his solo—and more introspection and exploration. The soloist is tasked with greater and greater invention from the song's chord changes. Dexter Gordon, the great expatriate tenor saxophonist, once introduced "Body and Soul" with these words: "All tenor players have to play this tune sometime in life. You can't escape it if you play tenor, you have to play this tune. (Laughs.) I'm sorry to say it but it's true, it's very true."[14]

Hawkins's record impacted performances far beyond simply "Body and Soul." Bluntly put, there is an entire school of saxophone playing exemplified by his often-studied solo, and its influence is so extensive that it is impossible to trace with any degree of adequacy. His manner of dispatching quickly with the melody and heading right into the improvisation is replicated, as noted earlier, in performances like Charlie Parker's two recorded takes of "Embraceable You" for the Dial label. Hawkins occasionally revisited "Body and Soul" under the guise of contrafacts. His 1944 recording of "Rainbow Mist" is similar in approach to his 1939 recording, but this time there isn't even a perfunctory reference to the song's melody.[15] It ends with a longish cadenza for Hawkins alone, an idea that was developed independently in another contrafact—the 1948 recording named "Picasso."[16] The track is a solo performance on the tenor saxophone—the first solo tenor recording in the history of jazz that I am aware of—and it dispatches with the melody line entirely but preserves its chord changes. Hawkins works through the harmonies, lingering on transitional chords, or building melodic phrases that never directly invoke "Body and Soul" but always approach the tune slantwise. Sonny Rollins, invoking Hawkins's two recordings, recorded his own solo saxophone version of "Body and Soul" in 1958, combining aspects of Hawkins's 1939 and 1948 recordings.[17] Between his introduction and coda, Rollins sticks close to the melody in his first chorus, before venturing out over the chord changes. Occasional allusions to the melody line help orient the listener and articulate the musical form. From this branch, a certain affinity is established between "Body and Soul" and the tenor saxophone.

THE AESTHETICS OF STANDARDS, OR HEARING DOUBLE 223

(3) Still another branch of the network forms around the Duke Ellington and Jimmy Blanton duet performance of "Body and Soul" from 1940.[18] Blanton, the brilliant young bassist who would die of tuberculosis at age twenty-three, takes the soloist's approach of Hawkins but displaces it onto the double bass. Blanton, playing the opening chorus *arco*, departs from the melody line as quickly as Hawkins did, and uses the rest of the chorus to play a series of brilliant improvisations over the chord changes. After a brief interlude by Ellington, Blanton returns on the bridge, and plays another half chorus, now pizzicato. His performance is a master class in state-of-the-art bass playing from 1940 and demonstrated that the instrument could do much more than keep time or hold down the low notes in the ensemble. Blanton's recording helped to establish the string bass as a soloist's instrument, and its impact is felt, again like Hawkins, in repertoire far beyond "Body and Soul."

In this respect, it might make sense to think of the Ellington and Blanton performance as prolonging the branch first opened by Hawkins. But this performance also opens up a new approach to the tune, as a vehicle for duet playing—especially where one of the duetters is the bass. Sarah Vaughan's 1978 recording (on Pablo) features her with the bassist Ray Brown.[19] It begins on the bridge, played in double-time, but transitions into ballad-tempo for the second chorus. Vaughan treats the melody line in a highly plastic manner, molding its pitches into new melodic profiles, and exploring the registral and timbral aspects of her remarkable voice. Her singing guides Brown even as she responds to Brown's prods and ideas. Unlike the Ellington and Blanton version, which featured Blanton's bass playing over Ellington's accompaniment, this duet is an equal billing where both Vaughan and Brown share the spotlight. A little over a decade later, Archie Shepp recorded a long duet version of "Body and Soul" with the bassist Richard Davis.[20] At nearly seventeen minutes long, the live recording allows ample space for both Shepp and Davis to wring from the chord changes melodic idea and to explore the timbral possibilities of their instruments. Shepp takes the first half of the recording, invoking—as his playing often does—the big growling sound of Coleman Hawkins or Ben Webster as well as the pointed abstractions of John Coltrane or John Gilmore—before handing things over to Davis. Davis's solo invokes Blanton's playing through allusion and through its protocols. Mirroring Blanton, Davis begins pizzicato but switches to arco for the second half of his solo, eventually cuing Shepp's final rubato chorus of the song.

(4) Finally, there is a branch associated with John Coltrane's rendition of "Body and Soul," recorded in 1960 but released on the 1964 album *Coltrane's Sound*.[21] Coltrane's version has a few distinctive features often replicated by others. He nudges the song from ballad-tempo to midtempo, while also slowing down the harmonic rhythm of the chords changes. Every bar is doubled. In so doing, the arrangement invokes aspects of Eldridge's performance—with its "long meter"—but without the use of "double-time." Much of the A-section is played with the bass holding a pedal point on scale degree $\hat{5}$, and the piano iterates an accompaniment pattern with a descending middle voice and repeated rhythmic figure. (You can hear it in the opening vamp, before Coltrane's entrance.) The bridge is also noteworthy for Coltrane's reharmonization of it—his use of "Coltrane Changes"—and his reworking of the melody line to fit this new harmonization. (It is similar in this respect to Coltrane's version of "But Not for Me," discussed earlier, but recorded at the same sessions.) It also has a rubato ending, where Coltrane plays a few cadenza-like figures, and a coda that invokes a cyclic motion of chords separated by the interval of a third, characteristic of "Coltrane Changes."

These distinguishing features appear in numerous subsequent recordings of "Body and Soul." Dexter Gordon took Coltrane's approach to the song and developed it in the many recordings he made of "Body and Soul" starting in the early 1970s and continuing up until his death. Gordon's versions tend to slow down Coltrane's tempo a notch, pushing the song back into the ballad range. He emphasizes the piano accompaniment's rhythmic pattern and descending figure and on the A-section, often doubling it on the saxophone. He also preserves Coltrane's reharmonized changes on the bridge. Gordon, not content to simply copy Coltrane, also developed a few chord substitutions of his own that tend to stick around from performance to performance. Recalling Hawkins's "Picasso" or Sonny Rollins's solo "Body and Soul," Gordon would often close the song with a solo chorus before leading into an ending that quoted Tadd Dameron's bebop ballad "If You Could See Me Now." Many of these features are crystallized in his performance of the tune on *Homecoming: Live at the Village Vanguard* and the soundtrack of the 1986 film *'Round Midnight*.[22]

Once these various topological shapes are identified, it is easy to hear how new performances of the song might touch on one or many branches. With this in mind, Joe Henderson's recording of "Body and Soul," from *The Standard Joe*—an album featuring numerous standards—is exemplary, a performance that is also a summation of the history of the song.[23] (My description is of take 1.) It begins with Henderson playing solo, invoking the solo tenor saxophone branch that includes Sonny Rollins and Coleman Hawkins. Bassist Rufus Reid and drummer Al Foster join Henderson at the bridge and lay into a standard ballad-tempo. At the end of the chorus, Henderson leads the band into long-meter double-time, invoking the branch first established by Chu Berry and Roy Eldridge. On the third chorus, where Al Foster shifts from brushes to sticks, the double-time groove is firmly established and Henderson's ideas become more adventurous. Because of the open, spacious sound of the ensemble—lacking a chord instrument in the rhythm section such as a piano or guitar—there is ample room for Henderson to improvise, and in so doing, to evoke associations with others who have played the standard. At times, Henderson's playing reminds one of Rollins because of its rhythmic and motivic focus; at other times, its harmonic density reminds one of Coltrane and his "sheets of sound." Yet Henderson's light and distinctive tenor tone—with agile leaps, beautifully placed altissimo notes, and rough puffs from the low register—remains uniquely identifiable, absorbing the protocols of the past without slavishly imitating them. After the bass solo, Henderson returns for another chorus, but drops back to the original ballad tempo in the final A-section. Then, like Dexter Gordon—who was himself building on Coltrane's protocols for "Body and Soul"—Henderson extends the final A-section into a cadenza for solo tenor. He even alludes to Coltrane's coda to "Body and Soul," with its cycling through a series chords with roots related by thirds.

Throughout the performance, Henderson not only adds a new node to the network of "Body and Soul" but evokes the network's history through his allusions to the network's central nodes and branching topology. It is a performance that does not simply attach itself to one of the branches in the network of "Body and Soul" but takes them up in turn. We need more than just a performance-to-performance comparison to evaluate Henderson's achievement; we must understand that this is simultaneously a performance *of the work* and a reflection *on the work* "Body and Soul," that is, on its emergence from a network of performances and on its distinct topology. Even though Henderson's performance is not a radical revision, it offers a new way of playing the tune by engaging the distinct topologies already in place; it is a performance that roves, alludes, ruminates, and gathers the past into a new configuration.

When a musician or knowledgeable listener begins to learn a standard, it takes time to become acquainted with the shape of the network as a whole. One might first encounter a specific branch (tied to a particular, favorite recording or performance) and other performances that are associated with it. To learn a standard is, in fact, to enter into a song's history of performance, and to get a feel for the way that it has been previously performed and the possibilities for its ongoing and future performance. These future performances are grounded not in a set of fixed protocols but rather in a collection of customs, or manners of executing some action. Each branch within a standard's network, packed with nodes and solidified through its dense webwork of edges, embodies the collective practices and shared protocols of prior performances. Replication is an act of substitution whose success or failure depends on specific, social contexts of use, but the terms by which a replication succeeds or fails ultimately depend on the tacit social background comprising acts of practical knowledge and collective histories. In this respect, "replication" is another word for what performance theorist Joseph Roach calls "surrogation," a cultural process that depends on the "three-sided relationship of memory, performance, and substitution."[24]

Although jazz performance is replicationally permissive, its space of possibilities is often constrained by its relation to the past, by the customary song-specific protocols embodied in a standard's branches. Radical replication often faces pushback because listeners, like musicians, grow accustomed to hearing standards in line with certain routines or protocols. For entrenched listeners, these protocols might be understood as work-determinative features that have crossed the line from sufficient to necessary. But that line can always be retread. For musicians who seek out a radical relationship with a song's history, who interrogate a song's protocols, the specific constraints embodied in these branches can be of ambiguous value: on one hand, they can stifle creativity, by canalizing performances into preset scripts; on the other hand, they can be spurs for rejecting established protocols, or for finding new and unusual ways of working within the protocols—even as they change them.

Sometimes the protocols can feel too strict or the customs too entrenched to dislodge, leading to the feeling that the repertoire of standards is bereft of new possibilities, that the music is no longer "alive," or that its utility is waning. The feeling that a standard has been "overplayed" is often the result of a performers' failure to negotiate the song's past history of performance in a compelling way. It might be a failure of imagination or a failure in execution, and in the face of such failures the listener might bemoan the fact that *we have heard this song before* and, even worse, we have *heard it played this way before*. And then, there are the moments of success, like Henderson's rendition of "Body of Soul." The aesthetic value of Henderson's performance is rooted in his skillful negotiation within and around these constraints. He evokes, indexes, and alludes to the wide extension of the song's network and its prominent branches, swinging through the canopy that they form. His performance engenders a new node with filament-like edges, widely out casting its tethers. In addition, Henderson evokes sounds, performers, and renditions that go beyond the nominated network of "Body and Soul" altogether, gesturing toward the history of the tenor saxophone and to performances and recordings scattered across the immense archive of jazz performance. He engages the "three-sided relationship of memory, performance, and substitution," through an act of replication that exceeds simple replacement or duplication; in its excess, it remakes the protocols and possibilities of further replication.

***

Henderson's "Body and Soul" is not a case of radical replication. Many of the properties typically deemed sufficiently work-determinative are present and easy to identify. But more and more, when contemporary jazz musicians play standards they tend to do so as an act of radical revision. Radical acts of replication foreground *both* the way that musicians situate themselves vis-à-vis the past *and* the imperative in jazz for musicians to develop their own style or to individuate themselves. The standard is an exemplary site where musicians grapple with the *twinned exigencies* of jazz performance: to be both part of a tradition and to "have a voice" that distinguishes one from that tradition.

As far as I know, the acclaimed jazz pianist Vijay Iyer has never recorded the standard "Body and Soul," but he did record a contrafact of it under the title "Habeas Corpus" on his album from 2003, entitled *Blood Sutra*.[25] Many of the most obvious work-determinative features of "Body and Soul" have been excised from "Habeas Corpus" and those that remain are obliquely referenced. Like "Body and Soul," Iyer's "Habeas Corpus" is in AABA form, and it opens with a vamp that has clear roots in John Coltrane's recording. Figure 6.1 compares the melody from the A-section of "Habeas Corpus"

Figure 6.1 Melodic comparison of "Body and Soul" with "Habeas Corpus," transposed to match pitch levels.

against the published sheet music of "Body and Soul." The original melody line is sententially shaped, with a basic idea ("my heart is sad and lonely") that repeats with transposition ("for you I sigh"). In the second appearance of the basic idea, a stepwise descent is added as a tail ("for you dear only"). That tail then becomes the basis for continuation, a skipping, descending line ("why haven't you seen it?") that leads to a cadential idea ("I'm all for you Body and Soul"). Iyer's "Habeas Corpus" pares away at the melody of "Body and Soul," excising the descending melodic tail of measure 4 and reducing the cadential idea to a series of oscillating semitones. But a measure-by-measure comparison will show how each idea from the melody of "Body and Soul" is chiseled out and set in stark relief. The basic idea is preserved, at the same pitch level, but with its large ending leap turned upside down. Iyer

THE AESTHETICS OF STANDARDS, OR HEARING DOUBLE 229

Figure 6.2. Opening vamps from John Coltrane, "Body and Soul" and Iyer, "Habeas Corpus."

follows the descending skips of the continuation (m. 5) but chromatically alters its first note, fills in gaps, and (again) reverses the ending upward leap.

These oblique references to the melody of Body and Soul, which harken back to both the sheet music and the long chain of replications that the melody has undergone, are combined with more specific references to John Coltrane's recording. Iyer, modeling his contrafact on Coltrane's version, opens with a vamp. Figure 6.2 compares the opening vamps of Coltrane's recording with Iyer's. Although the figuration and harmonizations might obscure this fact, two features are noteworthy: both are based around a chromatically descending line, and both are situated over pedal points. In Coltrane's version, the chromatic descent appears in an inner voice (doubled in octaves) from E♭ down to C. In Iyer's contrafact, the descent is in the topmost voice, beginning on B♯ and dropping to G♯. The rhythm of the descending line creates a polyrhythm against the pedal point. In Coltrane's version the dotted-quarter pulse is set up against the half notes in the bass, and the whole forms a tresillo-like pattern; in Iyer's version, the melody and pedal point make a polyrhythm of 4 against 5.

The B-section or bridge from "Habeas Corpus" is also modeled on Coltrane's reharmonization of "Body and Soul." When the two are compared, as in Figure 6.3, it is easy to see how the same processes that Iyer applied to the melody—paring down and reducing out properties—are applied to

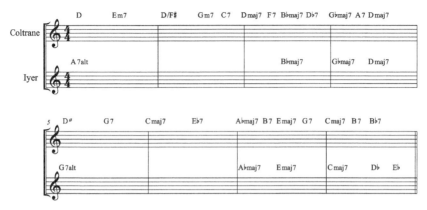

Figure 6.3 Bridge from John Coltrane, "Body and Soul" compared with Iyer, "Habeas Corpus."

Coltrane's chord changes. The stepwise ascent and prolongation of D major seen in measures 1 and 2 of the bridge are replaced with A7alt, D major's dominant. In measures 3 and 4, where Coltrane introduces the cyclic progression associated with "Giant Steps," Iyer similarly reduces. All the dominant harmonies that set up the arrival of B♭, G♭, and D major are stripped away, leaving only the feeling of cyclical motion but without all its trappings. A similar process is repeated in measures 5–8 of the bridge.

In his liner notes to the album *Historicity*, Iyer meditates on what it means to play standards.[26] His ideas depart from an epigram by the political philosopher Antonio Gramsci: "The starting-point of critical elaboration is the consciousness of what one really is, and is 'knowing thyself' as a product of the historical process to date which has deposited in you an infinity of traces, without leaving an inventory." Gramsci articulates how historical process and self-knowledge are related; "knowing thyself" depends on understanding the historical formation of how one came to be. Iyer applies that framework to his rumination on the meaning of the term *historicity*: "There are two main meanings for 'historicity': 1) the quality of being historically accurate, as opposed to fictitious or legendary; 2) a condition of being placed in the stream of history; also: a result of such placement." As he pointedly notes, "the second sense matters here." The idea of being "historically accurate"—of being a musical historicist or turning jazz into a museum of historical performance practice—is not Iyer's *desideratum*, nor even desirable. Rather, historicity is the condition of being placed into a stream of history, among the innumerable deposited traces that form the fabric and tissue of music's customs and protocols. In turning to the specific repertoire on the album—which, like *The Standard Joe*, is a recording of familiar pieces and "preexisting works"—Iyer writes, "You could see our covers as tributes, but we've also tried to augment each song with a fragment of ourselves. Each cover becomes a conversation between the original work and something else entirely." The musical logic is analogous to the grammatical logic of the conjunctive, of the *but* and *also* and *and*: a tribute to others, *but also* a piece of ourselves; a conversation between the original work *and* something else entirely.

The metaphor of the stream flows through the liner notes. The second meaning of "historicity" refers to being situated in the "stream of history," and the quote from Gramsci depicts the historical process as an infinity of traces, or as a deposit, like the sediment that is carried along and left behind in the unceasing onrush and outflow of water. Of course, the stream is also the "mainstream," that master metaphor that has often been used to enforce musical canons and bind the permissive practices of jazz to a set of established protocols.[27] The mainstream flows powerfully, and "without a doubt," Iyer writes, "it's the past that sets us in motion." But against the flow of the mainstream, which allows oneself to be simply carried along, Iyer displaces the metaphor: historicity is not the mainstream but rather "the swirl of undercurrents, the reason we brace ourselves as we step into the river." The imagery here evokes, once again, a twinned exigency: to gather oneself—and bracing is an act of self-gathering, of pulling oneself together in the face of potential forces of dispersion—even as one paces into the flux.

Flows and networks have affinities; both are dynamic structures that undergo constant transformation and movement. The topology of a standard is a dynamic depiction of the sedimented history of a song and its protocols—a meshwork, woven tightly and made tensile from its gathering of overlapping, intercalated performances. Topologies embody history, not as a stockpile of possibilities ("an inventory"), but as a force of corrigibility ("it's the past that sets us in motion"), as the grip of constraints, customs, protocols, and possibilities (realized and unrealized) that the jazz musician must, at some point, negotiate ("we brace ourselves as we step into the river"). This is how we come to terms with the condition of "historicity." The history of a standard is inscribed in its topology, and its shape impresses itself on practitioners and listeners as a feeling of both possibility and constraint. Topology is embodied in the condition of being historically situated, of acting within a milieu of performances that both inspire and impinge. In performance, this history is not only felt but a way a feeling; not only heard, but a way of hearing—what I call *hearing double*.

***

Hearing double is a mode where a listener hears a performance of music—whether at a concert or on a recording—against the background of its previous performances. When hearing double, the perception of the music currently filling one's ears is "shadowed" or "fringed" by other performances capable of being imaginatively auditioned. These other performances need not be heard with the same degree of perceptual detail and clarity that one experiences with a live performance or recording. Rather, these shadowed or fringed performances are akin to aural images—recollected or imagined sounds—that can be heard in the mind's ear.

Unlike a live performance or the playback of a recording, an aural image makes no actual sound available for others to hear. But it is sonic nevertheless insofar as it is a reference, a recollection, or an imagining of a stretch of sound. Sometimes the aural image is heard in the mind's ear distinctly, with its details intact. At other times, the aural image is heard vaguely, spectrally, or nebulously. It might even be heard schematically, where aspects of the recollected sounds are connected, but the whole is difficult to conjure up. At its most attenuated, the aural image might be so wispy as to be simply a feeling about how some music goes, a sense that "this piece of music" has been heard before yet cannot quite be placed. To borrow a term from phenomenology, these variations in the detail and texture of the aural image are manifested with various degrees of *fulfillment*. When an aural image is completely fulfilled, a listener might recall nearly every sonic detail of some previous performance or recording in their mind's ear; at its least fulfilled, a listener might hear only a framework, a chord progression, or a schema. No matter how it is manifested, the sound of an aural image is always contained within the echo chamber of one's imagination.

Unusual terms like "aural image" and its "degrees of fulfillment" might lead one to assume that this is some rare phenomenon saved only for expert listeners. In fact, aural images are as common and ubiquitous as any other act of imagination. They are simply a form of recall and phantasy in the auditory register. To give an example, I would wager that quite a few readers of this sentence can recall, in quite rich detail, the sound of the opening chord to the Beatles' "Hard Day's Night" or the sound of Paul McCartney's voice singing the pickup notes to "Hey Jude." Once those images have been recollected,

I would also wager that many can use them to initiate some form of "playback" in their mind's ear, where they can then hear the music that follows from these opening moments.[28] Hearing double is a mode of listening that exploits the ubiquity of the aural image. Moreover, it is a crucial mode of listening for those who attend to the genealogical, stylistic, or generic relations between one piece of music and another. As a listener's ears are filled with musical sound, aural images of related performances are evoked. There might be certain inflections, chord substitutions, or other aspects of the current performance that stir up the aural imagining of other, specific, previous performances. Hearing double is the perceptual and imaginative act of hearing how one piece of music is made out of another piece of music.

Although one might hear double in situations where it may not be requisite, there are specific kinds of music that solicit the listener to do so. For example, hearing double is crucial for understanding and appreciating "cover" songs. In the case of covers, we hear one musician intentionally play the music of another. When listening to a cover, the present performance is accompanied by an aural image of the original, prior performance. Listeners are expected not only to attend to the music that is sonically present, but to hear (in some more or less fulfilled manner) the relationship between the present performance and the original. In fact, the whole point of a cover, if it is to be recognized as such, is to invoke this mode of listening. For if a listener hears a cover without knowing the original, much of the interest in the cover is unavailable. Thus a cover is a performance that entails a particular mode of referential listening, where it is shadowed by an aural image.

No matter how radically it might transform its source material, a cover references a specific preceding performance or recording. In topological terms, a cover adds a new node to a network that refers primarily (if not uniquely) to a specific, precedent node. Consider Joe Cocker's cover of the Beatles' "With a Little Help from My Friends," from 1969.[29] What makes this cover estimable is the degree to which Cocker's arrangement alters the original tempo, changes the groove, and builds new levels of intensity and contrast into the song's formal units—and that is not to mention Cocker's gravelly, energetic vocal performance. Where the Beatles' song is intended as a jolly sing-along, sung by Ringo Starr (as the fictional Billy Shears), Cocker's version bends the genre toward acid rock and rhythm and blues. In so doing, it invokes not only the Beatles' original recording but other performances that are models for Cocker's reworking, like Vanilla Fudge's slowed-down covers of the Supremes' "Keep Me Hanging On" as well as many Beatles songs. Without the contrast between Cocker's performance and the aural image of the Beatles' performance, the aesthetic value of the cover version would simply be missed. The aesthetic value of the cover depends on hearing double.

Standards also require listeners to hear double but in a different way than covers. Standards are topologically distinct in that the work-determinative properties of standards emerge from *multiple nodes and branches in an extended network of performances*. In contrast, the work-determinative properties of covers are attached to *a single, original node and its fixed aural image*. In the performance of a standard, one or many previous nodes might be evoked alongside the present performance. The aural images evoked are manifold, culled from a much larger network of possible indices. In the case of covers, no matter how imaginative or radical they may be, the original performance, once established, is fixed; further nodes simply come afterward.

Thus, a standard is distinguished from a cover by the multiplicity of aural images that accompany it and the lack of a single, central node to which those aural images are fixed. Where a cover alludes to a specific original performance or inscription, the aural images evoked by a standard are distributed and diffuse. The full recognition of such allusions and evocations by a listener or performer depends on the factors such as one's knowledge of a song's history, on individual taste, and on familiarity with a large number of performances of both the specifically nominated song, related repertory, and stylistic and generic expectations. As a rule of thumb, we can apply this test: is there a single reference to which subsequent performances allude, and which guides future performances and their chains of replication? If so, we are probably dealing with a cover, not a standard.

Some songs that we might ordinarily talk about as standards turn out to be covers; and other songs that we do not typically think of as standards might indeed be so. Consider "Strange Fruit." The song, written for Billie Holiday and shaped by her performance and persona, was a fixed part of her repertoire. From her days at Café Society until her death, she performed the song often as a closing number, and recorded it a handful of times. "Strange Fruit" is so closely associated with Holiday—the timbre of her voice, her arrangement, and the slowly rising intensity of her haunting performance—that it is nearly impossible to hear someone sing the song without an evocation of Holiday and her aural image. This aural image may be more or less fulfilled, and it may be rooted in different periods of her career, but it is sure to be there. Thus, I would argue that "Strange Fruit" is more of a cover song than a standard. In contrast, a performance of "Body and Soul" may or may not invoke aural images of Holiday's own iconic performances of that song. I may hear an aural image of Holiday in a new performance of that tune, but my hearing is also likely to be crowded with additional aural images, allusions to the various branches of the song previously discussed. For that reason it is a standard.

In making this distinction I am not denigrating "Strange Fruit" or lionizing "Body and Soul." There is no intrinsic aesthetic value in being a standard as opposed to a cover. These are not terms of value or esteem, rather, they are descriptions of a song's musical network, and ultimately of its ontology. Different topological types can be identified by considering their distinct shapes, and the quantity and relation of aural images evoked during their performance. But we should also note that words such as "cover" and "standard" are assertions; that is, they are ways of eliciting others to consider the ontology and performance history of a song. Say, for example, I state the following sentence: "Although Jimi Hendrix played them both, 'Sgt. Pepper's' is a cover, while the 'Star Spangled Banner' is a standard." What I am claiming is not a matter of opinion but a way of asserting something about each song's history and about the mode of listening it solicits. Categorizing a song as a standard or as a cover is an implicit assertion about the relation of a performance to a network of previous performances. It is a claim about the quantity, significance, and relation of the aural images evoked, and about the historical constraints and possibilities that are being negotiated in the performance itself.

While I believe that the distinction between a cover and a standard is useful and meaningful, we must also recall that networks are corrigible. Songs accumulate nodes through additional performances, and the very act of accumulation can alter its work-determinative properties. Because networks are corrigible, the act of distinguishing between a cover and standard is ultimately an historical matter, best understood as a difference in degree than a strict difference in kind. For instance:

(1) There are cases where a profusion of covers produces a standard. When a song has had a sizable number of covers performed; when those covers have been imaginative and distinct enough to merit attention to their own properties; when these properties have become the basis for new chains of replication; and when those multiple additional performances have transformed the topology of the song's

network such that one precedent-setting node no longer holds sway—at that point, we have crossed the line from a song often covered to a standard. Leonard Cohen's "Hallelujah" comes to mind.

(2) There are cases where a cover eclipses its original and becomes the central node in the network, holding sway over all further chains of replication. We might think of Elvis Presley's cover of "Hound Dog," or many of Laura Nyro's songs from the late 1960s, which were more well-known by subsequent cover performances than by her original recordings.[30]

(3) And there are cases where something with the variability of a standard might become canalized into a cover, where a single node acquires enough force to dominate over a whole network. For instance, "In the Mood," discussed earlier, went through nearly a decade of transformations until Glenn Miller's recording eclipsed all others to become the central node in the network, the node evoked by all subsequent performances. In that sense, "In the Mood" is less a standard than a cover.

There can often be tremendous value in revisiting the performances eclipsed by a subsequent cover, as in the second and third cases, and in situating the eclipsing cover back into its proper chronology and context. This historical, and historicizing act, transforms an assumed original back into a cover by showing the chains of replication from which the assumed original was made. Such critical work often reveals what subsequent versions have borrowed, stolen, changed, transformed, omitted, elaborated, and embellished.

In either case, to appreciate and evaluate a standard or a cover requires listeners to hear double. To hear a cover *as a cover* is to hear the present performance fringed or shadowed *by a single, predominant aural image indexing a fixed, precedent-setting node*. To hear a standard *as a standard* is to hear the present performance fringed or shadowed *by multiple, equally predominant aural images indexing numerous nodes*. In this way, standards exceed covers in that hearing double becomes a case of hearing triple, or hearing quadruple, or *hearing multiples*. By evoking numerous aural images, standards are exemplary sites for hearing double.

***

The aural images that accompany the performance of a standard, while forming its background, are more than simply a backdrop; they affect the aesthetic evaluation of the present performance. At the moment when a musician calls a standard on the bandstand, they are nominating the present performance as part of a larger, pre-established network, and a wide range of possibilities and constraints are invoked. They have already placed their listener into a horizon of expectations to be fulfilled or evaded, a horizon that is always gesturing toward, to borrow Nathaniel Mackey's evocative phrase, "an insistent previousness evading each and every natal occasion."[31] For each new performance (for each birth of a new node or "natal occasion") there is a horizon of past performances ("an insistent previousness") that cannot be evaded or reduced away. That insistent previousness is the horizonality of the horizon, the impinging facticity of previous nodes that are experienced (understood, felt, and heard) as a force that constrains, challenges, and elicits the musician to respond with additional replications. How will the performance proceed and what will be its implicit protocols? How will it solicit a rehearing of work-determinative properties? How will it disclose new determinations and unheard, unnoticed aspects? How will it compel us to hear double, to hear in a way that roves across the network, following the filaments and webwork of replication? How will the addition of this performance to the network alter the topology of the network as a whole? New performances of a standard are thus evaluated in terms not only of the choices an improviser, performer, or arranger makes, but those that they could have made. Each reharmonization, substitution, or alteration is heard against this insistent horizon of constraints and possibilities. Unlike the aesthetics of "the musical work" under the guise of *Werktreue*—where works are often esteemed for their autonomy and formal unity—the evaluation of standards requires comparisons and relations with other performances and other works. Hearing double means hearing comparatively, against the background of a network of other performances, and making evaluations about how each performance contributes its singularity to a prior multiplicity of which it is a member.

Hearing double is crucial for understanding what is at stake in the performance of standards. To the neophyte or the uninitiated, to the listener who is unaware of a standard's "insistent previousness," all of this complex, virtual to and fro is simply opaque. They cannot hear the sonic but non-sounding music that shadows the present performance. Such a listener might enjoy the music or might be motivated to listen to more of it, but we could not say that they are yet immersed in the culture of standards or that they can hear *in the standard* its chains of replication and nomination. They have yet to acquire a repository of aural images. Without hearing double, the "three-sided relation of performance, memory, and substitution" is attenuated, if not severed. There is no emergence; there is no historical and cultural undercurrent to the listening; there is no reversal of foreground and background, no play of invention and acknowledgment. The uninitiated listener is left confronted with a brute particular—a single performance bereft of a network. At that moment, for that listener, the aesthetic value of the standard, not simply the performance, is unavailable.

***

Without hearing double, the uninitiated listener is also missing a feeling for agency. They cannot know what the musicians have *accomplished* without some sense of the insistent previousness with which they grapple. Consider the album *Thelonious Monk Plays the Music of Duke Ellington*, recorded in 1955 (and released the following year) for Riverside Records.[32] In the 1940s, Monk had been one of the architects of bebop but unlike Charlie Parker or Dizzy Gillespie, who rose to popular attention in the late 1940s, Monk's profile was less well-known. He remained a cult figure among jazz fans and musicians, known more as the composer of "'Round Midnight" and other tunes, than for his own performances. The story goes that many critics felt his own compositions were too difficult for the general public.[33]

Producer Orrin Keepnews viewed the recording sessions as an opportunity to bring renewed attention to Monk. Instead of featuring his "difficult" compositions, Monk could ease his way into the public's ear by performing familiar material. Monk's all-Ellington album was his first LP and his first recording as a leader that did not include any of his own compositions. (It was followed by *The Unique Thelonious Monk*, another record of standards.) After the release, some critics argued that the record represented a watering-down or making-palatable of Monk's style, an attempt to win fans by turning away from Monk's own compositions. In his biography of Monk, the historian Robin D. G. Kelley argues just the opposite: that Monk revered Ellington and that he was musically engaged throughout the preparation for the record.[34] For our purposes, the issue is moot, since the question of Monk's agency is not resolved by determining whether the project was his idea or someone else's. Rather, Monk's agency is demonstrated in the very fabric of his performance. In attending to his musical decisions—not only his arrangements and performances of Ellington's tunes, but his on-the-spot improvisations— a listener can hear the precise ways that Monk grapples with that "insistent previousness" that is internal to the ontology, and to the performance, of standards.

Thelonious Monk Plays the Music of Duke Ellington solicits us, as listeners, to hear double. To understand the record demands that we attend to Monk and his playing as an interpreter of material that, although not of his own invention, is well-known and evocative of numerous aural images. Monk's arrangements are heard against both the background of Ellington's ever-changing revisions of his own music, and the various performances and versions of Ellington's music by others. Monk's performance shifts our attention from his own body of work as a composer to the specific details of his piano playing and his musical decisions. Monk's own idiosyncratic pianism illuminates just how indebted he was to Ellington's work as a pianist. One can hear in Monk's playing Ellington's percussive attack; his manner of voicing chords and his layered, thick, two-handed harmonies; his habitual runs and flourishes; his prolific, judicious, and gorgeous use of dissonance; and his focused, jabbing pointillism.

Throughout the album, the listener can hear Monk as he listens to Ellington, as if we are listening at a second degree. Everyone who knows the album will recall Monk's way of playing the famous riff ("do wah do wah") from "It Don't Mean a Thing If It Ain't Got That Swing." Monk emphasizes the backside of the beat, slowly stretching the riff's triplet subdivisions into an evenly spaced duple feel. But what goes unremarked is that, at that moment, we can hear Monk hearing Ellington's music and assimilating it, refracting it through the prism of Monk's aesthetic and kinesthetic sensibility. Through emphasis or exaggeration, or by pushing and pulling against the beat—all the musical, muscular gestures that constitute the very elements of replication—we hear Monk hearing its rhythms, and how we too might rehear them. In his reharmonization of the dirge-like opening of "Black and Tan Fantasy," we hear how Monk hears possibilities for chord-substitution and reharmonization, how he can take something as distinct as the funeral melody and chordal accompaniment of "Black and Tan Fantasy" and invert its hierarchy, submerging its mournful tune under a wash of chromatic, roving chords.

Monk's performance of "Mood Indigo" is no exception, but with additional complexities.[35] The quantity of aural images evoked by a performance of "Mood Indigo" are greater than with "Black and Tan Fantasy," "It Don't Mean a Thing," or the other Ellington songs he recorded. "Mood Indigo," from 1930, was one of Ellington's earliest "hits," and it is easily recognizable

240   HEARING DOUBLE

for the haunting, distant sound of its first strain: a trio of trumpet, trombone, and clarinet.[36] To get that sound, Ellington inverted the traditional arranging techniques, voicing the chord with muted trombone in its highest register, clarinet in its lowest, and muted trumpet in between. The first strain is followed by a second, featuring the woody, chalumeau-register sound and liquid phrasing of Barney Bigard on clarinet.

In subsequent performances and recordings, Ellington, and his musical partner Billy Strayhorn, relentlessly rearranged "Mood Indigo," treating its various strains and characteristic timbres with far less fidelity than many of Ellington's interpreters would dare. It is worth tracing a few of most prominent changes that "Mood Indigo" underwent, in order to point out a significant detail about Monk's performance.

(1) Staring in the late 1930s, Ellington began to add an introduction to the song—typically played rubato on the solo piano—and to make drastic changes to the song's harmonization, instrumentation, and formal arrangement. On the 1940 Columbia recording, Ellington crystallizes these changes.[37] The piano introduction is played in right-hand octaves, leading into a statement of the melody arranged for the whole orchestra that displaces the simple three-part voicings of the 1930 recording. After Ivie Anderson's vocal chorus, Ben Webster's closes off the solos sections with a middle-register improvisation on the tenor saxophone.

(2) Ellington's 1945 Victor recording dissolves and reconstitutes the Columbia recording.[38] Kay Davis now performs the melody as a wordless vocal (linking "Mood Indigo" to the "Creole Love Call") over a radically new harmonization. This reworking of the tune includes sudden modulations to distant key areas, and a chromatically altered melody line to fit its new harmonization. Al Sears takes over Ben Webster's role, playing a dreamy solo over a cloud of dissonant chords, pinned in place by a pedal point.

(3) When given the opportunity at the end of 1950 to make a long-playing record for the Columbia Masterworks label (a new format at the time, and Ellington's first LP), Ellington and Strayhorn reimagine "Mood Indigo" as a set of variations.[39] In a fifteen-minute long meditation on the song, its two strains (the first for horn trio, the second for chalumeau clarinet) are turned, veritably, inside out. Behind the soloists, Ellington reharmonizes the song by building in dissonance, through

Figure 6.4 The end of the "retransition" from "Mood Indigo," from *Masterpieces by Ellington*.

Figure 6.5 Monk's introduction to "Mood Indigo," from *Thelonious Monk Plays the Music of Duke Ellington*.

distant modulations, or by means of pedal points to underpin roving harmonies. One variation even presents "Mood Indigo" as a waltz, in three-quarter time. But here is the detail that is relevant for Monk's version. Just preceding the final chorus—a reprise of the first strain for the trio of winds—there is an extended passage for solo piano.[40] At the very end of the passage, Ellington plays an arpeggiated figure over a chromatically rising bass line, arriving at a half-cadence and setting up the final return of first strain (Figure 6.4).

Monk, in his version of "Mood Indigo," develops this idea—he takes its ascending figuration and straight eighth-note patter but reworks it harmonically, submerging it under the shard bright, octave-rich dissonances in his right hand—and pushes it to the front of his arrangement. What was once a small transition in Ellington's arrangement now is radically replicated into a strident introduction. Monk's opening is reproduced in Figure 6.5.

In developing this idea, Monk selects out a particularly interesting moment in Ellington's playing and puts a spotlight on it—highlighting a moment where Ellington's piano-playing sounds most Monkish, and Monk's playing sounds most Ellingtonian. Hearing double can often generate this kind of paradox, where it feels as if the vector of influence has turned on itself and reversed direction, where time folds over to bring temporally disjunct moments into adjacency. I hear not only the present evoking aural images of the past, but I rehear the past by *hearing in past aspects their future manifestation.*

Monk's rediscovery by the jazz audience in the 1950s began with his Ellington album. And Ellington would also be "reborn" after his performance at the 1956 Newport Jazz Festival. Both would capture and hold the public's attention, and both would eventually end up on the cover of *Time* magazine. The two would even perform together at Newport in 1962. By attending to this little, detailed moment where we hear Monk simultaneously pay tribute to Ellington in the most Ellingtonian of ways—by revising and rearranging and transforming aspects of Ellington's pianism—we also attend to the replicational links that bind Monk to Ellington and Ellington to Monk. By listening to Monk listening to Ellington, we have an opportunity to revisit Ellington's recordings and hear how his pianism and compositions presage Monk. I do not believe that this is a trick of the ear. In the years following *Monk Plays Ellington*, Ellington began to record more albums as a pianist, like the famous *Money Jungle* and the underrated *Piano in the Foreground*. It is possible that this was just coincidence; but I would not be surprised if Monk's recording also made Ellington's pianism more accessible, more interesting, more *of interest*, even to Ellington himself. In the years following *Monk Plays Ellington*, Ellington began to use that retransitional bit, highlighted on Monk's recording, as *the opening idea* to initiate performances of "Mood Indigo." You can hear it on Ellington's collaborations with Coleman Hawkins, with Louis Armstrong, with Rosemary Clooney, and on airchecks and live performances throughout the 1960s.

***

Naturally, one could consider the agency of a composer and performer like Thelonious Monk via any of his recordings or performance. We need not confine ourselves to a record like *Monk Plays the Music of Duke Ellington*. But by attending to the way that Monk plays standards, we not only hear Monk perform but we also hear how his performance responds to the vast network of performances that precede him. That is one of the values of listening to standards: they are instances where we can hear how someone else hears by attending to their musical decisions—what to copy, what to excise, what to revise, and what to innovate. Consideration of musical agency adds an orthogonal dimension to hearing double; we not only hear the music in relation to a background of aural images and past performances, we can also hear what the musicians are hearing in the music that precedes them. We can hear how some of our finest musicians grapple with the twinned exigency of "historicity."

And yet the standard is diminishing. It plays a smaller and smaller role in the world of contemporary jazz. Although there are always exceptions, the most celebrated jazz musicians today are admired as much (if not more) for their compositions than for their performances of standards. It is a rare exception to see, for instance, a MacArthur Foundation "genius" grant given to a jazz performer whose repertoire is primarily that of standards.[41] The function of the standard as lingua franca among musicians or as a gatekeeper that determines one's entry into the community of jazz musicians has diminished in ways that are probably, all in all, salubrious. At the same time, the diminished role of the standard is supplemented with more composition, and that links jazz much more intimately with the production models of popular music and "new music." The obligation to play standards, whether real or merely perceived, can be a straitjacket on jazz performance. There are good reasons to imagine a world where the standard has passed on, whether it has been "assassinated" or simply died of natural causes. How many times do we need to hear "All the Things You Are" played in some uncommon time signature to make us feel that the standard has outlived its usefulness?

Perhaps it has, but I cannot leave it there. I feel compelled to acknowledge and to marvel at those performances of standards that snap into crisp focus the insistent previousness of the performances that came before, and that solicit us to recognize jazz's twinned exigency: the necessity to grapple with the past in a deliberate and explicit way *and* to demonstrate one's style, voice, or distinctness from that tradition. There are performances where a musician whom I could not quite follow—perhaps someone whom I could not quite hear on first listening or whose style seemed too mannered or idiosyncratic—suddenly makes their listening (and thus their musical sensibilities) available by means of the standard. There are moments where I can hear what another has been hearing all along. Those performances illuminate how we share a world of listening, even as the very act of the other's listening remains necessarily opaque, fleeting, and indirect. Performance, at times, can be elusive evidence; it can essay exteriorization. Standards are the best vehicle I know of for making one's hearing available to others, for offering a glimpse into the shared world of the audible (which is so much more than the sonic), and for reaffirming how the horizon of history is our matrix of musical possibilities and our insistent, inexorable constraint. That is what keeps me listening to standards.

Notes

Introduction

1. For an erudite and entertaining treatment of the history of the fakebook, see Barry Kernfeld, *The Story of Fake Books: Bootlegging Songs to Musicians* (Lanham, MD: Scarecrow Press, 2006).
2. Kelly and Sanders were musical collaborators and friends. See Ed Kelly and Pharoah Sanders, *Ed Kelly & Pharoah Sanders* (Evidence Music, 1993). CD.
3. That said, I believe there are important implications about musical ontology to be gained from the study of jazz that can be carried back to considerations of classical music, and to earlier repertoires and performance traditions. Some of those implications are touched upon in later chapters.
4. I have also learned a tremendous amount from reading Goehr's other books, and occasional revisitations to the issue of music ontology. In particular, I admire her reevaluation of Nelson Goodman's work, in essays and in the preface to the second edition of *Imaginary Museum*. I have also learned a tremendous amount from conversations with her, during my time at Columbia University and afterward.
5. See Lydia Goehr, *The Imaginary Museum of Musical Works: An Essay in the Philosophy of Music*, rev. ed. (New York: Oxford University Press, 2007); Goehr, "Three Blind Mice: Goodman, McLuhan, and Adorno on the Art of Music and Listening in the Age of Global Transmission," *New German Critique* 35, no. 2 (2008): 1–31; Georgina Born, "On Musical Mediation: Ontology, Technology and Creativity," *Twentieth-Century Music* 2, no. 1 (2005): 7–36; Alfred Gell, *Art and Agency: An Anthropological Theory* (Oxford: Clarendon Press, 2007); Theodor W. Adorno, *Current of Music: Elements of a Radio Theory* (Cambridge: Polity, 2009); Adorno, *Introduction to the Sociology of Music* (New York: Seabury Press, 1976); Adorno, *Negative Dialectics* (New York: Seabury Press, 1973).

   I have discussed questions of sound, music, and ontology elsewhere. See Brian Kane, "The Fluctuating Sound Object," in *Sound Objects*, ed. James A. Steintrager and Rey Chow (Durham, NC: Duke University Press, 2019), 53–70; Kane, "Sound Studies without Auditory Culture: A Critique of the Ontological Turn," *Sound Studies* 1, no. 1 (2015): 2–21.

Chapter 1

1. Allen Forte, *Listening to Classic American Popular Songs* (New Haven, CT: Yale University Press, 2001), xii.
2. Allen Forte, *The American Popular Ballad of the Golden Era, 1924–1950* (Princeton, NJ: Princeton University Press, 1995), 3.
3. Ibid., 197. Readers familiar with Purcell's *Dido and Aeneas* will recall its famous ground-bass lament. Whether readers agree with Forte's description of "My Funny Valentine" as a lament is perhaps less important than noting the wistful sighing quality of the descending inner voice. I thank James Hepokoski for this observation.
4. Ibid., 202.
5. For a similar case see Grover Sales, *Jazz: America's Classical Music* (New York: Da Capo Press, 1992).
6. Forte, *The American Popular Ballad of the Golden Era, 1924–1950*, 4–5.
7. Ibid., 4.
8. Ibid., 43.
9. Ibid., 334.
10. Ibid., 335.
11. Ibid., 333.
12. Musicologists writing about jazz at the time of Forte's publication had already offered pointed challenges to the very notion of structure as central to jazz studies. For example: Gary Tomlinson, "Cultural Dialogics and Jazz: A White Historian Signifies," in *Disciplining Music: Musicology and Its Canons*, ed. Katherine Bergeron and Philip Vilas Bohlman (Chicago: University of Chicago Press, 1992), 64–94; Rob Walser, "'Out of Notes': Signification, Interpretation, and the Problem of Miles Davis," in *Jazz among the Discourses*, ed. Krin Gabbard (Durham, NC: Duke University Press, 1995), 165–88. Tomlinson challenges the internalist notion that jazz focuses on musical structure by considering vernacular cultural approaches. Walser considers the problem of transcription and the reifying role it plays in the analysis of jazz improvisation.
13. Dealing squarely with the question of mediation, some musicologists have chosen to write about the "life of a song" or a collection of songs, tracing performance to performance relations. While these studies resist the classical ontology of the musical work in their focus on performance, and thus the mutability of a work, they rarely offer a direct philosophical engagement about matters of ontology. For example, Keith Waters, in his excellent book on the recordings of the Miles Davis Quintet, observes, "I am aware of the problems of ontology that arise from the idea of 'the composition,' that the notion of 'the composition' itself suggest a fixed or idealized entity at odds with the ways in which players freely and flexibly construct head statements. Rather than tend to those particular and interesting philosophical problems, I will use the word *composition* . . . in the way that jazz musicians generally do." Keith Waters, *The Studio Recordings of the Miles Davis Quintet, 1965–68* (New York: Oxford University Press, 2011), xi. This is perfectly understandable, since questions of ontology often lead away from the musicological and music theoretical concerns that motivate scholars

to write extended pieces on the "life of a song" in the first place. See: Ryan Raul Bañagale, *Arranging Gershwin: Rhapsody in Blue and the Creation of an American Icon* (New York: Oxford University Press, 2014); Todd Decker, *Who Should Sing "Ol' Man River"?: The Lives of an American Song* (New York: Oxford University Press, 2015); Will Friedwald, *Stardust Melodies: The Biography of Twelve of America's Most Popular Songs* (New York: Pantheon Books, 2002). Of course, there are exceptions such as: José Antonio Bowen, "The History of Remembered Innovation: Tradition and Its Role in the Relationship between Musical Works and Their Performances," *Journal of Musicology* 11, no. 2 (1993): 139–73; Bowen, "Recordings as Sources for Jazz: A Performance History of 'Body and Soul,'" in *Five Perspectives on "Body and Soul" and Other Contributions to Music Performance Studies*, ed. Claudia Emmenegger and Olivier Senn (Zürich: Chronos, 2011), 15–27; James Hepokoski, "From 'Young Bears' to 'Three-Letter Words': 'Anything Goes,' 1934–1962," in *A Cole Porter Companion*, ed. Don M. Randel, Matthew Shaftel, and Susan Forscher Weiss (Bloomington: Indiana University Press, 2015), 123–64.
14. Richard Rodgers and Lorenz Hart, "My Funny Valentine, from *Babes in Arms*" (New York: Chappell, 1937).
15. Forte, *The American Popular Ballad of the Golden Era, 1924–1950*, 197.
16. Richard Rodgers et al., *Babes in Arms* (Columbia Masterworks, 1951); Frank Sinatra, *Songs for Young Lovers* (Capitol, 1954).
17. For additional reflections on the cultural and musical significance of Columbia's studio recordings of American musical theater, see Hepokoski, "From 'Young Bears' to 'Three-Letter Words' "; Patrick King, "Spin: Goddard Lieberson and the Development of the American Musical Cast Recording" (M.A. thesis, Tufts University, 2014).
18. Forte, *The American Popular Ballad of the Golden Era, 1924–1950*, 333.
19. Andrew Kania, "All Play and No Work: An Ontology of Jazz," *Journal of Aesthetics and Art Criticism* 69, no. 4 (2011): 391–403; L. B. Brown, "Musical Works, Improvisation, and the Principle of Continuity," *Journal of Aesthetics And Art Criticism* 54, no. 4 (1996): 353–70.
20. Stephen Davies, *Musical Works and Performances: A Philosophical Exploration* (New York: Oxford University Press, 2001). In the rest of this chapter I will be focusing on Davies's notion of the "thin" work, although he is not the only proponent of this concept. See also J. O. Young and C. Matheson, "The Metaphysics of Jazz," *Journal of Aesthetics and Art Criticism* 58 (2000): 125–34. I choose to focus on Davies because his account of the thin musical work is the most developed and comprehensive account in the literature. More than many philosophers of music, Davies gives serious consideration to jazz and popular music. In what follows, I will be focusing on Davies as an exemplar of the theory of thin musical works. As will become clear, by rehearsing his argument I am not endorsing it.
21. Sinatra, *Songs for Young Lovers*.
22. Davies, *Musical Works and Performances*, 20.
23. Ibid.
24. Even in Nelson Goodman's nominalist account of musical works, these properties, which could not be strictly and definitely notated, were considered inessential in

judging the compliance between performances and scores. See Nelson Goodman, *Languages of Art: An Approach to a Theory of Symbols* (Indianapolis: Hackett, 1976).
25. Davies, *Musical Works and Performances*, 20.
26. Ibid.
27. Ibid.
28. Anonymous, *Volume 1 of over 1000 Songs* (Unidentified publisher, 1950s).
29. A brief note about terminology. I am using the word "incorrigible" in its philosophical and etymological sense as describing an object or thing that is unchanging or immutable. I will be using the term technically in what follows and do not intend any connotations of value, of "bad behavior," or the like.
30. Davies, *Musical Works and Performances*, 20.
31. Ibid., 21.
32. Ibid.
33. Ibid.
34. Although Davies does not explicate the term, by "vehicle," I assume he means a particular inscription or artifact capable of communicating work-determinative features.
35. Davies, *Musical Works and Performances*, 21.
36. Ibid.
37. Ibid.
38. Miles Davis, *Kind of Blue* (Columbia, 1959).
39. Davies, *Musical Works and Performances*, 21.
40. Miles Davis, *"Four" & More* (Columbia, 1964).
41. *The Complete Live at the Plugged Nickel 1965* (Columbia, 1995).
42. Although Freud had used the term earlier, the classical presentation of *Nachträglichkeit* appears in his case study on the "Wolf Man." See Sigmund Freud, *Three Case Histories* (New York: Simon & Schuster, 1996).
43. Davies offers some general conditions that must be met for a performance to instance more than one work: "The works in question must have [1] an independent existence but be historically related, [2] both works must be present throughout the entire performance, and [3] the performance should be no less accurate in instancing one than it is in instancing the other." Davies, *Musical Works and Performances*, 180. I will not go into the arguments supporting all three conditions, since my interest concerns whether musical works are corrigible by considering cases where works appear to thicken in properties. Rather, I focus on Davies's examples of performances that instance more than one work since they constitute a large portion of Davies's discussion of standards.
44. Ibid. Davies mistakenly identifies "Garland Razaf" as the composer of "In the Mood." In fact, Joe Garland composed the work, with lyrics by Andy Razaf.
45. Gunther Schuller, *The Swing Era: The Development of Jazz, 1930–1945* (New York: Oxford University Press, 1989). For an additional account, see Steve Sullivan, *Encyclopedia of Great Popular Song Recordings* (2013). While I rely on Schuller and Sullivan for providing the outline of this account, neither author comprehensively details the relationship of arrangement to arrangement or considers versions of the song after Miller's famous recording.

46. Schuller, *The Swing Era*, 674.
47. I could have called it the "In the Mood" riff but, since my purpose is to investigate Davies's claim that "In the Mood" was first a thin work, then placed into thicker arrangements, I do not want to beg any questions about the status of the RIFF. By coining a neutral term, I am, for the time, remaining agnostic about whether it should be identified with "In the Mood," or even what constitutes "In the Mood" as a work. While Schuller and Sullivan narrate the historical vicissitudes of the RIFF, they do not raise ontological questions about musical works since ontology is not their concern. However, retelling the history of the RIFF with an eye toward ontology helps further develop the argument about ontological *Nachträglichkeit*.
48. Wingy Manone, "Tar Paper Stomp" (Decca, 1938). This recording is a reissue of the original 1930 recording.
49. For more on Manone's recording session see Sullivan, *Encyclopedia of Great Popular Song Recordings*, 50.
50. Schuller, *The Swing Era*, 674.
51. This recording is available on Wingy Manone, *Wingy Manone and His Orchestra, 1936–1939, Vol. 1* (RCA Victor, 1988).
52. Fletcher Henderson, "Hot and Anxious" (Columbia, 1931). On Henderson's recording session see Sullivan, *Encyclopedia of Great Popular Song Recordings*, 50.
53. Jeffrey Magee, *The Uncrowned King of Swing: Fletcher Henderson and Big Band Jazz* (New York: Oxford University Press, 2005), 161.
54. Ibid., 162.
55. Don Redman, "Hot and Anxious" (Brunswick, 1932).
56. Their recording is available on Mills Blue Rhythm Band, *Mills Blue Rhythm Band 1934–1936* (Classics Records, 1993). For more on Garland and the Mills Blue Rhythm Band, see Sullivan, *Encyclopedia of Great Popular Song Recordings*, 50.
57. Schuller, *The Swing Era*, 386. Joe Garland played various reeds in the band in addition to composing and arranging. He should be included among Schuller's "strong roster" of musicians.
58. Anyone familiar with Miller's recording of "In the Mood' will recognize this strain, if they did not already get the hint from the chord progression of the second strain (Figure 1.16).
59. Edgar Hayes, *Edgar Hayes and His Orchestra, 1938–1948* (Classics, 1999). Again, for details on Hayes's recording session, see Sullivan, *Encyclopedia of Great Popular Song Recordings*, 50.
60. The slow version is available on Artie Shaw, *Artie Shaw & His Orchestra 1938, Vol. 2* (Hindsight Records, 1979). A quicker version is found on *Melody and madness, Vol. 1* (Phontastic, 1999). Sullivan, *Encyclopedia of Great Popular Song Recordings*, 50.
61. Schuller, *The Swing Era*, 674; Sullivan, *Encyclopedia of Great Popular Song Recordings*, 51.
62. *Encyclopedia of Great Popular Song Recordings*, 50.
63. Glenn Miller, "In the Mood" (Bluebird, 1939).
64. *The Glenn Miller Orchestra "Live" at the Glen Island Casino Summer 1939* (Magic, 1988).

65. While overshadowed for the public, insiders in the music business did not forget the previous history of the tune. In a letter to the editors of *Downbeat*, published on January 1, 1940, Manone claimed to be the author of "In the Mood." "The big noise around Broadway is about the big tune titled *In the Mood*," Manone writes. "It belongs to none other than Wingie Manone. Boy, I am sure glad that one of my numbers finally turned up after being on the shelf nine years. I am very sorry for a colored boy named Joe Garland who has his name on the number as composer and claims he wrote it in 1938 but I walked up to him and the Shapiro-Bernstein Music Publishing Co. with my original recording of this which I wrote and recorded for Gennett in Richmond, Ind. in the year 1930. Boy, those cats fell out when they saw this record.... That Gennett company went out of business years ago but little 'Wingie' saved the one and only record. It is called 'Tar Paper Stomp' and this will be a good Christmas present for me, yeah man! Please print this at your earliest.... Thanks and best wishes from WINGIE MANONE." The editors note that "both Garland and the publishers of 'In The Mood' deny Wingie Manone wrote the tune. They claim Manone's charges are groundless. —EDS."

On February 14, *Downbeat* published a response by jazz musician Fred Wacker commenting on the dispute. "Shapiro-Bernstein and Joe Garland know what they can do with *In the Mood*. The funny part of it is that Wingy Manone's right—he did make the tune 10 years ago on Champion. You can hear it as *Tarpaper Stomp* on a Decca reissue. The real payoff is that Fletcher Henderson also made it in 1930 as *Hot and Anxious* by the Baltimore Bellhops on Columbia. Credit where it's due and let Wingy and Fletcher fight it out. —FRED WACKER." See Wingy Manone, "Manone Says 'In the Mood' Is His Tune," *Downbeat* 7, no. 1 (1940): 2; Fred Wacker, "Wingy or Henderson Wrote *In the Mood*," ibid., no. 4: 10.

While the controversy was inflamed by the enormous popular success of "In the Mood," the close relationship of "Tar Paper Stomp" and "Hot and Anxious" had been noted two years earlier, when Decca reissued Manone's 1930 recording. In a *Downbeat* record review of the reissue, Paul Edward Miller writes, "*Tar Paper Stomp*, credited to Mannone [sic], turns out to be *Hot and Anxious* in a slightly different version. Who wrote it first I do now know, but I do know that Horace Henderson wrote the latter tune almost ten years ago." Paul Edward Miller, "Record Reviews," ibid. 5, no. 5 (1938): 14. In the end, nothing came of the controversy. See Sullivan, *Encyclopedia of Great Popular Song Recordings*, 50–51.

66. Joe Garland and Andy Razaf, "In the Mood" (New York: Shapiro, Bernstein & Co., 1939). Garland and Razaf are credited with the music and lyrics on all published versions, not the "Garland Razaf" that Davies names as the composer of the tune.

67. King Sisters and Alvino Rey, "In the Mood" (Bluebird, 1939).

68. Gene Krupa, *The Radio Years, 1940* (Jazz Unlimited, 1993).

69. John R. Williams, *This Was Your Hit Parade* (Rockland, ME: Courier-Gazette, 1973), 101; Bruce C. Elrod, ed., *Your Hit Parade and American Top Ten Hits*, 4th ed. (Ann Arbor, MI: Popular Culture, Ink, 1994), 63.

70. Bob Crosby, *Bob Crosby and His Orchestra* (Aircheck, 1978).

71. Benny Goodman, *"Camel Caravan" Broadcasts 1939, Vol. 2* (Phontastic, 1992).

72. Duke Ellington, *Ellington '55* (Capitol, 1955). For discographic information see "Ellingtonia," www.ellingtonia.com/discography/1951-1960/.
73. Ernie Fields, "In the Mood" (Rendezvous, 1960).
74. Joel Whitburn, *Top Pop Singles 1955–2002* (Menomonee Falls, WI: Record Research Inc., 2003), 145.
75. Moreover, the analytical processes that Forte has in mind, processes that reveal the "harmonic skeleton" with which jazz musicians make new versions, are not insulated from "sociology." In fact, they contribute to the growth of the network insofar as they spur additional performances and thus, potentially, influence future inscriptions in the network. As a theorist, Forte's own analytical reductions would be another node in this network, albeit ones that may ultimately have little sway over the network. It all depends on who reads his text and the influence that it ultimately exerts. As a hypothetical, imagine that Forte's analysis of "My Funny Valentine" is read by Brad Mehldau, who uses it as the basis for a compelling performance of the tune, one that emphases the linear confrontations of measures 30 and 31. Perhaps that performance becomes so widely replicated by jazz musicians that it becomes the standard way for jazz musicians to play the tune. A future ontologist studying the tune may then claim that those features are work-determinative. A future music theorist working on Mehldau's music may analyze his performance and glean some other structures, distinct from Forte's observations, and make a persuasive case for them. And the process goes on.
76. In this graph, I have condensed works and "vehicles" when appropriate, by notating them as solid diamonds.
77. Goodman, *Languages of Art*, 113.

Chapter 2

1. Whitney Davis, *Replications: Archaeology, Art History, Psychoanalysis* (University Park: Pennsylvania State University Press, 1996), 1. Throughout the text, I will use "replication" as a technical term in the sense defined above. Although "replication" is more unwieldy than the term "replica," I will avoid the latter for two reasons. First, replicas tend to imply exact replicas, and the exact duplication of an object's properties is not the focus of my discussion. Second, by avoiding the term "replica" I can be precise about the usage of the term "replication" and the meaning with which I employ it. While I am aware the term "replication" can denote both the process of making a substitute and the product that results from that process, I do not think the ambiguity is ultimately pernicious. The process of replication produces replications. Both process and product will be of concern for the ontological account presented below.
2. Ibid., 2.
3. Ibid.
4. Ibid.

5. I mean "grammar" in the sense that Wittgenstein employs it, as an expression of norms or a description of our typical usage of an utterance. Here, the social context provides the norms by which a replication is judged successful or unsuccessful. See Ludwig Wittgenstein, *Philosophical Investigations*, trans. G. E. M. Anscombe (New York: Macmillan, 1953).
6. For more on aspects and aspect-perception see: Stephen Mulhall, *On Being in the World: Wittgenstein and Heidegger on Seeing Aspects* (London: Routledge, 1990); Wittgenstein, *Philosophical Investigations*, Part II, section xi.
7. Johnny Green, Edward Heyman, and Robert Sour, "Body and Soul" (New York: Harms, 1930). As Green notes, the published sheet music for "Body and Soul" comes after quite a few initial performances. Originally written for Gertrude Lawrence, the song gained in popularity in England during its first months in circulation. According to Green, publishers approached him after the song had become a hit. See Green's interview in Fred Hall, *More Dialogues in Swing: Intimate Conversations with the Stars of the Big Band Era* (Ventura: Pathfinder, 1991).
8. "Body and Soul" migrated to the key of D♭, in no small part due to Coleman Hawkins's famous recording from 1939.
9. For a comprehensive ethnographic account of these practices, see Paul Berliner, *Thinking in Jazz: The Infinite Art of Improvisation* (Chicago: University of Chicago Press, 1994).
10. My introduction to "functional bass" and its virtues stems from conversations with Ian Quinn. I have modified his unpublished system for the purposes of this book. All shortcomings in its presentation and use are solely attributable to the author, not the inventor.
11. *Embellishing chords* are chords that have no harmonic-functional meaning of their own and typically appear between chords with functional interpretations. *Passing chords* are embellishing chords interpolated between two chords of the same function in different inversions. Thus, passing chords are non-functional chords that often generate parsimonious voice-leading or harmonize stepwise bass motion. In Figure 2.3, two D-minor chords bound the inverted A7. The D-minor chords are both subdominant in function but in different inversions. The A7 chord passes from subdominant harmony to subdominant harmony. It passes between S$\hat{2}$ and S$\hat{4}$ by harmonizing $\hat{3}$ in the bass. Since a passing chord is non-functional—that is, since it elaborates and embellishes other chords—it receives no functional label. Rather, as noted above, we will label it "P" for passing, and include the scale degree in the bass. As a rule, in functional-bass notation, all passing, neighbor, and embellishing chords will be placed in parentheses to show that they do not have harmonic-functional meaning. *Neighbor chords* are typically interpolated between two chords of the same function and same inversion. For instance, were the A7 of Figure 2.3 to be bounded by two instances of S$\hat{2}$, it would be a neighbor chord, not a passing chord.
12. Art Tatum, "Body and Soul," *Tatum Is Art—Piano Solo—1938-1939* (Musidisc, 1976). All solo piano transcriptions of "Body and Soul" are based on Franz Krieger, *Jazz-Solopiano: Zum Stilwandel am Beispiel ausgewählter "Body and Soul"–Aufnahmen von 1938–1992* (Graz: Akademische Druck- u. Verlagsanstalt, 1995). I have added

NOTES 253

a functional-bass analysis to his transcriptions. Where I disagree with Krieger's transcriptions or chord labels, I have changed them.
13. This could also be considered a diminished chord, vii°65, applied to the D minor chord that follows it. Both interpretations of the chord will work with the following discussion.
14. Or, alternatively, [ii vii°65→| ii6 V7 | I].
15. Art Tatum, "Body and Soul," *The Tatum Solo Masterpieces, Vol 1* (Pablo, 1975).
16. For a contemporary account of the use of chains of applied chords in jazz harmony, see Leonard Feather, *Inside Jazz* (New York: Da Capo Press, 1976), 55. The book was originally published as *Inside Be-Bop* in 1949 and contains many useful insights about jazz harmony from the period.
17. I do not want to give the impression that harmony is more important, or even essential, for replication in jazz. I am focusing on it here only in order to give an account of replication. Later, I will consider the relative importance of harmony and melody in the ontology of standards.
18. For a detailed account of the performance history of "Body and Soul," see Bowen, "Recordings as Sources for Jazz: A Performance History of 'Body and Soul.'"
19. Hank Jones, "Body and Soul," from *Have You Met Hank Jones?* (Savoy), 1956.
20. When introducing the tritone substitution a few paragraphs ago, I presented a progression very similar to this and made the argument that *D2♭ is a commonplace chord with dominant function in the jazz vocabulary.
21. Steven Strunk, in a seminal article on bop harmony, calls this a "II-V Elaboration." While I find Strunk's work on jazz harmony deeply insightful, I do not like the nomenclature of a "II-V elaboration," since it can lead to the confusion of II-V in the home key with the "local" II-V progressions. My terminology disambiguates these two scenarios. See Steven Strunk, "The Harmony of Early Bop: A Layered Approach," *Journal of Jazz Studies* 6, no. 1 (1979): 4–53.
22. I would argue that an unpacked chord, like an applied chord, does not have harmonic function because it embellishes the chord from which it was generated. However, like Strunk, I agree that one can elaborate, or unpack, a minor chord by adding a dominant-seventh chord to it. As Strunk notes, "Most frequently the object chord is a dominant seventh structure; less frequently the object chord is a chord functioning as II." In these cases, the minor chord is the embellished and not the embellishing chord. See ibid., 13.
23. Teddy Wilson, "Body and Soul," *Teddy Wilson and His Orchestra* (Classics), 1991.
24. Use of the leading-tone dominant chord is more common in post-bop repertory, as jazz composers sought ways of evading standard V-I progressions. A fascinating example is Wayne Shorter's composition, "E.S.P.," which resolves E7alt to Fmaj7 in measures 1–4, then resolves E7alt to E♭maj7 in measures 5–8. Thus E7alt is treated as both D$\hat{7}$ and *D$\hat{2}$♭. For a transcription of the tune with insightful analysis, see Waters, *The Studio Recordings of the Miles Davis Quintet, 1965–68*, 109–12.
25. While I have been trying to demonstrate how the sharing of a specific harmonic pattern allows for two morphologically distinct stretches of music to be substitutable for one another—in other words, to be in the relationship of replication—we could also

consider the issue the other way around. From an historical perspective, the fact that Wilson plays these changes at this particular spot in his performance of "Body and Soul" could be taken as evidence that he hears the leading-tone dominant-seventh as a valid substitute for V7. This may seem, at first, like a vicious circle, but it is not. Take two performances of "Body and Soul" as uncontroversial performances of the same work; by comparing them, we can recover aspects of historical modes of listening. That is, we can recover from Teddy Wilson's playing what chords counted as substitutes for other chords at that historical moment. From a philosophical perspective, by building on the historical knowledge that these two chords were understood by historical agents as substitutable, we can seek the preservation of a common pattern or aspect that mediates the relation of two musical artifacts.

26. Thelonious Monk, "Body and Soul," *The Complete Riverside Recordings* (Riverside, 1986). I have altered the chord labels from the Krieger's original transcription. For a different reading of the chords, see Krieger, *Jazz-Solopiano*, 215.

27. One might argue that the opening chord, C7♯9♭5, is really an "upper-structure" voicing, composed of an E♭-minor triad over a C-major triad (in this case, with no 3rd). The E♭-minor part of that chord would then have to function as S$\hat{2}$, the requisite subdominant harmony that seems to be missing. My objection to that interpretation would be that it would ask us to separate upper-structure voicings into possessing more than one functional role. What would be the criteria for doing so, and why would we choose, say, E♭ minor over C? If we were to abstain from choosing, what would it mean to hear two functions at the same time? With the importance that chordal roots have had in jazz harmony and its pedagogy, I have chosen to emphasize chordal roots in determining functional interpretations.

28. For more on this theme see Graham Harman, *Prince of Networks: Bruno Latour and Metaphysics* (Prahran, Victoria: Re.press, 2009), 64; Bruno Latour, *We Have Never Been Modern*, trans. Catherine Porter (Cambridge, MA: Harvard University Press, 1993), 89.

29. George Gershwin and Ira Gershwin, "But Not for Me" (New York: New World Music Corp., 1930).

30. My terminology here is borrowed from William Earl Caplin, *Classical Form: A Theory of Formal Functions for the Instrumental Music of Haydn, Mozart, and Beethoven* (New York: Oxford University Press, 1998).

31. The first take, performed at a moderately fast tempo, was released in 1954 on a Prestige 10″ record under the title *Miles Davis with Sonny Rollins*. Three years later, both takes were released on a 12″ LP entitled *Bags' Groove*, which also reissued other music Davis recorded in 1954. Aside from the need to fill the additional space of a 12″ LP, the two takes of "But Not for Me" are different enough to be of genuine musical interest. Unlike the brisk first take, the second take is much slower. Although hardly a ballad, it is played at a relaxed and moderate pace. In fact, the tempo of Davis's second take is almost identical to Chet Baker's vocal rendition of "But Not for Me," recorded and released early in 1954 on Pacific Jazz (LP PJ-1222), entitled *Chet Baker Sings*.

32. Davis's alteration of the incipit of "But Not for Me" makes it akin to other tunes in the repertoire, such as "Can't We Be Friends," "I Cover the Waterfront," "Our Delight," and "Our Love Is Here to Stay."
33. Recorded March 22, 1957. Red Garland, *Red Garland's Piano* (Prestige, 1957).
34. Hank Jones, "But Not for Me," *Have You Met Hank Jones?* (Savoy Records, 1957).
35. Ahmad Jamal, *Ahmad Jamal at the Pershing* (Argo, 1958). For a detailed transcription of Jamal's performance, transcribed by Alex Smith, see Jamal, *The Ahmad Jamal Collection* (Milwaukee: Hal Leonard, 1997).
36. Coleman Hawkins, "Body and Soul"(Bluebird, 1939).
37. Bowen, "Recordings as Sources for Jazz."
38. Ibid., 24. Bowen doesn't speak about Holiday's 1957 recording, which I have added to Figure 2.14, but her performance of the melody is remarkably similar to her 1940 recording. One notable addition is the neighbor note at the beginning of measure 3, a feature also heard in McVea's version.
39. Hawkins's version is not the only potential source for replications. A lower-neighbor d^1, first heard at the end of measure 2 in Blanton's recording, also appears in McVea. While it is probably safe to say that the g♭ was disseminated because of Hawkins's famous recording, more would have to be done to establish, say, Blanton's influence on McVea or on other recordings where the d^1 is present.
40. "Embraceable You" was in Parker's repertory and there are numerous live and studio recordings to consider. Take 2 (the released master) from the Dial recording session of October 28, 1947, is particularly radical in its excision of the melody. See Charlie Parker, *The Complete Savoy & Dial Master Takes* (Savoy, 2002).
41. James Moody and his Swedish Crowns, "Body and Soul / I'm in the Mood for Love" (Metronome Records, 1949). It is no coincidence that Moody's recording of "I'm in the Mood" is paired with "Body and Soul." Both ballads are played with little to no reference to the melody line and thus expose the chain of replications that links Hawkins to Parker to Moody.
42. John Coltrane, *My Favorite Things* (Atlantic, 1961).
43. *My Favorite Things* was culled from a number of recording sessions from late October 1960. Material from these sessions appeared on *Coltrane Jazz*, *Coltrane's Sound*, and *Coltrane Plays the Blues* in addition to *My Favorite Things*. The decision to release a record of "standards" was intentional on the part of Atlantic records.
44. See Keith Waters, "'Giant Steps' and the ic1 Legacy," *Intégral* (2010): 135–62; David Baker, *Modern Concepts in Jazz Improvisation* (Van Nuys: Alfred Music Publishing, 1990).
45. Aside from "Countdown," one could appeal to other compositions by Coltrane based on standards to demonstrate how the "Giant Steps" progression functions as prolongational and embellishing. A few examples from the same recording sessions as *My Favorite Things* are found on the album released as *Coltrane's Sound*: the first is "Satellite," based on "How High the Moon"; the second is Coltrane's reharmonization of the bridge on his version of "Body and Soul"; the last is "26-2," based on "Confirmation."

46. The interchangeability of parts in American popular music has been often noted. For a particularly vitriolic critique see the "Musical Analyses of Hit Songs" in Adorno, *Current of Music: Elements of a Radio Theory* (Malden, MA: Polity, 2009), 327–42. But Adorno wasn't telling anyone anything they didn't already know. For an insider's view, see Isaac Goldberg, *Tin Pan Alley: A Chronicle of the American Popular Music Racket* (New York: John Day Co., 1930).

Chapter 3

1. "There's little ambiguity in the openly commercial grounding of many American musical transactions," writes the musicologist Richard Crawford. "As we recognize 'business' as the very turf upon which American musical life has been constituted, we see more clearly that the musician's need to make a living has been the driving force behind two centuries of American music making. That recognition undermines confidence in a fixed border between 'commercial' and 'noncommercial' arenas. Moreover, as we come to appreciate the artistry of certain commercially driven American musicians—Irving Berlin is a good recent example—we are reminded that commercial motives do not necessarily overwhelm all others." Richard Crawford, *The American Musical Landscape: The Business of Musicianship from Billings to Gershwin* (Berkeley: University of California Press, 2000), 47.
2. Sy Oliver, "Opus One" (New York: Embassy Music Corp., 1945).
3. Richard Crawford has an illuminating discussion of "I Got Rhythm" organized around three different approaches to Gershwin's song: (1) "I Got Rhythm" as a "song played and sung by popular performers"; (2) as a "jazz standard"; and (3) as a "musical structure, a harmonic framework upon which jazz instrumentalists ... have built new compositions." Crawford, *The American Musical Landscape*, 218.
4. Does Parker's excision of the melody impact the question about what work is being performed? As argued in Chapter 2, the ontology of a work of jazz is not dependent on a set of essential work-determinative properties, such as a song's melody. Work-determinative properties are those properties that are sufficient for identifying and individuating a musical work. The relevant features are determined in relation to the social context of use and the holism of previous performances of a work. A consequence of this view is that we cannot assume that, broadly speaking, a presentation of the "melody" is essential when performing a work or producing a replication based on previous performances. There are numerous performances of standards where the melody has been sharply reduced—stated at the beginning and then quickly elided or occasionally alluded to—or simply excised altogether. In such cases the reduction or excision of the melody will often be accompanied by the preservation of the chord progression, which will take on work-determinative status.
5. For a short list of analyses see: Gary Giddins, *Visions of Jazz: The First Century* (New York: Oxford University Press, 1998), 261–83; Henry Martin, *Charlie Parker and Thematic Improvisation* (Lanham, MD: Scarecrow Press, 1996), 71–78; Thomas Owens, "Charlie Parker: Techniques of Improvisation" (PhD diss., University of

California, Los Angeles, 1974); Strunk, "The Harmony of Early Bop: A Layered Approach"; Frank Tirro, *Jazz: A History* (New York: W. W. Norton, 1977), 97; Martin Williams, "A Charlie Parker Masterpiece," *Downbeat* 37 (April 2, 1970).

6. Henry Martin identifies this motive as M in his analysis of this recording. But for Martin, the "essence of take 2's principal motive . . . is the interval of the minor seventh." Reducing the motive to an interval allows Martin to claim that almost any instance of a seventh is motivic. I worry that when a motive is reduced to such elementary musical material as an interval, it no longer has a sufficiently recognizable shape to do the work that motivic analysis is typically supposed to do — that is, to show how the music's surface and structure are organized. While I agree with him that his motive M—what I label as motive z—is important in Parker's solo, it is for different reasons, as my discussion makes clear. See Martin, *Charlie Parker and Thematic Improvisation*, 78–82.

7. In addition to Parker's live performances and studio recordings of "Embraceable You," we also have a remarkable recording of Parker playing along with Hazel Scott's solo recording of the song. See "Embraceable You" on Charlie Parker, *Bird in Time 1940–1947* (ESP-Disk, 2008).

8. One clear reference is found at measure 13 of Parker's solo, a quick nod to the lyrics "you and you alone."

9. Giddins, *Visions of Jazz*, 277.

10. A noteworthy example is the 1955 release of *Bird at St. Nick's*, which features a live performance of "Embraceable You" from 1950 beginning with the quotation from "A Table in the Corner." See Charlie Parker, *The Complete Dean Benedetti Recordings of Charlie Parker* (Mosaic Records, 1990); *Bird in Time 1940–1947*.

11. The session log is available online; see Charlie Parker Session Logs from November 26, 1945, Savoy Records (accessed June 5, 2023), https://jaybrandford.com/2015/05/31/charlie-parker-solo-transcription-meandering/.

12. Miles Davis, *Relaxin' with the Miles Davis Quintet* (Prestige, 1958). Of course, the title appears on the record sleeve and center label.

13. Frederic Ramsey and Charles Edward Smith, *Jazzmen* (New York: Harcourt, Brace, 1939), 71.

14. Ross Russell, *Bird Lives!: The High Life and Hard Times of Charlie (Yardbird) Parker* (New York: Charterhouse, 1973), 252.

15. Edward M. Komara, *The Dial Recordings of Charlie Parker: A Discography* (Greenwood, CT: Greenwood Press, 1998), 15. See Komara's Appendix 3 for a reproduction of Parker's list of titles.

16. Ashley Kahn, *Kind of Blue: The Making of the Miles Davis Masterpiece* (New York: Da Capo, 2000), 150.

17. The novelty of Coleman playing a "non-Coleman tune" was highlighted in advertisements for *This Is Our Music*. "Ornette Coleman's previous two Atlantic LPs caused an explosion whose repercussions are still being felt. They established him in the course of a year and half as the most important new voice in jazz. *This Is Our Music*, like the earlier LPs, features the brilliant original compositions of Ornette—plus his first recording of a non-Coleman tune: *Embraceable You*. This will be 1961's most

talked-about album. Don't miss it!" "Advertisement for Atlantic Records," *Downbeat* 28, no. 8 (1961). Aside from "Embraceable You," Coleman's group, featuring Paul Bley on piano, can be heard playing Charlie Parker's "Klactoveesedstene" and Irving Berlin's "How Deep Is the Ocean" on a bootleg recording, Ornette Coleman, *Complete Live at the Hillcrest Club* (Gambit Records, 2008). Neither matches the adventurousness of Coleman's "Embraceable You."
18. From the liner notes to *This Is Our Music* (Atlantic, 1960).
19. Ronald Atkins, "Review of *This Is Our Music*," *Jazz and Blues* 3, no. 3 (1973): 20.
20. Martin Williams, "Talking with Myself," *Evergreen Review* 8, no. 3 (1964): 83–84. Given his description of Parker's "Embraceable," Williams must be referring to the Dial recording, take A.
21. Philip Larkin, *All What Jazz: A Record Diary 1961–1971* (New York: Farrar, Straus & Giroux, 1985), 66.
22. Benny Carter, "Blindfold Test," *Downbeat* 28, no. 24 (1961): 39. To add insult to injury, Carter's "afterthought" to the blindfold test adds, "I should like to revise one rating. After hearing *Embraceable You* by the Ornette Coleman group, I'd like to raise the rating on Phil Woods' *Midnight Sun Never Sets* to 12!"
23. Don DeMichael, "Review of *This Is Our Music*," *Downbeat* 28, no. 10 (1961): 25. In one angry letter prompted by DeMichael's review, Virgil Matthews writes that Coleman's Embraceable You "is a thing of startling beauty. Apparently De Michael would have him blow Charlie Parker's versions of the tune." The critics, Matthews laments, "would prefer another Birdling to be added to the many we already have." See Virgil Matthews, "The Critic's Critic," *Downbeat* 28, no. 14 (1961): 10.
24. Eric Thacker, "Review of *Ornette!*," *Jazz and Blues* 3, no. 7 (1973): 19.
25. Gordon Jack, *Fifties Jazz Talk: An Oral Retrospective* (Lanham, MD: Scarecrow Press, 2004), 93.
26. Don DeMichael, "Jackson of the MJQ," *Downbeat* 28, no. 14 (1961).
27. Alun Morgan, "Review of *This Is Our Music*," *The Gramophone* (1961): 284.
28. Chris DeVito et al., *The John Coltrane Reference* (New York: Routledge, 2013), 588. The editors mention the existence of a private recording of La Roca playing "Impressions" with Coltrane's group, recorded at the Showboat in Philadelphia, sometime between July 18 and July 23, 1960. This is the earliest recorded evidence of Coltrane playing "Impressions."
29. John Coltrane, *Complete Live at the Sutherland Lounge 1961* (Rare Live Recordings), 2012. On the CD, there is a track identified as "Impressions #2." This is noted as an "unidentified composition" in DeVito et al., *The John Coltrane Reference*, 601 and 17. The composition bears certain similarities to "Impressions." Both are modal tunes, both are in D minor, and Coltrane approaches both tunes in a similar manner. However, calling it "Impressions #2" is too strong, I feel. The unidentified composition is in a complicated ABA form, not the simple twenty-four-measure AABA of "Impressions." Based on the recording from the Sutherland Lounge, the untitled composition is organized into three rotations of a twenty-four-measure ABA form. In the first rotation, the A-section contains eight bars of D-minor-seventh, the B-section has eight bars of B♭-dominant-seventh, and the final A-section has eight

more bars of D-minor-seventh. In the second and third rotations, the B-section is different: in the second rotation, A♭-minor-seventh and, in the third, B-minor-seventh. The Sutherland recording of the unidentified composition is incomplete, beginning during Coltrane's solo. Coltrane ends his solo in the middle of the second rotation, which causes some potential confusion in the band. Should they go on to rotation three or start with rotation one for McCoy Tyner's solo? Cued by Tyner, the band plays rotation one, in essence, jumping back to the top of the form. After Tyner's solo, Coltrane plays two more complete choruses (six rotations in all), bringing the performance to an end, but without anything that resembles a recognizable melody line. Given the similarities between the tunes, perhaps this was a variant on "Impressions," or a composition in progress. Its form resembles the ABA of Miles Davis's "Milestones," another recording on which Coltrane participated. If one could find out more information about this "unidentified composition," there would be interesting questions to ponder about the relationship between it and "So What" and "Milestones," questions that might help illuminate Coltrane's compositional process through chains of replication, and his practices of nomination.

30. John Coltrane, *Impressions* (Impulse, 1963).
31. Don DeMichael, "The Monterey Festival," *Downbeat* 28, no. 23 (1961): 13. DeMichael praises Montgomery's playing, especially his solo on "So What," and notes that neither Dolphy nor Coltrane "was as moving or as consistent as Montgomery." *Downbeat*, November 9, 1961, 12–13. See also DeVito et al., *The John Coltrane Reference*, 232.
32. The latter was apparently not recorded, perhaps because Coltrane's commercial recording was so well known, and Impulse records was interested in other materials from Coltrane's repertoire. DeVito et al., *The John Coltrane Reference*, 622.
33. Ibid., 632.
34. Even though these recordings have not been commercially released, the jazz scholar Barry Kernfeld has cataloged and described them. See Barry Kernfeld, "John Coltrane in Rudy Van Gelder's Studio," http://www.barrykernfeld.com/aop.htm.
35. DeVito et al., *The John Coltrane Reference*, 649–50; Kernfeld, "John Coltrane in Rudy Van Gelder's Studio."
36. "Strictly Ad Lib," *Downbeat* 30, no. 4 (1963): 47. The situation was not helped by Coltrane's tendency not to announce the song titles to the audience. See DeVito et al., *The John Coltrane Reference*, 240 and 700.
37. See, e.g., Harvey Pekar, "Review of *Impressions*," *Downbeat* 30, no. 24 (1963): 22.
38. Amiri Baraka, "John Coltrane–Cecil Taylor–Art Blakey," *Downbeat* 31, no. 6 (1964): 34.
39. And yet, even after the public baptism on the record sleeve, "Impressions" and "So What" are still, on occasion, being identified with each other. The guitarist Wes Montgomery was one of the first to regularly perform "Impressions" as part of his repertoire. Throughout 1965, on a European tour and at club dates in New York, Montgomery performed "Impressions" repeatedly. Throughout much of the latter half of 1965, Montgomery and the Wynton Kelly trio had taken up residence at the Half Note, where many sets were recorded by his label, Verve records, and broadcast on local radio as live "remotes." On November 5, two years after the release

of *Impressions*, a bootleg recording captures Montgomery opening his set with "Impressions" but, in an uncanny repetition of the events at Newport, that's not the way it is introduced by the announcer, WABC's Alan Grant:

> Alan Grant: This is a moment that many of our listeners, of course, and the people who are enjoying the show here at the Half Note have been waiting for ... as we bring to the stage let's have a big round of applause for Mr. Wes Montgomery. Wes! (Applause)
> Wes Montgomery: I'm here.
> AG: Wes, baby! Where are ya?
> WM: Whaaa ... I'm here. (Laughs)
> AG: (Laughs) All right, all right. The, uh, opening tune that we'll do will be "'Round Midnight ... (Pause, laugh)
> WM: "So What."
> AG: You wanna do "So What?" All right, we'll do that. We changed it. We'll do "So What." OK. "So What." Wes Montgomery with the Wynton Kelly trio. . . . (From a radio broadcast, November 5, 1965, WABC-FM)

After a quick bit of tuning, Montgomery taps off the tempo. Instead of playing "So What," the band plays a different tune: "Impressions." However, unlike Vega's introduction, where we can only circumstantially guess how he got the name of Coltrane's opening song, here we know the source. Montgomery calls the tune "So What" and relays it to Grant. Why? Since "Impressions" is a contrafact of "So What," and since Montgomery is the one playing the melody, is he simply being pragmatic in announcing the tune? Perhaps it is akin to a saxophonist telling the band to play "I Got Rhythm" while playing any number of alternative melodies written to fit the chord progression. If so, then "So What" here is functioning less like a work and more like a genre or type, a formulaic chord progression over which any number of different melodies could be placed. But it seems likely that Montgomery's nomination is part of a longer chain. Since he played with Coltrane at Monterey in 1960, early in the history of "Impressions" (from what we can tell), perhaps he is simply repeating the name that Coltrane was using at the time. Since Montgomery learned about the song before its moment of baptism—when it was still going under the working title "So What"—he appears to be prolonging Coltrane's pre-baptism practice. Verve records eventually released a recording of Montgomery playing "Impressions" from his stay at the Half Note, in 1969, a year after the guitarist's untimely death. The album, *Willow Weep for Me*, was a follow up to *Smokin' at the Half Note*, but many of the live tracks were overdubbed with strings and winds, a way of capitalizing on unreleased live material while presenting it in the overly orchestrated, easy listening style typical of Montgomery's final years at Verve. The officially released "Impressions," which was thankfully spared Claus Ogerman's heavy-handed arrangements, differs from the bootleg recording. Most important, when considering chains of nomination, it is labeled on the disc as "Impressions," although Richard Lamb, in the liner notes the album, wryly notes about "Impressions" that, "if the changes sound familiar, try Miles' title *So What?*" Since the record was released after Montgomery's death, we cannot hold him responsible for its public nomination.

40. Lewis Porter, *John Coltrane: His Life and Music* (Ann Arbor: University of Michigan Press, 1997), 218.
41. Gray's solo was later given lyrics by John Hendricks and appears on Lambert, Hendricks, and Ross, *Sing a Song of Basie*.
42. The unreleased version from 1958 is listed on Ahmad Jamal's website, and given slate number 9046. See "Ahmad Jamal Discography," https://ahmadjamal.com/#/complete-recordings/. This track was not issued on Ahmad Jamal, *The Complete Ahmad Jamal Trio Argo Sessions 1956–62* (Mosaic Records, 2010). The 1960 recording was released on *Happy Moods* and is also on the Mosaic set.
43. "The Lamp Is Low" first appeared on Your Hit Parade on August 5, 1939, for two weeks, peaking at number 6, then fell off for a week. It returned on August 26 and sat on the charts for the next six weeks, peaking at number 3. Although Porter asserts that the B-section is indeed a quote from Ravel, I am not so sure. While there are resemblances, the melody is neither as exact as the Gould quote, nor does it possess the same degree of evidence for a chain of replication.
44. Carl Woideck, *The John Coltrane Companion: Five Decades of Commentary* (New York: Schirmer Books, 1998), 45.
45. Gary Carner, *The Miles Davis Companion: Four Decades of Commentary* (New York: Schirmer Books, 1996), 27.
46. On Rocky Boyd, see Jack K. Chambers, *Milestones: The Music and Times of Miles Davis*, vol. 2 (New York: Da Capo Press, 1998), 40.
47. The album's center label also lists Pike as the composer.
48. Davis, while associated with modal jazz, did not invent the term. Keith Waters provides a cogent and synoptic account of the history and meaning of the term "modal jazz" in Waters, *The Studio Recordings of the Miles Davis Quintet, 1965–68*, 40–52.
49. Waters lists six characteristics of modal jazz, which are worth repeating here: "1. Modal scales for improvisation (or as a source for accompaniment); 2. Slow harmonic rhythm (single chord for 4, 8, 16, or more bars); 3. Pedal point harmonies (focal bass pitch or shifting harmonies over a primary bass pitch); 4. Absence or limited use of functional harmonic progressions (such as V-I or ii-V-I) in accompaniment or improvisation; 5. Harmonies characteristic of jazz after 1959 (suspended fourth—"sus"—chords, slash chords, harmonies named for modes: i.e., Phrygian, Aeolian harmonies); 6. Prominent use of melodic and/or harmonic perfect fourths." Ibid., 46. My account emphasizes some of these characteristics over others, a consequence of my focus on "So What," "Impressions," and related works.
50. "So What," *Newport in New York '72* (Cobblestone, 1972).
51. Alun Morgan, in a review of the album, notes the confusion. "'So What' is actually Coltrane's adaptation of the tune, and the label should have read 'Impressions.'" Alun Morgan, "Review of *The Jam Sessions, Vol. 4*," *Jazz and Blues* 3, no. 3 (1973): 26.
52. See Wes Montgomery, "Willow Weep for Me," *Smokin' at the Half Note* (Verve Records, 1968).
53. McCoy Tyner, *Trident* (Milestone, 1975).
54. Arthur C. Danto, *The Transfiguration of the Commonplace: A Philosophy of Art* (Cambridge, MA: Harvard University Press, 1981).

Chapter 4

1. Goodman, *Languages of Art*, 113.
2. Ibid. On syntactic conditions of notations see 130–41; on characters, see 141–43; on semantic conditions, see 148–54.
3. Ibid., 115.
4. Goodman deals with the obvious objections, like enharmonic spelling of notes. His theory is even robust enough to handle notational systems where there is more than one possible sonic realization—systems such as figured bass—so long as, given a sonic realization, the sound event is the member of one and only one character class.
5. Goodman, *Languages of Art*, 113.
6. All quotations in this paragraph are from ibid., 186.
7. Goehr, *The Imaginary Museum of Musical Works*; Theodore Gracyk and Andrew Kania, *The Routledge Companion to Philosophy and Music* (London: Routledge, 2011); Peter Kivy, *Introduction to a Philosophy of Music* (Oxford: Clarendon Press, 2002); Aaron Ridley, *The Philosophy of Music: Theme and Variations* (Edinburgh: Edinburgh University Press, 2004).
8. This way of formulating the basic commitments of realist philosophy is indebted to Harman, *Prince of Networks*, 72.
9. For a defense of a realist ontology of musical works that emphasized precisely this aspect, see Christopher Norris, *Platonism, Music and the Listener's Share* (London: Continuum, 2006).
10. Nicholas Wolterstorff, "Toward an Ontology of Art Works," *Noûs* (1975): 126. Wolterstorff's influential essay was expanded into a book. See Wolterstorff, *Works and Worlds of Art* (Oxford: Clarendon Press, 1980).
11. Wolterstorff, "Toward an Ontology of Art Works," 128.
12. Ibid.
13. Jerrold Levinson, *Music, Art, and Metaphysics: Essays in Philosophical Aesthetics* (Oxford: Oxford University Press, 2011), 63–88.
14. Ibid., 81.
15. "I propose that a musical work be taken to involve not only a pure sound structure, but also a structure of performing means. If the sound structure of a piece is basically a sequence of sound qualitatively defined, then the performing-means structure is a parallel sequence of performing means specified for realizing the sounds at each point. Thus a musical work consists of at least two structures. It is a compound or conjunction of a sound structure and a performing-means structure." In Levinson's tersest formulation, a musical work is a sound/performing-means structure-as-indicated-by-x-at-t. Ibid., 78.
16. Ibid., 86.
17. See "Platonism in Music: A Kind of Defense," and "Platonism in Music: Another Kind of Defense," in Peter Kivy, *The Fine Art of Repetition: Essays in the Philosophy of Music* (Cambridge: Cambridge University Press, 1993).
18. Ibid., 63.
19. Ibid., 66–73.

20. Peter Kivy, *Authenticities: Philosophical Reflections on Musical Performance* (Ithaca, NY: Cornell University Press, 1995), 158. Kivy continues, "If, of course, *enough* of such departures occur... we might want to say not merely that it is not a performance of W in this respect or that but that is not a performance at all, *tout court*."
21. Bruno Latour, *Pandora's Hope: Essays on the Reality of Science Studies* (Cambridge, MA: Harvard University Press, 1999), 69.
22. Ibid.
23. Ibid.
24. Ibid., 73.
25. William James, *Pragmatism and the Meaning of Truth*, cited in ibid., 74.
26. The saltatory view, by erasing the relations between each node (the equivalent of erasing all the mediating links in a chain), ends not with a network but rather a set or collection of objects. The problem now concerns categorization: what properties are shared by (or are typical of) all the members of this set? What properties are central and which are peripheral? For a category-based approach to standards see Lawrence Zbikowski, "Cultural Knowledge and Musical Ontology," in *Conceptualizing Music: Cognitive Structure, Theory, and Analysis* (New York: Oxford University Press, 2002).
27. Annemarie Mol, "Ontological Politics. A Word and Some Questions," *Sociological Review* 47, no. S1 (1999): 74–75.
28. Before the era of *Werktreue*, classical musicians had a robust practice of transcription. Transcriptions provide a unique historical milieu for investigating practices of replication. Rather than engage in abstract arguments about whether instrumentation is essential for musical works (thus, making transcriptions into new or derivative works), one should look at the historical practices of composers and listeners to understand the status of transcriptions. Were Liszt's transcriptions of Beethoven understood as artifacts substitutable for the original—that is, replications—or were they considered works of their own? It would be nice to let the historical agents answer this question, since it might tell us something about the way that practices of replication in classical music have become less permissive over time. At the same time, one might note that replication in jazz is also undergoing significant changes. If impermissive replication preserves morphology over time, and thus allows for the establishment of a musical museum culture, how are we to understand the museum-like practices of Wynton Marsalis, the Jazz at Lincoln Center Orchestra, and other attempts to recreate the sounds of jazz's past?
29. Robert R. Faulkner and Howard Saul Becker, *"Do You Know...?" The Jazz Repertoire in Action* (Chicago: University of Chicago Press, 2009).
30. Stated in terms of graph theory, chains of replication and chains of nomination provide the nodes and edges that constitute a network. Chains of replication generate a new node from a previous node, and they are linked together by means of edges. Each node possesses a particular topology, a shape that is unique—just like any performance, recording, score, or inscription is unique and identifiable as such. Edges, like nodes, have content, but of a different sort. When a new node is generated from a previous node by means of replication, their connecting edge represents the schematic

pattern or properties shared between nodes. Sometimes replication can be too generous in the way that it builds a network. Given the multiple contexts in which one thing can be substituted for another, replication proliferates like a weed. It needs the constraint of an additional practice. Nomination, when added to replication, helps to winnow down which nodes should be associated with one another and which should not. To call a performance by the name "Body and Soul" is to claim that some node n belongs to a specific network w. To call the same performance by a different name is to do just the opposite, to deny that n and w belong together. To be more specific, nomination asserts that *there is an edge between node* n *and network* w and that *the edge represents work-determinative properties*, not just any old replicated pattern. At the same time, nomination does not specify for us what those work-determinative properties are. It simply asserts that work-determinative properties are there to be found and solicits a listener to find them.

31. One way to evaluate this claim is to consider the explanatory scope of various ontological arguments. One fact that recommends the network model is that it can account for why works of classical music appear consistent and incorrigible, like exhibits in the "imaginary museum of musical works," by accounting for their practices of nomination and impermissive replication. And yet, philosophers who start from the presumed fixity of musical works, like Levinson or Kivy or Davies, are challenged to explain how jazz performances can be instances of works. The fact that the network-based theory can do more explanatory work, that is, that it has fewer premises and a wider extension, is a recommendation for its adoption. For more on the relationship of ontology and exemplification in artworks, see Kane, "Sound Studies without Auditory Culture: A Critique of the Ontological Turn."

32. Bruno Latour, *Science in Action: How to Follow Scientists and Engineers through Society* (Cambridge, MA: Harvard University Press, 1987).

33. Harman, *Prince of Networks*, 34.

34. Latour speaks often of a statement's fate being in the hands of others. See Latour, *Pandora's Hope*, 95.

35. This view is aligned with Lydia Goehr's trenchant observation that "I can never get down to a thin enough or simple enough version of the compositional condition without feeling I am putting aside the thickness that gives the thin ontological condition its significance in the first place." Goehr, *The Imaginary Museum of Musical Works*, xlix.

Chapter 5

1. Erik Barnouw, *The Golden Web* (New York: Oxford University Press, 1968), 3–4.
2. Naturally, there are problems in how lists of popular songs are tabulated, especially given that the entertainment industry was already segregating "Race records"—recordings by African American musicians—from other records. "Race records" were not included in *Your Hit Parade*'s tabulations, thus reinforcing forms of exclusion.

NOTES 265

3. Arnold Shaw, *Let's Dance: Popular Music in the 1930s* (New York: Oxford University Press, 1998), 47.
4. Ray E. Barfield, *Listening to Radio, 1920–1950* (Westport, CT: Praeger, 1996), 175–78.
5. The classic book on the early development of radio in America is Susan J. Douglas, *Inventing American Broadcasting, 1899–1922* (Baltimore: Johns Hopkins University Press, 1987). My account of is greatly indebted to Douglas's work. On WEAF see William Peck Banning, *Commercial Broadcasting Pioneer: The WEAF Experiment, 1922–1926* (Cambridge, MA: Harvard University Press, 1946).
6. Michael Jay Biel, "The Making and Use of Recordings in Broadcasting before 1936" (PhD diss., Northwestern University, 1977), 230.
7. Ibid., 230–31.
8. Quoted in Lawrence Wilson Lichty and Malachi C. Topping, *American Broadcasting: A Source Book on the History of Radio and Television* (New York: Hastings House Publishers, 1976), 458.
9. At a congressional hearing in 1929, chief radio inspector William Terrell offered a justification of the government's rationale for the Class B programming requirements. "The reason we did that was because at the beginning all the stations were turning to entertainments, and at the beginning the people were appreciating it. But later they were tiring of it, and if we had not checked it, it would have had an effect on broadcasting. So we created the special license and they had to have talent." Ibid., 550–51. On the response of amateur radio "hams" to their confinement to the shortwave bands, see Clinton B. DeSoto, *Two Hundred Meters and Down: The Story of Amateur Radio* (West Hartford, CT: American Radio Relay League, 1936).
10. Albin Zak, *I Don't Sound Like Nobody: Remaking Music in 1950s America* (Ann Arbor: University of Michigan Press, 2010), 13.
11. All quotes are from Federal Radio Commission, "Second Annual Report of the Federal Radio Commission" (Washington, DC: US Government Printing Office, 1928), 155–56 and 168.
12. Federal Radio Commission, "Radio Service Bulletin" (Washington, DC: US Government Printing Office, 1927), Order 16, August 31, 1927.
13. Federal Radio Commission, "Radio Service Bulletin" (Washington, DC: US Government Printing Office, 1929), December 31, 1929, 10–11.
14. Federal Communications Commission, "Rules and Regulations, Part 1: Rules of Practice and Procedure" (Washington, DC: US Government Printing Office, 1939), §3.407e.
15. Biel, "The Making and Use of Recordings," 814.
16. Ibid., 642.
17. Ibid., 643.
18. Zak, *I Don't Sound Like Nobody*, 23–24.
19. Robert David Leiter, *The Musicians and Petrillo* (New York: Bookman Associates, 1953), 68ff.
20. Russel Sanjek, *American Popular Music and Its Business: The First Four Hundred Years* (New York: Oxford University Press, 1988), 3:170.
21. Ibid.

22. Zak, *I Don't Sound Like Nobody*, 27.
23. Biel, "The Making and Use of Recordings," 641–42.
24. Duncan MacDougald Jr., "The Popular Music Industry," in *Radio Research, 1941*, ed. Paul Lazarsfeld and Frank Stanton (New York: Duell, Sloan & Pearce, 1941).
25. Ibid., 93.
26. George Thomas Simon, *The Big Bands*, rev. ed. (New York: Macmillan, 1971), 59.
27. Ibid., 60.
28. MacDougald, "The Popular Music Industry," 93.
29. Ibid., 94.
30. Ibid., 95.
31. Ibid., 96.
32. David Suisman, *Selling Sounds: The Commercial Revolution in American Music* (Cambridge, MA: Harvard University Press, 2009), 167.
33. By the 1950s, *Your Hit Parade* often began with this standard announcement: "The top tunes all over America, as determined by *Your Hit Parade* survey, which checks the best sellers in sheet music, and phonograph records, the songs most heard on the air, and the songs most played on the automatic coin machines. An accurate, authentic tabulation of America's taste in popular music." Transcribed from the June 2, 1956, broadcast on NBC.
34. Details about the affidavit and *Your Hit Parade*'s tabulation procedures come from "Sheet, Air Plugs & Parade Reports," *Billboard*, January 13, 1945, 14.
35. MacDougald, "The Popular Music Industry," 69.
36. See ibid.; Goldberg, *Tin Pan Alley: A Chronicle of the American Popular Music Racket*; Abel Green, *Inside Stuff on How to Write Popular Songs* (New York: Paul Whiteman Publishers, 1927).
37. MacDougald, "The Popular Music Industry," 109.
38. In an acknowledgment, MacDougald thanks Adorno for his help in the essay's "theoretical organization" and final "formulation." Ibid., 65.
39. Ben Yagoda, *The B Side: The Death of Tin Pan Alley and the Rebirth of the Great American Song* (New York: Riverhead Books, 2015), 71.
40. MacDougald, "The Popular Music Industry," 91.
41. Zak, *I Don't Sound Like Nobody*, 20.
42. Ibid.
43. Horace Stern, "Waring V. WDAS Station, Inc.," in *327 Pa. 433 (Pa. 1937)*, Supreme Cournt of Pennsylvania (1937), 1.
44. Ibid., 4; and Zak, *I Don't Sound Like Nobody*, 21.
45. Zak, *I Don't Sound Like Nobody*, 23.
46. Ibid., 21.
47. The term "earwitness" is borrowed from R. Murray Schafer. For Schafer, earwitnesses are crucial for constructing a history of the soundscape since they are "writing about sounds directly experienced and intimately known." The descriptions of earwitnesses "constitute the best guide available in the reconstruction of soundscapes past." R. Murray Schafer, *The Soundscape: Our Sonic Environment and the Tuning of the World* (Rochester, VT: Destiny Books, 1994), 8–9.

48. Ibid., 7.
49. For a critique of the notion of the soundscape, see Ari Y. Kelman, "Rethinking the Soundscape: A Critical Genealogy of a Key Term in Sound Studies," *The Senses and Society* 5, no. 2 (2010): 212–34.
50. Whitney Davis, *A General Theory of Visual Culture* (Princeton, NJ: Princeton University Press, 2011). Chapter 9 is particularly trenchant for my argument.
51. Lynn Abbott and Doug Seroff, *Ragged but Right: Black Traveling Shows, Coon Songs, and the Dark Pathway to Blues and Jazz* (Jackson: University Press of Mississippi, 2007).
52. One might consider, for instance, Louis Armstrong. Growing up in New Orleans in extreme poverty, and with only a limited education, Armstrong's early training in music came through instruction at the Home for Colored Waifs, and through his mentor, "King" Joe Oliver. He was not a strong reader of music at the time that he was hired by Fletcher Henderson in the mid-1920s, although his brilliant solos stand out on the handful of recordings with Henderson. In contrast, Lil Hardin, the pianist in King Oliver's band and (eventually) Armstrong's spouse, was trained in music at Fisk University, with great facility in reading music and writing musical scores. Like so many women in jazz, Hardin's role behind the scenes of Armstrong's famous Hot Five recordings has been generally neglected. As she pushed Armstrong to lead his own group, and to compose original music, she was also notating and arranging it.
53. The history of Black emancipation in America is often tied to literacy; in many slave narratives, the act of learning to read and write grounds accounts of self-development and self-realization. For a brilliant challenge to the coupling of literacy and emancipation, see Daphne A. Brooks, "'Puzzling the Intervals': Blind Tom and the Poetics of the Sonic Slave Narrative," in *The Oxford Handbook of the African American Slave Narrative*, ed. John Ernest (New York: Oxford University Press, 2014).
54. These musicians often had complex relationships with their Black predecessors and influences, sometimes acknowledging their influences and sometimes disavowing what they had learned and imitated. In the case of Whiteman, see Joshua Berrett, *Louis Armstrong and Paul Whiteman: Two Kings of Jazz* (New Haven, CT: Yale University Press, 2004).
55. Paul Whiteman and Mary Margaret McBride, *Jazz* (New York: J. H. Sears & Co., 1926), 117–19.
56. Almost anything can be "jazzed," claims Whiteman, although in some cases it is inappropriate. "Onward, Christian Soldiers . . . should not be jazzed . . . [and] nether would we jazz the 'Tannhäuser' march nor any of the lovely operatic arias." Ibid., 121.
57. Biel, "The Making and Use of Recordings," 994.
58. Ibid., 993.
59. Allegedly, Benny Goodman paid Al Jarvis $500 to plug his discs before his famous arrival at the Palomar Ballroom in California. Arnold Passman, *The Deejays* (New York: Macmillan, 1971), 77–78.
60. Sometimes the competing versions would arrive immediately on the heels of the first release. Yagoda tells a story of Mitch Miller's producing a version of "Tzena, Tzena,

Tzena" two days after Gordon Jenkins and The Weavers' disc was first released. Yagoda, *The B Side*, 133.

61. The saturation of the soundscape with recordings, and their role in fixing a song's aural image, impacted audiences' expectations about live performance. As Elijah Wald notes, the singer Vaughn Monroe was mocked by a reviewer in 1941 for presenting himself as a recording artist and modeling his live performance on his recordings. According to the reviewer, "Vaughn let the lads and lassies know that he knew that their great acquaintance with his band came from records, so he confined the bulk of his show to his diskings." As Wald correctly notes, "For older audiences, the idea that a live performer would essentially go onstage as the touring version of his or her own recordings was pretty strange, but younger fans took it for granted. So musicians now had a new responsibility: not only to play as well as they could and entertain the audience, but also to fulfill the expectations of fans who often knew their records better than they did." Elijah Wald, *How the Beatles Destroyed Rock 'n' Roll: An Alternative History of American Popular Music* (New York: Oxford University Press, 2009), 126–27.

62. Yagoda, *The B Side*, dust jacket and 128. Musicologist Albin Zak tells a similar story, minus the lament. "The 1950s marked a radical transformation in American popular music.... The sudden flood of records from the margins of the music industry left impressions on the pop soundscape that would eventually reshape long-established listening habits and expectations, as well as conventions of songwriting, performance, and recording." Zak, *I Don't Sound Like Nobody*, dust jacket.

63. For an insightful discussion of Sam Phillips's work, see *I Don't Sound Like Nobody*, 100–4.

64. The ideal of fidelity was always a something of a fiction, even if the belief or disbelief in it shaped actual studio practice, as well as the marketing and reception of recordings. From their inception, recordings mediated the reality that they ostensibly indexed. For more see Jonathan Sterne, *The Audible Past: Cultural Origins of Sound Reproduction* (Durham, NC: Duke University Press, 2003).

65. Zak, *I Don't Sound Like Nobody*, 162.

66. Theodore Gracyk, *Rhythm and Noise: An Aesthetics of Rock* (Durham, NC: Duke University Press, 1996), 1. He notes, "Rock's most distinctive characteristic within popular music may lie in the realm of ontology." Gracyk includes rock and roll as a style of rock music; while the distinction is well-founded and important for his argument, it is not relevant to my discussion. I will use the terms synonymously for the sake of clarity.

67. Ibid., 13.

68. Ibid. For example, Peter Guralnick writes with an attention to the sound of those early records: "There is a crisp authority to Scotty Moore's lead guitar, Elvis's rhythm is ringing and clear, and the bass gallops along in slap-happy fashion.... The sound is clean, without affectation or clutter . . . with a kind of thinness and manic energy.... The sound was further bolstered by a generous use of echo, a homemade technique refined independently by Sam Phillips . . . with sewer pipes and bathroom

acoustics." Cited in ibid., 15. See Peter Guralnick, *Lost Highway: Journeys & Arrivals of American Musicians* (Boston: Little, Brown, 1999).
69. Gracyk, *Rhythm and Noise*, 14. My emphasis. The point holds for other early rock recordings as well. "Consider the Beatles' recording of 'Twist and Shout.' The raw sound of [John] Lennon's voice at the end of a twelve-hour recording session is essential to its effect." Ibid., 14–15.
70. At the time Gracyk wrote *Rhythm and Noise*, Springsteen's album was widely available in three formats: LP, cassette, and compact disc. I am modifying his account for timeliness, but without changing its argument. Ibid., 21.
71. Ibid., 21.
72. Ibid., 32–33. This potentially abstract worry is concretized in the case of Taylor Swift, who has embarked on a large project of re-recording and re-releasing her early catalog, of which she is no longer the owner. See Jon Caramanica et al., "Taylor Swift Remade 'Fearless' as 'Taylor's Version.' Let's Discuss," *New York Times*, April 10, 2021, C2.
73. For a more extensive account of the "copy" record, and the specific case of LaVern Baker, see Wald, *How the Beatles Destroyed Rock 'n' Roll*, 175–76.
74. Interview with Snooky Lanson in Elrod, *Your Hit Parade and American Top Ten Hits*, 9.
75. On Dizzy Gillespie, bebop, and jazz musicians as artists, see Eric Porter, *What Is This Thing Called Jazz?: African American Musicians as Artists, Critics, and Activists* (Berkeley: University of California Press, 2002), Chapter 2.
76. On the question of bebop and cultural initiation, one might take their bearings from Langston Hughes, Amiri Baraka, and Dan Burley. All three understand bebop (and its contemporary African American cultural manifestations) as requiring initiation, as harboring secrets that can only be unlocked by those with the proper interpretive and experiential key. Hughes, writing in the voice of Jess B. Semple, the fictional everyman Harlemite, claims that Bop comes from the police and their violence toward Black people. Semple, when stopped and questioned by the cops upon walking through a white neighborhood, says: "If my answers don't satisfy them, BOP! MOP! . . . BE-BOP! If they don't hit me, they have already hurt my soul. *A dark man shall see dark days.* Bop comes out of them dark days. That's why real Bop is mad, wild, frantic, crazy—and not to be dug unless you've seen dark days too. Folks who ain't suffered . . . think Bop is nonsense." Langston Hughes, *The Best of Simple* (New York: Hill & Wang, 1961), 118–19. Baraka, in his autobiography, describes his first encounter with bebop and the time it took to become familiar with it: "I listened to BeBop after school, over and over. At first it was strange and the strangeness itself was strangely alluring. BeBop! I listened and listened." After becoming initiated, Baraka comes to describe bebop as "A new language a new tongue and vision for a generally more advanced group in our generation. BeBop was a staging area for a new sensibility growing to maturity." Amiri Baraka, *The Autobiography of LeRoi Jones* (New York: Freundlich Books, 1984), 57–58. Although Burley doesn't write about bebop directly, his brilliant writings on jive illuminate the patois, spirit, and its encoded cultural messages that one finds in jive's contemporary, bebop. "[Jive] is a medium of escape, a safety valve for people

pressed against the wall for centuries, deprived of the advantages of complete social, economic, moral and intellectual freedom . . . a protest of a people given half a loaf of bread and then dared to eat it; a people continually fooled and bewildered by the mirage of a better and fuller life. Jive is a defense mechanism, a method of deriving pleasure from something the uninitiated cannot understand. It is the same means of escape that brought into being the spirituals . . . [and] the blues songs of protest. . . . Jive provides a medium of expression universal it is appeal. . . . It is language made vivid, vital and dynamic." Dan Burley, *Dan Burley's Jive* (DeKalb: Northern Illinois University Press, 2009), 11. Substitute the word "bebop" for "jive" and you have a shoe that fits quite well. Burley himself was no stranger to the beboppers; you can see him playing boogie-woogie in Dizzy Gillespie's film *Jivin' in Be-Bop*, from 1947. Also, Scott DeVeaux's discussion of bebop and the "avant-garde" touches on many of the key issues about bebop, the avant-garde, and cultural initiation. See Scott DeVeaux, *The Birth of Bebop: A Social and Musical History* (Berkeley: University of California Press, 1997), 20–21.
77. "All the Things You Are" appeared in *Broadway Melody* (1944), "Star Eyes" in *I Dood It* (1943), and "Stella by Starlight" in *The Uninvited* (1944).
78. For instance, Bob Redcross's acetate recordings from 1943 capture Parker practicing along with Benny Goodman's recording of "China Boy" and Hazel Scott's recording of "Embraceable You." I think there is no reason to assume that Parker did not practice along with other recordings, or radio programs, or even juke boxes. For more on Parker and his relationship with popular music, see Brian Priestley, "Charlie Parker and Popular Music," *Annual Review of Jazz Studies* (2009): 83–99.
79. Amiri Baraka, *Black Music* (New York: Quill, 1967), 107.
80. Ibid., 105.
81. Amiri Baraka, *Blues People: Negro Music in White America* (New York: William Morrow, 1963), 212. Baraka, in a confessional mode, includes himself in this group.
82. Ibid., 214.
83. Ibid., 217.
84. Ibid., 218.
85. Ibid., 217.
86. Baraka, *Black Music*, 194.
87. For example, Carl Brauer, in an affirmative review of Anthony Braxton's *In the Tradition*, an album of standards from a musician known for his compositions and extended improvisations, writes, "the resulting recording shows another side of Braxton . . . as he eschews his own compositions for a series of jazz classics. The critics who think Braxton isn't a jazz musician (if that's really important) should finally be silenced." Carl Brauer, "Review of Anthony Braxton, in the Tradition," *Cadence*, June 1977, 34.
88. Baraka, *Black Music*, 54.
89. Ibid., 107.
90. Ibid., 105.
91. Ibid., 174.
92. Ibid., 55.

93. Abbott and Seroff, *Ragged but Right*, 127ff. According to Abbott and Seroff, a review first noted that "Ma Rainey assassinates the blues," in 1915, but the term had been around previously. In 1911, there was mention in the major trade publication for traveling black theatrical and minstrel shows, the *Indianapolis Freeman*, that the comedy team of "Dude" Kelley and Amon Davis are "assassinators of the blues, as they style themselves." See ibid., 130 note 75. Of special interest is the 1915 advertisement for Rainey and Rainey, "Assassinators of the Blues," also from the *Indianapolis Freeman*, reproduced on page 134.
94. Baraka, *Black Music*, 31.
95. Ibid., 110.
96. There is more to Baraka's claim than I address, but it would be a shame to leave it undiscussed. Baraka's selection of "This Nearly Was Mine" as the "best tune" on the album is both a provocation and response his fellow jazz critics. "This" is selected to challenge the claims, common at the time, that Taylor's music was not really rooted in the "jazz tradition," that his music is too "classical," that it "doesn't swing," or that its musical language is more indebted to European atonality than to jazz harmony. In his review of *The World of Cecil Taylor*, Baraka makes the argument that Taylor's performance is "traditional" jazz in the sense that the act of using "materials and ideas that are perhaps cultural inheritances" and "work[ing them] over into something for himself" is "about as 'traditional' as any really fresh and exciting jazz music can be." In other words, Taylor is "traditional" insofar as he is participating in a culture of permissive musical replication, even as he is radicalizing it or even transforming it entirely. Ibid., 110–11.
97. My understanding of a "criterial question" is indebted to Stanley Cavell's work on Wittgenstein, and especially to Stephen Mulhall's exposition of Cavell's work. See Stanley Cavell, *The Claim of Reason: Wittgenstein, Skepticism, Morality, and Tragedy* (New York: Oxford University Press, 1979); Stephen Mulhall, *Stanley Cavell: Philosophy's Recounting of the Ordinary* (Oxford: Clarendon Press, 1998).
98. To reiterate an earlier point, what is interesting about this kind of radical replication is not that we can produce rigid rules that determine for us where one work ends and another begins, but that they force us to account for why ontological determination is often fraught, and to understand the reasons behind it.
99. By August 1966, *Billboard* magazine called the Beatles' song "Yesterday" a "modern standard" with over 175 versions available by everyone from Lawrence Welk to Xavier Cugat to the Supremes. See Wald, *How the Beatles Destroyed Rock 'n' Roll*, 223.

Chapter 6

1. Kania, "All Play and No Work: An Ontology of Jazz."
2. Ibid., 391–92.
3. Ibid., 400.
4. To reformulate it, the musical work in jazz is both the condition and consequence of performances. Kockelman's account of ontology emphasizes the way that ontologies

are always both "grounded in and grounding of one's own worlds," while also "subject to reframing through one's experience in such worlds." In this respect, "ontologies are not only the roots and fruits of representation of the world ... they are also the roots and fruits of residence in the world." Paul Kockelman, *Agent, Person, Subject, Self: A Theory of Ontology, Interaction, and Infrastructure* (New York: Oxford University Press, 2013), 3.
5. In 1980, Gary Giddins described it as "the most recorded American popular song of all time (nearly 3000 versions)," and there have likely been a few thousand more versions recorded since then. Although I disagree with Giddins about the overall topology of "Body and Soul"'s network, my discussion of the song is informed by and indebted to his essay. Gary Giddins, "50 Years of Body and Soul," in *Reading Jazz: A Gathering of Autobiography, Reportage, and Criticism from 1919 to Now*, ed. Robert Gottlieb (New York: Vintage Books, 1999), 1006.
6. Chu Berry and His "Little Jazz" Ensemble (feat. Roy Eldridge), "Stardust / Body and Soul" (Commodore, 1938).
7. Giddens, "50 Years of Body and Soul," 1008.
8. Cozy Cole and his Orchestra, "Body and Soul" (Savoy, 1944).
9. Art Tatum Trio, "Body and Soul" (Comet, 1944).
10. Cole's recording is from January 1944 and Tatum's is from June. See Nat "King" Cole, "Body and Soul" (Capitol, 1944).
11. James Moody, "Body and Soul," *Flute 'n the Blues* (Argo, 1956).
12. Coleman Hawkins and His Orchestra, "Body and Soul" (Bluebird, 1939).
13. Benny Carter, on the album *Further Definitions*, arranged the first A-section of Hawkins's performance for a quartet of saxophones, including Hawkins himself! Eddie Jefferson's vocalese version, from the 1968 album *Body and Soul*, adds lyrics to Hawkins's solo that tell the story of Hawkins's career and why he was "the king of the saxophones." It is a pretty flat-footed performance, plodding and predictable, but—like almost all jazz vocalese—an act of canonization that turns improvisations into "sacred" texts. See Benny Carter and His Orchestra, "Body and Soul," *Further Definitions* (Impulse!, 1962); and Eddie Jefferson, "Body and Soul," *Body and Soul* (Prestige, 1968). For more on the impact of Hawkins's "Body and Soul" on other performances of the standard, see Friedwald, *Stardust Melodies*, 167.
14. Dexter Gordon, "Body and Soul," *Fried Bananas* (Gearbox Records, 1972). Gordon made "Body and Soul" into a regular part of his repertoire starting in the early 1970s, and his arrangement of the song combines aspects of John Coltrane's recording (discussed below) with those of Hawkins.
15. Coleman Hawkins and His Orchestra, "Rainbow Mist" (Apollo, 1944).
16. Coleman Hawkins, "Picasso" (Clef, 1948).
17. Sonny Rollins, "Body and Soul," *Sonny Rollins and the Big Brass* (Metrojazz, 1958).
18. Duke Ellington and Jimmy Blanton, "Body and Soul" (Victor, 1940).
19. Sarah Vaughan, "Body and Soul," *How Long Has This Been Going On?* (Pablo, 1978).
20. Archie Shepp and Richard Davis, "Body and Soul," *Body and Soul* (Enja, 1991).
21. John Coltrane, "Body and Soul," *Coltrane's Sound* (Atlantic, 1964).

22. Dexter Gordon, *Homecoming: Live at the Village Vanguard* (Columbia, 1990); *Round Midnight: Original Motion Picture Soundtrack* (Columbia, 1986).
23. Joe Henderson, "Body and Soul," *The Standard Joe* (Red, 1991).
24. Joseph Roach, *Cities of the Dead: Circum-Atlantic Performance* (New York: Columbia University Press, 1996), 2.
25. Vijay Iyer, "Habeas Corpus," *Blood Sutra* (Artists House, 2003).
26. Vijay Iyer Trio, *Historicity* (ACT, 2009). Liner notes are available online at https://vijay-iyer.com/albums/historicity/ (accessed June 8, 2023).
27. "Mainstream jazz," as it is sometimes called, is closely attached to the repertory of standards. See Mark Tucker, "Mainstreaming Monk: The Ellington Album," *Black Music Research Journal* 19, no. 2 (1999): 227–44.
28. On a personal note, certain recordings that I have been listening to since my teens—and that remain with me—can be recalled with almost complete fulfillment. In my mind's ear I can hear, for instance, the introduction to Miles Davis's "So What," from *Kind of Blue*. The image includes not only the pitches and rhythms played by the piano and bass, but also the timbre of the bass on the recordings, and the sense of space (or reverberation) on the recordings. As the bass player starts the head, I can hear the timbre and wash of Jimmy Cobb's cymbals and anticipate the sound of the horns when they make their entrance. As for the solos, I can playback in my head Miles Davis's solo, or imagine the opening phrase of Cannonball Adderley's alto solo, and then follow it through a chorus or two.

    Kind of Blue was one of the first jazz records I purchased. For me, as an avid jazz listener and performer for many years, a record like *Kind of Blue* functioned as a central text for study. Just as writers or poets might be able to recite passages of prose or stanzas of verse from memory, jazz musicians can recite others' recordings and improvisations. The aural image is simply a way of gesturing toward the human ability to imaginatively recollect sounds to which they have become attached.
29. Joe Cocker, "With a Little Help from My Friends," *With a Little Help from My Friends* (A&M, 1969).
30. Just to name a few songs first recorded by Nyro, and subsequently covered: "Wedding Bell Blues" (5th Dimension), "Stoned Soul Picnic" (5th Dimension), "Eli's Coming" (Three Dog Night), "And When I Die" (Blood, Sweat, and Tears), and "Stoney End" (Barbra Streisand).
31. Nathaniel Mackey, *Bedouin Hornbook* (Lexington: University Press of Kentucky, 1986), 34.
32. Thelonious Monk, *Thelonious Monk Plays the Music of Duke Ellington* (Riverside, 1956).
33. See Tucker, "Mainstreaming Monk: The Ellington Album."
34. Robin D. G. Kelley, *Thelonious Monk: The Life and Times of an American Original* (New York: Free Press, 2010), 192–93.
35. If we were to stick only to Ellington's own recordings and performances of "Mood Indigo," we'd have to say that the song is already, in the topological sense of the term, a standard. I recall Martin Block once saying that "Mood Indigo" was not a song but a *tradition*.

36. Ellington recorded "Mood Indigo" for three different labels in 1930. The Brunswick recording was released with the title "Dreamy Blues." See [Duke Ellingon] The Harlem Footwarmers, "Mood Indigo" (Okeh, 1930); [Duke Ellingon] The Jungle Band, "Dreamy Blues" (Brunswick, 1930); Duke Ellington and His Cotton Club Orchestra, "Mood Indigo" (Victor, 1930).
37. Duke Ellington and His Famous Orchestra, "Mood Indigo" (Columbia, 1940).
38. Duke Ellington, "Mood Indigo" (RCA, 1945).
39. Duke Ellington and His Orchestra, "Mood Indigo," *Masterpieces by Ellington* (Columbia, 1951).
40. Walter van de Leur says that this passage is played by Strayhorn, that he's the soloist, but I have not found any additional corroborating evidence. See Walter van de Leur, *Something to Live For: The Music of Billy Strayhorn* (Oxford: Oxford University Press, 2002), 117.
41. Every rule has its exception, like the exceptional Cécile McLorin Salvant.

Discography

Baker, Chet. *Chet Baker Sings*. Pacific Jazz 1222, 1956. LP.
Berry, Chu, and His "Little Jazz" Ensemble (feat. Roy Eldridge). "Stardust / Body and Soul." Commodore 1502, 1938. 78 rpm.
Carter, Benny, and His Orchestra. "Body and Soul." *Further Definitions*. Impulse! A-12, 1962. LP.
Cocker, Joe. "With a Little Help from My Friends." *With a Little Help from My Friends*. A&M Records SP-4182, 1969. LP.
Cole, Cozy, and His Orchestra. "Body and Soul." Savoy 501, 1944. 78 rpm.
Cole, Nat "King." "Body and Soul." Capitol 20010, 1944. 78 rpm.
Coleman, Ornette. *Complete Live at the Hillcrest Club*. Gambit Records, 2008. CD.
Coleman, Ornette. *This Is Our Music*. Atlantic SD-1353, 1961. LP.
Coltrane, John. "Body and Soul." *Coltrane's Sound*. Atlantic 1419, 1964. LP.
Coltrane, John. *Complete Live at the Sutherland Lounge 1961*. Rare Live Recordings, 2012. CD.
Coltrane, John. *Impressions*. Impulse! A-42, 1963. LP.
Coltrane, John. *My Favorite Things*. Atlantic 1361, 1961. LP.
Crosby, Bob. *Bob Crosby and His Orchestra*. Aircheck Records 17, 1978. LP.
Davis, Miles. *Bag's Groove*. Prestige 7109, 1957. LP.
Davis, Miles. *The Complete Live at the Plugged Nickel 1965*. Columbia CXK 66955, 1995. CD.
Davis, Miles. *"Four" & More*. Columbia 9253, 1964. LP.
Davis, Miles. *Kind of Blue*. Columbia CL 1355, 1959. LP.
Davis, Miles. *Miles Davis with Sonny Rollins*. Prestige 187, 1954. LP.
Davis, Miles. *Relaxin' with the Miles Davis Quintet*. Prestige 7129, 1958. LP.
[Ellington, Duke] The Harlem Footwarmers. "Mood Indigo." Okeh 8840, 1930. 78 rpm.
[Ellington, Duke] The Jungle Band. "Dreamy Blues (Aka Mood Indigo)." Brunswick 4952, 1930. 78 rpm.
Ellington, Duke. *Ellington '55*. Capitol W521, 1955. LP.
Ellington, Duke. "Mood Indigo." Columbia 35427, 1940. 78 rpm.
Ellington, Duke, and His Cotton Club Orchestra. "Mood Indigo." Victor 22587, 1930. 78 rpm.
Ellington, Duke, and His Famous Orchestra. "Mood Indigo." RCA-Victor LPM-6009, 1945. 78 rpm.
Ellington, Duke, and His Orchestra. "Mood Indigo." *Masterpieces by Ellington*. Columbia ML-4418, 1951. LP.
Ellington, Duke, and Jimmy Blanton. "Body and Soul." Victor 27406, 1940. 78 rpm.
Fields, Ernie. "In the Mood." Rendezvous Records 110, 1959. 45 rpm.
Garland, Red. *Red Garland's Piano*. Prestige PRLP 7068, 1957. LP.
Goodman, Benny. *"Camel Caravan" Broadcasts 1939. Vol. 2*. Phontastic NCD 8818, 1992. LP.

Gordon, Dexter. "Body and Soul." *Fried Bananas*. Gearbox Records 1535, 1972. LP.
Gordon, Dexter. *Homecoming: Live at the Village Vanguard*. Columbia C2K 46824, 1990. LP.
Gordon, Dexter. *Round Midnight: Original Motion Picture Soundtrack*. Columbia SC 40464, 1986. LP.
Hawkins, Coleman, and His Orchestra. "Body and Soul." Bluebird B-10523, 1939. 78 rpm.
Hawkins, Coleman, and His Orchestra. "Picasso." *The Essential Coleman Hawkins*. Verve Records 8568, 1964. LP.
Hawkins, Coleman, and His Orchestra. "Rainbow Mist." Apollo 751, 1944. 78 rpm.
Hayes, Edgar. *Edgar Hayes and His Orchestra, 1938–1948*. Classics 1053, 1999. CD.
Henderson, Fletcher. "Hot and Anxious." Columbia 2449-D, 1931. 78 rpm.
Henderson, Joe. "Body and Soul." *The Standard Joe*. Red Records RR 123248-2, 1991. CD.
Iyer, Vijay. "Habeas Corpus." *Blood Sutra*. Artists House – AH 9, 2003. CD.
Iyer, Vijay, Trio. *Historicity*. ACT 9489-2, 2009. CD.
Jamal, Ahmad. *Ahmad Jamal at the Pershing*. Argo 628, 1958. LP.
Jamal, Ahmad. *The Complete Ahmad Jamal Trio Argo Sessions 1956–62*. Mosaic Records MD9-246, 2010. CD.
Jefferson, Eddie. "Body and Soul." *Body and Soul*. Prestige PR7619, 1968. LP.
Jones, Hank. *Have You Met Hank Jones?* Savoy Records MG12084, 1956. LP
Kelly, Ed, and Pharoah Sanders. *Ed Kelly & Pharoah Sanders*. Evidence Music 22056-2, 1993. CD.
King Sisters and Alvino Rey. "In the Mood." Victor PBS-042247, 1939. 78 rpm.
Krupa, Gene. *The Radio Years 1940*. Jazz Unlimited 2021, 1993. CD.
Manone, Wingy. "Jumpy Nerves." *Wingy Manone and His Orchestra, 1936–1939*. Vol. 1. RCA Victor LPM 10123, 1988. LP.
Manone, Wingy. "Tar Paper Stomp." Decca 7425, 1938. 78 rpm.
Miller, Glenn. "In the Mood." *The Glenn Miller Orchestra "Live" at the Glen Island Casino Summer 1939*. Magic DAWE 31, 1988. CD.
Miller, Glenn. "In the Mood." Bluebird B-10416, 1939. 78 rpm.
Mills Blue Rhythm Band. *Mills Blue Rhythm Band 1934–1936*. Classics Records 710, 1993. CD.
Monk, Thelonious. "Body and Soul." *The Complete Riverside Recordings*. Riverside Records RCD-022-2, 1986. CD.
Monk, Thelonious. *Thelonious Monk Plays the Music of Duke Ellington*. Riverside Records RLP-12-201, 1956. LP.
Montgomery, Wes. "Willow Weep for Me." *Smokin' at the Half Note*. Verve Records 8633, 1968. LP.
Moody, James. "Body and Soul." *Flute 'n the Blues*, Argo LP-603, 1956. LP.
Moody, James, and His Swedish Crowns. "Body and Soul / I'm in the Mood for Love." Metronome Records B502, 1949. 78 rpm.
Parker, Charlie. *Bird in Time 1940–1947*. ESP-Disk 4050, 2008. CD.
Parker, Charlie. *The Complete Dean Benedetti Recordings of Charlie Parker*. Mosaic Records MD7-129, 1990. CD.
Parker, Charlie. *The Complete Savoy & Dial Master Takes*. Savoy Jazz 17149, 2002. CD.
Redman, Don. "*Hot and Anxious*." Brunswick 1344, 1932. 78 rpm.
Rodgers, Richard, Lorenz Hart, Mary Martin, and Lehman Engel. *Babes in Arms*. Columbia Masterworks 4488, 1951. LP.

Rollins, Sonny. "Body and Soul." *Sonny Rollins and the Big Brass*. Metrojazz E1002, 1958. LP.
Shaw, Artie. *Artie Shaw & His Orchestra 1938. Vol. 2*. Hindsight Records HSR-140, 1979. LP.
Shaw, Artie. *Melody and Madness. Vol. 1*. Phontastic 7609, 1999. LP.
Shepp, Archie, and Richard Davis. "Body and Soul." *Body and Soul*. Enja Records CD 7007-2, 1991. CD.
Sinatra, Frank. *Songs for Young Lovers*. Capitol H-488, 1954. LP.
Tatum, Art. "Body and Soul." *Tatum Is Art—Piano Solo—1938–1939*. Musidisc JA-5177, 1976. LP.
Tatum, Art. "Body and Soul." *The Tatum Solo Masterpieces*. Vol. 1. Pablo Records 2310-723, 1975. LP.
Tatum, Art, Trio. "Body and Soul." Comet T2, 1944. 78 rpm.
Tyner, McCoy. "Impressions." *Trident*, Milestone 9063, 1975. LP.
Various. "So What." *Newport in New York '72*. Cobblestone CST 9032-6, 1972. LP.
Vaughan, Sarah. "Body and Soul." *How Long Has This Been Going On?* Pablo Records 2310-821, 1978. LP.
Wilson, Teddy. "Body and Soul." *Teddy Wilson and His Orchestra*. Classics 620, 1991. CD.

References

Abbott, Lynn, and Doug Seroff. *Ragged but Right: Black Traveling Shows, Coon Songs, and the Dark Pathway to Blues and Jazz*. Jackson: University Press of Mississippi, 2007.
Adorno, Theodor W. *Current of Music: Elements of a Radio Theory*. Malden, MA: Polity, 2009.
Adorno, Theodor W. *Introduction to the Sociology of Music*. New York: Seabury Press, 1976.
Adorno, Theodor W. *Negative Dialectics*. New York: Seabury Press, 1973.
"Advertisement for Atlantic Records." *Downbeat* 28, no. 8 (April 13, 1961): 1.
"Ahmad Jamal Discography." Accessed June 5, 2023. www.ahmadjamal.com/#/complete-recordings/.
Anonymous. *Volume 1 of over 1000 Songs*. Unidentified publisher, 1950s.
Atkins, Ronald. "Review of *This Is Our Music*." *Jazz and Blues* 3, no. 3 (June 1973): 20.
Baker, David. *Modern Concepts in Jazz Improvisation*. Van Nuys, CA: Alfred Music Publishing, 1990.
Bañagale, Ryan Raul. *Arranging Gershwin: Rhapsody in Blue and the Creation of an American Icon*. New York: Oxford University Press, 2014.
Banning, William Peck. *Commercial Broadcasting Pioneer: The WEAF Experiment, 1922–1926*. Cambridge, MA: Harvard University Press, 1946.
Baraka, Amiri. *The Autobiography of LeRoi Jones*. New York: Freundlich Books, 1984.
Baraka, Amiri. *Black Music*. New York: Quill, 1967.
Baraka, Amiri. *Blues People: Negro Music in White America*. New York: William Morrow, 1963.
Baraka, Amiri. "John Coltrane–Cecil Taylor–Art Blakey." *Downbeat* 30, no. 6 (February 27, 1964): 34.
Barfield, Ray E. *Listening to Radio, 1920–1950*. Westport, CT: Praeger, 1996.
Barnouw, Erik. *The Golden Web*. New York: Oxford University Press, 1968.
Berliner, Paul. *Thinking in Jazz: The Infinite Art of Improvisation*. Chicago: University of Chicago Press, 1994.
Berrett, Joshua. *Louis Armstrong and Paul Whiteman: Two Kings of Jazz*. New Haven, CT: Yale University Press, 2004.
Biel, Michael Jay. "The Making and Use of Recordings in Broadcasting before 1936." PhD diss., Northwestern University, 1977.
Born, Georgina. "On Musical Mediation: Ontology, Technology and Creativity." *Twentieth-Century Music* 2, no. 1 (2005): 7–36.
Bowen, José Antonio. "The History of Remembered Innovation: Tradition and Its Role in the Relationship between Musical Works and Their Performances." *Journal of Musicology* 11, no. 2 (1993): 139–73.
Bowen, José Antonio. "Recordings as Sources for Jazz: A Performance History of 'Body and Soul.'" In *Five Perspectives on "Body and Soul" and Other Contributions to Music Performance Studies*, edited by Claudia Emmenegger and Olivier Senn, 15–27. Zürich: Chronos, 2011.

Brauer, Carl. "Review of Anthony Braxton, *In the Tradition*." *Cadence*, June 1977, 1.
Brooks, Daphne A. "'Puzzling the Intervals': Blind Tom and the Poetics of the Sonic Slave Narrative." In *The Oxford Handbook of the African American Slave Narrative*, edited by John Ernest, 391–414. New York: Oxford University Press, 2014.
Brown, L. B. "Musical Works, Improvisation, and the Principle of Continuity." *Journal of Aesthetics and Art Criticism* 54, no. 4 (1996): 353–70.
Burley, Dan. *Dan Burley's Jive*. DeKalb: Northern Illinois University Press, 2009.
Caplin, William Earl. *Classical Form: A Theory of Formal Functions for the Instrumental Music of Haydn, Mozart, and Beethoven*. New York: Oxford University Press, 1998.
Caramanica, Jon, Joe Coscarelli, Jon Pareles, Ben Sisario, and Lindsay Zoladz. "Taylor Swift Remade 'Fearless' as 'Taylor's Version.' Let's Discuss." *New York Times*, April 10, 2021.
Carner, Gary. *The Miles Davis Companion: Four Decades of Commentary*. New York: Schirmer Books, 1996.
Carter, Benny. "Blindfold Test." *Downbeat* 28, no. 24 (November 23, 1961): 39.
Cavell, Stanley. *The Claim of Reason: Wittgenstein, Skepticism, Morality, and Tragedy*. New York: Oxford University Press, 1979.
Chambers, Jack K. *Milestones: The Music and Times of Miles Davis*. Vol. 2. New York: Da Capo Press, 1998.
Crawford, Richard. *The American Musical Landscape: The Business of Musicianship from Billings to Gershwin*. Updated ed. Berkeley: University of California Press, 2000.
Danto, Arthur C. *The Transfiguration of the Commonplace: A Philosophy of Art*. Cambridge, MA: Harvard University Press, 1981.
Davies, Stephen. *Musical Works and Performances: A Philosophical Exploration*. New York: Oxford University Press, 2001.
Davis, Whitney. *A General Theory of Visual Culture*. Princeton, NJ: Princeton University Press, 2011.
Davis, Whitney. *Replications: Archaeology, Art History, Psychoanalysis*. Philadelphia: Pennsylvania State University Press, 1996.
Decker, Todd. *Who Should Sing "Ol' Man River"?: The Lives of an American Song*. New York: Oxford University Press, 2015.
DeMichael, Don. "Jackson of the MJQ." *Downbeat* 28, no. 14 (July 6, 1961): 4.
DeMichael, Don. "The Monterey Festival." *Downbeat* 28, no. 23 (November 9, 1961): 12–13.
DeMichael, Don. "Review of *This Is Our Music*." *Downbeat* 28, no. 10 (May 11, 1961): 25.
DeSoto, Clinton B. *Two Hundred Meters and Down: The Story of Amateur Radio*. West Hartford, CT: American Radio Relay League, 1936.
DeVeaux, Scott. *The Birth of Bebop: A Social and Musical History*. Berkeley: University of California Press, 1997.
DeVito, Chris, Yasuhiro Fujioka, Wolf Schmaler, David Wild, and Lewis Porter. *The John Coltrane Reference*. New York: Routledge, 2013.
Douglas, Susan J. *Inventing American Broadcasting, 1899–1922*. Baltimore: Johns Hopkins University Press, 1987.
"Ellingtonia." Accessed June 5, 2023. www.ellingtonia.com/discography/1951-1960/.
Elrod, Bruce C., ed. *Your Hit Parade and American Top Ten Hits*. 4th ed. Ann Arbor, MI: Popular Culture, Ink., 1994.
Faulkner, Robert R., and Howard Saul Becker. *"Do You Know . . . ?" The Jazz Repertoire in Action*. Chicago: University of Chicago Press, 2009.

Feather, Leonard. *Inside Jazz*. New York: Da Capo Press, 1976.
Federal Communications Commission. "Rules and Regulations, Part 1: Rules of Practice and Procedure." Washington, DC: US Government Printing Office, 1939.
Federal Radio Commission. "Radio Service Bulletin." Washington, DC: US Government Printing Office, 1927.
Federal Radio Commission. "Radio Service Bulletin." Washington, DC: US Government Printing Office, 1929.
Federal Radio Commission. "Second Annual Report of the Federal Radio Commission." Washington, DC: US Government Printing Office, 1928.
Forte, Allen. *The American Popular Ballad of the Golden Era, 1924-1950*. Princeton, NJ: Princeton University Press, 1995.
Forte, Allen. *Listening to Classic American Popular Songs*. New Haven, CT: Yale University Press, 2001.
Freud, Sigmund. *Three Case Histories*. New York: Simon & Schuster, 1996.
Friedwald, Will. *Stardust Melodies: The Biography of Twelve of America's Most Popular Songs*. New York: Pantheon Books, 2002.
Garland, Joe, and Andy Razaf. "In the Mood." New York: Shapiro, Bernstein & Co., 1939.
Gell, Alfred. *Art and Agency: An Anthropological Theory*. Oxford: Clarendon Press, 2007.
Gershwin, George, and Ira Gershwin. "But Not for Me." New York: New World Music Corp., 1930.
Giddins, Gary. "50 Years of Body and Soul." In *Reading Jazz: A Gathering of Autobiography, Reportage, and Criticism from 1919 to Now*, edited by Robert Gottlieb, 1006-13. New York: Vintage Books, 1999.
Giddins, Gary. *Visions of Jazz: The First Century*. New York: Oxford University Press, 1998.
Goehr, Lydia. *The Imaginary Museum of Musical Works: An Essay in the Philosophy of Music*. Rev. ed. New York: Oxford University Press, 2007.
Goehr, Lydia. "Three Blind Mice: Goodman, McLuhan, and Adorno on the Art of Music and Listening in the Age of Global Transmission." *New German Critique* 35, no. 2 (2008): 1-31.
Goldberg, Isaac. *Tin Pan Alley: A Chronicle of the American Popular Music Racket*. New York: John Day Co., 1930.
Goodman, Nelson. *Languages of Art: An Approach to a Theory of Symbols*. Indianapolis: Hackett, 1976.
Gracyk, Theodore. *Rhythm and Noise: An Aesthetics of Rock*. Durham, NC: Duke University Press, 1996.
Gracyk, Theodore, and Andrew Kania. *The Routledge Companion to Philosophy and Music*. New York: Routledge, 2011.
Green, Abel. *Inside Stuff on How to Write Popular Songs*. New York: Paul Whiteman Publications, 1927.
Green, Johnny, Edward Heyman, and Robert Sour. "Body and Soul." New York: Harms, 1930.
Guralnick, Peter. *Lost Highway: Journeys & Arrivals of American Musicians*. Boston: Little, Brown, 1999.
Hall, Fred. *More Dialogues in Swing: Intimate Conversations with the Stars of the Big Band Era*. Ventura, CA: Pathfinder, 1991.
Harman, Graham. *Prince of Networks: Bruno Latour and Metaphysics*. Prahran: Re.press, 2009.

Hepokoski, James. "From 'Young Bears' to 'Three-Letter Words': 'Anything Goes,' 1934–1962." In *A Cole Porter Companion*, edited by Don M. Randel, Matthew Shaftel, and Susan Forscher Weiss, 123–64. Bloomington: Indiana University Press, 2015.

Hughes, Langston. *The Best of Simple*. New York: Hill & Wang, 1961.

Iyer, Vijay. Liner notes to *Historicity* (ACT, 2008). Accessed June 8, 2023. https://vijay-iyer.com/albums/historicity/.

Jack, Gordon. *Fifties Jazz Talk: An Oral Retrospective*. Lanham, MD: Scarecrow Press, 2004.

Jamal, Ahmad. *The Ahmad Jamal Collection*. Transcribed by Alex Smith. Milwaukee: Hal Leonard, 1997.

Kahn, Ashley. *Kind of Blue: The Making of the Miles Davis Masterpiece*. New York: Da Capo Press, 2000.

Kane, Brian. "The Fluctuating Sound Object." In *Sound Objects*, edited by James A. Steintrager and Rey Chow, 53–70. Durham, NC: Duke University Press, 2019.

Kane, Brian. "Sound Studies without Auditory Culture: A Critique of the Ontological Turn." *Sound Studies* 1, no. 1 (2015): 2–21.

Kania, Andrew. "All Play and No Work: An Ontology of Jazz." *Journal of Aesthetics and Art Criticism* 69, no. 4 (2011): 391–403.

Kelley, Robin D. G. *Thelonious Monk: The Life and Times of an American Original*. New York: Free Press, 2010.

Kelman, Ari Y. "Rethinking the Soundscape: A Critical Genealogy of a Key Term in Sound Studies." *The Senses and Society* 5, no. 2 (2010): 212–34.

Kernfeld, Barry. "John Coltrane in Rudy Van Gelder's Studio." Accessed June 5, 2023. www.barrykernfeld.com/aop.htm.

Kernfeld, Barry. *The Story of Fake Books: Bootlegging Songs to Musicians*. Lanham, MD: Scarecrow Press, 2006.

King, Patrick. "Spin: Goddard Lieberson and the Development of the American Musical Cast Recording." MA thesis, Tufts University, 2014.

Kivy, Peter. *Authenticities: Philosophical Reflections on Musical Performance*. Ithaca, NY: Cornell University Press, 1995.

Kivy, Peter. *The Fine Art of Repetition: Essays in the Philosophy of Music*. Cambridge: Cambridge University Press, 1993.

Kivy, Peter. *Introduction to a Philosophy of Music*. Oxford: Clarendon Press, 2002.

Kockelman, Paul. *Agent, Person, Subject, Self: A Theory of Ontology, Interaction, and Infrastructure*. New York: Oxford University Press, 2013.

Komara, Edward M. *The Dial Recordings of Charlie Parker: A Discography*. Westport, CT: Greenwood Press, 1998.

Krieger, Franz. *Jazz-Solopiano: Zum Stilwandel am Beispiel ausgewählter "Body and Soul"—Aufnahmen von 1938–1992*. Graz: Akademische Druck- u. Verlagsanstalt, 1995.

Larkin, Philip. *All What Jazz: A Record Diary 1961–1971*. New York: Farrar, Straus & Giroux, 1985.

Latour, Bruno. *Pandora's Hope: Essays on the Reality of Science Studies*. Cambridge, MA: Harvard University Press, 1999.

Latour, Bruno. *Science in Action: How to Follow Scientists and Engineers through Society*. Cambridge, MA: Harvard University Press, 1987.

Latour, Bruno. *We Have Never Been Modern*. Translated by Catherine Porter. Cambridge, MA: Harvard University Press, 1993.

Leiter, Robert David. *The Musicians and Petrillo*. New York: Bookman Associates, 1953.

Leur, Walter van de. *Something to Live For: The Music of Billy Strayhorn*. New York: Oxford University Press, 2002.

Levinson, Jerrold. *Music, Art, and Metaphysics: Essays in Philosophical Aesthetics*. New York: Oxford University Press, 2011.

Lichty, Lawrence Wilson, and Malachi C. Topping. *American Broadcasting: A Source Book on the History of Radio and Television*. New York: Hastings House Publishers, 1976.

MacDougald, Duncan, Jr. "The Popular Music Industry." In *Radio Research, 1941*, edited by Paul Lazarsfeld and Frank Stanton, 65–109. New York: Duell, Sloan & Pearce, 1941.

Mackey, Nathaniel. *Bedouin Hornbook*. Lexington: University Press of Kentucky, 1986.

Magee, Jeffrey. *The Uncrowned King of Swing: Fletcher Henderson and Big Band Jazz*. New York: Oxford University Press, 2005.

Manone, Wingy. "Manone Says 'In the Mood' Is His Tune." *Downbeat* 7, no. 1 (January 1, 1940): 2.

Martin, Henry. *Charlie Parker and Thematic Improvisation*. Lanham, MD: Scarecrow Press, 1996.

Matthews, Virgil. "The Critic's Critic." *Downbeat* 28, no. 14 (July 6, 1961): 2.

Miller, Paul Edward. "Record Reviews." *Downbeat* 5, no. 5 (May 1938): 14.

Mol, Annemarie. "Ontological Politics. A Word and Some Questions." *The Sociological Review* 47, no. S1 (1999): 74–89.

Morgan, Alun. "Review of *The Jam Sessions, Vol. 4*." *Jazz and Blues* 3, no. 3 (June 1973): 26.

Morgan, Alun. "Review of *This Is Our Music*." *The Gramophone*, November 1961, 284.

Mulhall, Stephen. *On Being in the World: Wittgenstein and Heidegger on Seeing Aspects*. London: Routledge, 1990.

Mulhall, Stephen. *Stanley Cavell: Philosophy's Recounting of the Ordinary*. Oxford: Clarendon Press, 1998.

Norris, Christopher. *Platonism, Music and the Listener's Share*. London: Continuum, 2006.

Oliver, Sy. "Opus One." New York: Embassy Music Corp., 1945.

Owens, Thomas. "Charlie Parker: Techniques of Improvisation." PhD diss., University of California, Los Angeles, 1974.

Parker, Charlie. Session Logs from November 26, 1945, Savoy Records. Accessed June 5, 2023. https://jaybrandford.com/2015/05/31/charlie-parker-solo-transcription-meandering/.

Passman, Arnold. *The Deejays*. New York: Macmillan, 1971.

Pekar, Harvey. "Review of *Impressions*." *Downbeat* 30, no. 24 (August 29, 1963): 22.

Porter, Eric. *What Is This Thing Called Jazz?: African American Musicians as Artists, Critics, and Activists*. Berkeley: University of California Press, 2002.

Porter, Lewis. *John Coltrane: His Life and Music*. Ann Arbor: University of Michigan Press, 1997.

Priestley, Brian. "Charlie Parker and Popular Music." *Annual Review of Jazz Studies* 14 (2009): 83–99.

Ramsey, Frederic, and Charles Edward Smith. *Jazzmen*. New York: Harcourt, Brace & Co., 1939.

Ridley, Aaron. *The Philosophy of Music: Theme and Variations*. Edinburgh: Edinburgh University Press, 2004.

Roach, Joseph. *Cities of the Dead: Circum-Atlantic Performance*. New York: Columbia University Press, 1996.

Rodgers, Richard, and Lorenz Hart. "My Funny Valentine, from *Babes in Arms*." New York: Chappell, 1937.

Russell, Ross. *Bird Lives!: The High Life and Hard Times of Charlie (Yardbird) Parker*. New York: Charterhouse, 1973.
Sales, Grover. *Jazz: America's Classical Music*. New York: Da Capo Press, 1992.
Sanjek, Russel. *American Popular Music and Its Business: The First Four Hundred Years*. Vol. 3. New York: Oxford University Press, 1988.
Schafer, R. Murray. *The Soundscape: Our Sonic Environment and the Tuning of the World*. Rochester: Destiny Books, 1994.
Schuller, Gunther. *The Swing Era: The Development of Jazz, 1930–1945*. New York: Oxford University Press, 1989.
Shaw, Arnold. *Let's Dance: Popular Music in the 1930s*. New York: Oxford University Press, 1998.
"Sheet, Air Plugs & Parade Reports." *The Billboard*, January 13, 1945, 14.
Simon, George Thomas. *The Big Bands*. Rev. ed. New York: Macmillan, 1971.
Stern, Horace. "Waring V. WDAS Station, Inc." 327 Pa. 433 (Pa. 1937). Supreme Court of Pennsylvania, 1937.
Sterne, Jonathan. *The Audible Past: Cultural Origins of Sound Reproduction*. Durham, NC: Duke University Press, 2003.
"Strictly Ad Lib." *Downbeat* 30, no. 4 (February 14, 1963): 12, 45–47.
Strunk, Steven. "The Harmony of Early Bop: A Layered Approach." *Journal of Jazz Studies* 6, no. 1 (1979): 4–53.
Suisman, David. *Selling Sounds: The Commercial Revolution in American Music*. Cambridge, MA: Harvard University Press, 2009.
Sullivan, Steve. *Encyclopedia of Great Popular Song Recordings*. Lanham, MD: Scarecrow Press, 2013.
Thacker, Eric. "Review of *Ornette!*" *Jazz and Blues* 3, no. 7 (October 1973): 19.
Tirro, Frank. *Jazz: A History*. New York: W. W. Norton, 1977.
Tomlinson, Gary. "Cultural Dialogics and Jazz: A White Historian Signifies." In *Disciplining Music: Musicology and Its Canons*, edited by Katherine Bergeron and Philip Bohlman, 64–94. Chicago: University of Chicago Press, 1992.
Tucker, Mark. "Mainstreaming Monk: The Ellington Album." *Black Music Research Journal* 19, no. 2 (1999): 227–44.
Wacker, Fred. "Wingy or Henderson Wrote *In the Mood*." *Downbeat* 7, no. 4 (February 15, 1940): 10.
Wald, Elijah. *How the Beatles Destroyed Rock 'n' Roll: An Alternative History of American Popular Music*. New York: Oxford University Press, 2009.
Walser, Rob. "'Out of Notes': Signification, Interpretation, and the Problem of Miles Davis." In *Jazz among the Discourses*, edited by Krin Gabbard, 165–88. Durham, NC: Duke University Press, 1995.
Waters, Keith. "'Giant Steps' and the Ic4 Legacy." *Intégral* 24 (2010): 135–62.
Waters, Keith. *The Studio Recordings of the Miles Davis Quintet, 1965–68*. New York: Oxford University Press, 2011.
Whitburn, Joel. *Top Pop Singles 1955–2002*. Menomonee Falls, WI: Record Research, 2003.
Whiteman, Paul, and Mary Margaret McBride. *Jazz*. New York: J. H. Sears & Co., 1926.
Williams, John R. *This Was Your Hit Parade*. Rockland, ME: Courier-Gazette, 1973.
Williams, Martin. "A Charlie Parker Masterpiece." *Downbeat* 37 (April 2, 1970): 34–35.
Williams, Martin. "Talking with Myself." *Evergreen Review* 8, no. 3 (August–September 1964): 83–85.

Wittgenstein, Ludwig. *Philosophical Investigations*. Translated by G. E. M. Anscombe. New York: Macmillan, 1953.

Woideck, Carl. *The John Coltrane Companion: Five Decades of Commentary*. New York: Schirmer Books, 1998.

Wolterstorff, Nicholas. "Toward an Ontology of Art Works." *Noûs* 9 (1975): 115–42.

Wolterstorff, Nicholas. *Works and Worlds of Art*. Oxford: Clarendon Press, 1980.

Yagoda, Ben. *The B Side: The Death of Tin Pan Alley and the Rebirth of the Great American Song*. New York: Riverhead Books, 2015.

Young, J. O., and C. Matheson. "The Metaphysics of Jazz." *Journal of Aesthetics and Art Criticism* 58 (2000): 125–34.

"Your Hit Parade." Originally broadcast on NBC, June 2, 1956. Radio broadcast.

Zak, Albin. *I Don't Sound Like Nobody: Remaking Music in 1950s America*. Ann Arbor: University of Michigan Press, 2010.

Zbikowski, Lawrence. "Cultural Knowledge and Musical Ontology." In *Conceptualizing Music: Cognitive Structure, Theory, and Analysis*, 201–42. New York: Oxford University Press, 2002.

Index

For the benefit of digital users, indexed terms that span two pages (e.g., 52–53) may, on occasion, appear on only one of those pages.

Tables and figures are indicated by *t* and *f* following the page number

"26-2" (Coltrane), 103

Abbott, Lynn, 185–86
adequatio rei et intellectus model, 140–41
Adorno, Theodor, 9–10, 174–77
African Americans
    freedom struggle of, 201, 202–3
    hard bop and, 202–3
    musical literacy and, 184–87
    in Oakland, 2–3
    permissive replicational practices among music of, 186–89, 198–99
    "race records" and, 170–71, 185–86
    segregation and discrimination against, 155–56, 184, 187
    traveling shows at turn of twentieth century and, 185–86
"Alice in Wonderland" (standard), 91
"All Blues" (Davis), 106–7
"All My Loving" (The Beatles), 212–13
allographic art, 125–27
"All the Things You Are" (standard), 1, 93–94, 95, 200, 243
"All Too Soon" (Ellington), 5
American Bandstand (television show), 198
American Federation of Musicians (AFM), 164–66, 199
American Tobacco Company, 171–72
Anderson, Ivie, 240
Armed Forces Radio, 157, 164–65
Armstrong, Louis
    "Body and Soul" recording (1930) of, 219–20
    Ellington's collaborations with, 242
    Gillespie's critiques of, 199
    hot jazz and, 188–89
    musical training of, 267n.52
    permissive forms of musical replication and, 189–90
    race records and, 170–71
ASCAP (American Society of Composers, Authors, and Producers), 102, 171
"Ascension" (Coltrane), 211
auditory culture
    definition of, 181–82
    musical ontology and, 11–12, 180, 195–96, 214
    replication and, 183–84
    social context and, 184
    sonic ontologies and, 183
    soundscapes and, 181–82, 197, 211–12, 214–15
aural images
    aesthetic evaluation and, 236–37
    cover songs and, 233–35, 236
    fulfillment and, 232–33
    hearing double and, 232–33, 236
    networks of competing recordings and, 191–92
    recall and fantasy involved in, 232–33
    recording technology and, 193
    standards and, 234–35, 236–37, 239
Austin High School Gang, 187–88
autographic art, 125–26, 195

Babes in Arms (Rogers and Hart), 24–25
Bach, Johann Christoph, 133–34
Baker, Chet, 24–25, 84–85, 151–52, 202
Baker, LaVern, 196–97
baptism. *See under* nomination

Baraka, Amiri (LeRoi Jones)
  African American freedom struggle and, 201, 202–3
  Coltrane reviews by, 114–15, 204
  free jazz and, 201–2, 203–4
  on hard bop and cool jazz, 202–3
  jazz standards and, 202–4, 205–6
  on musical "assassins," 203–6
  Tin Pan Alley and, 201–2
Barfield, Ray, 157
Basie's Beatle Bag (Count Basie), 212–13
The Beatles, 197, 212–13, 232–34. *See also specific songs*
bebop
  avant-garde and, 200–1
  contrafacts and, 95, 200
  Gillespie and, 199
  melody and, 87
  Monk and, 75–76, 200, 238
  origins of, 199
Benecke, Tex, 49–50
Berendt, Joachim-Ernst, 114
Berlin, Irving, 18, 192
Berry, Chu, 147–48, 219–21, 225
"Besame Mucho" (Dorsey), 170
Biel, Michael, 165–66
Bigard, Barney, 239–40
Billboard magazine, 156–57, 168–69, 170–72
The Birdcage (Oakland jazz club), 2–3
"Bird of Paradise" (Parker), 95
Black, Bill, 193
Black Americans. *See* African Americans
"Black and Tan Fantasy" (Ellington), 239–40
black boxes (Latour), 149–50
Black Music (Baraka), 201
Blakey, Art, 114–15
Blanton, Jimmy, 86–87, 219, 223–24
blindfold tests, 100–1
Block, Martin, 191–92
Blood Sutra (Iyer), 227–29
"Blue Moon," 197
Blues People (Baraka), 201, 202
"Blue Suede Shoes," 197
"Body and Soul" (standard)
  Armstrong's recording (1930) of, 219–20
  Art Tatum Trio recording (1944) of, 220–21
  aural images and, 234–35
  bebop and, 71–72
  Blanton's recording (1940) of, 86–87, 86f, 219
  Coltrane's recording (1960) of, 224–25, 227–30, 229f, 230f
  contrafacts and, 222, 227–31
  Cozy Cole and His Orchestra recording (1944) of, 220
  duet playing and, 223–24
  Eldrige and Berry's recording (1938) of, 219–20, 221–22, 224
  Ellington and Blanton recording (1940) of, 223–24
  Gordon's recording (1976) of, 224–25
  "Habeas Corpus" and, 227–30, 228f, 229f, 230f
  harmony and chord progression in, 63–64, 65–67, 68–76, 76t, 77–78, 79–80, 86–87, 91, 183–84, 221, 224–25
  Hawkins's recording (1939) of, 71, 78–79, 86f, 86–87, 219, 221–24, 225
  Henderson's recording (1991) of, 225–27
  Holiday's recordings (1940 and 1957) of, 86f, 86–87, 219, 234–35
  "Humoresque" and, 220–21
  jazz standard status of, 1, 71, 234–35
  Jones (Hank) recording (1956) of, 71f, 71–72, 76, 76t, 77f, 77–78, 219
  key of, 71
  McVea's recording (1957) of, 86f, 86–87, 219
  melody of, 63–64, 86–87, 222, 223–24, 227–29
  Monk's recording (1961) of, 74f, 74–78, 75f, 76t, 77f, 80, 86, 200–1
  Moody's recording (1956) of, 221
  network of performances of, 77f, 78, 219–27
  nomination and, 107–8, 147–48, 221
  opening three measures as model in, 63–64, 64f, 65–67, 68f, 68, 70–71, 86f, 86–87
  opening vamps of, 229f, 229
  "Picasso" and, 222, 224
  "Rainbow Mist" and, 222

INDEX

replication and, 60, 63–64, 65–67, 69–72, 74–80, 76t, 86–87, 91, 107–8, 136–37, 183–84, 200–1, 219, 226–29
Rollins's recording (1958) of, 222, 224–25
second A-section in, 67f, 67, 68–70, 69f
sheet music of, 227–29, 228f
Shepp and Davis recording (1989) of, 223–24
solos in, 219–24, 225
string bass and, 223
Tatum's recording (1938) of, 65–67, 66f, 67f, 76t, 77f, 219
Tatum's recording (1953) of, 68f, 68, 76t, 77f, 219
tempo of, 219–22, 223–25
tenor saxophone and, 221–22, 226–27
as "thin work," 77–78
unpacked chords and, 71–73
Vaughan's recording (1978) of, 223–24
Wilson's recording (1941) of, 72f, 73–74, 76t, 77f, 77–78, 219
Boone, Pat, 212
Born, Georgina, 8–10
Born to Run (Springsteen), 195
Bowen, José, 86f, 86–87
Boyd, Rocky, 116–17, 120–22, 121f
Brown, Ray, 223–24
Brubeck, David, 202
"Buddy Bolden's Blues," 186–87
Burleigh, Harry, 186–87
"But Not for Me" (standard)
 B-section of, 91–92
 chorus of, 81–82
 Coltrane's recording (1961) of, 87–88, 89f, 89–92, 142–43, 224
 Davis's recording (1954) of, 83–85, 89–90, 91–92, 151–52
 first A section of, 81f, 82–83
 formal analysis of, 81–82, 82f
 Gershwin's original arrangement of, 81–82, 83, 84–85, 89–90, 142–43, 151–52
 Girl Crazy musical and, 81–82
 harmonization of, 82–86, 87–88, 89–90, 91–92
 Jamal's recording of, 84–85, 91–92
 Jones (Hank) performance (1956) of, 83–84, 85–86

 lead sheet for, 29, 30f
 Lewis recording (1960) of, 83–84
 melody of, 81–82, 87–88, 90, 91–92
 network of performances of, 85–86
 Real Book version of, 83–84, 84f
 Red Garland Trio's recording (1957) of, 83–84, 85–86
 replication and, 85–86, 90–92
 sheet music of, 81–82, 83
 tempo of, 83–84

Café du Nord (San Francisco jazz club), 4
Calloway, Cab, 45–46
"Can't Buy Me Love" (The Beatles), 212–13
Capitol Records, 164–65
Carson, David B., 159–60
Carter, Benny, 111, 176–77
CBS Radio, 162–63
chains of nomination. *See under* nomination
chains of replication. *See under* replication
Chambers, Jack, 116–17
"Chansonette," 188
Charles, Denis, 208–10
The Charlie Parker Story (Parker), 101–2
"Chasing the Trane" (Coltrane), 201–2
"Chelsea Bridge" (Ellington), 220
"Cherokee" (Parker), 95, 102
Cherry, Don, 201–2, 204–5
circulating reference, 138–41
Clarke, Kenny, 83
classical music
 Adorno on radio broadcasts of, 174
 music ontology and, 8, 26–27
 replication and, 147
 as "thick works," 29, 31
Clooney, Rosemary, 242
Cocker, Joe, 233–34
Cohen, Leonard, 235–36
Cole, Cozy, 220
Cole, Nat "King," 4, 5, 200. *See also* King Cole Trio
Coleman, George, 36–37
Coleman, Ornette
 "Embraceable You" recording (1960) by, 109–11, 144, 145–46, 203–4
 free jazz and, 201–2, 203–4
 "Free Jazz" recording (1961) of, 211

Coles, Johnny, 221
Coltrane, John. *See also specific songs*
  "Body and Soul" recording (1960) of, 224–25, 227–30, 229f, 230f
  Boyd and, 116–17, 120–21
  "But Not for Me" recording (1961) by, 87–88, 89f, 89–92, 142–43, 224
  "Coltrane Changes" in musical compositions and, 87–88, 142–43, 224
  free jazz and, 201–2, 203
  "Impressions" performance by quintet (1961) of, 112–13
  jazz standards as an enduring part of the repertoire of, 203–4
  John Coltrane Quintet and, 112–13
  Kind of Blue and, 113, 117
  Lincoln Center performance (1963) of, 114–15
Coltrane's Sound (Coltrane), 224
The Complete Riverside Recordings (Monk), 74
compulsory license, 169–70, 177, 191–92
"Confirmation" (Coltrane), 103
Connick Jr., Harry, 83–84
contrafacts
  bebop and, 95, 200
  "Body and Soul" and, 222, 227–31
  definition of, 95
  "Embraceable You" and, 95–96, 101–2, 105–6, 108–9
  "I Got Rhythm" and, 95
  "Impressions" and, 123
  nomination and, 95, 100–1, 103, 108–9
  replication and, 100–1
cool jazz, 202
Copyright Act of 1909, 169–70, 177–79
"Cottontail" (Ellington), 220
Count Basie, 52, 186–87, 212–13
"Countdown" (Coltrane), 88f, 88–89
cover songs, 233–36
Crawford, Richard, 256n.1
"Creole Love Call" (Ellington), 186–87, 240
Crosby, Bing, 170, 198
Crosby, Bob, 51, 58f
Crouch, Stanley, 116

Dameron, Tadd, 224
"Dance Rhythm," 188
Danto, Arthur, 123
Darin, Bobby, 52–53
Davies, Stephen
  on "In the Mood," 40–41, 50, 53–54, 55
  on model performances' ability to communicate musical prescriptions, 33–35
  on musical ontology of works designed for performance, 28–30
  musical structure in the theories of, 57
  on one performance's ability to be two musical works, 40–41, 41f, 53, 55, 248n.43
  on oral transmission of musical works, 32–33
  on scores' ability to communicate musical prescriptions, 31–32, 33–34
  on "thickness" of classical music, 29
  "thick works" defined by, 28
  "thin works" defined by, 27, 28
  on work-determinative properties, 30–31, 37–38, 79–80, 135–36, 146
Davis, Arthur, 112–13
Davis, Kay, 240
Davis, Miles. *See also specific songs*
  Boyd and, 116–17
  "But Not for Me" recorded (1954) by, 83–85, 89–90, 91–92, 151–52
  chains of nomination and, 106–7
  cool jazz and, 202
  "If I Were A Bell" and, 103
  "My Funny Valentine" recorded by, 24–25, 29–30
Davis, Whitney, 61, 181–82
Davis, Wild Bill, 84–85
Decca, 164–65, 170–71
DeMichael, Don, 111
Déserts (Varèse), 29
"Diminuendo and Crescendo in Blue" (Ellington), 44
disc jockeys (DJs), 191–92, 211–13
Dolphy, Eric, 114–15
"Donna Lee" (Parker), 95
"Don't Blame Me" (standard), 200
"Don't Worry about Me" (standard), 91
"Don't You Know?" (Reese), 52–53

"Doodlin'" (Silver), 2–3
Dorsey, Jimmy, 170, 175
"Doxy" (Rollins), 204–5
"Dreamy Blues" (Ellington), 103
Dunn, Joe, 42
duplication, 195–98, 211. *See also* replication

Ease It! (Rock Boyd Quintet), 116–17, 121*f*
Edison, Harry "Sweets," 121–22
Edison Thomas, 193
Edwards, Joan, 157–59, 158*t*
Eldridge, Roy, 147–48, 219–22, 224, 225
Ellington, Duke. *See also specific songs*
    Beatles music recordings by, 212–13
    blues music structures and, 44
    collaborations during 1960s by, 242
    "In the Mood" recording (1954) of, 52, 58*f*, 149–50
    "light music" and, 176–77
    Monk's recording of the music of, 238–40, 241–43, 241*f*
    Newport Jazz Festival performances (1956 and 1962) of, 242
    pianist work by, 239, 242
Ellington '55 (Ellington), 52
embellishing chords, 252n.11
"Embraceable You" (standard)
    Coleman's recording (1960) of, 109–11, 144, 145–46, 203–4
    contrafacts and, 95–96, 101–2, 105–6, 108–9
    Gershwin's original arrangement of, 95*f*, 96–100, 98*f*, 102, 109–10
    harmony and chord progression in, 87, 100–1, 109–10, 111–12
    "I'm in the Mood for Love" and, 106
    lead sheet of, 95*f*
    "Meandering" and, 99–102, 104, 108–9, 200–1
    melody of, 87, 95–100, 104, 109–10
    motives in, 95–99, 95*f*
    nomination and, 100–1, 104, 108–9
    Parker's Montreal performance recording (1953) of, 97–100
    Parker's "Take A" Dial recording (1947) of, 87, 95–101, 96*f*, 98*f*, 108–10, 222
    Parker's "Take B" Dial recording (1947) of, 95–96, 97–101, 97*f*, 98*f*, 108–10, 222
    "Quasimodo" and, 105–6, 108–9, 200–1
    replication standards and, 111–12, 200–1
    solos in, 95–96, 96*f*, 97–99, 97*f*
    "A Table in the Corner" and, 95–99, 200
    work-determinative properties of, 104
Europe, James Reese, 186–87
Evans, Bill, 35–36, 106–7, 116–17, 118*f*
"Every Time We Say Goodbye" (Porter), 87–88
"Excerpts" (Coltrane), 114–15
"Experiment in Modern Music" (Whiteman), 188

fakebooks, 1, 29, 57–58
"Fascinating Rhythm" (Gershwin), 40
Feather, Leonard, 100–1
Federal Communications Commission (FCC), 190–91
Federal Radio Commission (FRC), 161–62, 164–65
Fields, Ernie, 52–53, 57, 58*f*
Fifth Symphony (Beethoven), 29
Fillmore District (San Francisco), 4
Fitzgerald, Ella, 84–85, 212–13
"Flamenco Sketches" (Davis), 106–7
The Fleetwoods, 52–53
"Flying Home" (Goodman), 52
"Fools Rush In" (standard), 91
Forrest, Jimmy, 103
Forte, Allen
    Great American Songbook and, 17–18
    musical structure in the theories of, 57, 251n.75
    music-analytic approach to popular music and, 21–22
    "My Funny Valentine" and, 18–20, 19*f*, 23, 24–25
    as performer of popular music, 23
    on protean nature of standards, 22, 26
    Schenkerian theory and, 17, 21, 23
    on taking popular music seriously, 21
Foster, Al, 225
Four and More (Davis), 36*f*
free jazz, 201–2, 203–4, 211

"Free Jazz" (Coleman), 211
Freud, Sigmund, 38–39

Gaillard, Slim, 4
Garland, Joe
 "In the Mood" arrangement of, 41–42, 47–50, 54–56, 58–59, 58f, 149–50, 151–52
 Miller and, 49–50
 Mills Blue Rhythm Band and, 45–46, 47–48
 Shaw and, 48–49
 "There's Rhythm in Harlem" arrangement of, 45–48, 50, 54, 55–56, 58f, 149–50
Garner, Errol, 84–85
Gell, Alfred, 9
Geller, Herb, 111–12
Gershwin, George
 "But Not for Me" arrangement of, 81–82, 83, 84–85, 89–90, 142–43, 151–52
 death of, 81–82
 "Embraceable You" arrangement of, 95f, 96–100, 98f, 102, 109–10
 Great American Songbook and, 18
Gershwin, Ira, 95f
Getz, Stan, 83–84
Giant Steps (Coltrane album), 88
"Giant Steps" (Coltrane song), 87–90, 229–30
Gibbs, Georgia, 196–97
Giddins, Gary, 95–96, 99–100, 219–20
Gillespie, Dizzy, 72–73, 95, 101–2, 199–200, 238
Gilmore, John, 223–24
Girl Crazy (musical), 81–82
Gitler, Ira, 116–17
Godfrey, Arthur, 191
Goehr, Lydia, 8–10
Goodman, Benny, 40, 51–52, 58f
Goodman, Nelson
 on allographic *versus* autographic art, 125–26, 195
 nominalist view of music and notation of, 126–28, 129, 130–31, 133, 134–35, 195
 sorites paradox and, 128–29

unchangeability of musical works for, 134–36
"Good Rockin' Tonight," 197
Gordon, Dexter, 221–22, 224–25
Gormé, Eydie, 84–85
Gould, Glenn, 147
Gould, Morton, 84–85, 115–17, 115f, 118–20, 119f, 120f, 123
Gracyk, Theodore, 194–97
Gramsci, Antonio, 230–31
Gray, Wardell, 115–16, 115f
"Great American Songbook," 17–18, 20, 90–91, 192, 214
Great Depression, 163–64
Green, Johnny, 63, 76t, 77f
"Greensleeves" (standard), 204
Grimes, Tiny, 220–21
"Groovin' High" (Gillespie), 95

"Habeas Corpus" (Iyer), 227–30, 228f, 229f, 230f
Haden, Charlie, 109–10, 111
Haley, Bill, 198
"Hallelujah" (Cohen), 235–36
Hamilton, Jimmy, 52
Hammerstein, Oscar, 87–88, 109–10, 207f
Hancock, Herbie, 36–37, 121–22
Hand, Learned, 179, 190–91
"Happy-Go-Lucky Local" (Ellington), 103
hard bop, 2–3, 202–3
"Hard Day's Night" (The Beatles), 232–33
Hart, Lorenz, 24–25
Hawkins, Coleman
 "Body and Soul" recording (1939) of, 71, 78–79, 86–87, 86f, 219, 221–24, 225
 Ellington's collaborations with, 242
 "Picasso" and, 222, 224
 "Rainbow Mist" and, 224
Hayes, Edgar, 47–48, 48f, 49f, 50, 54–55, 58f
hearing double
 aural images and, 232–33, 236
 background of previous musical performances and, 232, 236–37
 cover songs and, 233–34, 236
 historicity and, 242–43
 network-based ontology and, 10–11

standards and, 236–38, 239
vectors of influence and, 241–42
Heath, Percy, 83
Henderson, Fletcher, 45, 51–52, 170–71, 176–77, 187–88
Henderson, Horace, 44–46, 58*f*, 149–50
Henderson, Joe, 225, 226–27
Henderson, Rick, 52
Hendrix, Jimi, 235
"Hey Jude" (The Beatles), 232–33
Higgins, Billy, 201–2, 204–5
Hines, Earl, 84–85
Historicity (Iyer), 230–31
Holiday, Billie, 26, 86–87, 86*f*, 219, 234–35
Homecoming: Live at the Village Vanguard (Gordon), 224
"Honeysuckle Rose" (Waller), 32–33
"Hot and Anxious" (standard)
    choruses in, 44–45
    ending of, 44–45
    Henderson (Horace) arrangement of, 44–46, 58*f*, 149–50
    Henderson (Fletcher) recording (1931) of, 45, 51–52
    "In the Mood" and, 54, 55–56, 58*f*
    introductory strain in, 44, 44*f*
    Redman's recording (1932) of, 45–47, 50, 58*f*
    RIFF in, 44–45, 54
    second strain in, 45, 45*f*
    solos in, 44–45
    "Tar Paper Stomp" and, 44–45, 149–50
    "There's Rhythm in Harlem" and, 45–46, 55–56, 149–50
    third strain in, 44–45, 45*f*
Hot Five recordings (Armstrong), 188–89
hot jazz, 189
"Hound Dog," 197–98, 236
"How High the Moon" (standard), 200
"Humoresque" (Dvořák), 220–21
Husserl, Edmund, 9

"I Can't Get Started" (Gillespie), 72–73
"I Didn't Know about You" (Ellington), 5
"If I Were a Bell" (standard), 103
"If You Could See Me Now" (Dameron), 224
"I Get a Kick out of You" (standard), 91

"I Got Rhythm" (Gershwin), 32–33, 95, 106, 115–16
"I Hadn't Anyone till You" (standard), 91
"I'll Never Smile Again" (standard), 91
"I Love You" (standard), 170
"I'm in the Mood For Love" (Moody), 87, 106
Impressions (Coltrane album), 113–15, 121–22
"Impressions" (Coltrane song)
    B-section of, 121–22, 122*f*, 123*f*
    European tour performances (1961) of, 114
    "Excerpts" and, 114–15
    harmony and chord structure of, 117–18, 118*f*, 119
    Monterey Jazz Festival performance (1961) of, 113–14
    Newport in New York '72 recording of, 121–22
    Newport Jazz Festival performance (1961) of, 112–13
    nomination and, 113–15, 117, 121–22, 123–24
    opening of, 113*f*, 114–15
    "Pavanne" and, 115–17, 118–19, 120–21
    replication and, 115–17, 120–21, 123, 124
    solos in, 113, 114–15
    "So What" and, 112–16, 117–18, 121–22, 123, 259–60n.39
    Sutherland Lounge performance (1961) of, 113
    tour performances (1962-1964) of, 114–15
    Tyner recording (1975) of, 122
    Village Vanguard recording (1961) of, 113–14, 116–17, 201–2
    "Why Not" and, 116–17, 120–22, 123
"Inchworm" (standard), 204
"Indian Summer" (standard), 5
"In the Mood" (standard)
    Bob Crosby and the Bobcats' radio performance (1940) of, 51, 58*f*
    choruses in, 49–50
    coda's trumpet fanfare in, 49–52
    Davies on, 40–41, 50, 53–54, 55

"In the Mood" (standard) (cont.)
  diminuendo in, 49–52
  Ellington's recording (1954) of, 52, 58f, 149–50
  Fields's recording (1959) of, 52–53, 58f
  Garland's arrangement of, 41–42, 47–50, 54–56, 58–59, 58f, 149–50, 151–52
  Goodman's radio recording (1940) of, 51–52, 58f, 149–50
  Hayes's recording (1938) of, 47–48, 48f, 49f, 54–55, 58f
  Henderson (Fletcher) arrangement of, 51–52
  "Hot and Anxious" and, 54, 55–56, 58f
  jazz standard status of, 40, 71
  "Jumpy Nerves" and, 43–44, 58f
  King Sisters recording (1939) of, 50–51, 58f
  Krupa's radio performance (1940) of, 51, 58f, 149–50
  Miller's arrangement of, 41–42, 45, 49–51, 52, 54–55, 58f, 149–50, 151–52
  Miller's recording (1939) of, 45–48, 49–50, 54–55, 56–57, 58f, 149–51, 236
  network of performances of, 57–59, 58f, 149–50, 236
  nomination and, 103
  pedal points in, 45, 49–53
  Razaf's lyrics for, 50
  replication and, 63
  RIFF of, 41–42, 45–46, 47–48, 49–50, 51–56, 63, 149–51
  Schuller on, 41–42
  Shaw's radio performances of, 48–49, 54–55
  sheet music of, 50, 56, 58f, 149–50
  solos in, 47–50, 51–53, 54–55
  tags in, 47–48, 49–50, 52–53
  "Tar Paper Stomp" and, 42–44, 53–54, 55–56, 58–59, 58f, 103
  "There's Rhythm in Harlem" and, 45–46, 47–48, 50, 55–56, 58f, 149–50
  as "thick work," 53
  as "thin work," 41–42, 53–56, 57, 58–59
  as "two works at once," 41, 53, 55
  work-determinative properties of, 150–51

Your Hit Parade and, 51
"Invitation" (standard), 2–3, 151–52
"It Don't Mean a Thing If It Ain't Got That Swing" (standard), 239–40
"It's Love-Love-Love" (standard), 170
"I've Got You under My Skin" (standard), 91
"I Want to Hold Your Hand" (The Beatles), 212–13
Iyer, Vijay, 227–31, 228f, 229f, 230f

Jackson, Frank, 4–6
Jackson, Milt, 111–12
Jamal, Ahmad
  "But Not for Me" recorded by, 84–85, 91–92
  "My Funny Valentine" recorded by, 29–30
  "Pavanne" arrangement by, 115–16, 118–19, 119f
James, Michael, 110
James, William, 141–42
Jarvis, Al, 191–92
jazz standards. *See* standards
Johnson, James Rosamond, 186–87
Johnson, J.J., 105–6
Jones, Elvin, 112–13
Jones, Etta, 83–84
Jones, Hank
  "Body and Soul" recording (1956) of, 71–72, 71f, 76, 76t, 77–78, 77f, 219
  "But Not for Me" recording (1956) of, 83–84, 85–86
Jones, Isham, 189
Jones, LeRoi. *See* Baraka, Amiri
Jones, "Papa" Jo, 83–84
Jones, "Philly" Jo, 116–17
Jones, Thad, 112–13
jukeboxes, 164–65, 170–72
"Jumpy Blues," 43–44
"Jumpy Nerves" (Manone), 43–45, 58f

Kahn, Ashley, 106–7
Kania, Andrew, 215–18
KDKA (Pittsburgh radio station), 159–60
"Keep Me Hanging On" (The Supremes), 233–34
Keepnews, Orrin, 238–39

Kelley, Robin D. G., 238–39
Kelly, Ed, 3
Kern, Jerome, 18
Kind of Blue (Davis), 35–37, 36*f*, 106–7, 113. *See also specific songs*
King Cole Trio, 170–71
King Sisters, 50–51, 57, 58*f*, 170
Kirk, Rahsaan Roland, 121–22
Kivy, Peter, 133–35, 146
"Klactoveesedstene" (Parker), 105–6
Klink, Al, 49–50
"Ko Ko" (Paker), 95
Krupa, Gene, 51, 58*f*, 149–50

"The Lamp Is Low" (Gould), 116
Languages of Art (Goodman), 125, 129
Lanson, Snooky, 197–98
Larkin, Philip, 111
La Roca, Pete, 113, 116–17, 120–21
Latour, Bruno, 138–41, 142–43, 149
"Laura" (standard), 91
lead sheets, 1–2, 29
Levinson, Jerrold, 132–35, 146, 149
Lewis, Ramsey, 83–84
"Little Pony" (Gray), 115–16, 115*f*
Live at the Pershing (Jamal), 84–85
Live at the Village Vanguard (Coltrane), 201–2
Lombardo, Guy, 26, 170, 189
London, Julie, 84–85
"Long Ago and Far Away," 93–94, 157–59, 158*t*
long meter, 219–20, 224
Lunceford, Jimmy, 115–16, 118–19

MacDougald Jr., Duncan
 Adorno and, 174
 arrangers' role in popular music and, 176–77, 179–80
 essential properties of musical works on radio and, 174–75
 on promotion cycle for popular songs, 167, 168–69
 on song pluggers, 167–68, 173–74
Macero, Teo, 106–7
Mackey, Nathaniel, 236–37
"Mack the Knife" (Darin), 52–53
Maddalena, Freddy, 4–5

Magee, Jeremy, 44
"Main Stem" (Ellington), 170–71
Make Believe Ballroom (radio program), 191–92
Mandel, Johnny, 175–77, 179–80, 182–83
Manone, Wingy, 42–45, 53–54, 58*f*, 103, 250n.65. *See also* "Tar Paper Stomp" (Manone)
Martin, Henry, 257n.6
Martin, Mary, 24–25, 151–52
McBride, Mary Margaret, 187–88
McCartney, Paul, 232–33
McVea, Jack, 86–87, 219
"Meandering" (Parker)
 chord progression in, 100–1, 104
 "Embraceable You" and, 99–102, 104, 108–9, 200–1
 motives in, 99–100, 104
 nomination and, 100–3, 104, 108–9
 solos in, 99–102
 work-determinative properties of, 104
mechanical rights, 169–70, 177
"Melancholy Baby" (standard), 201–3, 205–6
Miller, Glenn
 Garland and, 49–50
 Glenn Island Casino booking (1939) of, 49–50, 56
 "In the Mood" arrangement of, 41–42, 45, 49–51, 52, 54–55, 58*f*, 149–50, 151–52
 "In the Mood" recording (1939) of, 45–48, 49–50, 54–55, 56–57, 58*f*, 149–51, 236
 "Pavanne" arrangement by, 115–16, 118–19, 120*f*
Miller, Mitch, 192–93
Mills, Irving, 45–48
Mills Blue Rhythm Band, 45–46, 47–48, 58*f*
Mobley, Hank, 116–17
modal jazz, 3, 117–18, 119, 261n.49
Mol, Annemarie, 145–46
Money Jungle (Ellington), 242
Monk, Thelonious
 bebop and, 75–76, 200, 238
 "Body and Soul" recording (1961) by, 74–78, 74*f*, 75*f*, 76*t*, 77*f*, 80, 86, 200–1

Monk, Thelonious (*cont.*)
  Ellington music recorded (1955) by, 238–40, 241–43, 241*f*
  Five Spot performance (1963) by, 205–6
  Newport Jazz Festival performances of, 242
Montgomery, Wes, 113–14, 122, 259–60n.39
"Mood Indigo" (Ellington), 103, 186–87, 239–42, 241*f*
Moody, James, 87, 106, 221
Moore, Scotty, 193
Morgan, Alun, 111–12
Mozart, Wolfgang, 29
"Mr. Blue" (The Fleetwoods), 52–53
Mulligan, Gerry, 24–25
Murray, Sunny, 109–10
musical literacy, 184–87
musical ontology
  accidental properties and, 151–52
  allography and, 126–27
  ambulatory model and, 141–44, 149, 151–52
  arrangements and, 133–34
  auditory culture and, 11–12, 180, 195–96, 214
  changeability of musical works and, 135–36
  criterial questions and, 210–11
  definition of, 7–8
  discovery-creation distinction and, 134
  essential properties and, 134–36, 146, 150–52
  indication and, 132–34
  initiated types and, 132, 133–35
  model performances and, 33–35, 34*f*
  Nachträglichkeit and, 38–39, 56
  networks and, 9, 39, 136, 138, 143–46, 177
  The New Sound (1950s) and, 194
  nominalism and, 127, 129, 130–31, 134–35, 136, 137, 138, 144, 182
  norm-kinds and, 131–32
  notation and, 126–28
  oral transmission of musical works and, 32–33, 33*f*
  performance-determinative properties and, 28–29
  performance-instance distinction and, 133
  realism and, 127, 129–31, 132, 133, 134, 135–36, 137–38, 141–42, 144–46, 148–49, 151–52
  recording technology and, 194–95
  saltatory model and, 141–44
  scores and, 31–32, 32*f*, 33–34
  sociology and, 57–58
  sorites paradox and, 128–29, 134
  thick works and, 28, 55
  thin works and, 27, 28, 38–39, 55, 56, 135–36
  work-determinative properties and, 28–29, 30–31, 38–39, 150–51
Music You Want (radio program), 190–91
Mutual radio network, 162–63
My Favorite Things (Coltrane album), 87–88
"My Favorite Things" (Coltrane song), 109–10, 113–15, 204
"My Funny Valentine" (standard)
  Babes in Arms as the first appearance of, 24–25
  Davis's recording of, 24–25, 29–30
  Forte's analysis of, 18–20, 19*f*, 23, 24–25
  hard bop and, 202
  Jamal's recording of, 29–30
  linear structures in, 18–20, 19*f*, 23
  Martin's recording of, 24–25, 151–52
  published arrangements of, 24–26, 25*f*
  Rogers's original arrangement of, 151–52
  Sinatra's recording of, 24–25, 28, 151–52
"My Heart Stood Still" (Rodgers), 18
"My Little Brown Book" (Ellington), 5
"Mystery Train," 197

Nachträglichkeit, 38–39, 56, 77–78, 135–36, 141–42
naming. *See* nomination
Nance, Ray, 52
National Association of Performing Artists (NAPA), 178–79
NBC radio network, 162–64
Neidlinger, Buell, 208
networks
  "But Not for Me" and, 85–86

corrigibility of, 235
cover songs and, 233–34
emergent properties and, 148–49, 182, 217–18
essential properties and, 151
identity and individuation questions and, 144–45
"In the Mood" and, 57–59, 58f, 149–50, 236
jazz standards and, 7, 8, 10–11, 151–52, 155, 217, 218, 226, 231–32, 234, 235–37
musical ontology and, 9, 39, 136, 138, 143–46, 177
replication and, 143–44, 218
soundscapes and, 170–71
thin works and, 57
topology and, 218–19, 225–26, 231–32, 236–37
work-determinative properties and, 143–44
"Newport in New York" (Coltrane), 123
Newport in New York '72 (album), 121–22, 123
Newport Jazz Festival (1961), 112–13
The New Sound (1950s)
bifurcation of jazz and popular music and, 190, 199–200
duplication and, 196–97
musical ontology and, 194
radio broadcast of phonography and, 190–91
recorded music and, 190
replication possibilities reduced under, 190
representational fidelity requirements reduced in, 193
sound as work-determinative property of, 195–97, 198–99
sound recording technical and conceptual changes and, 192–94
soundscape of, 190, 195–96
Tin Pan Alley displaced by, 192
"new thing" (free jazz), 201–2, 203–4, 211
"Nica's Dream" (Silver), 2–3
"Night Train" (standard), 103
nominalism. *See under* musical ontology

nomination
assertion and, 104, 109–10, 121–22
baptism and, 102–3, 104, 113–14, 121
"Body and Soul" and, 107–8, 147–48, 221
chains of nomination and, 60, 102–3, 105–8, 109–10, 112, 114, 121, 123, 124, 136, 144–45, 147, 197, 206, 217
commercial implications of, 93–94
contrafacts and, 95, 100–1, 103, 108–9
copyright and royalty issues involved in, 102, 103
"Embraceable You" and, 100–1, 104, 108–9
"Impressions" and, 113–15, 117, 121–22, 123–24
information retrieval and, 93–94
Kind of Blue songs and, 106–7
lyrics and, 93–94
"Meandering" and, 100–3, 104, 108–9
ontology and, 100–1, 102–3, 124, 136, 144, 145–46
"Quasimodo" and, 105–6
replication and, 100–1, 106–10, 108t, 112, 124, 206
social nature of, 10
solicitation and, 104, 109–10, 121–22
substitutability and, 104
transmission and, 103–4, 121
withholding of names and, 103
work-determinative properties and, 104, 147–48
Nyro, Laura, 236

Oakland (California), 2–3, 5–6
"Oleo" (standard), 204–5
Oliver, King, 103
Oliver, Sy, 94
"Once I Loved" (standard), 91
"One o'Clock Jump" (Count Basie), 52
"On Green Dolphin Street" (standard), 2–3
ontology. *See also* musical ontology
aesthetics and, 215
circulating reference and, 138–41
emic approach to, 215–17
epistemology and, 130
historical understandings of, 8, 9–10

ontology (*cont.*)
  jazz genre as a whole and, 215–18
  jazz standards and, 7–8, 10–11, 23–24, 26–27, 29–30, 59, 78, 80, 92, 94–95, 100–1, 136, 182
  nomination and, 100–1, 102–3, 124, 136, 144, 145–46
  ontological politics and, 145–46
  replication and, 90–91, 106, 124, 136, 141–42, 144, 145–46
  social nature of, 10
  sonic ontology and, 183
"Opus No. 1" (Oliver), 94, 103
Original Dixieland Jazz Band, 187–88
"Ornithology" (Parker), 200
"Out of Nowhere," 2–3

"Pale Moon," 188
Parker, Charlie. *See also specific songs*
  ballads as core part of repertoire of, 200
  contrafacts and, 95
  death of, 101–2
  protocols of musical replication and, 200–1
Pass, Joe, 83–84
Paul, Les, 192–93
Pavane pour une infante défunte (Ravel), 116, 123
"Pavanne" (Gould), 84–85, 115f, 115–17, 118–21, 119f, 120f, 123
Peatman, John, 171–72
Performance Trust Fund, 164–65
Petrillo, James Caesar, 164–65
Petty, Norman, 192–93
Phillips, Sam, 192–93
phonography
  American Federation of Musicians and, 164–66
  announcements required before radio broadcasts from, 161–63, 164–65, 190–91
  concerns regarding deception and, 161–62
  copyright law and, 178–79
  Federal Radio Commission report (1928) on, 161–62
  government regulation of radio and, 159–61, 172–73, 189–90

Great Depression and, 163–64
increased radio broadcasts during "New Sound" era of, 190–91
network radio during jazz standard era and, 157–60
radio network policies regarding, 162–63
record companies and, 163–66
royalty income and, 163–65, 169–70
soundscapes and, 166–67, 191–92
Piano in the Foreground (Ellington), 242
"Picasso" (Hawkins), 222, 224
Pike, Dave, 116–17
Pike's Peak (Pike), 116–17
Platonism, 59, 127, 129–30, 131–34, 148–49, 150
"Poinciana," 5
"Poor Butterfly" (standard), 91
popular music industry. *See under* soundscapes
Porter, Cole, 5, 87–88, 170, 192
Porter, Lewis, 116
Porter, Robert, 2, 4
Presley, Elvis, 192–93, 194, 197–98, 212, 236
"Prisoner of Love" (standard), 91

"Quasimado" (Parker), 105f, 105–6, 108–10, 200–1

"race records," 170–71, 185–86
radio. *See also Your Hit Parade*
  Class A and Class B licenses for, 159–61
  commercial sponsors and, 155–56, 162–63
  copyright law and, 178–79
  drive week and, 168–70
  frequency spectrum for, 159–60
  Great Depression and, 163–64
  network radio's emergence during 1920s and, 155–56
  phonography during jazz standard era and, 157–60
  Radio Act of 1912 and, 159–60
  Radio Act of 1927 and, 161
  remote segments and, 168–69, 175, 182–83

soundscape of network radio and, 155–56, 166–67, 175, 182–83, 189–90, 197
television's displacement as dominant medium and, 190, 192
union musicians employed by, 164–65
wireless telephony and, 159–60
World War II and, 155–56, 157, 164–65
"Rainbow Mist" (Hawkins), 222
Rainey, Gertrude "Ma," 185–86, 204–5
Rainey, Will, 204–5
Ramsey Jr., Frederic, 103
Ravel, Maurice, 116, 123
Razaf, Andy, 50
RCA Victor records, 190–91
realism. *See under* musical ontology
Reboppers, 99–100
"Red Clay" (standard), 3
Red Garland Trio, 83–84, 85–86
Redman, Don, 45–47, 50, 58*f*
Reese, Della, 52–53
Reid, Rufus, 225
replication
  analogical likeness and, 183–84
  aspectual nature of artifacts and, 62–63
  auditory culture and, 183–84
  "Body and Soul" and, 60, 63–64, 65–67, 69–72, 74–80, 76*t*, 86–87, 91, 107–8, 136–37, 183–84, 200–1, 219, 226–29
  "But Not for Me" and, 85–86, 90–92
  chains of replication and, 60, 85–86, 92, 100–1, 106–8, 109–10, 112, 115–16, 117, 121, 123, 124, 136–38, 141–43, 144–45, 147, 197, 206, 217, 218, 219, 234, 236
  chord progressions and, 64, 65–67, 86, 100–1
  classical music and, 147
  constrained forms of, 196–99
  contrafacts and, 100–1
  cover songs and, 236
  definition of, 61, 136–37
  duplication and, 196–97, 211
  harmony and, 79–80
  hiatus and, 142–43
  "Impressions" and, 115–17, 120–21, 123, 124
  "In the Mood" and, 63
  material differences between, 61–62
  melody and, 86
  morphological likeness and, 183–84
  musical literacy and, 184–87
  networks and, 143–44, 218
  nomination and, 100–1, 106–10, 108*t*, 112, 124, 206
  "Pavanne" and, 115*f*, 115–16
  permissive forms of, 92, 151–52, 184, 186–90, 197, 198–99, 211, 226
  radical replication and, 80, 90–91, 92, 109–10, 183–84, 206, 210–11, 226, 227
  reduction compared to, 62–63
  social context of use and, 10, 62, 75–77, 78–80, 136–37, 151, 184, 226, 235–36
  standards and, 64, 145–46, 147, 151–52, 184, 234, 235–37
  substitutability and, 61–63, 104, 136–37, 196–97
  surrogation and, 226
  unpacked chords and, 71–73
  work-determinative properties and, 79–81, 90–92, 107–8, 121–22, 141–42, 226, 227
Rhapsody in Blue (Gershwin), 18, 188
"Rhythm Changes" (chord progression in "I Got Rhythm"), 3, 32–33, 95, 106, 115–16
Roach, Joseph, 226
Roberts, Marcus, 83–84
rock and roll, 194–96, 197–98, 211–12
Rodgers, Richard, 18, 24–25, 84–85, 87–88, 109–10, 151–52, 205–6, 207*f*. *See also specific songs*
Rogers, Shorty, 202
Rollins, Sonny, 83–84, 201–2, 203–5, 222, 224–25
"Roll Over Beethoven," 197
Roper, Elmo, 166–67
"'Round Midnight" (Parker), 2–3
"Route 66" (standard), 4
Russell, Ross, 105–6

Sanders, Pharoah, 3
San Fernando Valley (Crosby), 170
San Francisco (California), 4
"Savoy Tea Party" (Parker), 102
"Savoy Truffle" (The Beatles), 212–13

Schafer, R. Murray, 180–81
Schenker, Heinrich, 17, 18–21, 24–25, 83
Schoenberger, John, 188
Schuller, Gunther, 41–44, 45–46, 58–59
Sears, Al, 240
second avant-garde. *See* free jazz
Seroff, Doug, 185–86
Shaw, Artie, 48–50, 54–55, 58*f*, 200
Shaw, Billy, 105–6
Shepp, Archie, 223–24
"Shine" (Armstrong), 219–20
"Shiny Stockings" (standard), 3
"A Ship without a Sail" (Rodgers), 18
Silver, Horace, 2–3, 83
Sinatra, Frank, 24–25, 28, 151–52, 157–59, 158*t*, 198
"Sing, Sing, Sing" (Goodman), 51
"Slaughter on Tenth Avenue" (Rodgers), 84–85
Smith, Bessie, 170–71, 187–88, 189–90
Song for Young Lovers (Sinatra), 24–25
song pluggers
  disc jockeys and, 191–92
  "drive week" and, 168–69
  enticements offered to bandleaders by, 167–68
  improvisation in performances by, 23–24
  "remotes" and, 168–69
  soundscapes and, 167–68, 171–74, 176
  Tin Pan Alley and, 57–58
sorites paradox, 128–29, 134
soundscapes
  acoustic design and, 180–81
  analogical likenesses and, 182–83
  arrangers and, 165–66, 176
  auditory culture and, 181–82, 197, 211–12, 214–15
  bandleaders and, 167–68
  competitive promotion of multiple recordings of same top song and, 170, 172–73
  Copyright Act of 1909 and, 169–70, 177
  definition of, 180–81
  disc jockeys and, 191–92
  jazz standards and, 10–11, 166–67, 172–73, 187, 189–90, 211–13, 214–15
  jukeboxes and, 170–71
  listeners and, 173–80
  live performance and, 165–67, 172–73, 191–92
  morphological likenesses and, 182–83
  network-based musical ontology and, 176
  network radio and, 155–56, 166–67, 175, 182–83, 189–90, 197
  "New Sound" and, 190, 195–96
  performers' creative contributions and, 178–80
  phonography and, 166–67, 191–92
  popular music industry and, 167–68
  "race records" and, 170–71
  regional variation and, 170–71
  song pluggers and, 167–68, 171–74, 176
  sonic ontologies and, 183
  standardization of tastes and, 173–74
  television's displacement of radio as dominant medium and, 192
  thick *versus* thin musical works and, 174–75
  Your Hit Parade and, 168–69, 171, 175
South Pacific (Rodgers and Hammerstein), 109–10, 205–6
"So What" (Davis)
  bridge of, 117
  Four and More recording of Lincoln Center performance of, 36*f*, 36–37
  harmony and chord progression in, 117–18, 118*f*, 119
  "Impressions" and, 112–16, 117–18, 121–22, 123, 259–60n.39
  Kind of Blue recording (1959) of, 35–37, 36*f*, 113, 117–18, 118*f*
  modal jazz and, 117–18
  nomination and, 121–22
  "Pavanne" and, 116, 119–20
  Plugged Nickel performance (1965) of, 36*f*, 37
  as "thin work," 35–38, 36*f*, 77–78
  "Why Not" and, 116–17
  work-determinative properties of, 37–38
Spector, Phil, 192–93
"Spring is Here" (standard), 202
Springsteen, Bruce, 195
Stafford, Jo, 170

The Standard Joe (Joe Henderson), 225, 230–31
standards
  aesthetic value of, 214–15, 218
  aural images and, 234–35, 236–37, 239
  "black boxes" and, 149–50
  Cole and, 5
  covers and, 234–36
  diminished role in contemporary jazz of, 243
  hearing double and, 236–38, 239
  jazz musicians' learning of, 1–3, 243
  lead sheets and, 1–2
  model performances and, 35
  networks and, 7, 8, 10–11, 151–52, 155, 217, 218, 226, 231–32, 234, 235–37
  Oakland jazz scene and, 2–3, 5–6
  ontology of, 7–8, 10–11, 23–24, 26–27, 29–30, 59, 78, 80, 92, 94–95, 100–1, 136, 182
  perpetuation and stabilization of, 152
  protean nature of, 6–7, 26, 27
  replication and, 64, 145–46, 147, 151–52, 184, 234, 235–37
  songs contrasted with, 7
  soundscapes and, 10–11, 166–67, 172–73, 187, 189–90, 211–13, 214–15
  as "thick works," 152
  work-determinative properties of, 80–81, 86, 218, 234, 236–37
"Star Eyes" (standard), 2–3, 200
Starr, Ringo, 233–34
Staton, Dakota, 83–84
"Stella by Starlight" (standard), 1, 151–52, 200
Stern, Horace, 178–80
Stewart, Rex, 44
Stewart, Slam, 220–21
"Stompin' at the Savoy" (Webb), 52
"Straighten Up and Fly Right" (Cole), 5, 170–71
"Strange Fruit" (Holiday), 234–35
Stravinsky, Igor, 29
Strayhorn, Billy, 240–41
Suisman, David, 169–70
"Sunny" (standard), 3
The Supremes, 233–34
sweet jazz, 189
Swing Era, 41–42, 44, 157, 167–68, 199

"A Table in the Corner" (standard), 95–99, 200
"Tar Paper Stomp" (Manone)
  "Hot and Anxious" and, 44–45, 149–50
  "In the Mood" and, 42–44, 53–54, 55–56, 58f, 58–59, 103
  introductory strain of, 42f, 42, 44–45
  "Jumpy Nerves" and, 44
  RIFF of, 42–44, 43f, 53–54
Tatum, Art
  ballads as core part of repertoire of, 200
  "Body and Soul" recording by trio (1944) of, 220–21
  "Body and Soul" recording (1938) of, 65–67, 66f, 67f, 76t, 77f, 219
  "Body and Soul" recording (1953) of, 68f, 68, 76t, 77f, 219
  performance-determinative properties of music and, 30–31
Taylor, Cecil
  free jazz and, 201, 203–4
  Lincoln Center performance (1963) of, 114–15
  "This Nearly Was Mine" recording (1961) by, 109–10, 205–6, 208–11, 209t
"Tequila" (The Champs), 52–53
Terry, Clark, 52
"That's the Blues, Old Man" (Ellington), 103
Thelonious Monk Plays the Music of Duke Ellington (Monk), 238–40, 242–43
"There's Rhythm in Harlem"
  Garland's arrangement of, 45–48, 50, 54, 55–56, 58f, 149–50
  "Hot and Anxious" and, 45–46, 55–56, 149–50
  "In the Mood" and, 45–46, 47–48, 50, 55–56, 58f, 149–50
  RIFF in, 45–46, 46f, 47f, 54
  second strain in, 46–47, 47f
  solos in, 46–47
  third strain in, 46–47, 48f
thick works
  classical music and, 29, 31
  Davies's definition of, 28
  "In the Mood" and, 53
  jazz standards and, 152

thick works (*cont.*)
  performance-determinative properties and, 40
  thin works contrasted with, 28–30
  work-determinative properties and, 29–30
thin works
  "Body and Soul" and, 77–78
  Davies's definition of, 27, 28
  "In the Mood" and, 41–42, 53–56, 57, 58–59
  networks and, 57
  performance-determinative properties and, 30–31, 39
  popular and jazz music as, 29–30, 31
  "So What" and, 35–38, 36*f*, 77–78
  thick works contrasted with, 28–30
  work-determinative properties and, 29–30, 37–38, 39–40, 58–59, 79–80, 135–36
This Is Our Music (Coleman), 109–11, 257–58n.17
"This Nearly Was Mine" (Rodgers), 109–10, 205–11, 207*f*, 209*t*, 271n.96
"Thou Swell" (Rodgers), 18
Tin Pan Alley
  Baraka on, 201–2
  "black boxes" as building units of, 149–50
  chord progressions and, 69–70
  decline in popularity during 1950s of, 192
  Great American Songbook and, 18
  Hollywood films and, 57–58
  musical production and publication apparatus supporting, 23–24
  replication and, 64
  small musical units within songs and, 90–91
  song pluggers and, 57–58
  "thin works" and, 29, 57–58
Titian, 125–26
"To a Wild Rose" (standard), 188
topology. *See under* networks
Townsend, Irving, 106–7
"Tune Up" (Davis), 88–89, 88*f*, 91
Turrentine, Stanley, 83–84
"Tweedle Dee" (LaVern Baker and Georgia Gibbs recordings), 196–97

"Twist and Shout," 197
Tyner, McCoy, 112–13, 117–18, 118*f*, 122, 258–59n.29

"Under a Blanket of Blue" (standard), 91
The Unique Thelonious Monk (Monk), 238–39
unpacked chords, 71–73, 253n.22

Vallee, Rudy, 189
Vanilla Fudge, 233–34
Varèse, Edgar, 29
Vaughan, Sarah, 4, 84–85, 223–24
V-discs, 164–65
Vega, Mort, 112–13
Venus and Cupid with an Organist (Titian), 125–26
Victor Record Review (radio program), 190–91

Waller, Fats, 32–33
Walters, George, 42
Waring, Fred, 178–79
"Warming Up a Riff" (Parker), 102
Washington, Dinah, 84–85
"Watermelon Man" (standard), 2–3
WDAS radio station, 178–79
WEAF (New York City radio station), 159–60
Webb, Chick, 52
Webster, Ben, 4, 220, 223–24, 240
Weinstock, Bob, 103
Werktreue, 8, 147, 236–37
"Where or When" (Rodgers), 18
"Whispering" (Whiteman), 95, 188
Whiteman, Paul, 18, 26, 95, 179, 187–90. *See also specific songs*
"Why Not" (standard), 116–17, 118–22, 121*f*, 123
Wiley, Lee, 81–82
Williams, Martin, 110, 111–12, 116
Williams, Tony, 121–22
Wilson, Teddy, 72*f*, 73–74, 76*t*, 77–78, 77*f*, 219
"With a Little Help from My Friends" (Cocker performance of Beatles Song), 233–34

WNEW radio station (New York City), 179
Wolterstorff, Nicholas, 131–33, 146
Workman, Reggie, 112–13
The World of Cecil Taylor (Taylor), 205–6, 209*t*, 271n.96
World War II, 155–56, 157, 164–65

Yagoda, Ben, 192
"You Are Too Beautiful" (Rodgers), 18
Young, Lester, 115–16
Your Hit Parade (radio and television program)
    arrangements of songs on, 157–59, 158*t*
    audience size for, 166–67, 168–69, 171
    cancellation (1958) of, 198–99
    countdown format of, 156–57
    "In the Mood" and, 51
    lawsuits by music publishers against, 171–72
    Lucky Strike Extras on, 156–57
    popularity of, 155, 157
    replication and, 189
    rock and roll and, 197–98
    soundscapes and, 168–69, 171, 175
    staff band as performer of songs on, 157–59
    tabulation system of, 171–73
    transition to television (1950) of, 197–98
    World War II and, 157

Zak, Albin, 178–80, 193–94, 195–96